POLITICAL MESSAGING IN MUSIC AND ENTERTAINMENT SPACES ACROSS THE GLOBE

VOLUME 2

Edited by

Uche Onyebadi
Texas Christian University

Series in Politics

VERNON PRESS

In the Americas:
Vernon Press
1000 N West Street, Suite 1200,
Wilmington, Delaware 19801
United States

In the rest of the world:
Vernon Press
C/Sancti Espiritu 17,
Malaga, 29006
Spain

Series in Politics

Library of Congress Control Number: 2022939755

ISBN: 978-1-64889-433-6

Cover design by Vernon Press using elements designed by pikisuperstar/Freepik and rawpixel.com/Freepik.

TABLE OF CONTENTS

ACKNOWLEDGMENT

Evidently, being the editor of an academic publication is a merited honor. But, it is an accomplishment that must acknowledge and celebrate everyone who contributed in whatever measure towards its production.

So, I am immensely indebted to all chapter authors from various parts of our world, most of whom I did not know prior to the commencement of this project, and I still have not met in person even at this point. Nonetheless, they believed in this book project and did their best to contribute towards its success. I also appreciate and treasure the support of my family, friends, colleagues and mentors.

And, in a special way, I express my profound gratitude to God who continuously provides me with the inspiration and energy to succeed in multiple endeavors.

Uche Onyebadi, Ph.D.
Texas Christian University
Texas, USA

FOREWORD

Lyombe Eko

Texas Tech University, USA

Music and entertainment consist of culture-specific narrative re-presentations and reenactments of the human condition, and of lived experience. While music is said to be a universal language, it, like entertainment, is produced, disseminated, and consumed within the contextual parameters of specific historical periods, political, and cultural geographies. One of the oldest instances of the instrumentalization of music and performance in history is recorded in the Hebrew Torah (1 Samuel: 18). After David had killed Goliath the giant, the women of all the cities of Israel came out singing, playing tambourines, dancing, and celebrating David's military prowess, while denigrating the achievements of King Saul, a man of unstable temperament. This nationwide political performance drove King Saul into murderous jealousy that ultimately unraveled his reign.

A more recent political performance of the rituals of political messaging occurred in China in 1989. Protesting students in Tiananmen Square erected a 10-metre-tall (33 ft) statue of the Goddess of Democracy and Freedom, and demanded more freedom and democracy in China. The students proceeded to recite parodic chants and mocking rhymes of Paramount Leader, Deng Xiaoping, and Premier, Li Peng. Tiananmen Square became a stage where for close to three months, dissatisfied students performed rituals of dissent, and presented counter-narratives and discourses of political defiance that CNN and other media outlets broadcast live to television audiences around the world. This was political theatre and messaging at its best. Three months after the demonstrations and metaphorical worshipping of the Goddess of Democracy began, the Chinese People's Liberation Army, the armed wing of the Chinese Communist Party, crushed the student demonstrations with extreme violence leading to heavy loss of student life.

As these examples demonstrate, political messaging through music and entertainment has been part of human society from time immemorial. That is because music and entertainment are spaces where diverse mentalities, collective memories, cultural expressions, and identitarian assertions are set forth. This two-volume collection of case studies and analyses of instrumentalizations of music and entertainment for purposes of political messaging from Afghanistan to Zimbabwe, demonstrate that the phenomenon is cross-cultural, global, and of contemporary relevance. It is mostly prevalent in geographies or territorialities of repression, jurisdictions where explicit and overt criticism of the government, the president, political leaders, political parties, ethnic groups, religions, or prophets can lead to dire legal and extra-legal consequences. As such, musicians, comedians, artists, and entertainers have to tread carefully to avoid offending the powers that be, those who have the ability to use the coercive power of the state to persecute and victimize their critics. Public political communicators in these kinds of authoritarian contexts embed their messages in humor, metaphors, analogies, and other literary techniques. This is the process of communicational couching, the subtle embedment and dissimulation of political messages–counter-discourses, counter narratives, and counter-communication–within the lyrics of music and entertainment content for purposes of eliciting desired responses from audiences. The trick is not to arouse the ire of the powers that be. Music and entertainment in which subtle or overt political satire and messages are embedded and couched do double duty as instruments of resistance and subversion.

The chapters in this two-volume book take the reader on an insightful scholarly safari of heuristic analyses of the instrumentalization of music and entertainment for purposes of political messaging in multiple politico-cultural geographies around the globe. The case studies span a broad spectrum of realities and politico-cultural contexts. They range from the appropriation of highbrow Western classical music in the United States, where it was presented anew as a weapon of activism in the struggle for civil rights, to the emergence of morbid "Pashto Terror Songs" in the killing fields at the Pashtun Belt which lies at the intersection of Pakistan and Afghanistan, the world's contemporary crucible of incessant war, gender inequality, and massive human rights violations. Analyses of the instrumentalization of classical music as an act of resistance in the cauldron of racism and racial discrimination in the United States, stand in stark contrast with the morbid songs of terror that have emerged from the "merchants of death" at the Pakistan-Afghanistan border. These two case studies serve as "book ends" that bracket diverse case studies of the deployment of music in the service of critical political communication in multiple political and cultural geographies around the world. The chapters within these "book ends" provide points of access to diverse narratives and case studies of the deployment of popular music and entertainment as instruments of resistance and subversion in a variety of politico-cultural contexts. The chapters are an eclectic and insightful collection of analyses that span multiple political and cultural geographies of communication around the globe. Written by a diverse group of scholars from all continents, they amount to re-presentations, novel presentations of instances of the instrumentalization of music and entertainment as the thin edge of the wedge of resistance, defiance, subversion, and identitarian affirmation. Taken together, the chapters present anew, good, bad, and unorthodox political and social uses to which music and entertainment are put, given their diversity and almost inexhaustible carrying capacity.

In oppressive politico-cultural contexts, music and entertainment are often the only avenues for the expression of dissent, the only instrument for the communication of counter-discourses and messages of resistance. As the chapters demonstrate, music and entertainment give voice to the marginalized "Other" from the Caucasus to the Caribbean. They not only describe and explain reality, they are satirical weapons that judge lived experience in specific politico-cultural contexts. This is because in critical and satirical political communication, to sing is to sting, to portray is to betray, to perform is to deform, to narrate is to berate, to describe is to ascribe, and to act is to attack. The case studies of political messaging in entertainment contained in these volumes do it all. They range from the performance of resistance in the Philippines– deployment of music and theatre as context-specific forms of dissent– to the transformation of entertainment spaces into places for projecting socio-political messaging and bringing into existence alternative, affirmative visions of society in the United States. The collection also includes analyses of Rastafarian military symbolism in performances of Reggae, the music of resistance par excellence, as well as the content of *cinéma engagé* or engaged political films in India. The unifying theme of the case studies in both volumes is the problem of autocracy; political and cultural repression, militarism, corruption, and societal injustice.

These diverse chapters offer new insights and avenues that make political communication varied, relevant, global, and open to new approaches. As such, they are bound to stimulate more global, interdisciplinary engagements and research endeavors in political communication and freedom of expression. This compendium enables us to view politics through the prism of music and entertainment. Their premise is that politics and political messaging are too important to be left to professional politicians, political scientists, and journalists. Music and entertainment in which subtle or overt political satire and messages are embedded or couched are as relevant objects of analysis as other forms of political communication.

Lyombe Eko (Ph.D.) is a Professor of Media Law, Comparative & International Communication in the Department of Journalism and Creative Media, College of Media and Communication, Texas Tech University, Lubbock, TX – USA. He is the author of *The Charlie Hebdo Affair & Comparative Journalistic Cultures* (https://link.springer.com/book/10.1007%2F978-3-030-18079-9#authorsand affiliationsbook).

PREFACE

Uche Onyebadi

Texas Christian University, USA

Contemporary political communication research is still overly concerned with investigating institutions and structures, processes, political participation and civic engagement, voter education, political cognitions and behaviors, etc. No doubt, these are legitimate, epistemological research subjects. However, these important areas of inquiry only emphasize the transmission, reception, and effects dimensions of the *political* content of this eclectic discipline, almost precluding its instrumental, functional, and *communicational* components. Decades earlier, Denton and Woodward (1998, p. 10) had also noted that "the crucial factor that makes communication 'political' is not the source of the message, but its content and purpose." Therefore, the need for an expansion of the intellectual and research frontiers of political communication cannot be clearer or more compelling.

While advocating the expansion of the present and restricted boundaries of political communication inquiry, Professor Wayne Wanta, a political communication scholar of international recognition and former president of the Association for Education in Journalism and Mass Communication (AEJMC), noted that what is *communicated* through music, for instance, possibly has longer-lasting and stronger influence on audiences, than a typical evening news bulletin. This is because, "The average person would never recite verbatim a news text from an evening newscast" (Wanta, 2019, p. xii), while the same person will not only commit the lyrics of a politically charged piece of music to memory, but will easily recall the words and probably act on them.

Quite notably, political communication research is gradually witnessing an evolution from what was solely the *political* to the inclusion of the *content and instrumentalization* of the *communication* through a variety of platforms. This movement has been greatly enabled by the advent of the Internet and all forms of social media which empower people to share political ideas across the spectrum. Contemporary political audiences are no longer passive recipients of political messages from contestants for political office, the legacy news media, political advertisements, and institutional or individual stakeholders in society. Members of this audience now horizontally discuss and share ideas about politics and its concomitant issues, and can use their platforms and self-selected membership of often exclusive political organizations, to motivate and campaign for concerted action on any political issue of interest to them.

This book, *Political messaging in Music and Entertainment Spaces Across the Globe,* is conceptualized as supporting this unique push toward the extension of the horizon of political communication research, by focusing and emphasizing political messaging (content) through music and entertainment spaces (platforms), and from a global perspective. It offers researchers and students of political communication a compendium of well-researched, valuable, and rich insights into how political messaging is constructed, instrumentalized, and disseminated through forms that are outside the orbit of mainstream research in the discipline.

The globalist perspective that underlies this book is a recognition of the fact that the forms of entertainment and music used for political messaging are not limited to constructs and experiences in the United States and other developed nations in the Western world. For instance, Bassem Raafat Mohamed Youssef, an Egyptian surgeon-turned comedian, conceptualized and hosted a satirical news program titled *El-Bernameg* (2011-2014), to expose the ills of successive governments in Egypt. Not only was the program successful and widely acclaimed in the country, he was nicknamed the *Jon Stewart* of Egypt. Stewart is a notable American satirist and former host of the popular *Daily Show* program on US Comedy Central television. However, when the Egyptian authoritarian leadership deemed him as too critical of government's highhandedness and corruption, Youssef had to escape into exile in the United States, as it became clear to him that his life was in danger.

In their article, *Producing Journalistic News Satire: How Nordic Satirists Negotiate a Hybrid Genre,* Koivukoski and Ödmark (2020) noted how Finnish and Swedish news satirists use their platforms to encode strong political messages to their audiences. Baym (2005), discussed how Jon Stewart's "fake news" *Daily Show* impacted audiences through discussing political issues in a satirical manner. Needless to point out that Volodymyr Oleksandrovych Zelensky, the man whose comedy show titled *Servant of the People* where he played the role of a fake Ukrainian president, ended up being sworn in as the 6th Ukrainian president in May, 2019. Finally, the global impact of the late Bob Marley's political lyrics as well as the politically charged music of the late Nigerian musician, Fela Aníkúlápó Kuti, also attest to the powerful political messaging that is disseminated through music.

Having edited two books that address political messaging through the instrumentality of music[1], and being cognizant of the severely limited books in this genre that include Love (2006), Street (2012) and Garratt (2019), it became obvious to me that music alone cannot sufficiently provide the

---

[1] Music as a Platform for Political Communication (2017) and Music and Messaging in the African Political Arena (2019).

pedestal upon which the latitude of research on the *communication* aspect of political communication can be firmly established. As Michael D. Carpini (2000) noted, the entertainment space offers some people the opportunity to learn and form opinions about political affairs. The concept of *Music and Entertainment*, which encompasses comedy, drama, literature and other forms of art and popular culture, is therefore a more virile and broader platform for political messaging as advocated in this book.

As the title suggests, chapter contributors to *Political Messaging in Music and Entertainment Spaces Across the Globe* come from various countries and continents. The focus is equally transnational. Interest generated upon publishing the call for chapter contributions was remarkable, such that the editor and publisher decided to publish the title in two volumes.

Below are insights into each chapter:

Chapter Summary [Volume 1]

Chapter 1: *Z/Sarsuwelas*: Music, theater, and the mediation of political dissent in the Philippines

Rodelio C. Manacsa
Zeny Sarabia-Panol

Political messaging via the theater and music, the authors contend, is an indirect, mediated process. They examine how Filipino activist artists appropriated the Spanish colonialist tradition of artistic Zarzuela and created an indigenous version, the Z/Sarsuwelas, as an instrument to fight injustices in society and resist the excesses of the political class and overlords in the Philippines.

Chapter 2: Bringing Spirituals onto the Classical Music stage in the service of African American Civil Rights

Julia Schmidt-Pirro

In the 1800s and early 1900s America, classical music was considered the exclusive enclave of Caucasian musicians and composers. However, three African Americans - Marian Anderson (1897–1993), Paul Robeson (1898–1976) and William Grant Still (1895-1978) – shattered this mystique by essentially turning their folk songs – the Spirituals - into classical music and concerts that attracted acclaim and recognition across the entire spectrum of classical music in the country. In this chapter, the author examines how the works of these African American classical music icons provided the templates used for the civil rights activism of later years.

Chapter 3: "I Am More Than My Body!:" Politicizing the Female Masquerade performance in the West Indian Carnival

Cherry-Ann M. Smart

West Indian carnivals are usually associated with musical performances, dancing and merriment. What is often ignored, or sidelined, is the politicization that lies underneath the glitz and razzmatazz the carnivals often showcase. In this chapter, the author sheds light on the Trinidad and Tobago carnival, highlighting the politicization, abuse of power and inequalities against the Female Masquerade participants in the extravaganza, and the political messaging embedded in such disrespect and disregard.

Chapter 4: Military Rhetoric: Making sense of political messaging in Reggae music

Kameika S. Murphy

Underlying Reggae music is something the author identifies as "military symbolism" in performances. When these symbolisms are understood within the context of the Rastafarian philosophy that guides Reggae music, and the model of resistance that historically emerged out of the 1831 Baptist War of emancipation in Jamaica, it becomes clear that Reggae is a space for political messaging, not just a forum for musical entertainment. This is the author's contention as expressed in this chapter.

Chapter 5: Revisiting the role of Popular Culture in supporting the anti-Apartheid Movement (1970s-1980s)

Archie W. Simpson

South Africa's system of apartheid was officially introduced in the country after the May 1948 election victory of the Afrikaner Nationalist Party led by Daniel François Malan. That system of official racial segregation turned out to be a festering sore on the conscience of the international community. This chapter examines how all forms of popular culture were used by nation-states, individuals and organizations across the world to fight the obnoxious apartheid system, leading to the 1994 general elections that heralded the end of apartheid policy. And, with the victory of the African National Congress in the election, Nelson Mandela became the first black president of South Africa.

Chapter 6: Political music in Brazil: An examination of Punk Rock in Brasília, 1979-1985

Silvio César Tamaso D'Onofrio
Henrique César Tamaso D'Onofrio
Marta Fernanda Tamaso D'Onofrio

Brazil was governed by authoritarian regimes in the 1970s and 1980s. Censorship was perhaps at its peak in the country in this period. In this chapter, the authors took a historical view of how Punk Rock bands in the country used the platform of the music genre known as Rock of Brasília, to continue performing their art and spreading their political ideology and messaging, in spite of the restrictions imposed by their government.

Chapter 7: Political Messaging in Indian Cinema: Core or Periphery?

Usha Rani

This chapter traces the evolution of the political content of the film industry in India, "based on the premise that film producers in states in the country where communist political parties are in power, tend to produce politically engaging films." The author uses two states – West Bengal and Kerala – to test this hypothesis. These are states where communist-leaning political parties have been dominant in power. The author concludes that while political communication was at the heart of films produced in these states decades earlier, that is no longer the case in the content of films produced in the states in modern times. Political messaging is now at the periphery of the contents of those films.

Chapter 8: Musicians and Political songs in the struggle for freedom in Zimbabwe

Bhekinkosi J. Ncube

When Zimbabwe became independent in 1980, expectations within and outside the country were that the political agitations that resulted in independence and freedom would recede into history. The story, however, turned out to be different. The author of this chapter takes a look at the use of protest music and political agitation in post-colonial Zimbabwe to challenge the shortcomings and excesses of the country's president, Robert Mugabe (now deceased). Here, the musician in focus is Desire Moyo who goes by the stage name, Moyoxide.

Chapter 9: Stylistic vernacular jingles in political messaging: An analysis of Igbo language jingles in Nigeria's General Elections (2019)

Cecilia A. Eme
Benjamin I. Mmadike

Using vernacular radio jingles in political messaging appears to be a most effective instrument to ensure that the messages are clearly understood by their intended audiences because of the presence of shared meaning between the encoders and decoders of the messages in a local setting. It is against this backdrop that the authors investigated the stylistic components of vernacular radio jingles in Nigeria's 2019 general elections, restricting themselves to the examination of how three main political parties in the country used such jingles for political campaign messaging in a designated state in the eastern region of Nigeria.

Chapter 10: Performative sites of resistance: A challenge to oppression through artistic entertainment

Rachael Cofield
Douglas L. Allen

According to its authors, the objective in this chapter is to "challenge societal oppressions by transforming entertainment spaces into places for projecting socio-political messaging and bringing into existence alternative, affirmative visions of society and place." The authors brought this to fruition by specifically evaluating the political messaging in the performances of two marginalized communities: the queer burlesque dancers of Metropolitan Studios in downtown Atlanta (USA) and Black members of the Florida A&M University band. They conclude that, "Such performances seek to project more affirmative counter-narratives into society and display more inclusive, justice-oriented articulations of space and performance."

Chapter 11: Chile's Nueva Canción and the Pinochet Regime: Censoring political messages in music

Kelly Grenier

Chile's former dictator, Augusto Pinochet, wielded absolute power in many respects. One area where he most noticeably cracked down on dissenting voices and imposed strict censorship was on what is generally referred to as political music and its musicians. Perhaps acknowledging the power of music, the former dictator paid particular attention the country's Nueva Canción movement. In this chapter, the author examines Pinochet's censorship by focusing attention on the Nueva Canción and arguably its foremost artist, Violeta Parra, and how the government hounded musicians who opposed Pinochet into exile.

Chapter 12: Zimbabwe: Zimbabwe: Music, performance, and political lyrics as "cure" for post *Bhalagwe* trauma

Mphathisi Ndlovu
Khanyile J. Mlotshwa

State-sponsored terrorism against an indigenous group of people is not a new historical phenomenon. But, what happened in Zimbabwe between 1983 and 1987, was as phenomenal as it was unprecedented. An estimated number of 20,000 Zimbabweans of Matabeleland origin were killed in this pogrom known as the Gukurahundi massacre. The authors revisited this gruesome event through the songs of Zimbabwean musician, Bongani Mncube, who used his platform to memorialize the killings that subsequent Zimbabwean governments have failed to officially acknowledge.

Chapter Summary [Volume 2]

Chapter 1: Stirring up "Good Trouble:" Black songs of protest and activism in 21st century US

Dorothy M. Bland
Marquita S. Smith

The Black Lives Matter (BLM) and the other social justice movements that originated from the US and spread all over the world, stimulated the creativity of Black musicians in the US in using their platforms to join the protest for racial equality. However, such politically charged music and songs of protest pre-date the BLM and protest against the 2020 killing of George Floyd by a Minneapolis police officer. The authors of this chapter look back at protest music in 21st century United States, and also paid particular attention to three prominent entertainment awards/shows of the modern era - the Black Entertainment Television, the 35th annual Stellar Awards, and the 15th installment of the BET Hip Hop Awards – to highlight the contributions of Black artists in stirring up "good trouble" in the fight against racial oppression and injustices in the country.

Chapter 2: Speaking for the "Other:" Reinforcing the Jezebel stereotype in Alexander McCall Smith's No. 1 Ladies' Detective Agency

Ann White-Taylor

Who speaks for the oppressed? And, are those speakers truly authentic in their self-styled, self-imposed mission to speak for others without belonging to the group they claim to represent? This chapter shines light on Alexander McCall Smith's, No. 1 Ladies' Detective Agency book series to challenge the political stereotypes about African women who are usually characterized as morally bankrupt and "bad girls" in society. The author provides a counter narrative in the works of several writers of African origin that challenge the negative stereotype of African women by people who pretend to be qualified to "speak for" the maligned ladies, but indeed denigrate them.

Chapter 3: Human Rights and redemptive-corrective justice in Bob Marley's music

Kevin Barker

A lot of literature exists on the music of the late global Reggae music icon, Robert "Nesta" Marley. However, not much has been written about his philosophy of redemptive justice against the backdrop of his Rastafarian beliefs. This chapter addresses this important but understudied area, and highlights the iconic artist's conception of justice. According to the author of this chapter, Marley clearly articulates and communicates his conceptualization of human rights and redemptive-corrective justice in his Reggae music.

Chapter 4: Framing contesting Nationalisms, Resistance, and Triumph in Ethiopian popular music

Dagim A. Mekonnen
Zenebe Beyene

No matter the particular regime in which they find themselves, either in a military dictatorship or a democratically elected government that acts more like a military junta, Ethiopian musicians have never ceased to produce songs with political themes and lyrics that celebrate nationalism and challenge the establishment. More recently, however, such themes have veered into ethno-nationalism sentiments. This chapter therefore focuses on, and analyzes, the songs with such centrifugal ethno-nationalistic themes and political messaging that threaten to further fragment the manifestly unstable Ethiopian polity.

Chapter 5: Interpreting Feminism through sounds of resilience in the U.S.: An analytical approach to music from the 19th to the 21st centuries

Ngozi Akinro
Jenny J. Dean

The authors of this chapter describe their work as an analysis of the political and feminist messages that "challenge hegemonic narratives" with the intention to *"spread positivity about feminism." They uniquely explore the music of twelve outstanding U.S. female musicians from the 19th to the 21st centuries, and conclude that although the selected songs express different messages based on the period in which they were composed and released, they all have the same focus: acknowledging and communicating messages that advance "the role and place of the female gender," and promoting the rights of women in spite of the dominant patriarchal society in which they live and work.*

Chapter 6: Broadcasting populism: An examination of Venezuelan Community TV and participatory democracy

Elena M. De Costa

What is the role of the mass media in Latin America? Specifically, what are the expectations of public broadcasting in this region? In answer to these and related questions, the author investigates the concept of community media in a socialist environment in Venezuela under the late President Hugo Chávez. The former Venezuelan leader promoted state-sponsored media in order to counter the monopoly of private media stations in the country, in what was described as giving a voice to people at the grassroots of Venezuelan society, as a form of mass participatory democracy. The setbacks in this approach to media democratization are addressed by the author.

Chapter 7: Music and violence: The complexity and complicity of Pashto "songs of terror"

Muhammad Farooq
Syed I. Ashraf

How do cultural songs romanticize militarization, violence and death? The authors untangle this apparent contradiction in their analysis of the Pashto songs among people who live in a cultural setting at the Pashtun Belt region that straddles Pakistan and Afghanistan. They argue that the twin technologies of death and destruction – Drone strikes deployed by modern war technology and the suicide bombings used by the militants to fight their vastly armed enemies – have invariably led to the emergence of local songs that have produced a peculiar genre that is called "songs of terror" in a region that has witnessed untold "musicalization of death" and unceasing, systemic violence. Thus, songs as cultural artefacts, have transformed into avenues for political messaging and "celebration" of death in what the authors call a necrospace where organized violence has become the societal norm.

Chapter 8: Political messaging in the Anatolian-Pop: How has this music genre transformed Turkey's socio-political landscape?

Yavuz Yildirim
Mehmet Atilla Güler

In Turkey, the Anatolian Pop music popped up in the 1960s with political and social messages that transformed the music scene in the country. In this chapter, the authors trace the history of this music genre, examine the top musicians and songs that made waves in Anatolian Pop, provide insights into how the new music brand tells stories about inequalities in the system, and challenge the Western hegemonic concepts and capitalist ideals that had crept into the country and impacted the pristine way of life of the people, all in a situation of censorship of thought and arts in Turkey.

Chapter 9: Praise songs amidst political chaos: Assessing the impact of "Hope Your Justice Will Arrive" on Hong Kong's 2019 Social Movement

Wendy Chan. W. Lam

The 2019 social movement protest in Hong Kong over the controversial extradition bill to China was unique in many ways. One of the ways the protests attracted global attention was when a Christian praise song turned out to be a hit tune and went viral on the Internet, and motivated young audiences to share the song online. The author of this chapter examined the YouTube song, "Hope Your Justice Will Arrive," with specific focus on a textual analysis of the comments left on the Internet by Hong Kong audiences in response to this song.

Chapter 10: From political stump to messaging through music: A study of Madzore's political songs in Zimbabwe

Faith Bahela

It is not often that politicians quit their soapbox and take to music to disseminate their political messages to larger audiences. In Zimbabwe, this was done by Paul Madzore, a former opposition politician who used his voice and music to join the teeming population of citizens the government described as "subversive" elements in the country. Using Foucault's theory of discourse, the author of this chapter explored Madzore's songs, and how they became "a site where political identities are renegotiated and reconstructed as the opposition party is valorized whilst delegitimizing ZANU-PF," the country's ruling party since independence in 1980.

Chapter 11: Political songs, advertising, and development messaging: An assessment of music in promoting socio-economic growth in Tiv society (Nigeria)

Terna P. Agba

This chapter makes the linkage between music and songs, political messaging and socio-economic development in society. Using a purposive sample of songs by four prominent Tiv musicians, the author employed the development communication theory to assess the political content of the musicians, and how the themes in their popular songs were aimed at facilitating the human and socio-economic and political development of their native Tiv land.

References

Baym, G. (2005). The Daily Show: Discursive Integration and the Reinvention of Political Journalism. *Political Communication, 22(3)*, 259-276. DOI: 10.1080/10584600591006492

Carpini, M.D.. (2000). In search of the informed citizen: What Americans know about politics and why it matters, *The Communication Review, 4*(1), 129-164. DOI: 10.1080/10714420009359466

Denton, R.E. & Woodward, G.C. (1998). *Political Communication in America.* Praeger.

Garratt, J. (2019). *Music and Politics: A critical introduction.* United Kingdom: Cambridge University Press.

Koivukoski, J. & Ödmark, S. (2020). Producing Journalistic News Satire: How Nordic Satirists Negotiate a Hybrid Genre. *Journalism Studies, 21*(6), 731-747. DOI: 10.1080/1461670X.2020.1720522

Love, N. S. (2006). *Musical Democracy.* Albany, NY: State University of New York Press.

Street, J. (2012). *Music and Politics.* Malden, MA – USA: Polity Press.

Wanta, W. (2019). Foreword. In U. Onyebadi, (2019) (Ed.). *Music and Messaging in the African Political Arena* (pp. xiii-xiv). Hershey PA, USA: IGI Global. DOI: 10.4018/978-1-5225-7295-4

CHAPTER 1

Stirring up "Good Trouble:" Black songs of protest and activism in 21st century U.S.

Dorothy M. Bland

Frank W. and Sue Mayborn School of Journalism,
University of North Texas, USA

Marquita S. Smith

School of Journalism and New Media,
University of Mississippi, USA

Abstract

Given the ongoing struggle for racial and social justice in the United States and the disproportionate impact of the novel coronavirus pandemic on people of color, Black artists are creating compelling messages using the power of music to protest what they see as injustice across various genres, from Gospel to Hip Hop. During the summer of 2020, social justice protests were held around the globe in the wake of George Floyd's killing in Minneapolis by police, and celebrities, from DaBaby to Tamela Mann, shared songs of protest during Black Entertainment Television's 2020 Awards Show, the 35th annual Stellar Awards Show, and the 15th installment of the BET Hip Hop Awards Show. In the last half of that turbulent year, these musical protests flowed alongside the rise of the international Black Lives Matter Movement. This qualitative study used a theoretical framework at the intersection of critical race theory, framing, and the rhetoric in protest songs to analyze the lyrics, videos, and how the performances were received in news media. While there is a growing body of literature about protest music over the last century, this is arguably the first academic study this decade to examine protest songs and videos performed at three major music awards shows highlighting mostly Black artists in 2020.

Keywords: Black music, protest songs, Black Lives Matter Movement, Black Entertainment Television, BET Awards, Stellar Awards, Hip Hop Awards

***

Introduction

Black singers, artists, entertainers, and others in the music industry, and across various genres, from Gospel to Hip Hop, are creating compelling messages using the power of music, video, and other creative acts to protest what they see as injustice. Social justice protests erupted around the globe during the summer of 2020 in the wake of George Floyd's killing on May 25 in Minneapolis. On Tuesday, June 2, 2020, music industry marketing veterans, Jamilla Thomas and Brianna Agyemang, organized a social media initiative known as #TheShowMustBePaused, which later came to be known as social media's #Blackout. Thomas and Agyemang's campaign featured lots of black boxes and platitudes. The social media effort resulted in major confusion. However, their goal was to disrupt business as usual while holding accountable major corporations and music industry executives who benefit from the labor and struggles of Black talent. However, some media critics noted that the initiative turned out to be a "big fail" (McNamara, 2020, para. 4). The same day, Spotify debuted its Black Lives Matter playlist, and James Brown's 1968 hit, "Say It Loud - I'm Black and I'm Proud," experienced a 15,740% increase, going from "just over 2,000 combined audio and streams" (Unterberger, 2020, para. 2) on May 26 to 375,000 streams on June 2. Kendrick Lamar's "Alright," which was described as a "modern civil rights anthem" (Unterberger, 2020, para. 3) in *Billboard*, and Childish Gambino's "This is America," also both broke a million streams that day. Lamar's "Alright," was originally released in 2015, and the video features powerful black and white imagery of police violence. The video went viral after protestors started chanting lyrics from the song in Cleveland, the city where 12-year-old Tamir Rice was killed in 2014. In "This is America," the 2018 video opens with a shirtless Childish Gambino shooting a hooded and handcuffed black guitarist, then children dragging the body away. According to Johnson (2018), "Our normalization of racist violence has come at the cost of not only black lives, but black innocence" (para 2).

In 2020, a number of major industry players including Epic Records, Sony Music, Universal Music, the Recording Academy, Apple Music, Amazon Music, Sirius XM and TikTok voiced support for diversity initiatives and more inclusion. TikTok was credited as offering one of the "more comprehensive plans" with a pledge of $3 million to aid Black communities (Blisten & Spanos, 2020).

Other entertainers exercised their right to petition and the power of the purse to support their causes. Star performers such as John Legend, Common, Lizzo, and The Weeknd "signed an open letter urging local governments to defund the police in favor of increasing spending on health care, education and other community programs" (Blisten & Spanos, 2020, para. 17). Beyoncé, who was honored with the BET 2020 Humanitarian Award, and her husband JayZ donated more than $1.5 million to Black Lives Matter and other civil rights initiatives, and The Weeknd donated more than $500,000 to support equal and social justice causes (Herwees, 2016). As Beyoncé accepted the award she told viewers: "We need to vote like our lives depend on it, because it does" (Landrum, 2020, para. 1).

A wide spectrum of Black celebrities, from DaBaby to Tamela Mann and Burna Boy shared songs of protest and social activism during Black Entertainment Television's 20th Awards, the 35th annual Stellar Awards and the BET Hip Hop Awards. These musical protests flowed alongside the rapid rise of the Black Lives Matter Movement without a live audience in a glitzy mega venue for the BET 2020, Stellar, and BET Hip Hop Award shows due to concerns about the events becoming super spreaders of the novel coronavirus. Nonetheless, the BET 2020 Awards show was historic as it marked the 20th anniversary year for the show and the first time the show aired live via simulcast on CBS in prime time in the United States. BET was founded by Robert Johnson in 1979 (Pulley, 2004), and is now part of the Paramount conglomerate. The 2020 BET Awards attracted more than 3.7 million viewers. On BET social, it attracted more than 30 million views and #BETAWARDS more than doubled its views year-over-year (BET Press, 2020). Now an international offering, the show was broadcast in parts of Africa, Europe, and Asia. For example, viewers in Nigeria, South Africa, France, the United Kingdom, and South Korea expanded the audience. On display across the globe, performers sang, rapped, and spoke to the masses through their musical productions.

The transformative power and influence of music are historically well-documented. Unlike many other forms of communication, music is capable of transcending boundaries. Mingo (2019) articulated music as a transgressive tool of resistance as follows:

> I use the term transgressive here to refer to the active crossing of socially constructed boundaries particularly within the Black Christian community in ways that expanded opportunities for public participation and leadership from marginalised persons within the community. Historically, gender, race, class, and sexuality have limited participation in predominant forms of public communication including preaching, speaking, and publishing. (p. 92)

For hundreds of years, songwriters have penned verses of protest. In fact, Edet (1976) asserted that it is human to protest. Lyrics told stories of slavery, mass lynching, segregation, chain gangs, mass incarceration, and poverty. All of these themes and more have been communicated in protest music, lyrics, and rhythms. These musical soundtracks not only highlighted the pain and suffering of the Black experience, but also often narrated social movements. That power to narrate should not be underestimated. Keiger (2020) posited that protest songs are aligned with advocacy journalism.

Thus, this qualitative study uses a theoretical framework at the intersection of critical race theory, framing, and the rhetoric in protest songs to analyze their lyrics, and how the BET 2020, Stellar, and BET Hip Hop Award performances were received in the news media. While there is a growing body of literature about protest music over the last century, this chapter fills the gap in the 21st century with a focus on how 22 performances, including four cypher performances, from these shows highlight the Black experience and protests during the Black Lives Matter Movement as documented in the news media.

Literature Review

History of Black Protest Music

According to *The New York Times'* "1619 Project," the history of Black protest music in the United States is traceable to the arrival of slaves in 1619 (Morris, 2019). A variety of music and media scholars (Darden, 2014; Edet, 1976) have chronicled the history of Black protest and sacred music. For example, Darden wrote that songs paying tribute to "the forebears of Monkey, Rabbit, High John de Conquer Stagger (or Stack-O) Lee, John Henry" were considered "nonsense" songs by slave owners as long as slaves toiled in the fields (p. 3). Beyond offering some encouragement and solace to the toiling slaves, the work songs on the fields often expressed the news of the day as well as protested current conditions of the enslaved (Edet, 1976). Overseers often ignored the lyrics as long as the slaves continued to produce.

After the introduction of Christianity to the slaves, the work songs added "the heroic stories of Moses, Daniel and Jesus, heroes who led their people from physical bondage to freedom" (Edet, 1976, p. 3). For example, the spiritual, "Go Down Moses," has a chorus of "Let my people go!" and Darden argues that it speaks of "righteous anger," (Darden, 2014, p. 92), toward slave owners. The song "Swing Low, Sweet Chariot," which was performed at Harriet Tubman's funeral in 1913, was also considered one of the Underground Railroad conductor's favorites, as it spoke to the importance of escaping hardship for a better life. Today, many Black congregations continue to sing adaptations of such Negro Spirituals.

African-American protest music and the social conditions which accompanied those tunes can be heard from the Civil War to the Black Revolution. After slavery, a new genre of music emerged, featuring the Gospel song. "These deeply religious songs contained few overt words of protest. Some of them, however, such as 'I Been Buked and I Been Scorned,' seemed to epitomize the black man's struggle in America" (Edet, 1976, p.38). Still, some scholars suggest that any acknowledgement of pain and sorrow experienced by Blacks, although shared as hymns and songs of faith, protested the current circumstances of their community.

After the Civil War, the musicianship of the Blues spanned the South. The Blues told stories of economic and relationship struggles. During the Great Depression, even Blacks who worked menial jobs found themselves without work, and the Blues lamented their poverty. The Blues music also highlighted the hardships and inequities of many in the Black community, especially the plight of the Black man. Thought leader W.E.B. Du Bois called the Reconstruction period from 1867 to 1877 the "Mystic Years," focusing on the progress of Blacks in education, politics, and financial stability (Lewis, 2014). But history tells a different tale of severe hardship and suffering within the Black community. Edet (1976) remarked that the beginning of this time period could instead be called "The Years of Misery."

Over the decades, the musical selections promoted truth and documented protests. At the dawn of the 20th century, John and James Johnson turned the poem originally written by James Weldon Johnson into "Lift Every Voice and Sing," which is now popularly known as the Black National Anthem. U.S. Rep. James Clyburn, a Democrat from South Carolina, announced plans in January 2021 to introduce legislation to make the song the national hymn (Prince, 2021). The song speaks of struggle, yet optimism is evidenced by these lyrics:

> Sing a song full of the faith that the dark past has taught us,
> Sing a song full of the hope that the present has brought us.
> Facing the rising sun of our new day begun,
> Let us march on 'til victory is won. (NAACP, 2021)

Moving into the 20th century, Darden also found ties between labor unions and protest spirituals, and Lawrence Gellert cataloged hundreds of "Negro Songs of Protest" in 1936. They included "Let's Go to de Buryin,'" part of the lyrics reading: "Cap'm kill my buddy, let's go to de buryin'/Heah a mighty rumblin,' let's go to de buryin" (Darden, 2014, p. 66). As the lynchings of Blacks were common in the South, Abel Meeropol is credited with penning the "Strange Fruit" song, which was recorded by Billie Holiday in 1939. Holiday, a legendary jazz and swing singer, was inducted into the Grammy Hall of Fame in 1973 and the National Rhythm and Blues Hall of Fame in 2017 for her work. Her life was marked by drug abuse, and her story has been featured in several films, including the *United States vs. Billie Holiday*, which was a biopic released in 2021. In her autobiography, Holiday wrote that the "Strange Fruit" song reminded her of how her father died. This lyric passage with imagery provides powerful reminders of the dangers faced by Blacks in the South:

> Southern trees bear strange fruit
> Blood on the leaves and blood at the root
> Black bodies swinging in the southern breeze
> Strange fruit hanging from the poplar trees.

> (in Darden, 2014, p. 93)

The same year that "Strange Fruit" was recorded, Marian Anderson made history when she gave a national Easter Sunday radio concert on the steps of the Lincoln Memorial in Washington, D.C. In addition to "America," she performed a variety of songs ranging from "Ave Maria" to "My Soul's Been Anchored in the Lord." She remained active in the Civil Rights Movement for decades and sang at the inaugurations of Presidents Dwight Eisenhower and John F. Kennedy. Anderson, a contralto, was the first Black to perform at the Metropolitan Opera in 1955. She earned numerous awards including the Presidential Medal of Freedom and a Grammy Lifetime Achievement Award. While Anderson was a trailblazer, other music celebrities and entertainers followed in her footsteps by recording protest songs and lending their support in high-profile venues and offering financial support to various protest movements. For example, Mahalia Jackson was the first Black Gospel artist to sing in New York Carnegie Hall in 1950.

By the 1960s, Black R&B recording artists were being recognized for contributing songs of protests such as Sam Cooke's "A Change is Gonna Come" in 1963, and Nina Simone's "Mississippi Goddam" in 1964, where she unleashed her fury after the assassination of Medgar Evers, a civil rights activist, and the Birmingham, Alabama, Baptist Church bombing in which four Black girls were killed (Morgan, 2020). Shortly after the assassination of Martin Luther King Jr., James Brown released "Say It Loud, I'm Black and I'm Proud." In 1971, tunes such as Gil Scott-Heron's "The Revolution Will Not Be Televised" and Marvin Gaye's "What's Going On" respectively spoke to the growing restless and potential uprising of Black folks upset with their absence on television as well as a response to police brutality (Carter et al., 2020). In the last quarter of the 20th century, Hip Hop became a stronger presence with groups such as N.W.A.'s "F*** the Police," making waves on the *Billboard* charts in 1988 and Public Enemy's "Fight the Power" released in 1989. Both songs are part of the Gangsta Rap genre and address growing racial tension among Blacks, law enforcement, and largely white power structures.

Over the years, Hip Hop has evolved with artists expressing even more violence and sex in lyrics. Today's entertainers may in some cases be considered more "gangsta" in tone and rhetoric. Much of the Hip Hop discourse analysis among scholars has fallen into three areas: lyrics and visual representation, historical analysis, and the "black public sphere, with an emphasis on the impact of social, economic, geopolitical forces in the black diasporic cultural expressions" (Fitts, 2008, p. 216). Over the last quarter century, scholars such as Kilson (2003) and McWhorter (2003) have called Hip Hop destructive to Black culture while others such as Boyd (2002) and Ginwright (2004) have praised it for being empowering. Charnas (2011) chronicled the rise of the Hip Hop business, which has become a global, multi-billion dollar industry "spanning music, language, film television, books, fashion, sports and politics" (p. ix). Goldman Sachs "has forecast that music revenue is expected to double to about

$131 billion by 2030" (Hale, 2019, para. 1). This is significant as R&B and Hip Hop music represent the most consumed genres, and Blacks have huge influence on pop culture around the globe.

Within the Hip Hop genre, cyphers also have become increasingly popular and known for improvisation. Watkins and Caines (2015) wrote:

> To cypher is to rap, break, beatbox tightly together in a circle where each person just might get a moment in the spotlight. To cypher is to borrow and to lend, to playfully freewheel through whilst taking an exacting care for each word and carefully considering all the sounds, meanings, and interpretations. It is to fight back, to borrow, to steal, to represent, and to collaborate, whilst suddenly—surprisingly—at times aggressively claiming your own voice, your own right to speak. (para. 2)

In 2016, *Rolling Stone* documented 22 protest anthems related to the Black Lives Matter Movement. They range from "Don't Shoot," which was released after Michael Brown's 2014 killing in Ferguson, and featured 10 rappers and four R&B singers, to "I Can't Breathe," which was released by Ellisha and Steven Flagg, siblings of Eric Garner who died after a chokehold at the hands of New York Police officers in 2014 (Spanos & Grant, 2016). It is noteworthy that megastars such as Kendrick Lamar and Beyoncé have added their voices to the protest with songs such as "Freedom" in 2016 and "Fear" in 2017. "We are sick and tired of the killings of young men and women in our communities," Beyoncé wrote in a statement on her website. "It is up to us to take a stand and demand that they stop killing us" (Knowles-Carter, 2016). Scholars Orejuela and Shonekan (2018) compiled case studies around the Black Lives Matter movement and music, from campus protests at the University of Missouri in 2016 to the go-go music scene in Washington, D.C. Music scholar, Portia K. Maultsby, wrote that the Black Lives Matter movement is a "contemporary expression of both pride and resistance" and music has been "central to the sociopolitical movements of black Americans who continue to fight all forms of institutional racism" (in Orejuela & Shonekan, p. ix). Beyond social-cultural influences, music continues to garner support for popular movements for equity and social justice.

Music remains a vital part of the social, cultural, and political fabric of the U.S., and indeed the world. From Africa, all throughout the diaspora, artists are still making protest music. In a long-standing tradition, musicians out of Nigeria collaborated with international musicians and rallied around protests to "End Sars." The recent popularity of local rapper Falz highlights the continuation of protest music in Nigeria. His lyrics and passion are welcomed by youth or the next generation. Inspired in part by Nigerian activist and king of the Afrobeat, Fela Kuti, his latest album *Moral Instruction (Falz, 2019)*, shouts anti-corruption messaging: "Is he the messiah? Or are we to look out for another?" His involvement in the #EndSARS protests and growing popularity in London and the U.S. is creating more global context for the Black Lives Matter movement, and the fact that these lives matter everywhere, including Nigeria.

After a video surfaced showing a special anti-robbery police squad called SARS killing a man on the street in Lagos, musicians Runtown and Falz tweeted about protesting the senseless killing and violence. Soon, U.S. celebrities such as P Diddy, entrepreneur, rapper and producer, Trey Songz, R&B artist, and Viola Davis, Oscar-winning actress, followed the hashtag and began tweeting their support. What these stars understood, earlier than most U.S. media did, was that this was an iteration of the Black Lives Matter movement. Despite the continued police brutality and violence, the protest music of Nigeria remains transcendental. People around the world are uniting and creating the sounds of a global soundtrack that speak out against police brutality and oppression.

In this literature review, we have attempted to highlight some of the powerful soundtracks that gave voice and supported decades of popular movements demanding civil rights and social justice in the U.S. In the wake of the racial reckoning of 2020, amid the national elections and a global pandemic, songs have provided a common language which affirmed, inspired, and called to action like-minded communities.

> The impact of David Bowie, Prince and Bob Dylan, for example, on diversity awareness and legislative reform relating to sexuality, gender and racial equality respectively is still felt; with the latter receiving a Nobel Prize in 2016 for 'having created new poetic expressions within the great American song tradition.' The influence of these composers and performers reached far beyond the concert hall. (Shaw, 2018, p. 301)

The artistry in that common language has not only garnered the Noble Prize in Literature but has also harvested a Pulitzer Prize in Music.

Kendrick Lamar achieved greatness as the first rap artist to earn a Pulitzer Prize in music in 2018 for his album titled, *DAMN*, which also earned five Grammys (Flanagan, 2018). A combination of personal accountability and political engagement, this LP debuted at the top of the *Billboard 200* chart — then remained in the top 10 for more than 25 consecutive weeks. Entertainers' ability to set agendas through song lyrics and visual images is evidenced.

Method and Theory

This is a qualitative content analysis of the music award shows outlined in this study. This method of examining data qualitatively was perhaps best articulated by Creswell and Guetterman (2021). In this regard, the authors watched the two-hour live broadcast of the 2020 BET Awards show on June 28, the Stellar Gospel Music Awards' 35th-anniversary show on August 23, and the BET Hip Hop Awards on October 27, all in 2020. Each show was also watched multiple times later via

YouTube. After watching the shows independently, the authors met virtually, in line with the Centers for Disease Control's (CDC) social and physical distance guidelines to combat the spread of the COVID-19 pandemic, to discuss songs with strong protest and activism themes. After reaching an agreement on 22 performances for the study, those performances were reviewed again and coded for title, performer, genre, and gender. The performances were reviewed at least three more times to identify recurring themes, images, and gender of primary performers. The performances, including four cyphers, are listed in Table 1.1 below.

Table 1.11: 2020 Musical Award Shows – Title, Artist, Gender, and Genre

Awards Show	Title	Artist	Gender	Genre
BET 2020	I Just Wanna Live	Keedron Bryant	Male	Gospel
BET 2020	Fight the Power (Remix)	Public Enemy, Nas, Rapsody, Black Thought	Males & Females	Hip Hop
BET 2020	We Will Never Break	John Legend	Male	R&B
BET 2020	Let Go & Black Habits (Medley)	Sir & D-Smoke	Male	Hip Hop
BET 2020	Rockstar (Remix)	DaBaby	Male	Hip Hop
BET 2020	Young, Gifted & Black	Jennifer Hudson	Female	R&B
BET 2020	Perfect Way to Die	Alicia Keys	Female	R&B
BET 2020	The Box	Roddy Rich	Male	Hip Hop
BET 2020	Something Has to Break	Kierra Sheard & Karen Clark Sheard	Female	Gospel
BET 2020	Savage	Megan Thee Stallion	Female	Hip Hop
BET 2020	People	Jonathan McReynolds	Male	Gospel
BET 2020	Worldwide Beautiful	Kane Brown	Male	Country
Stellar	We Gon' Be Alright	Ty Tribett	Male	Gospel
Stellar	Bridge Over Troubled Water	CeCe Winans	Female	Gospel
Stellar	Touch From You	Tamela Mann	Female	Gospel
BET Hip Hop	Monsters You Made	Burna Boy & Chris Martin	Male	Hip Hop
BET Hip Hop	Try Jesus	Tobe Nwigwe	Male	Hip Hop
BET Hip Hop	Money Maker	2Chainz featuring Lil Wayne	Male	Hip Hop
BET Hip Hop	The Cypher (political)	Polo G, Chika, Jack Harlow, Flawless Real Talk, Rapsody	Males & Females	Hip Hop
BET Hip Hop	The Cypher (ladies first)	Teyana Taylor, H.E.R., Erykah Badu, Brandy	Females	Hip Hop
BET Hip Hop	The Cypher (reggae)	Beenie Man, County Killer, Koffee, Skip Marley, Shenessa	Males & Females	Hip Hop
BET Hip Hop	The Cypher (newcomers)	Ade, Buddy, Flo Mill, Deante Hitchcock	Males & Females	Hip Hop

Themes in all three shows centered on racial equality and justice for Black and brown Americans.

The three award shows were selected because they aired on BET, which is marketed as the premiere channel for Black programming. Nielsen researchers have found that African Americans watch "37% more television than any other" racial/ethnic group (Obenson, 2019, para. 1). In addition to coding by genre, the researchers also looked at primary performers by gender. Building on the work of Emerson (2002), who explored the representation of Black women in videos, the researchers coded for the presence of violence and scantily clad entertainers showcasing sexuality. Song lyrics and videos were selected for further analysis if they addressed issues of racism, identity politics, or social justice. For this study, we analyzed frames communicated through 22 songs and performances. Accordingly, through the lens of framing theory, this chapter explores the symbiotic relationship between music and public policy, identity politics, and social justice. "In essence, framing theory suggests that how something is presented to the audience (called 'the frame') influences the choices people make about how to process that information" (Davie, 2020, para.2). Moreover, frames are used to organize or construct message meaning.

In communication theory, typically a frame references how media organizations present or convey information, especially news. Scholars have described framing as a form of agenda setting where audiences are told what to think about and how to process the issue. Goffman posited that social frameworks are built on natural frameworks (Metts & Cupach, 2008). He stated that frameworks and frames in communication heavily influence how people interpret, process, and receive data or information. Additionally, Metts and Cupach (2008) wrote that Goffman promoted the notion that individuals are capable users of frameworks on a daily basis, although they may not be aware that they do so. For instance, people listening to music or viewing music award shows are likely processing messages even in their subconscious. For this study, the authors adopted the framing techniques by Fairhurst and Sarr (1996), along the following key factors:

- Metaphor: Using comparison to frame an idea or concept.
- Stories (myths, legends): Creating a lasting descriptive narrative to frame a topic.
- Tradition (rituals, ceremonies): Engaging in cultural mores that infuse significance in the day-to-day. This is often tied to artifacts.
- Slogan, jargon, catchphrase: Invoking a frame with a refrain that's relatable and memorable.
- Artifact: Promoting symbols with intrinsic value – a visual/cultural phenomenon beyond its simple meaning.
- Contrast: Describing an object in terms of what it is not.

- Spin: Presenting a concept in such a way as to convey a value judgement (positive or negative). This spin may or may not be obvious.

Within these frames, musical performances were evaluated on their contributions to critical race and rhetoric theories. Both theories offer guides for understanding how protest songs support and forward social justice movements while connecting and creating lasting narratives for communities. First, Critical Race Theory (CRT) analyzes and challenges mainstream narratives in law, history, and popular culture that reinforce traditional values and norms. (Bell, 1992; Delgado & Stefancic, 2013; Matsuda, 1996). "Through counter-telling, CRT seeks to destabilize 'stock stories' that valorize the legitimacy of dominant groups" (Adams, Bell & Griffin 2016, p.17).

Findings

The 22 performances selected for analysis in this study range from Gospel to Hip Hop. Overall, more male artists than female artists were featured in the protest songs in the study. As indicated in Table 1, there were 11 prominent male artists, seven prominent female artists and four performances featured both male and female artists. Also, it is noteworthy that female rapper Rapsody performed in both the BET 2020 and the BET 2020 Hip Hop Awards shows. The genre that got the most play in the study was Hip Hop, which included four cyphers with more than 20 artists in the BET Hip Hop Awards show. Here is the breakdown by genre for the performances in the study: Hip Hop (12), Gospel (6), R&B (3) and Country (1). While male vocalists dominated performances at two of the three shows in the study, it is noteworthy that Brandy recruited entertainers Teyana Taylor, H.E.R., and Erykah Badu for the "Ladies First" cypher that featured all female artists rapping to "I Wanna Be Down." Male artists dominated the other cyphers that featured a wide range of talent from reggae legends such as Skip Marley and Bounty Killer to activism newcomers like Polo G and Jack Harlow. On the BET 2020 Awards, there were seven male Hip Hop artists and two female artists (Megan Thee Stallion and Rapsody) coded in the protest songs. The second most popular genre in the study was Gospel with six songs. Three of those songs were sung by female artists. Only three of the protest songs in the study fell into the R&B category, and two of those songs were performed by female artists.

While the cyphers typically featured four or more artists rapping, most of the other songs in the study featured a single artist as the vocalist. As for the visual imagery in videos, particularly those involving Hip Hop artists, more than half were elaborately staged productions with dancers and other performers. For example, Megan Thee Stallion's remix performance of "Girls in the Hood" and "Savage" initially did not seem much like a protest song based on the lyrics with a small army of scantily-clad and rump-shaking female dancers in a desert scene, but the image of a clenched fist symbolic of Black Power with an outline of red and green pushed it into the protest category, visually. To build on the literature review, this next section explores the genres and frames used to express the Black experience in protest songs and music videos during the turbulent year of 2020. Additionally, the researchers explore how the protest songs and videos in the BET 2020, Stellar, and BET Hip Hop Awards shows build on previous narratives about the Black experience in the U.S. The authors found that the protest songs performed at the awards shows sought to demarginalize African Americans through lyrics and visuals decentering whiteness.

Discussion

The year 2020 left the nation nostalgic for better times – stability and economic prosperity – and in need of a soundtrack expressing a range of emotions in turbulent times. People were desperately in need of inspiration, and some awards shows moved to virtual settings due to the pandemic. The BET 2020, Stellar, and BET Hip Hop Award shows featured the best from all genres. The music and lyrics resonated with the masses and narrated both quietly and loudly the story of Blacks in America. Still, the authors attempted to take a more complex review to the music, lyrics and visual cues used in protest music written in response to the racial reckoning, involving the killing of unarmed Black people and turmoil of 2020.

BET 2020 Awards Show

Given the fact that the BET 2020 Awards show took place the month after George Floyd's killing and much of the nation was wrestling with travel restrictions related to the COVID-19 pandemic, it was not surprising to see the 2020 BET Awards Show had a strong focus on protest songs. The show opened with Keedron Bryant, who was a 12-year-old at the time of the show, singing "I Just Wanna Live." The song was written by his mother after watching the viral video of a Minneapolis policeman pressing his knee on Floyd's neck for 9 minutes and 29 seconds. The lyrics were particularly powerful and spoke to his fear and ongoing struggle as noted by this passage:

> I'm a young black man
> Doing all that I can (Can)
> To stand
> Oh, but when I look around
> And I see what's being done
> To my kind (Kind)
> Every day (Day)
> I'm being hunted as prey

My people don't want no trouble
We've had enough struggle
I just wanna live
God protect me. (Bryant, 2020)

Days before the BET 2020 Awards show aired, Bryant signed a recording deal with Warner Records. The company agreed to donate 100 percent of net profits from that song to the NAACP (Associated Press, 2020). Bryant's performance went viral with celebrities such as former U.S. President Barack Obama, NBA star LeBron James and actress Lupita Nyong'o praising him on social media. As of January 31, 2021, Bryant had 2,500 followers on Twitter, a YouTube channel with about 58,200 subscribers, more than 89,459 followers on Facebook, and more than 415,000 followers on Instagram. The exponential following on Instagram is likely driven by the fact that Instagram users tend to skew younger. Bryant has also appeared on the *Little Big Shots* TV show featuring children, and was a finalist for Nickelodeon and *Time's* 2020 "Kid of the Year" contest. Bryant's song also was among 60 songs that made Spotify's Black Lives Matter playlist. By December 2020, Spotify reported more than 64 million streams of the Black Lives Matter playlist, and the company has pledged to donate "up to $10 million to organizations that are focused on the fight against racism, injustice, and inequity around the world" (Spotify, 2020).

While Bryant's performance opened the awards celebration, Chuck D and Flavor Fav of Public Enemy also performed with Nas, Black Thought and Rapsody, Jahi, and YG for an updated rendition of "Fight The Power." Again, that song was released in 1989 as part of the soundtrack for Spike Lee's movie *Do the Right Thing*. The original rhymes were powerful then, and speak to the current culture. The historic background provided context for young viewers on the history of riots and the meaning of the iconic Black Power fist. "The value of a black life is the cost of going to Wendy's," they sang, and that line resonated as a young Black person's life is equated to a little more than $4. This opening used powerful framing and agenda setting for the awards show. The opening also deployed all of the seven frames promoted in the Fairhurst and Sarr (1996) framework: metaphor, stories, tradition, slogan, artifact, contrast, and positive spin. The lyrics in this opening performance engaged in powerful storytelling, but the chants and refrains of "Fight the Power" is a slogan that has resonated with African Americans since the song was released more than three decades ago. "Fight the Power" ranked #1, #3, #20 on U.S. *Billboard* Charts; #29 in the UK; #30 in the Netherlands – all in its first year of release (Lentini, 2020). The protest song was introduced globally and remains one of Public Enemy's best-known songs. In 2001, the Recording Industry Association of America ranked "Fight the Power" at #288 in the "Songs of the Century" (Lentini, 2020).

Let Go

The opening scene highlighted a performance involving a Black dancer in front of a wrecked, burned car, as a police officer equipped in riot gear joined. Then, D Smoke began his new song "Let Go," an emotional response written the day George Floyd was killed by Minneapolis police officers. "I reach out despite the feeling they out to kill us/ Get rowdy 'bout the Pesos/ The solution for this whole institution/ Just to breathe, we need to let go," sings Sir. This powerful response and metaphor articulated grief and collective understanding. Next, D Smoke smoothly transitioned into "Black Habits," where he sang the chorus with Jackie Gouche: "Black magic (black magic), black excellence (black excellence)/ Black habits (black habits), this black medicine (yeah), everything/ Black Chucks, black tux, everything, everything." This song turned the word Black from just a color into a feeling or a culturally lived experience. It was more than just the absence of color, but it was a vibe. To be Black is a beautiful thing, to understand the culture and rich history of a people. This song puts a positive frame or spin on the interpretation of the word Black, it is more than just a negative stereotype. Blackness supersedes any title. In the same way the classic James Brown anthem, "I'm Black and I'm proud," affirmed a people, "Black Habits" promotes Black identity and pride.

The Box

This song, which was performed by Roddy Ricch, details his life's journey. The box is used as different metaphors throughout the production. A dominant metaphor focused on his desire to leave a life of crime and the justice system behind him. The box may describe how white Americans see African Americans: in a box, or better yet, through one. The lyrics suggest that if Blacks are on television or within a place far enough for white people to feel safe or in a space where they provide entertainment then they are OK. Is it possible for Whites to view Blacks outside of that frame? This song is about breaking out of that box, becoming more than entertainers or statistics. Released as a single off his album, "*Please Excuse Me for Being Antisocial*," *The Box* became Ricch's highest-charting song worldwide. The song topped US *Billboard* Hot 100 at number one for eleven weeks, while also landing at the top of the 200 *Billboard* songs and albums in January of 2020 (A. Brown, 2020). Ricch also had international notoriety, topping charts in Canada, Hungary, and New Zealand. The song about success, money, and influence also landed in the top five in both Ireland and the United Kingdom. The frames used in this Hip Hop song are metaphors that tell stories.

While Gospel artists had the Stellar Awards, the vocalists made their presence known at the more secular production. As noted earlier, Gospel music has a strong tradition of protest, and the duo of Kierra Sheard and her mother, Karen

Clark Sheard, were decked out in black when they performed "Something Has to Break" during the BET 2020 Awards. In the spirt of the Gospel tradition, Jennifer Hudson performed, "Young, Gifted and Black." These lyrics were simple and still relevant. The song was written by Weldon Irvine and Nina Simone in 1965. Simone recorded it first, and Aretha Franklin later re-recorded it in 1972 on an album that was Top 10 Gold-certified. The album won Franklin a 1972 Grammy Award for Best Female R&B Vocal Performance of the Year. With strong Gospel musicality, this anthem has always been a song of pride and celebration. Simone penned this song to honor her friend, Lorraine Hansberry. Hansberry, the author famous for her play *A Raisin in the Sun*, inspired the song. After Hansberry's death in 1965, a collection of her works was published under the title *To Be Young, Gifted and Black*. This production was also made into an off-Broadway play. James Baldwin wrote about it this way in 1969: "I had never in my life seen so many black people in the theatre. And the reason was that never before, in the entire history of American theater, had so much of the truth of black people's lives been seen on the stage. Black people had ignored the theater because the theater had always ignored them" (Nemiroff, 1995, p. xviii).

One may have expected this song to be much longer, but it was not. It didn't need to be long and exhaustive to express the meaning of the song, being young, gifted and Black. Within the frame of both stories and spin (Fairhurst & Sarr, 1996), this song promotes Black intellectualism and pride. It speaks to youth declaring that their skin color, heritage, and culture are valuable and sacred even if the world sees it as less. The message: It is important to love the skin you're in and to maintain a positive self-image despite the negative stereotypes sometimes perpetuated in the media. In her virtual BET performance, Hudson channeled Aretha Franklin beginning her solo, while playing the piano. With strong Gospel music undertones, her performance was a precursor to the trailer promoting the movie, *Respect*, where she stars in the biopic of the legendary Aretha Franklin. *Respect*, titled after Franklin's 1967 hit, had originally been scheduled to be released in August 2020, but was shifted at the start of the pandemic to the Martin Luther King Jr. holiday weekend. MGM pushed back the debut of the movie a second time, and the movie was scheduled for release a year later, August 2021. Franklin selected Hudson, who won a supporting actress Oscar for *Dreamgirls*, for the role prior to her death in 2018. While the song, "Young, Gifted and Black" honors Franklin, the affirmation and encouragement that the lyrics provided in the middle of the Black Lives Matter Movement should not go unnoticed.

Another powerful performance at the BET Awards was Alicia Keys's "Perfect Way to Die." Keys gave a thoughtful and passionate performance with strong visuals. In addition to showcasing larger than life murals, honoring George

Floyd and Breonna Taylor, both killed by police officers in 2020, the artist streamed in the background the names of dozens of Blacks who died in police shootings or race-tinged episodes. Names highlighted in colorful chalk included Tamir Rice, Stephon Clark, Botham Jean, Darius Tarver, and Ahmaud Arbery.

Keys's lyrics below speak to the pain and anguish of a Black mother losing a child, and are particularly poignant since George Floyd pleaded for his "mama" in his final minute of life.

> Simple walk to the corner store
> Momma never thought she would be getting a call from the coroner
> Said her son's been gunned down, been gunned down
> Can you come now?........
> And she's stuck there singing:
> Baby, don't you close your eyes
> This could be our final time
> And you know I'm horrible at saying goodbye
> And I think of all you could've done
> At least you'll stay forever young
> I guess you've picked the perfect way to die. (Keys, 2020)

The lyrics highlight a mother's lament and tell the story of losing a son to the city streets. Keys is known for her activism through song and music, but this parental perspective was unexpected. Some critics referred to her performance honoring the murdered Black men and women as haunting. At the end of her performance, Keys took a knee showing humility and solidarity for the Black Lives Matter Movement for equal justice. Her decision to kneel was a visual symbol, which also entered a contentious political debate. Former NFL quarterback Colin Kaepernick took a near career-ending stance when he decided to protest police brutality and systemic racial injustice. He has reported that his decision to kneel in protest during the pregame National Anthem began with one man, Mario Woods. Woods was shot and killed by police in his San Francisco neighborhood (Coombs et al., 2020). It was reported that the 26-year-old had suffered 21 gunshot wounds, including two in the head. According to authorities, Woods was a stabbing suspect with a criminal record.

Nine months later, Kaepernick took a seat during the playing of the "Star-Spangled Banner" ahead of his San Francisco 49ers entering the field. His demonstration sparked a national protest of kneeling during football games. Seattle Seahawk and Green Beret, Nate Boyer, suggested to Kaepernick that kneeling would be more respectful to the nation's military, the ex-quarterback explained (Coombs et al., 2020). Other Black athletes joined the protest, which quickly became politicized as then-President Donald Trump encouraged owners of teams to fire athletes who chose to kneel in protest. Several frames were present within Keys's performance. Keys provided a powerful use of story (Fairhurst & Sarr, 1996) expressed in the lyrics, combined with the haunting refrain: "I guess you've picked the perfect way to die." This catchphrase resonated with listeners as she sang the song.

DaBaby's "Rockstar" was about truth-telling. In his lyrics, DaBaby admits that he does rap about guns and shootings, but he wants his listeners to be better. He doesn't talk about the police shootings as a Black or white issue, but as a societal issue. Both he and Roddy Ricch performed the song at the BET Awards. The single was released in April as part of DaBaby's third studio album, *Blame It On Baby*. However, as racial tensions mounted throughout the summer, the song was re-released in June as a Black Lives Matter remix, following the response to the deaths of Ahmaud Arbery, George Floyd, Breonna Taylor, and other African Americans in police custody. He expresses in "Rockstar" that no one is above the law, not even rock stars such as himself and Roddy Ricch. They realized that at the end of the day, regardless of their wealth and fame, they will always be African-American men, and they need their own forms of protection. Regardless, all police see is the color of their skin, not their popularity or financial status. In his BET Awards performance, dancers wore shirts that read: "I am Trayvon Martin," "Black Lives Matter," "Hands Up. Don't Shoot," and "More Love." The production ended with "In Loving Memory of All the Lives Lost to Racism and Police Brutality." Obvious frames used here included the power of story and the artifacts displayed on shirts and throughout the performance. DaBaby's "Rockstar" was noted as the *Billboard's* 2020 song of the summer. The song held the top spot for 13 out of 15 weeks on *Billboard's* song of the summer tracking list. For seven of those weeks, the track was also No.1 on the Hot 100 chart (Dinges, 2020).

Megan Thee Stallion, in her first-ever appearance at the BET Awards, performed a few minutes from two songs: "Girls in the Hood" and "Savage Remix." First, she launched into her newly released single, "Girls in the Hood," which samples N.W.A.'s classic "Boyz-n-the-hood" (N.W.A. is known for their protest anthems against police brutality). While Megan Thee Stallion's lyrics don't directly say protest, they do so indirectly. Called a next wave feminist, she is all about progress and freedom for women. Her powerful rhymes encourage girls to run the world, while her more subtle video images speak to the Black Lives Matter Movement with a flag with those words in red, and another waving flag during the "Savage" video that suggests Black power. Even when we sometimes do not recognize it as such, artists are finding ways to disrupt the narrative and speak truth to perceived power. The representation of the fist, regardless of the song topic, is important. Her media production framed awareness and influence through the use of strong visuals and symbolic artifacts.

Additionally, the rapper created a slogan from her 2018 hit titled, "Hot Girl." Social media was filled with #HotGirlSummer featuring young women's achievements and contributions. The slogan "hot girl summer in 2020," is about independence and sexual freedom; what a far cry from more than a century ago when women had no voting rights.

Kane Brown, a Black male country music artist, also made history when he performed "Worldwide Beautiful," an anthem focused on racial reconciliation on the BET 2020 Awards show (Parton, 2020). His performance appeared to be a bridge from Gospel recording artist Jonathan McReynolds's performance of "People," which offered pleas for forgiveness and healing from less-than-kind people at the awards show. Female country music artists were notably absent from the performances, although Mickey Guyton, a Black country music singer, released "Black Like Me" in 2020. Notably, she spoke out about being called the N-word and other indignities (Yahr, 2020) in the song.

John Legend's "Never Break" is a song about empowerment, strength, and unity. He sings: "No matter what may come our way. We will never break. We will never break. Built on a foundation. Stronger than the pain. We will never break. As the water rises. And the mountains shake. Our love will remain." The song, originally penned to lament his wife's pregnancy loss, certainly tells a personal story, but also communicates a powerful message for national reconciliation in such a politically polarized environment. The visuals and lyrics from this song really helped bring viewers into the empty damp warehouse where Legend performed. The visuals in the song showed combinations of African Americans gathering together, a lot of smiles, laughter, and joy. Even as one man is being arrested, he is still joyous. There is not a single video nor picture of just a singular African American in this video. Unity and togetherness and community are the main points in this song. His frame: Together we can.

BET Hip Hop Awards

The BET Hip Hop Awards had a much different vibe than Legend's R&B performance. The show showcased four cyphers, which typically involve rappers freestyling in small groups, whose performances were thick with social justice and protest messages. For example, in a political cypher, Polo G rapped about tension between the police and Black people: "They really the threat, but that's how they portray me...When you spit the truth, they try to view it as hate speech." (Curto, 2020, para. 3). Jack Harlow, a white Louisville resident, rapped about protests in his hometown over Breonna Taylor's killing: "Last we heard, they reviewin' the evidence / Same old song and we all know the rest of it / 2020 turned the whole country to pessimists / You ain't said a word, what the hell do you represent?" (Curto, 2020, para. 3). The fear that many Blacks experience because of their skin's melanin was addressed by Flawless Real Talk with these words: "Knowin' that my skin could be the death of me/I could be the next to be/Killed by the people that were sworn to be protectin' me." (Curto, 2020, para. 3). While some folks are worried about the "Supreme" as in the Supreme Court of the United States, Flawless Real Talk rapped, "I'm worried about supremacy," a reference to the rise of the white supremacy movement in the United States. Rapsody, who earned the Hip Hop Awards lyricist of the year, closed that cypher with this verse: "Martin had a dream, pop / Breonna couldn't dream, pop," she opened, miming gunshots on her head. "Jammin' with an attitude, they never ever charge cops / When they aimin' at our body, blop-blop-blop-blop-blop." (Curto, 2020, para 3). Another cypher featuring industry newcomers paid tribute to Pop Smoke, a 20-year-old rapper from New York who was killed in a robbery at his Hollywood Hills home in February 2020 (Queally, 2020). In the newcomers' cypher, Deante Hitchcock rapped about black trauma, yet emphasized the value of the Black family with this passage: "My black kid gon' have a black mama/ And they gon' look to me like superhero/ Like the Black Panther and the Black Mamba" (2020 BET Hip Hop Awards Cypher Lyrics). In a reggae cypher, which featured legends such as Skip Marley and Bounty Killer, Marley encouraged people to keep on marching because "We're gonna change the globe / With everything we know / And bless up to the ancestors for paving the road" (Curto, 2020, para. 2).

The performance of "Monsters You Made" by Nigerian songwriter and rapper Burna Boy with Coldplay's Christopher Martin was one of two performances on the Hip Hop Awards that featured a white vocalist. The protest footage was striking in the video and the messaging was clear as members of Burna Boy's band wore black t-shirts with #StopPoliceBrutality in red and white letters across their chests. The "Monsters You Made" speaks not only to concerns about police brutality, but to economic disparities as noted in these lyrics:

It's like the heads of the state
Ain't comprehending the hate
That the oppressed generate
When they've been working like slaves
To get some minimum wage
You turn around and you blame
Them for the anger and rage
Put them in shackles and chains
Because of what they became
We are the monsters you made. (Burna Boy, 2020)

In addition to addressing policing and economic disparities, Burna Boy's performance sent a message of Black solidarity as he ended the performance with members of his band holding their fists in the air. The performance ended with a list of Tiyane Kazeem and other Nigerians killed by SARS and the message of "#EndPoliceBrutality."

The BET Hip Hop Awards were broadcast less than a week before the November 3, U.S. presidential election and many of the performers in the study weaved in the importance of social justice and voting in their performances. For example, 2 ChainZ wore a red and white Clark Atlanta University sweatshirt, offered a shoutout to historically Black colleges and universities, called for locking up the officers who killed Breonna Taylor, and added: "make sure you vote" in his opening monologue to "Money Maker," a sexually explicit song. Although 2 ChainZ's performance included female dancers twerking and grinding for the cameras in BAFU crop tops and short shorts, the performance also included a greater message with street signs to honor George Floyd and Breonna Taylor. In contrast to the sexualized 2 ChainZ performance, Tobe Nwigwe's performance of "Try Jesus" also visually sent a plea for justice while reminding the audience that he's willing to fight for what is right. His performance included a variety of modestly robed female backup singers, and he sported the faces of Breonna Taylor and George Floyd on the front of his garb.

The Stellar Awards

It was fascinating to see that a Hip Hop style performance also opened the 35th annual Stellar Awards for Gospel music with Tye Tribett and a mix of female and male dancers in ripped black overalls, sweaters and gold chains singing "We Gon' be Alright." It appeared to be a step to engage millennials and younger audiences in Gospel music. Tribett ended his energetic performance with showcasing "Christ Matters" on the back of his jean jacket. The song's chorus spoke of the persistence and perseverance of Black folks over generations.

Black also was the chosen color for Cece Winans's formal gown with a sequined blazer as she performed a moving rendition of "Bridge Over Troubled Water" in a traditional church sanctuary as part of a tribute to the late John Lewis, a member of the U.S. House of Representatives and Democrat representing the state of Georgia. Her performance was a fitting tribute to the congressman who died in July 2020, and almost lost his life when he was beaten by law enforcement officers as he tried to march across the Edmund Pettus Bridge in 1965 at Selma, Alabama, as part of a civil rights protest. There is now a movement to rename the bridge to honor Lewis (Trent, 2020). Winans's performance also showed how Lewis has been a bridge to civil rights progress, as there were images of Lewis with the "John Lewis Freedom Parkway" street sign, and Lewis being awarded the Presidential Medal of Freedom from former President Barack Obama. Although it was not part of the BET or Stellar Awards, it is worth noting that Bebe and Marvin Winans sang a special song they titled

"Good Trouble" to honor Lewis's legacy and life's work as a civil rights leader and activist at his funeral in Atlanta in July 2020.

The lyrics from Tamela Mann's emotional performance of a "Touch From You" also spoke of the trials and tribulations often found in Gospel music. Again, as mentioned in the literature section of this study, Gospel music along with the Blues and Jazz often shared stories of the conditions within the community. During her performance, she encouraged listeners to "to sing our freedom's song" while calling on the Lord for help. It was striking to see more than a dozen framed black and white photos of Blacks who have been killed or murdered ranging from the 1955 lynching of Emmett Till, who was wrongfully accused of flirting with a white woman in Mississippi, to Botham Jean, who was killed by a white female police officer while having some ice cream in his Dallas apartment in 2018. During the song, Mann asked, "Can you hear the voices of people crying" for justice?

Conclusion

In our review of relevant literature on this topic, we demonstrated the power of songs and protests throughout the last century. Again, our findings narrowly explored the power of framing theory in songs and videos featured on the virtual 2020 BET Awards, Stellar Awards, and BET Hip Hop Awards. However, artists provided a variety of ways to understand the year in music. In 2020, the resurgence of Black Lives Matter protests prompted more sounds of protests and calls for action on social justice. Musical performers from all genres showcased outrage, regret, resilience, mourning and unity. Our study was limited and only focused on a narrow scope of performers. However, a future study could be more in-depth, focusing on artists across more styles, genres, and performances by non-Blacks. In fact, the National Public Radio (NPR) published a work entitled, *2020 Was the Year of Protest Music* featuring 20 songs that certainly pushed back against police brutality and assaults on human dignity.

Even songs that debuted prior to 2020 landed on a best-of soundtrack, circling back to a variety of media playlists offering powerful lyrics that reframed a narrative. For example, the FDT lyrics which debuted in 2016 reflect the boldness of Hip Hop culture in an age when freedom of speech is often debated. The song title stands for "F--- Donald Trump" and was recorded by Rapper YG and the late Nipsey Hussle when the controversial and self-proclaimed billionaire was a presidential candidate. In his MTV review, Turner (2016) wrote:

> YG is still in Compton, but we hear him starting to see the ways that national political turmoil has seeped into the streets he walks everyday.

Still, Brazy's final tracks aren't simply directed at black people – they form a rallying cry for Blacks, Mexicans, Muslims, and all people caught in the vitriolic crosshairs of Donald Trump. It's about galvanizing unity among all who oppose his oppressive and un-American ideals. The song is a middle finger to those who deny the humanity of immigrants and a rejection of the idea that we, as Black people, are going to stand aside and watch this happen. (para. 3)

YG performed at the 2020 BET Awards with several other Hip Hop artists who opened the show with the classic Public Enemy song, "Fight the Power."

The anti-President Trump anthem, FDT, was alleged to have been censored under pressure from the former president's Secret Service detail. Rapper YG said they threatened to pull the album *Still Brazy* off the shelves if he didn't revise the lyrics which mentioned that the former president's racist rhetoric was dividing the nation and an open assault on Black and brown people (Turner, 2016). Although the song was originally released on March 30, 2016, prior to Trump's victory in the November 2016 election, it was played throughout his term as a protest to his political victory and subsequent actions and speeches with racial undertones. The song was also a rallying cry for unity among the Black and brown communities. During the coverage of the 2020 election, the song resurfaced again on major media stations from FOX News to CNN. This time, however, it was an anthem of celebration for those dancing in streets from Georgia to California rejoicing over the pronouncement of the winning ticket of President Joseph Biden and Vice President Kamala Harris. These rappers certainly created what Fairhurst and Sarr (1996) had described as a memorable and relatable catchphrase, and it indeed resonated with a younger and more diverse population. Building on their catchphrase, G-Eazy and Macklemore made a sweltering remix titled "F---Donald Trump Part II." The FDT lyrics ushered in the next upsurge of anti-Trump sentiments.

That 2016 Hip Hop production continues to provide critical commentary and adds to the narrative of former President Trump's regime. We believe many of the songs featured in our study will have staying or lasting power, giving voice to the uncertainty of the global pandemic, grieving the hundreds of thousands who died at the hand of COVID-19. The songs bemoan the financial distress of businesses and individuals, emphasize the complications of hurricanes and wildfires, acknowledge the anguish of those who died from unjust police brutality and highlight the capitol insurrection of Jan. 6, 2021.

It is also noteworthy that the National Museum of African American Music (NMAAM) officially opened on Martin Luther King Jr. Day, January 18, 2021, delayed from its originally scheduled opening in Fall 2020, due to the global pandemic. This is the world's first museum dedicated to Black music and a testament to the resilience of Black people.

Since 1619, enslaved African American people understood the power of music, specifically the capability of songs to penetrate the soul and fortify the heart. Those touring the 56,000-square-foot museum will have the opportunity to visit "the only museum in the world dedicated to preserving and celebrating more than 50 music genres and styles that were created, influenced or inspired by African-Americans, including Spirituals, Blues, Jazz, Gospel, R&B, and Hip Hop" (Kelly, 2020). The museum's seven galleries use technology to provide visitors with more than 1,500 artifacts, including clothing and memorabilia, to help illustrate how entertainment, sports, and social justice all intersect in the narratives of African-American music and history.

The fact that the NMAAM is located in Nashville, which is considered the nation's capital for country music, speaks volumes. This lyrical passage from Kane Brown's song, "Worldwide Beautiful" is evidence that there's more opportunity for healing:

> You're missing every color, if you're only seeing black and white
> Tell me how you're gonna change your mind if your heart's unmovable
> We ain't that different from each other
> From one to another,
> I look around and see worldwide beautiful. (K. Brown, 2020)

Music will continue to be a viable tool for true expression. Future researchers should plan to chronicle the many genres and messages that are conveyed in social, political and equity protest songs for years to come. Additionally, researchers could evaluate the power of artists to be social documentarians or journalists. And those who have an interest in more global contexts should follow musicians in West Africa, especially Nigeria where the late Fela Kuti's musical protest legacy remains.

Will the next generation of musicians be as defiant? Unfortunately, not everyone is a fan of today's protest music. The condescending tone with which some elders dismiss the sounds of Hip Hop and more edgy musical productions, suggests that profanity, violence, and misogyny have become increasingly common on the music scene. Researchers definitely should examine the evolution of protest songs from poems to Jazz and Rap renditions.

References

Adams, M. E., Bell, L. A. E., & Griffin, P. E. (2016). *Teaching for diversity and social justice.* New York: Routledge.

Associated Press. (2020, June 18). *Keedron Bryant, 12-year-old Behind George Floyd's Anthem, Signs with Warner Records*. Billboard. https://www.billboard.com/pro/keedron-bryant-signs-warner-records/

Bell, D. (1992). *Faces at the bottom of the well: The permanence of racism*. New York: Basic Books.

BET Press. (2020, June 29). *The "BET Awards" 2020 triumphs with an extraordinary celebration of Black culture* [Press release]. https://www.betpressroom.com/press-release/the-bet-awards-2020-triumphs-with-an-extraordinary-celebration-of-black-culture/

Blisten, J., & Spanos, B. (2020, June 3). *Platitudes and Protest: How the music industry responded to Blackout Tuesday*. Rolling Stone. https://www.rollingstone.com/pro/features/blackout-tuesday-music-industry-1009501/

Boyd, T. (2002). *The New H.N.I.C.: The Death of Civil Rights and the Reign of Hip Hop*. New York: New York University Press.

Brown, A. (2020, January 13). L.A. rapper Roddy Ricch tops Billboard albums and singles charts. *Los Angeles Times*. https://www.latimes.com/entertainment-arts/music/story/2020-01-13/roddy-ricch-tops-billboard-hot-100-with-the-box

Brown, K. (2020, June 4). Worldwide Beautiful [Song]. *Genius*. https://genius.com/Kane-brown-worldwide-beautiful-lyrics

Bryant, K. (2020, May 27). I Just Wanna Live [Song]. *Genius*. https://genius.com/Keedron-bryant-i-just-wanna-live-lyrics

Burna Boy. (2020, August 13). Monsters You Made [Song]. *Genius*. https://genius.com/Burna-boy-monsters-you-made-lyrics

Carter, B., Chinen, N., Powers, A., Redmond, S. L., & Wang, O. (2020, June 26). *We insist: A century of black music against state violence*. NPR. https://www.npr.org/2020/06/26/883334741/we-insist-a-century-of-black-music-against-state-violence

Charnas, D. (2011). *The big payback: The history of the business of hip hop*. New American Library.

Coombs, D. S., Lambert, C. A., Cassilo, D., & Humphries, Z. (2020). Flag on the play: Colin Kaepernick and the protest paradigm. *Howard Journal of Communications, 31*(4), 317–336.

Creswell, J. W., & Guetterman, T. C. (2021). *Educational research: planning, conducting and evaluating quantitative and qualitative research*. Pearson.

Curto, J. (2020, October 28). Brandy recruited an all-women lineup for her 2020 BET hip hop awards cypher. *Vulture*. https://www.vulture.com/2020/10/bet-hip-hop-awards-2020-cyphers.html

DaBaby. (2020). Rockstar [Song]. *Blame it on Baby*. Interscope Records & South Coast Music Group.

Darden, R. (2014). *Nothing but love in God's water*. Pennsylvania State University Press.

Davie, G. (2020, November 11). Framing Theory [Web log post]. Retrieved from https://masscommtheory.com/theory-overviews/framing-theory/

Delgado, R., & Stefancic, J. (2013). *Critical race theory: The cutting edge*. (3rd ed.). Temple University Press.

Dinges, G. (2020, September 8). It's official: Rapper DaBaby's "rockstar" is Billboard's song of the summer 2020. *USA Today*. Retrieved January 10, 2021, from https://www.usatoday.com/story/entertainment/music/2020/09/08/2020-song-summer-ababys-rockstar-takes-top-honors/5750400002/

D Smoke & SiR. (2020). Let go [Song]. Woodworks/Empire.

Edet, E. M. (1976). One hundred years of black protest music. *The Black Scholar, 7*(10), 38–48. https://doi.org/10.1080/00064246.1976.11413848

Emerson. (2002). "Where my girls at?" Negotiating black womanhood in music videos. *Gender & Society, 16*(1), 115–135.

Fairhurst, G. T., & Sarr, R. A. (1996). *The art of framing: Managing the language of leadership*. San Francisco: Jossey-Bass Publishers.

Falz. (2019). *Moral Instruction* [Album]. BahdGuys Entertainment Limited.

Fitts, M. (2008). "Drop it like it's hot:" Culture industry laborers and their perspectives on rap music video production. *Meridians: Feminism, Race, Transnationalism, 8*(1), 211–235. https://doi.org/10.2979/mer.2007.8.1.211.

Flanagan, A. (2018, April 16). *Kendrick Lamar's DAMN wins historic Pulitzer prize in music*. NPR. https://www.npr.org/sections/therecord/2018/04/16/602948758/kendrick-lamars-damn-wins-historic-pulitzer-prize-in-music

Ginwright, S. (2004). *Black in school: Afrocentric reform, urban youth, and the promise of hip- hop culture*. Teachers College Press.

Hale, K. (2019, February 6). Goldman Sachs bets on hip hop and millennials for music revival. *Forbes*. https://www.forbes.com/sites/korihale/2019/02/06/goldman-sachs-bets-on-hip-hop-and-millennials-for-music-revival

Herwees, T. (2016, February 8). Beyoncé and Jay Z donate $1.5 million to the Black Lives Matter movement. *Good*. https://www.good.is/articles/jay-z-beyonce-black-lives-matter-funds

Irvin, W., & Simone, N. (1969). To be young, gifted and black [Song]. RCA Victor.

Johnson, T. (2018, May 8). Donald Glover's 'This is America' is a nightmare we can't afford to look away from. *Rolling Stone*. https://www.rollingstone.com/music/music-news/donald-glovers-this-is-america-is-a-nightmare-we-cant-afford-to-look-away-from-630177/

Keiger, D. (2020, July 29). How protest songs echo – and sometimes lead – the stories of our time. *Nieman Story Board*. https://niemanstoryboard.org/stories/how-protest-songs-echo-and-sometimes-lead-the-stories-of-our-times/

Kelly, B. MP&F Strategic Communications. (2020, December 7). *National museum of African American music to open Jan. 18, 2021* [Press release]. https://nmaam.org/wp-content/uploads/2021/01/Museum_Opening_Release__1272020.pdf

Keys, A. (2020, June 19). *Alicia Keys – Perfect Way to Die* [Video]. Genius. https://genius.com/Alicia-keys-perfect-way-to-die-lyrics

Kilson, M. (2003, July 17). The pretense of hip hop black leadership. *The Black Commentator*. https://blackcommentator.com/50/50_kilson_pf.html

Lamar, K. (2015). Alright [Song]. On *To Pimp a Butterfly*. Interscope Records.

Landrum, L. (2020, June 29). Tributes and politics: How artists used 2020 BET awards platform. *The Christian Science Monitor*. https://www.csmonitor.com/The-Culture/2020/0629/Tributes-and-politics-How-artists-used-2020-BET-Awards-platform

Lentini, L. (2020, November 4). The 35 best songs of the last 35 years. *Spin*. https://www.spin.com/2020/11/the-35-best-songs-of-the-last-35-years

Legend, J. (2020). Never break [Song]. On *Bigger Love*. Columbia Records Group.

Lewis, S. (2014). Reading Olive Schreiner Reading WEB Du Bois. *Research in African Literatures*, *45*(2), 150-167.

Mann, T. (2020). Touch from you [Song]. On *Overcomer*. Tillymann Music Group.

Matsuda, M. (1996). *Where is your body? And other essays on race, gender and law*. Boston: Beacon Press.

McNamara, M. (2020, June 15). Column: White celebs rush to amplify Black Lives Matter. The results are mixed to embarrassing. *Los Angeles Times*. https://www.latimes.com/entertainment-arts/story/2020-06-15/black-lives-matter-white-celebrities-support

McWhorter, J. H. (2003). *How hip hop holds blacks back*. *City Journal*. https://www.city-journal.org/html/how-hip-hop-holds-blacks-back-12442.html?wallit_nosession=1

Megan Thee Stallion. (2019). Hot girl summer [Song]. 300 Entertainment.

Metts, S., & Cupach, W. (2008). Face theory: Goffman's dramatistic approach to interpersonal interaction. In L. A. Baxter, & D. O. Braithwaite (Eds.), *Engaging theories in interpersonal communication: Multiple perspectives* (pp. 203-214). SAGE Publications, Inc., https://dx.doi.org/10.4135/9781483329529.n15

Mingo, A. (2019). Transgressive leadership and theo-ethical texts of black protest music. *Black Theology*, *17*(2), 91-113.

Morgan, T. (2020, June 23). *11 anthems of black pride and protest through American history*. History. https://www.history.com/news/black-music-slavery-protest

Morris, W. (2019, August 14). Music Black culture appropriation. *New York Times Magazine Interactive*. https://www.nytimes.com/interactive/2019/08/14/magazine/music-black-culture-approproation.html

NAACP. (2021). NAACP history: Lift every voice and sing. https://www.naacp.org/naacp-history-lift-evry-voice-and-sing/.

Nemiroff, R. (Ed.). (1995). *To be young, gifted, and Black: Lorraine Hansberry in her own words*. Vintage.

Obenson, T. (2019, March 22). With more black stars on TV than ever, where do BET, OWN, and other black networks fit in? *IndieWire*. https://www.indiewire.com/2019/03/bet-own-oprah-tv-one-bounce-black-tv-networks-1202032679/

Orejuela, F., & Shonekan, S. (2018). *Black Lives Matter & music: Protest, intervention, reflection*. Indiana University Press.

Parton, C. (2020, June 29). Kane Brown makes history on the 2020 BET Awards. *Sounds Like Nashville*. https://www.soundslikenashville.com/music/kane-brown-makes-history-2020betawards/#:~:text=Kane%20Brown%20made%20history%20over,a%20track%20on%20the%20show

Public Enemy. (1989). Fight the Power [Song]. Motown.

Prince, R. (2021, January 4). Clyburn wants to amplify 'Lift Every Voice.' *Journal-Isms*. http://www.journal-isms.com/2021/01/clyburn-wants-to-amplify-lift-every-voice/

Pulley, B. (2004). *The billion dollar BET: Robert Johnson and the inside story of Black Entertainment Television*. John Wiley & Sons.

Queally, J. (2020, July 13). Four charged with murder in slaying of Pop Smoke. *Los Angeles Times*. https://www.latimes.com/california/story/2020-07-13/four-charged-with-murder-in-slaying-of-rapper-pop-smoke

Roddy Ricch. (2019). The Box [Song]. On *Please Excuse Me for being Antisocial*. Atlantic.

Shaw, J. (2018). From Beethoven to Bowie: Identity framing, social justice and the sound of law. *International Journal for the Semiotics of Law-Revue Internationale de Sémiotique Juridique, 31*(2), 304–324.

Spanos, B., & Grant, S. (2016, July 13). Songs of Black Lives Matter: 22 new protest anthems. *Rolling Stone*. https://www.rollingstone.com/music/music-lists/songs-of-black-lives-matter-22-new-protest-anthems-15256/

Spotify. (2020, June 1). *Spotify Stands with the Black Community in the Fight Against Racism and Injustice*. https://newsroom.spotify.com/2020-06-01/spotify-stands-with-the-black-community-in-the-fight-against-racism-and-injustice/

Trent, S. (2020, July 26). John Lewis nearly died on Edmund Pettus Bridge. Now it may be renamed after him. *Washington Post*. https://www.washingtonpost.com/history/2020/07/26/john-lewis-bloody-sunday-edmund-pettus-bridge/

Turner, D. (2016, July 7). *YG takes on Donald Trump and killer cops on still brazy*. MTV News. http://www.mtv.com/news/2902531/yg-still-brazy-trump-cops/

Unterberger, A. (2020, June 5). Protest songs by Kendrick Lamar, James Brown & more experience enormous streaming increases. *Billboard*. https://www.billboard.com/articles/business/chart-beat/9396644/protest-songs-streaming-increase-kendrick-lamar-childish-gambino

Watkins, P., & Caines, R. (2015). Cyphers: Hip hop and improvisation. *Critical Studies in Improvisation*.https://www.criticalimprov.com/index.php/csieci/article/view/3518/3588

Yahr, E. (2020, June 9). How the country music industry is responding to George Floyd's death and facing its own painful truths. *Washington Post*. https://www.floyd-reaction/

YG & Nipsey Hussle. (2016). F—k Donald Trump [Song]. On *Still Brazy*. Def Jam.

CHAPTER 2

Speaking for the "Other:" Reinforcing the Jezebel stereotype in Alexander McCall Smith's *No. 1 Ladies' Detective Agency*

Ann White-Taylor

University of Arkansas at Pine Bluff, USA

Abstract

This chapter argues that Alexander McCall Smith, author of *The No. 1 Ladies' Detective Agency* book series, stereotypes African women by allowing characters who are considered morally acceptable to refer to African women who are considered morally unacceptable as "bad girls," a derogatory term used in the series to describe sexually-promiscuous women. While the books, written more than 50 years after Botswana gained independence from Britain, present the southern African country in some positive ways, the novels are fraught with western stereotypes of African women, particularly that of the Jezebel stereotype or what Jewell (1993) called the "hypersexual bad-black-girl." In referring to some of the women in the books and the Home Box Office television series this way, McCall Smith, a white British writer, reinforces the stereotype by allowing the main characters to label some African women as "bad girls." However, the characters who are labeled as "bad" are seldom allowed to speak, and when they do speak, they also reinforce the stereotype. Thus, these characters have no means of defending themselves from the stereotype that has been thrust upon them. While McCall Smith has said that he has no problem speaking for African women because he was born in Africa (Sin Africa), Alcoff (1991) asserts that in the practice of speaking for, as well as speaking about others, one is "engaging in the act of representing the other's needs, goals, situations, and in fact, who they are."

Keywords: Bad girls, glamour girls, subaltern, stereotypes, Jezebel, South Africa, Botswana, lady detectives

***

Introduction

In a telling scene from the first episode of the HBO television series, *The No. 1 Ladies' Detective Agency* (Curtis & Minghella, 2009), Grace Makutsi, who has earned the highest score ever on the "general typing and secretarial examinations at Botswana Secretarial College with a grade of 97 percent," is interviewing for a position in an agency.

Precious Ramotswe, the agency's owner, who is surprised because she had been expecting someone quite different, says to Grace: "When someone says secretary, one thinks of someone…"

Grace interjects, saying: "In a tight skirt who will soon be disgracing herself under a desk with her boss in ways that only God knows how she can still look at herself in a mirror."

Precious responds: "Not quite, not always."

Grace continues:

> But often, I cannot tell you the number of times I have applied for jobs with my 97 percent and found myself in competition with a girl with 42 percent and a very short skirt, and every time, it is a short skirt who gets the job (Curtis & Minghella, 2009).

The scene is indicative of the way Grace and Precious discuss who they often refer to as "bad girls" or "glamorous girls" in the television series based on the books written by British writer, Alexander McCall Smith. While the books, written more than 50 years after Botswana gained independence from Britain, present the southern African country in some positive ways, they are fraught with western stereotypes of African women, particularly that of the Jezebel or what Jewell (1993) has called the "hypersexual bad-black-girl" image. By allowing Grace and Precious to describe some African women as "bad girls," McCall Smith, who was described by a reporter for *The Atlantic* as a "very white, very male Scotsman" (Gritz, 2010, para. 1) with thinning gray hair and light blue eyes, reinforces the myth of the over-sexualized black woman or the Jezebel stereotype. One of the negative images of African American women that permeated southern American literature during the 19th and early 20th centuries, the Jezebel stereotype is derived from the biblical story of Jezebel, who was married to King Ahab of Israel. Gaines (1999) writes that Jezebel was so disruptive to Israelite social order and religious ways that she is called a harlot, although the scriptures do not provide examples of adulterous behavior. According to Gaines (1999), an explanation for the accusation of promiscuity is that biblical authors sometimes connect pursuing false gods with chasing false lovers. A relationship with a foreign deity is similar to an extramarital affair; both are immoral and offer only sham affection or protection.

Wells (2018) writes that this image of Jezebel is still prevalent and is embedded in how society characterizes black girls.

While McCall Smith allows Precious and Grace to label some South African women characters in his book series as bad girls, the bad girls are seldom allowed to speak. However, when these characters do speak, they also reinforce the Jezebel stereotype. Hungwe's (2006) study of what constitutes respectability in South African women is useful for this chapter. In her research, Hungwe chronicles how women in the former colony of Southern Rhodesia and contemporary Zimbabwe were and still are defined as "respectable" or "unrespectable." Hungwe defined a "respectable" woman in Zimbabwean society as one who is treated with deferential esteem, and who is perceived as an honorable and dignified member of her community or society. An "unrespectable" woman, however, is seen as dishonorable and lacking in dignity; she will attract social opprobrium and her behavior may not be emulated (p. 33). According to Hungwe, ideas of what black South African women should be grew out of colonial notions of what makes women respectable or unrespectable. The early colonial era, roughly up to the 1920s, was characterized by the same notions of respectability that had existed during pre-colonial times. Women could garner respect through marriage, bearing children within wedlock, or earning money for the patriarchal family unit. Generally, respectable women (of all races) were expected to be virgins before marriage and chaste within marriage. Unmarried rural women who had children (especially if they did so after visiting or moving to the towns) earned the wrath of their elders and were branded as prostitutes. After the 1920s, Zimbabwean women began to migrate to towns, becoming receptionists, secretaries, telephone operators, housemaids, nannies, vegetable vendors, sex workers, dressmakers, and "shebeen queens" (brewers of home-made beer) (Hungwe, 2006).

In McCall Smith's book series, Precious Ramotswe and Grace Makutsi certainly see themselves as respectable women. "She was a good detective, and a good woman," (1988, p. 4) McCall Smith (1998) writes of Precious in the first chapter of the *No. 1 Ladies' Detective Agency*, the first book in the series. Later in the book, she is described by her father as good woman: "Precious was like her mother, who was a good fat woman" (p. 43). Because she is considered a good woman, Precious is respected by others in her community. Not only is she a business owner, but she gained some wealth through an inheritance from her father, who was revered in his community. Her inheritance allows her to buy a nice home and marry a "good" man who is also a business owner and adopts two children.

While Grace does not come from a wealthy family, she worked to put herself through business college earning 97 percent on her final exams, one of the highest scores in the school's history, a fact that she expresses often. However, what merits discussion here by McCall Smith is why none of the students who have attended the Botswana Secretarial College ever scored higher than 97 percent. After graduating from the Botswana Secretarial College, Grace is hired by Precious to work as a receptionist in her detective agency, a position that is considered respectable for South African women. In *The Kalahari Typing School for Men* (2002) McCall Smith writes:

> Whenever she walked past the Botswana Secretarial College, Mma Makutsi felt a surge of pride. She had spent six months of her life at the college during which time she had scraped an existence, working part time as a night waitress in a hotel (a job which she hated) and struggling to stay awake during the day. Her resolve and her persistence had paid off, and she would never forget the strength of the applause at the graduation ceremony when, before the proud eyes of her parents, who had sold sheep to pay for the journey down to Gaborone, she had crossed the stage to receive her secretarial diploma as the leading graduate of the year. Her life, she suspected, would involve no greater triumph than that. (p. 84)

Grace's position in the detective agency allows her to care for an ill brother and send money home to her family, something that also is considered respectable. Grace becomes even more respectable in later books in the series when she marries a wealthy business owner, which considerably increases her standing in the community. Grace, however, believes that her station in life improved because she did not indulge in the kind of behavior that is attributed to bad girls. She has a certificate from a business college, and because of this, she can earn a living in a respectable manner.

Because Grace and Precious are characterized as respectable South African women, McCall Smith gives them authority to label South African women who have not achieved their standard of respectability as "bad girls." In a chapter titled, "An Excellent Type of Girl" in the book, *Morality for Beautiful Girls* (2001), Grace is asked to help screen entrants for a local beauty competition. In the chapter, McCall Smith categorizes good and bad girls. He wrote: "It had not been difficult to identify Motlamedi as unsuitable for the important office of Miss Beauty and Integrity. . . it was rare for Mma Makutsi to feel sure about somebody on a first meeting, but there was no doubt in her mind that Motlamedi was, quite simply, a bad girl" (p. 203). McCall Smith further writes:

> This description was very specific; it had nothing to do with bad women or bad ladies – they were quite different categories. Bad women were prostitutes; bad ladies were manipulative older ladies, usually married to older men, who interfered in the affairs of others for their own selfish ends. The expression bad girl, by contrast, referred to somebody who was usually rather younger (certainly under thirty) and whose interest

was in having a good time. Indeed, there was a subcategory of bad girls, that of good time girls. These were girls who were mainly to be found in bars with flashy men, having what appeared to be a good time. (p. 203)

McCall Smith clearly characterizes Grace as a good girl:

At the other end of the spectrum were girls who worked hard and who were appreciated by their families. They were the ones who visited their elders; who looked after the smaller children, sitting for hours under a tree watching the children play; and who in due course trained to be nurses or, as in Mma Makutsi's case, undertook a general secretarial training at the Botswana Secretarial College. Unfortunately, these good girls, who carried half the world upon their shoulders, did not have much fun. (p. 203)

Grace comes to the following conclusion about women who enter beauty competitions:

There was no doubt that Motlamedi was not a good girl, but was there any possibility, Mma Makutsi now glumly asked herself, that any of the others might prove to be much better? The difficulty was that good girls were unlikely to enter a beauty competition in the first place. It was in general, not the sort of thing that good girls thought of doing. (p. 203)

Later in the chapter, Grace has a moment of triumph when she shows her list of contestants to a male who works as an apprentice in Mr. J. L. B. Matekoni's auto repair shop. Matekoni is the husband of Precious Ramotswe. "This is a fine list of girls!" he said enthusiastically. "These are some of the best girls in town. Or at least three of them are the best girls in town. Big girls, you know what I mean, big, excellent girls. These are girls that we boys are very appreciative of. We approve of these girls. Oh yes! Too much!" (p. 204).

Looking at women in Zimbabwe, Hungwe (2006) writes that one of the ways in which patriarchy has been entrenched in Zimbabwean society is by dividing women, offering them limited power and social approval in exchange for behavior strictly policed along binary lines. Women who are thus divided, and who label and insult each other, continue to service patriarchal structures.

In McCall Smith's books, several conversations between Precious and Grace help label women in Botswana as respectable or unrespectable. For example, in *In the Company of Cheerful Ladies* (2004), Grace spies Violet Steptoe, a former classmate who scored only 40 percent on her examinations at the Botswana Secretarial College, at a dance class.

Grace muses:

Yes, it was her; one of the women from her year at the Botswana Secretarial College, one of those fun-loving glamorous girls who ended up getting barely 50 percent, and there she was, dancing with a confident and attractive man. (p. 91)

Violet's only comment here is: "So!" shouted the glamorous girl. "So there you are! Grace Makutsi!"

Later, during the same class, Grace runs into Violet in the ladies room: "And you Violet? What have you been doing? Did you manage to find a job?"

She was one of the worst of the glamorous, empty-headed set at the Botswana Secretarial College, and here she was applying powder to her face in the aptly named Powder Room of the President Hotel. (p.125)

The implication of this remark was that those who got barely 50 percent in the final examinations might be expected to experience some difficulty in finding a job. This, however, was not lost on Violet.

Find a job? She retorted? Mma (pronounced Ma), I had them lining up to give me a job! I had so many offers that I could think of no way of choosing between them. So you know what I did? You want to know?
I looked at the men who were offering the jobs and I chose the best-looking one, she announced. I knew that that was how they would choose their secretary, so I applied the same rule to them! Hah! (p. 125)

In episode 2 (Curtis & Minghella, 2009), of the HBO series, Grace runs into Violet again, this time while Grace is investigating a case for the detective agency.

Violet tells Grace:

I have a great position. High marks aren't everything you know, Grace. I have my own techniques. My boss is a great man. He bought me this bag (she shows Grace her handbag) as a matter of fact. So, I get all the perks.

Because Violet is one of the few "bad girls" who speak, her comments bring to mind several questions. Who is Violet Steptoe? Why does she feel the need to depend on men for her survival? What does she feel about her own self-worth? The reader learns nothing about Violet's background because she is not given an opportunity to tell her story. As a result, McCall Smith allows readers to learn what they know about Violet through Precious and Grace. Thus, McCall Smith provides Violet with no means of resisting the stereotype that is thrust upon her.

Here, this author examined some subaltern studies to understand if the myth of the over-sexualized black woman or the bad black girl is reflected in some of McCall Smith's female characters in *The No. 1 Ladies' Detective Agency* book series and the HBO television series. Alcoff (1991) asserts that in the practice of speaking for, as well as the practice of speaking about others, one is "engaging in the act of representing the other's needs, goals, situation, and in fact, who they are" (p. 9). In doing so, one is participating in the construction of their subject-positions. Mardorossian (1999) notes that the premises of the colonialist discourse do not falter and lose ground when the black subalterns speak, but paradoxically when they are silenced and stereotyped.

Understanding this type of characterization is crucial, Busia (2012) asserts, because women of African descent, in general, have not always even been seen as a subset of "women" (p.100), but somehow of a species apart from female humanity. This is also important Bush (1996) explains, because white representations of black women have frequently been at odds with the realities of their lived experiences. Disentangling fact from fiction is complicated by the fact that, during the colonization process, white patriarchal and racist culture reconstructed the black woman as the "ultimate other" (p. 420). For these reasons, this type of representation is important to African women and women in the black diaspora because images of black sexuality that originated in the 16th century have continued to the present day in various forms. And although these images differ in terms of historical and cultural specifics, the stereotype of the sensuous black female is omnipresent (Marshall, 1996). Therefore, recognition of these myths is important not only for African women, but for all women in the black diaspora.

Mitchell and Feagin (1995) assert that people of color have consistently used all means at their disposal as tools of opposition, sometimes influencing and reshaping the dominant culture in the process. Under conditions of oppression, subordinate groups tend to emphasize existing cultural concepts, norms, and practices that are in opposition to the majority group's culture. In time, new elements of oppositional culture develop and become interwoven with the traditional beliefs and practices of oppressed peoples. Thus, non-European groups, including African Americans in the United States, often draw on their own cultural resources to resist subjugation under oppressive circumstances. In these instances, these groups will develop an oppositional culture that embodies a coherent set of values, beliefs, and practices that mitigate the effects of oppression and reaffirms that which is distinct from the majority culture.

Alexander McCall Smith and the *No. 1 Ladies' Detective Agency*

Alexander McCall Smith was born in 1948, in Bulawayo, Southern Rhodesia (later known as Zimbabwe), where his father worked as a public prosecutor in what was then a British colony. The youngest of four children, McCall Smith spent his childhood in Southern Rhodesia and attended the Christian Brothers College in Bulawayo. He left Africa at age 17 and enrolled at the University of Edinburgh, where he earned an LLB, then a Ph.D in Law (Petruso, n.d.). He became a law professor in Scotland, and it was in this role that he returned to Africa, first to Swaziland (now known as Eswatini) and then in 1980, he went to

Botswana where he helped found the law school and taught law at the University of Botswana. While in Botswana, he also put together and wrote Botswana's criminal code. Though McCall's codification was not put into law, it was later published as *The Criminal Law of Botswana* and still proved to be very important to legal issues in that country (Petruso, n.d).

At 50, McCall Smith published *The No. 1 Ladies' Detective Agency*, his first book. The *No. 1 Ladies' Detective Agency* series revolves around Precious Ramotswe, a divorced African woman who sells her inheritance and opens a private investigation agency in Botswana's capital city, Gaborone. Precious calls her agency the No. 1 Ladies' Detective Agency as she tells her father on his death bed, "because it will be the best one in Botswana, the No. 1 Agency" (*The No. 1 Ladies' Detective Agency*, 1998, p. 6). Published in 1998, the book was the first in a series that now includes 21 other books. McCall Smith's books have sold millions of copies in English and have been translated into 40 languages (Gaotlhobogwe, 2011). In 2009, a television series based on the books was created by HBO Entertainment in association with The Weinstein Co., and the BBC produced a seven-part series that was aired on HBO (Memmott, 2009). The other books in the series are listed in the appendix section of this chapter.

Speaking for the "Other"

In an interview published in *The Atlantic* (Gritz, 2010), McCall Smith was asked this question: "Your *Ladies'* Detective books are written in the very convincing voice of an African woman. How are you able to inhabit a character who is so different from you?" McCall Smith's response was:

> I suppose it's part of being a novelist that one has to be able to imagine what it's like to be another person. After a while, one can imagine what it's like to be virtually anyone. But obviously, one has to have a certain amount of experience of the world one's characters live in, and I have lived in Africa.

McCall Smith assumes that because he has lived in Africa, he knows enough about subaltern Africans to write about them. However, Achebe (1995) asserts that to the colonial mind it was always of utmost importance to be able to say: 'I know my natives,' a claim which implied two things at once: that the native was really quite simple and that understanding him and controlling him went hand in hand – understanding being a pre-condition for control and control constituting adequate proof of understanding (p. 74). Likewise, Alcoff (1991) explains that a speaker's social location has an epistemically significant impact on that speaker's claims and can serve to authorize or deauthorize one's speech. She asserts that when one is speaking for others, one may be describing their situation and thus also speaking about them. In fact, it may be impossible to speak for others without simultaneously conferring information about them.

Similarly, when one is speaking about others, or simply trying to describe their situation or some aspect of it, one may also be speaking in place of them, that is, speaking for them.

Pieterse (1990) explains that while decolonization in a political sense has occurred, and a process of intellectual decolonization has taken place in the sense that critical perspectives on colonialism have become more and more common, what remains to be addressed is cultural decolonization. The legacy of several hundred years of western expansion and hegemony manifested in racism and exoticism continues to be recycled in western cultures in the form of stereotypical images of non-western cultures (p. 9). And while buzzwords such as "postcolonialism" and "political correctness" ostensibly inform interaction with culture and history, the colonial legacy continually asserts itself in popular culture and reinscribes a politics of power in the landscape (van Eeden, 2004).

Images of Africans in Western Films and Books

Gugler (2003) explains that with the assumption of colonial control, European voices came to dominate the discourse about Africa. Since colonial days, films produced in the U.S., Europe, and South Africa have propagated images of black Africa dominated by people of European descent with whom Western viewers could easily identify with. The portrayal of Africans repeated and reinforced negative stereotypes; they appeared as barbaric, savage, and bloodthirsty; as servants, mostly incompetent; or simply as part of the décor. Harding (2003) notes that in order to construct an image of some place, person, or thing of which "we have no direct experience, we rely heavily on visualization presented by others and made available to us" (p.69). The same is true for Africa and the role of early photography in setting up a bank of seemingly definitive images of Africa and its people, crucial in both the colonial and the missionary enterprise. When the moving image of Africa followed, the same elements identified by these early still photographers were repeated and embellished, and visual characters, by now familiar, were again presented. As Bhabha (1983) writes, this fixity as a sign of cultural/historical/racial difference in the discourse of colonialism is a paradoxical mode of representation that connotes rigidity and an unchanging order as well as disorder, degeneracy, and daemonic repetition. Likewise, the stereotype, which is its major discursive strategy, is a form of knowledge and identification that vacillates between what is always 'in place' (p.18-36), already known and something that must be anxiously repeated.

Ukadike (1990), however, notes that colonialist representation began long before the invention of motion pictures. In various forms, vicious misrepresentation of Africans and authentic traditional African values existed in the literary works of Rider Haggard and other European writers and scholars. The European colonizers were hell-bent on telling the world that colonialism was a valuable philanthropic "civilizing mission" (p. 31) inspired by the necessity to stamp out ignorance, disease, tyranny, and usher in the "best" (p. 31) cultural patterns. Along these same lines, Stam and Spence (2000) assert that colonialist representation is rooted in a vast colonial intertext, a widely disseminated set of discursive practices. Long before the first racist images appeared on the film screens of Europe and North America, the process of colonialist image-making, and resistance to that process, resonated throughout Western literature. Colonialist historians, speaking for the 'winners' of history, exalted the colonial enterprise at bottom little more than a gigantic act of pillage whereby whole continents were bled of their human and material resources as a philanthropic 'civilizing mission' (p. 316).

Recognition of this type of stereotyping in western films is also important, as Cameron (1994) explains, because with the chief colonial powers among the creators of early motion pictures, it was not surprising that the content of cinema would reflect the content of a colonial "received wisdom" (p.12). For filmmakers working on location in Africa, the window through which they saw the continent was a colonial one. What these celluloid images suggest is that consciously or not, the filmmakers were acting as cultural colonialists by reinforcing and legitimizing Western political practices in Africa. These images contribute to viewing audiences' misperceptions of Africa and Africans, and help to perpetuate and strengthen racist and colonialist modes of thinking (Dunn, 1996).

In America, European racist texts found a new haven. Edgar Rice Burroughs, for example, created dime store novels in which he created fictional images of Africa and, although he never set foot on African soil, his legendary character, Tarzan, was to fascinate generations of Americans and audiences everywhere (Ukadike, 1994). In 1921, *Tarzan, the Ape Man* found his voice. Four decades after most of Africa became independent, Hollywood continues to promote a white man dominating his African surroundings. Newer versions of the Tarzan movies continue to be made, both for the big screen and the home video market. Not only Tarzan movies, but most Western films set in Africa have similarly, if more subtly, put down Africans (Gugler, 2003).

Stereotypes of African Women

Hungwe (2006) writes that the distinction made between "respectability" and "unrespectability" among South African women serves a patriarchal agenda. As long as women occupy space allocated to them, they remain "respectable," but once they start redefining public and private terrain, they run the risk of being judged as depraved and "unrespectable" in the eyes of society. What is more, it can be argued that some women actively participate in this form of policing. As is usually the case in patriarchal social structures, women who oppress, demonize, and marginalize other women usually have some small amount of power or authority bestowed upon them by patriarchal structures; or they benefit from certain patriarchal practices, as in the case of older women throughout Africa who earn an income by performing female genital cutting or mutilation.

Collins (1990) explains that one of the core concepts of black feminist consciousness is controlling the negative images of African American women as a way of creating a self-defined black women's standpoint. This is important for producers of African American cultural products since stereotypical portrayals of African American women have been essential to the political economy of domination fostering black women's oppression. Collins (1990) submitted that:

> Therefore, challenging these controlling images has long been a core theme in black feminist thought. As part of a generalized ideology of domination, these controlling images of black womanhood take on special meaning because the authority to define these symbols is a major instrument of power. (p. 67-68)

Despite efforts of African American women writers to create more positive images of black women, the Jezebel stereotype has remained stable. She is still opportunistic, one-dimensional, and sexually deviant as ever (Campbell, et al., 2008). As Wyatt (1997) explains, the negative stereotypes of the past are the negative stereotypes of today:

> The stereotype of the promiscuous black woman persists whether we are standing at a bus stop with our children, on our way to church dressed in our Sunday best, studying in the library for a class, sitting in a business suit testifying before a congressional committee, or standing in a hotel lobby. Age, dress, appearance, and even economic status have much less to do with our image than do race and gender. (p. 29)

Collins (1990) asserts that controlling images of black women are not simply grafted onto existing social institutions, but are so pervasive that even though the images themselves change in the popular imagination, black women's portrayal as the "other" persists. Despite the pervasiveness of controlling images, African American women have resisted in a variety of ways (hooks, 1992; Gilkes, 1983), specifically by recording black women's reactions to controlling images, confronting controlling images forwarded by institutions internal and external to the African American community, and by developing redefinitions of beauty.

Images of African Women in the Media

Shohat (1991) writes that western cinema not only inherited and disseminated colonial discourse, but also created a system of domination through monopolistic control of film distribution and exhibition in much of Asia, Africa, and Latin

America. Shohat further asserts that Third World women – when not inscribed as metaphors for their virgin land as in Bird of Paradise – appear largely as sexually hungry subalterns. As a result, hegemonic western representation has been locked into a series of Eurocentric articulations of power.

The Jezebel Stereotype or the "Bad Black Girl"

Berry and Manning-Miller (1996) explain that although the number of media images and the variety of messages about African Americans have increased in recent years, many critics and scholars have found that most remain problematic. Modern stereotypes of African American women are too often reminiscent of the Jezebel stereotype or the sexually aggressive African American woman. Scholars have identified four variations of interrelated, socially-constructed, controlling images of black womanhood that dominated southern antebellum literature before and after the American Civil War: the mammy, Aunt Jemima, Sapphire, and Jezebel (Collins, 1990). Among these, the most damaging has been the Jezebel stereotype. White (1999) writes that the Jezebel stereotype, which became one of the most prevalent images of black women in antebellum America, was "molded into a peculiarly American mythology" (p. 27) during the era of slavery. Many antebellum Southerners were convinced that slave women were lewd and lascivious, that they invited sexual overtures from white men, and that any resistance they displayed was mere feigning.

Jewell (1993) has characterized Jezebel as a tragic mulatto with "thin lips, long straight hair, slender nose, thin figure and fair complexion" (p. 46), the heroine in much of the literature of 19th and early 20th century southern antebellum literature by African American women writers. The character is considered tragic because she is the product of a white father, usually the slave master, and his African American female slave, and is not completely accepted in African American or white society. Pilgrim (2002), however, asserts that the conceptualization of Jezebel as the tragic mulatta is too narrow. While it is arguable that the "tragic mulatto" and "Jezebel" share the reputation of being sexually seductive, and both are antithetical to the desexualized Mammy caricature, it is a mistake to assume that only, or even mainly, fair-complexioned black women were sexually objectified by the larger American society. From the early 1630s to the present, black American women of all shades have been portrayed as hypersexual "bad-black-girls" (Jewell, 1993, p. 46). Thus, African women of all hues are susceptible to being stereotyped as Jezebel.

Jewell (1993) writes that when the reference is rooted in slavery, the slave owners who coerced female slaves or offered them harsh alternatives if they were unwilling to submit to the owner's whims attributed these liaisons to the hyper-sexuality of the female slave who was purported to be the aggressor or seducer. Therefore, Jezebel or the "bad-black-girl" (p. 37) has been used to depict black women as eager, available, and willing sexual partners. Jezebel's sexual aggression, fertility, and libidinous self-expression were considered limitless and concretized black female subordination, justifying the rape of African women by white men. According to this portrayal, the African woman truly enjoyed being ravaged by her master and his sons so that abusing her was simply satisfying her natural desires (Simms, 2001).

Institutional Sites for Transmitting Controlling Images

Collins (1990) asserts that institutional sites within and outside of the black community have been essential in transmitting controlling images of black women. Higginbotham (1989) further explains that the tendency to transmit images from institutional sites in the black community has its roots in the racial uplift movement of the late nineteenth and early twentieth centuries. "Race work" or "racial uplift" equated normality with conformity to white middle-class models of gender roles and sexuality. Thus, many black women linked mainstream domestic duties, codes of dress, sexual conduct, and public etiquette with both individual success and group progress. Black leaders argued that "proper" and "respectable" behavior proved blacks worthy of equal civil and political rights. Conversely, nonconformity was equated with deviance and pathology and was often cited as a cause of racial inequality and injustice (Higginbotham, 1992).

Method

This study used the textual analysis method to examine *The No. 1 Ladies' Detective Agency* HBO series and the novels to determine if McCall Smith reinforces the western myth of the Jezebel stereotype by allowing two of the main characters, Precious and Grace, to speak for other African women they describe as "bad girls" or "glamour girls." The secondary objective was to determine if, by silencing the "bad girls" characters, McCall Smith provides them with no means of resisting the stereotype.

In his 1994 study, *White Screens Black Images: Hollywood from the Dark Side*, Snead identified three tactics that perpetuate black stereotypes: mythification, marking, and omission. Mythification involves mythifying whites as powerful and civilized, and ensuring that blacks appear meek and uncivilized. Marking is a tactic in which the color black is repeatedly over-determined, and omission is exclusion by reversal, distortion, or some other form of censorship. In this research, Snead's tactic of omission is used to help determine if by omitting the voices of women who have been described as "bad girls" or "glamour girls," McCall Smith reinforces the Jezebel stereotype. Since the voices of most of the characters described as "bad girls" are omitted, readers and viewers of the series and the books can only determine who they are by what is said about them.

McKee (2003) defines textual analysis as a way for researchers to gather information about how other human beings make sense of the world. It is a methodology – a data-gathering process – for those researchers who want to understand the ways in which members of various cultures and subcultures make sense of who they are, and of how they fit into the world in which they live. Thus, it is useful for researchers working in cultural studies, media studies, mass communication, and perhaps even in sociology and philosophy. As a result, by seeing the variety of ways in which it is possible to interpret reality, individuals also understand their own cultures better because they can start to see the limitations and advantages of their own sense-making practices. For this research, this author adapted McKee's (2001) step-by-step guide for completing a textual analysis:

1.   Choosing a topic for research.
2.   Developing specific research questions.
3.   Listing texts relevant to the study. (For this research, the author read each of the books in the McCall Smith series and noted words and phrases relevant to this study. The most relevant phrases were "bad girls" and "glamour girls". In some instances, the phrase "no good" was used when referring to some of the women in the books. The author also examined the characters who used the phrases, how they used them, and to whom the phrases were directed toward).
4.   Finding additional texts that might be relevant to the study. (For this part of the research, the author examined other detective novels by South African writers. While there are several detective novels written by black and white South African men, only one of them featured a female detective).
5.   Gathering the texts.
6.   Watching examples of related television programs and examining how particular textual elements work in each one.
7.   Watching other programs in the same genre and noting how they work. (For this research, this author found no programs other than the *No. 1 Ladies' Detective Agency* HBO series that featured women detectives in Botswana, South Africa).
8.   Getting as much sense as possible of the wider meaning of the texts.
9.   Returning to the relevant texts for interpretations, sense-making and meaning.

Findings and Analysis

Jewel (1993) identified the Jezebel stereotype as a "bad girl," and if McCall Smith's characterizations of African women can be believed, many women in Botswana are "bad girls." That there are many such women in Botswana is even inferred by characters other than Precious and Grace. In the first book in the series, Precious is talking with Alice Busang, who has come to the agency for help in determining if her husband is having an affair. Here is the conversation, beginning with Precious:

> He goes to bars, does he?
> Yes.
> That's where they meet them. They meet these women who hang about in bars waiting for other women's husbands. This city is full of women like that." (*No. 1 Ladies' Detective Agency*, 1998, pg. 140)

McCall Smith does not specify who these women are and it is clear that Alice Busang does not know who they are either. However, by referring to them as "these women who hang about in bars waiting for other women's husbands" she infers that they are women who prey on married men. She also says, "the city is full of women like that." In this way, Alice Busang stereotypes all Botswana women who frequent bars as bad women.

In the first episode of the television series, Grace tells Precious:

> There were many glamorous girls at the College. These were the ones who did not do very well. They got fifty percent or just over. They used to go out three or four nights a week and many would meet older men, who would have more money and a nice car. These girls did not care that these men were married. They would go out with these men and dance in bars. Then, what would happen, Mma?

Mma Ramotswe shook her head and said:

> I can imagine.
> They would tell these men to leave their wives. And the men would say that this was a good idea, and they would go off with these girls. And there would be many unhappy women who now would not be able to get another man because the men only go for young glamorous girls and they do not want an older woman.

In *Morality for Beautiful Girls*, Precious is speaking with the organizer of a local beauty competition who said:

> Yes, some very bad things have happened. Last year, two of our beauty queens were found to be bad girls. One was arrested for prostitution in one of the big hotels. Another was shown to have obtained goods under false pretenses and to have used a credit card without authorization. There were letters in the paper. There was much crowing. They said things like: Are these girls the right sort of girls to be ambassadors for Botswana? (p. 159)

What is omitted here are the voices of the women who Precious and Grace assume visit bars looking for married men or those who enter beauty competitions. Readers do not know why the women visit bars or enter beauty competitions, and since the women do not speak, it could be assumed that Grace and Alice Busang's assessments are true.

In another example, a client asks Precious for help in determining if his younger brother is being poisoned by his wife. After Grace convinces Precious to take the case, the government man tells Grace: "And you, Mma. You are a clever lady. If you ever decide that you are tired of being a private detective, come and work for the government. The government needs women like you. Most of the women we have working for the government are no good" (*Morality for Beautiful Girls*, 2001, Kindle edition).

Here, even highly-placed government officials condemn many Botswana women who work for the government as being bad girls. The official says: "They sit and paint their nails. I have seen them. You would work hard, I think" (2001, Kindle edition). Described as wearing oversized glasses and having bad skin, Grace does not fit the "bad girl" stereotype, and most men do not find her attractive. He assumes that Grace does not lure men to her bed and cannot be a threat to the good men of Botswana.

In *Morality for Beautiful Girls* (2001), Grace, discusses the scale she uses to rate bad girls:

> This description was very specific; it had nothing to do with bad women or bad ladies-they were quite different categories. Bad women were prostitutes; bad ladies were manipulative older ladies, usually married to older men, who interfered in the affairs of others for their own selfish ends. The expression bad girl, by contrast referred to somebody who was usually rather younger (certainly under 30) and whose interest was in having a good time. (Kindle edition)

Grace also developed subcategories for bad girls: "Indeed there was a subcategory of bad girls, that of good-time girls. These were girls who were mainly to be found in bars with flashy men, having what appeared to be a good time" (*Morality for Beautiful Girls*, 2001, Kindle edition).

The bad girls are often described as pretty, lazy (none of them do much work), and according to Grace, spend their days scheming to get a rich man. The bad girls are not only described as being pretty, but as having lighter skin. Jewell (1993) has characterized Jezebel as a tragic mulatta with "thin lips, long straight hair, slender nose, thin figure and fair complexion." However, Pilgrim (2002) asserts that the conceptualization of Jezebel as the tragic mulatta is too narrow. While it is true that the "tragic mulatta" and "Jezebel" share the reputation of being sexually seductive, and both are antithetical to the desexualized Mammy caricature, it is a mistake to assume that only, or even mainly, fair-complexioned black women were sexually objectified by the larger American society. From the early 1630s to the present, black American women of all shades have been portrayed as hypersexual "bad-black-girls" (Jewell, 1993). Thus, African women of all hues are susceptible to being stereotyped as Jezebel.

In another instance, in *Morality for Beautiful Girls* (2001), Precious asks Grace to take over the management of her husband's office:

> We were taught how to do that at college, said Mma Makutsi. They sent us one day to an office that was in a very bad way, and we had to sort it out. There were four of us - myself and three pretty girls. The pretty girls spent all their time talking to the men in the office while I did the work. I worked until eight o'clock at night. The other girls all went off with the men to a bar at five o'clock and left me there. (Kindle edition)

Precious responds:

> They are useless girls, those girls, she said. There are too many people like that in Botswana these days. But at least you know that you have succeeded. You are an assistant detective and what are they? Nothing, I should think.

In one passage in *Tears of the Giraffe* (2000), Precious is in the office of J.L.B. Matekoni, the man she eventually marries, and notices that some of the calendars on the walls have pictures of scantily-clad women on them. She says:

> They were ridiculous calendars, with all those far-too-thin ladies sitting on tyres and leaning against cars. Those ladies were useless for everything. They would not be good for having children, and not one of them looked as if she had her school certificate, or even her standard six. They were useless good-time girls, who only made men all hot and bothered, and that was no good to anybody. If only men knew what fools of them these girls made; but they did not know it and it was hopeless trying to point it out to them. (p. 9)

Even Precious does not entirely escape the stigma of being labeled a "bad girl."

Reminiscing about her failed marriage to her abusive ex-husband Note Mokoti, Precious says to herself:

> She could have said no at this point, which is what her father wanted her to say. But she did not want to say that. She lived for her meetings with Note Mokoti. She wanted to marry him. He was not a good man, she could tell that, but she might change him. And, when all was said and done, there remained those dark moments of contact, those pleasures he snatched from her, which were addictive. She liked that. She felt

ashamed even to think of it, but she liked what he did to her, the humiliation, the urgency (*No. 1 Ladies' Detective Agency*, 1998, p. 54)

In episode 1 of the HBO series (2009), Precious decides to take Alice Busang's case, but rather than use covert observation or other forms of private detection, she decides to set a seductive trap to catch Alice's husband cheating. Imitating the same action that she accused bad girls of engaging in, she goes to a bar that Alice's husband is known to frequent. She invites the strange man into her home and offers him something to drink. Putting on a record of soft music, she begins to gyrate her body sensuously. She suggests that he take a picture of them kissing so that she can have something to remember him by. At this point, she believes that she has all of the evidence that she will need to convince Alice Busang that her husband is a philanderer. When she shows the photo to his wife, Alice Busang becomes enraged:

> This is you, is it not? Kissing my husband?
> I am playing a part to demonstrate that your husband is
> unfaithful.
> How dare you kiss my Kremlin, you thief! You Jezebel! You
> have stolen my husband from under my nose.

Precious, astounded by Alice Busang's accusations, tries to comfort the angry wife:

> But you wanted proof . . .
> Proof that my husband is unfaithful. Not proof that you are
> the fattest tart in Gaborone!

Precious's action here indicates that none of the women in Botswana are immune to the bad girl stereotype. Although Precious is considered a woman of good moral standards, McCall Smith does not hesitate to have her act in the same way as the women Precious and Grace characterized as bad.

Conclusion

In her study of respectability and unrespectability, Hungwe (2006) writes that:

> Women who sing the patriarchal tune are presented as champions of women's causes, at the same time that they serve their masters' cause. These are the respectable women, the ones who know their rightful position. Thus the distinction between respectable and unrespectable women in terms of age, class, race, and marital status has the lasting effect of ensuring that women carry their burdens with strength and do not present a united front as women in Zimbabwean gender struggles. (p. 45)

This can be applied to women in Alexander McCall Smith's *No. 1 Ladies' Dectective Agency* series. Indeed, Precious Ramotswe and Grace Makutsi, with their colonialist opinions of women they consider morally inferior to themselves, only serve to slow the advancement of women's rights in Botswana. Whether consciously or unconsciously, Hungewe writes (2006), there is no doubt that some women participate in defining and bestowing the labels of respectability and unrespectability on Zimbabwean women.

To counter the negative cultural representations discussed in this chapter, African feminist filmmakers have argued for films that are grounded in African feminism. Ellerson (2000) has called this effort the African women in the cinema movement, a concept that must be analyzed within the context of social, political, and cultural structures in Africa. It must be discussed within the specific conventions of cinematic practices that have emerged in Africa since the inception of what has come to be called African cinema. In *Sisters of the Screen* (2000), Ellerson asserts that the dominant idea of cinema as the feature film projected on a large screen viewed by large audiences does not portray the reality of African cinema in general, and even less so the cinema of African women.

For African women, writing has also been essential to effective resistance to negative stereotypes. *African Women Writing Resistance: An Anthology of Contemporary Voices* (de Hernandez, et al., 2010) quotes Ellen Banda-Aaku, saying: "Writing exposes the many challenges African women are resisting in the world today, and speaking out brings issues to the forefront so we are forced to question or address them" (p. 7). "By writing we become more aware of the values and beliefs holding us back, as well as those that can move us forward. Only by writing can we tell the story of the African woman. If we don't tell our story, who will?"

In the same volume, (de Hernandez, et al., 2010) quotes Diana Adesola Mafe as saying: "writing is resistance, an opportunity to voice my non-compliance. Here I can make up for all those moments where I wish I had said something. Here I can anchor those past (and future) experiences, deconstruct them, learn from them, and perhaps most importantly, share them" (p. 8).

South African writers must also resist the negative stereotypes that have been pervasive in African American literature. An example, Collins (2004) asserts, are the legions of young black women who dance, strut, and serve as visually appealing props in rap and hip-hop music videos:

> The women in these videos typically share two attributes – they are rarely acknowledged as individuals and they are scantily clad. One black female body can easily replace another, and all are reduced to their bodies. (p. 128)

Ironically, displaying nameless, naked black female bodies had a long history in Western societies, from the display of enslaved African women on the auction block under chattel slavery to representations of black female bodies in contemporary film and music videos. (p. 128)

In a 2009 USA Today article, reporter Robert Bianco writes of the *No. 1 Ladies' Detective Agency* HBO series:

> And there you have the larger, sweetly put point, and one of the reasons some will find the series as precious as its heroine. As much as anything, *Ladies'* is McCall's attempt to counter some of the stereotypes many of us have about Africa, and to share and explain the affection he has for a world where gentility and formality still have a place. You'll hear it as much as see it: Contractions are seldom used, women refer to each other as 'my sister,' and people address each other with honorifics and last names.

Bianco makes no mention of the many times the two main women characters in the novels refer to other women in Botswana as "bad" or the derogatory way in which they use the terms "glamorous" and "pretty" to describe some South African women. Perhaps as a white American, he does not the grasp the idea that some of the language in the books perpetuates stereotypes that black women of African descent have been battling since the beginning of the slave trade. As Young (1996) asserts, since slavery, African females have been represented as not pure, not feminine, not fragile, but strong, sexually-knowing, and available.

However, African and African American scholars and writers have done much to counter the negative stereotypes by presenting images and writings that do much to resist such images. One example is Malebo Sephodi's 2017 novel, *Miss Behave,* which challenges society's deep-seated beliefs about what it means to be an obedient woman (*The Reading List,* 2018). Another African woman who is writing against the stereotypes is Angela Makholwa, regarded as the first black author to write crime fiction in South Africa. Her debut novel, *Red Ink,* published in 2013, is a psychological thriller that tells the story of fictional public relations consultant and ex-journalist, Lucy Khambule, as she investigates a horrifying series of rapes and murders in Johannesburg. Makholwa followed this up with *The 30th Candle,* an exploration into the sexuality of women in modern times. *The Black Widow Society,* published in 2014, is set around a secret organization established by three black businesswomen in an effort to liberate women from abusive relationships by carrying out hits on their abusive partners. For her work, Makholwa was shortlisted for the Alan Paton Award and the Barry Ronge Fiction prize (Samanga, 2016).

References

Achebe, C. (1995). Colonialist criticism. In B. Ashcroft, G. Griffiths, & H. Tiffin (Eds.), *The Post-Colonial Studies Reader* (pp. 57–61). London and New York: Routledge.

Alcoff, L. (1991). The Problem of Speaking for Others. *Cultural Critique, 20,* 5–32. https://doi.org/10.2307/1354221

Berry, V., & Manning-Miller, C. L. (1996). *Mediated Messages and African-American Culture: Contemporary Issues.* Sage Publications.

Bhabha, H. K. (1983). The Other Question. *Screen, 24* (6), 18–36. https://doi.org/10.1093/screen/24.6.18

Bianco, R. (2009). She's Precious, 'No. 1 Ladies' Detective Agency' is perfect. *USA Today.* http://usatoday30.usatoday.com/life/television/reviews/2009-03-26-ladies-detective-agency_N.htm

Bush, B. (1996). History, memory, myth? Reconstructing the history (or histories) of black women in the African Diaspora. *Nature Society and Thought, 9*(4), 419–444.

Busia, A. P. A. (2012). Women and the Dynamics of Representation: Of Cooking, Cars, and Gendered Culture. *Feminist Africa, 16,* 98–117. http://www.agi.ac.za/agi/feminist-africa/16

Cameron, K. M. (1994). *Africa on film: Beyond black and white.* New York: Continuum.

Campbell, S., Giannino, S., China, C., & Harris, C. (2008). I love New York: Does New York love me? *Journal of International Women's Studies, 10*(2), 20–28.

Collins, P. (1990). *Black feminist thought: Knowledge, consciousness, and the politics of empowerment.* New York: Routledge.

Collins, P. (2004). *Black Sexual Politics: African Americans, Gender, and the New Racism.* New York and London: Routledge.

Curtis, R. [Writer], & Minghella, A. [Writer] (2009). Episode one, pilot. In T. Bricknell [Director]. *The No. 1 Ladies' Detective Agency* [TV series episode]. Botswana, Africa, British Broadcasting Corporation and Home Box Office.

de Hernandez, J. B., Dongola, P., Jolaosho, O., & Serafin, A. (2010). African women writing resistance: An introduction. In P. Dongala, O. Jolaosho, A. Serafin, J. B. de Hernandez, P. Dongala, O. Jolaosho, & A. Serafin (Eds.), *African Women Writing Resistance: An Anthology of Contemporary Voices* (pp. 3–11). Madison, WI: The University of Wisconsin Press.

Dunn, K. (1996). Lights. . .camera. . .Africa: Images of Africa and Africans in western popular films of the 1930s. *African Studies Review, 39*(1), 149–175.

Ellerson, B. (2000). *Sisters of the Screen: Women of Africa on Film, Video, and Television.* Trenton, N.J. and Asmara, Eritrea: Africa World Press.

Gaines, J. H. (1999). *Music in the Old Bones: Jezebel Through the Ages.* Carbondale, IL: Southern Illinois University Press.

Gaotlhobogwe, M. (2011). *McCall Smith - getting into Mma Ramotswe's head is easy.* https://www.mmegi.bw/arts-culture/mccall-smith-getting-into-mma-ramotswes-head-is-easy/news

Gilkes, C. (1983). From slavery to social welfare: Racism and the control of black women. In A. Swerdlow & H. Lessinger (Eds.), *Class, Race, and Sex: The Dynamics of Control* (pp. 288–300). Boston: G.K. Hall.

Gritz, J. R. (2010). *A conversation with Alexander McCall Smith. The Atlantic.* https://www.theatlantic.com/entertainment/archive/2010/06/a-conversation-with-alexander-mccall-smith/57709/

Gugler, J. (2003). *African Film: Re-imagining a Continent.* United Kingdom: James Currey Ltd.

Harding, F. (2003). Africa and the moving image: Television, film and video. *Journal of African Cultural Studies, 16*(1), 69–84.

Higginbotham, E. (1989). Beyond the sound of silence: Afro-American women in history. *Gender and History, 1*(1), 50–67.

Higginbotham, E. (1992). African-American women's history and the metalanguage of race. *Signs, 17*(2), 251–274.

hooks, B. (1992). *Black Looks: Race and Representation.* Boston: South End Press.

Hungwe, C. (2006). Putting them in their place: "respectable and "unrespectable" women in Zimbabwean gender struggles. *Feminist Africa: Subaltern Sexualities, 6,* 33–47. http://www.agi.ac.za/agi/feminist-africa/06

Jewell, K. S. (1993). *From Mammy to Miss America and Beyond: Cultural Images and the Shaping of U.S. Social Policy.* London and New York: Routledge.

Mardorossian, C. (1999). Shutting up the subaltern: Silences, stereotypes, and double-entendre in Jean Rhys's Wide Sargasso Sea. *Callaloo, 22*(4), 1071–1090.

Marshall, A. (1996). From sexual denigration to self-respect: Resisting images of black female sexuality. In D. Jarrett-Macauley (Ed.), *Reconstructing Womanhood, Reconstructing Feminism* (pp. 5–35). London and New York: Routledge.

McKee, A. (2001). A beginner's guide to textual analysis. *Metro Magazine,* 138–149.

McKee, A. (2003). *Textual Analysis. A Beginner's Guide.* London, Thousand Oaks, CA, and New Delhi: Sage Publications.

Memmott, C. (2009). *McCall Smith has many books brewing, just like bush tea. USA Today.* http://usatoday30.usatoday.com/life/books/news/2009-12-07-mccallsmith07_CV_N.htm.

Mitchell, B.L., & Feagin, J.R. (1995). America's racial-ethnic cultures: Opposition within a mythical melting pot. In B. P. Bowser, T. Jones, & G. A. Young (Eds.), *Toward the Multicultural University* (pp. 65–86). Westport, CT: Praeger.

Petruso, A. (n.d.). *Alexander McCall Smith.* Encyclopedia of World Biography. https://www.notablebiographies.com/newsmakers2/2005-La-Pr/McCall-Smith- Alexander.html.

Pieterse, J. N. (1990). *White on Black: Images of Africa and Blacks in Western Popular Culture.* New Haven and London: Yale University Press.

Pilgrim, D. (2002). *Jezebel stereotype.* Jim Crow Museum of Racist Memorabilia. https://www.ferris.edu/HTMLS/news/jimcrow/jezebel/index.htm

Samanga, R. (2016). *Celebrating 8 of the most influential black South African women writers: These phenomenal black women changed South Africa's literary game.* OkayAfrica. https://www.okayafrica.com/south-africa-influential-black-women-writers/

Shohat, E. (1991). Gender and culture of empire: Toward a feminist ethnography of the cinema. *Quarterly Review of Film & Video, 13*(1-3), 45–84.

Simms, R. (2001). Controlling images and the gender construction of enslaved African Women. *Gender and Society, 15*(6), 879–897.

Smith, A. M. (1998). *The No. 1 Ladies' Detective Agency*. New York: Pantheon Books.

Smith, A. M. (2000). *Tears of the Giraffe*. New York: Anchor Books.

Smith, A. M. (2001). *Morality for Beautiful Girls*. New York: Anchor Books.

Smith, A. M. (2002). *The Kalahari Typing School for Men*. New York: Anchor Books.

Smith, A. M. (2004). *In the Company of Cheerful Ladies*. New York: Pantheon Books.

Snead, J. (1994). *White Screens, Black images: Hollywood from the Dark Side*. New York and London: Routledge.

Stam, R., & Spence, L. (2000). Colonialism, racism and representation: An introduction by Robert Stam & Louise Spence. In J. Hollows, P. Hutchings, & M. Jancovich (Eds.), *The Film Studies Reader* (pp. 315–322). London and New York: Arnold and Oxford University Press Inc.

The Reading List (2018). *'I wrote it for black women but men are finding value in it' – Malebo Sephodi chats about her new book Miss Behave*. https://readinglist.click/sub/i-wrote-it-for-black-women-but-men-are-finding-value-in-it-malebo-sephodi-chats-about-her-new-book-miss-behave/

Ukadike, N. F. (1994). Reclaiming Images of Women in Films from Africa and the Black Diaspora. *Frontiers: A Journal of Women Studies, 15*(1), 102–122. https://doi.org/10.2307/3346615

Ukadike, N. F. (1990). Western film images of Africa: Genealogy of an ideological formulation. *The Black Scholar, 21*(2), 30–48.

van Eeden, J. (2004). The Colonial Gaze: Imperialism, Myths, and South African Popular culture. *Design Issues, 20*(2), 18–33. http://www.jstor.org/stable/1512077

Wells, A. (2018, November 2-4). *Unearthing Jezebel: Reconstructing the Jezebel's and the black women's narratives* [Conference Presentation]. REA Annual Meeting, Washington D.C., United States. https://religiouseducation.net/papers/proceedings-REA2018.pdf

White, D. G. (1999). *Ar'nt I a Woman?: Female Slaves in the Plantation South*. Revised Edition. New York: W.W. Norton & Co.

Wyatt, G. E. (1997). *Stolen Women: Reclaiming our Sexuality, Taking Back Our Lives*. New York: John Wiley & Sons, Inc.

Young, L. (1996). *'Race,' Gender and Sexuality in the Cinema*. New York: Routledge.

Appendix

Books in the series: *No. 1 Ladies' Detective Agency* (1998), *Tears of the Giraffe* (2000), *Morality for Beautiful Girls* (2001), *The Kalahari Typing School for Men* (2002), *The Full Cupboard of Life* (2003), *In the Company of Cheerful Ladies* (2004), *Blue Shoes and Happiness* (2006), *The Good Husband of Zebra Drive* (2007), *The Miracle at Speedy Motors* (2008), *Tea Time for the Traditionally Built* (2009), *The Double Comfort Safari Club* (2010), *The Saturday Big Tent Wedding Party* (2011), *The Limpopo Academy of Private Detection* (2012), *The Minor Adjustment Beauty Salon* (2013), *The Handsome Man's De Luxe Café* (2014), *The Woman Who Walked in Sunshine* (2015), *Precious and Grace* (2016), *The House of Unexpected Sisters* (2017), *The Colors of all the Cattle* (2018), *To the Land of Long Lost Friends* (2019), and *How to Raise an Elephant* (2020).

CHAPTER 3

Human rights and redemptive-corrective justice in Bob Marley's music

Kevin Barker

Kingston University, UK

Abstract

In the oral-literary traditions of Afro-Caribbean societies, Bob Marley's iterations of justice in his music, an expression of Rastafarian ethics, offer analytical tools for a constant revisiting of the meaning of being independent in a postcolonial world, and the terms upon which reconciliation, peace, and the good life could be achieved. While this has an immediate local footing in Jamaica, where the genre of reggae music was created, Bob Marley's ideas of justice resonate well beyond his country. Much has been said about Marley's Pan-Africanism, his ideas of social democracy, his referencing of violence and peace, and his affirmations of self-identity. Indeed, it is commonplace to speak of Marley's ethics in terms of justice. This chapter, therefore, addresses Marley's communication of ideas of justice in the field of human rights. It is argued that Bob Marley communicates a distinctive conception of justice, labelled here as *redemptive-corrective justice*. It is suggested that, from *Soul Rebels* (1970) to *Confrontation* (1983), Marley laid the basis for a popular philosophy of redemptive-corrective justice framed in a public historicist-poeticist tradition, one in which more recent artists, such as Chronixx now practice. After introducing the positioning of Bob Marley's work in scholarly discourse, this chapter is then arranged in three sections: part one, on Marley's methodology; part two, on his signification of justice; and finally, part three, on the function of redemptive-corrective justice.

Keywords: Bob Marley, redemptive justice, corrective justice, human rights, historic wrongs

***

Introduction

Bob Marley, through his music, provides the ground on which to tease out an idea of redemptive justice in postcolonial spaces, and in ways that communicate in global, universal terms. From his contemporary, Peter Tosh, to his own offspring, Damian "Jr Gong" Marley, Bob Marley's preoccupation with justice as redemption remains palpable in postcolonial spaces. The iconic "Redemption Song" from the album *Uprising* (1980), "Blackman Redemption" and "I Know" from the album *Confrontation* (1983) echo the mantra of self-redemption chanted in "Get up, Stand up" from the album *Burning* (1973). Marley's idea of justice takes the personal as its starting point – the point of view that those who would not otherwise see justice should self-affirm, step up or speak up to effect change; that justice is not elsewhere. In some ways, the presentation of redemption as personal-political is partly a signal that people in wretched circumstances are partly implicated in their own oppression, at least as far as this kind of awakening is actively avoided. Redeeming oneself is an essential part of the journey out of oppression, and equally too for those who wield the power of injustice.

Bob Marley's iterations of justice set to music as invocatory texts – that is, texts that function as calls to self-reflection, self-reformation, the grounding of agency, and the raising of consciousness — are important tools that enable black peoples to (re)read their lives and inscribe new foundations. Such self-reflective invocations disturb and re-imagine the power relations that ascribe the qualities of oppressed groups placed outside the much-heralded corrective forces of law in liberal legal thought. This will be further elucidated in Part 3 of this chapter. In Marley's idea of justice, the redemptive and the corrective are inseparable and enduring. Considered through the lens of law and culture (Chase, 1986; Chase, 1994; Coombe, 2005; Kahn, 1999; MacNeil, 2007; Post, 1991; Redhead, 1995; Sarat, 2011; Sarat & Kearns, 1998; Sarat & Simon, 2003), this chapter positions Marley's philosophical fragments in song as engagements with the constitutive relations between the popular and the state; between the popular and the texts of law in which justice is constantly re-examined.

This chapter is not focused on the musical techniques or the religious/theological traditions in Marley's work, notwithstanding the cue from Rastafarian ethics as an "ideological corrective" in popular consciousness in the diaspora (Savishinsky, 2014, p.19). Rather, it focuses on the messages communicated and presented in the lyrical content of his songs as philosophical fragments. Indeed, much of the alleged European foundations of Western philosophy consist of fragments of its founders. Such treatment of Bob Marley's work in philosophical terms is not unprecedented. Stephens (1999) positioned Bob Marley in the philosophical emancipatory tradition inhabited by Frederick Douglass. Marley's philosophizing has also been located within the same tradition of Marcus Garvey, articulating the positions through which the lives of the peoples of Africa and of African descent may be made better (Campbell, 1987; Dawes, 2002), as literary-cultural praxis (Cooper, 1995; Pollard, 1980; Wint & Cooper, 2003), in turn, a significant part of the historicist-poeticist tradition in Caribbean Philosophy (Henry, 2000; Hodges, 2005), as radical redemptive poetics (Bogues, 2003), and as a thinker in the construction of the Black Atlantic (Gilroy, 2005).

This philosophical tradition of emancipation set out to question the basis of trans-Atlantic chattel slavery perpetrated on black people, the racial hierarchies that defined the human chattel as black for the functioning of plantation societies in the Americas, and to raise the consciousness of masters and enslaved alike to accelerate the process of corrective justice. A significant point of emphasis in this tradition has been on the urgency of undoing injustice through self-redemption: avoiding complicity in oppression, active resistance to the manifestations of oppression, and resetting the mentalities of those who occupy oppressive spaces. The point of departure in this chapter is in the shift of focus from questions that emerge from the colonial/postcolonial condition that informed Bob Marley's music, to questions that inform the liberal institutional discourses on doing justice for historic wrongs through corrective justice mechanisms, such as tort systems and human rights regimes. In the language and register of Rastafari, such state-centric institutional arrangements are typically labelled "Babylon System" (Chevannes, 1998; Davidson, 2008), with purposes that have been at odds with justice. Marley's work is very much within this radical tradition of human rights discourse. Yet his presence there is not without instructive tension.

Paul Gilroy (2005) highlights this tension in his reading of Marley's global appeal. Gilroy labels Marley's lyrical textuality as a "cosmopolitan pattern [that] altered the fields of political force around national (sic) states and national cultures" (p.229). He rightly locates this in a tradition that was (and remains) "simultaneously and inextricably both poetic and political" (p. 229), a condition of thought shaped by chattel slavery in plantation societies. In his global reach and reification, the rebel exemplified in Marley is at once resistance and universalism (Alleyne, 1994). Gilroy sees musicality as the technology of universalism through which Bob Marley's lyrics should be read as messages of the universality of human rights and non-discrimination on account of race. Yet, this positioning of Marley as a cosmopolitan is at some distance from his idea of justice as a radical grounding of resistance, one that challenges faith in the institutionality of cosmopolitanism, and its complicity with colonial and postcolonial oppression. Thus, calls for justice and rights as universal claims are quite compatible with vested racializations of law and power. That tension in the global, cosmopolitan messaging of justice exposes the nakedness of unrepentant liberal human rights discourse in two ways: the faith in ideals (utopian visions of justice) and the utility of forgetting the legacy of colonialism and trans-Atlantic chattel slavery. Marley's idea of redemptive justice challenges this twined position.

The most apparent formulation of Marley's notion of redemption is one that comes through the workings of Jah (God) and, crucially, through actualization on Earth. Though it is plausible to note some references to redemption in the afterlife, the root of Marley's notion of redemption is organic and earthbound, notwithstanding references to Mount Zion (the Rastafarian notion of heaven). The universally popular, "Get up, Stand up," on the album, *Burning* (1973), invokes the defence of natural rights, not as aspirational ideals, but as rights that should be part of concrete experience; not as a matter of faith, but as the basis of collective action in the here and now (Gallardo, 2003). The good life that rights actualization would provide is not the preacher's heaven to come, but heaven on Earth. That good life is not dependent on divine intervention upon God's return. The good life is to be experienced and must be fought for in this lifetime. In "Get up, Stand up," Marley sang:

> Preacher man don't tell me heaven is under the earth
> I know you don't know what life is really worth
> Is not all that glitters is gold and half the story has never been told
> So now you see the light, stand up for your rights.
> Come on.

> Get up, stan' up, stand up for your rights
> Get up, stan' up, stand up for your rights

> Most people think great God will come from the sky
> Take away everything and make everybody feel high
> But if you know what life is worth, you would look for yours on earth
> And now you see the light, you stand for your rights.

This organic earthbound articulation of redemptive justice forms the basic philosophical framework for Marley's body of work that comments on a myriad of dimensions of injustice and the possibilities of overcoming them. It is, too, a comment on secular radical natural law theory that underpins human rights discourses in postcolonial spaces. This radical perspective on human rights raises important questions about the imperial and colonial legacy that resist the politics of forgetting and the complacency of a utopian vision of human rights. Through this reframing of Bob Marley's music, resources may be found to re-interpret those parts of his message that have been oversimplified in terms of mere violence or violent resistance on the one hand and peace/pacification on the other (Gilroy, 2005). For instance, it allows a reading of "Chant Down Babylon" on the *Confrontation* (1983) album that lends coherence and consistency in a principled approach to redemptive justice across his albums as well as application in particular instances of intervention. Such interventions merit the label "corrective justice" – the ultimate teleological import of redemption, raising stronger and more enduring capacities to rectify injustices.

It is worth turning briefly to the institutional bases on which the problem of justice for historic public wrongs rests, to the extent that these wrongs were of concern to Marley. As will become clear later in this chapter, Marley not only commented on the conditions associated with the colonial-postcolonial state, but he also communicated a call to redemptive action. Such a call is inextricably bound up with corrective justice. Yet this call encounters fundamental problems with the conception and practice of corrective justice established in liberal institutional mechanisms for righting wrongs. Such problems with corrective justice are even more pronounced when such wrongs are historical. The scholarship on this is central in the current debate about correcting injustices, particularly in view of the material and symbolic manifestations that troubled Marley. His idea of redemptive-corrective justice opens up further lines of critique that address these challenges. Indeed, it would be a mistake to confine Marley's messaging to the political, to its rhetorical effect, and lose sight of its ultimate target, the praxis of corrective justice. His is a popular communicative reasoning (the politics of raising popular consciousness) which is also directed at the institutionalisation of (in)justice in the form of the colonial/postcolonial state. It is in the latter that the praxis of corrective justice has been embodied, and with which current discourses on historic public wrongs must contend, not least on the question of reparations.

Corrective justice has been the subject of much discussion on questions of addressing wrongs. In Western legal theory, it has largely focused on private law, principally tort law, as the theoretical basis of *correcting* wrongs or harms (see for example Gardner, 2011; Colman, 1992; Colman, 1995; Weinrib, 2012; Perry, 1992; Posner, 1981; Ripstein, 2007). Beyond the narrow focus on bringing such claims in law, the position of corrective justice in the wider discourse of what to do about relations within social and economic structures comes into contention with the more dominant debate about retributive justice (Benson, 1992). Further, though not widely discussed in such terms in the public square, the tension between the claims on the state to correct, especially historic wrongs and the sanctity or dignity of the individual, is sufficiently remarkable (Ripstein, 2006). This is significant when one considers the typical rejoinders in the debate about the utility and practicality (let alone the philosophical basis) of reparations for trans-Atlantic chattel slavery (Gifford, 2019). Not least, the number of limbs in reparations claims raise specific questions about apology (Hershovitz, 2011) and the interconnections with unjust enrichment (Sinel, 2011). One who has been wronged is justified in seeking the reversal of this misfortune (or the reversal of the material effects of actionable wrongs), subject, of course, to identifying a wrongdoer. The liable party is required to re-allocate from their pot of wrongful advantage to that of the other party who suffered the loss or harm, or from whom they had been unjustly enriched. Yet, this seemingly reasonable approach to correcting wrongs runs into difficulties when the claim in question is heavily weighed down by the politics of history, the politics of forgetting, and the politics of memory. The dominant institutional position in Western legal systems is to require the parties in such cases of reparatory justice to relieve themselves of the weight of history. Typically, the weight of history is bundled with death (only living victims can claim), traceability (only direct descendants can claim), and remoteness (the harms alleged are too far removed from the "lawful" practice in question and from the obligations and sensibilities of the current nation-state and its citizens).

Yet corrective justice is much more than the rather narrow framing at the level of individual private relations. This is a recurring theme in Marley's music, and an important point not lost on some theorists on corrective justice. Note that Robert Cover (1983, p. 33) speaks of "redemptive constitutionalism," inviting a much broader and inclusive sense. The capacity to do corrective justice is grounded in constitutive terms, a required dimension of the constitutional order – the original starting point of corrective justice is an immanent public matter. As such, corrective justice is anterior to any institutional arrangement set up in its name. With that in mind, it is instructive that the juridification of corrective justice in Western societies is notable for its blind spots on historic public wrongs. Sourced in Aristotelian ethics (Brickhouse, 2014), and as presented principally in modern private law theory (especially torts) (Gardner, 2011), there is some divergence in the discourse on the relationship between corrective justice and redistributive justice. Aristotle viewed them as separate and independent of each other; some theorists accept that position while others insist that corrective justice enables distributive justice (Beever, 2013, p.71). In other words, a wrong or harm suffered is evidence of wrongful redistribution that must be *corrected*. The authoritative mechanism for corrective justice is then vested in legal institutions. Marley, too, is preoccupied with this challenging imperative. His is one that reaches beyond private social and economic relations, which has important redemptive tasks, and into public, constitutive recognition, with clear implications for reparative state-citizen relations. Unlike the public-oriented corrective constitutionalism, the individual private-level variety of corrective justice constructed in private law reduces the capacity for redressing historic public wrongs, the sorts of wrongs that are direct consequences of systematic state-sanctioned and/or state-directed injustice.

Indeed, in addition to Cover (1983), the more inclusive framings of corrective justice shift outwards from private wrongs (micro) to public wrongs (macro) in recognition of wrongs visited on (historically marginalised) groups, peoples, and populations. Such inclusive shifts identify the contexts of injustice that mirror expectant calls for justice, most notably on slavery and reparations (Lyons, 2013; Lyons, 2004; Copp, 2010). Others position the pastness of public wrongs as the basis for taking more inclusive corrective justice seriously. As Podunavac (2001) puts it: "Corrective justice is markedly oriented to the past and to the necessity for punishing, compensating for, correcting and eliminating the bad effects of the old regime and its actors" (p.165). An important aspect of this inclusive conception of corrective justice is the recognition of its legal and political elements, a conception in which the legal and the political, though separable for the convenience of exposition and application, are inseparable for making sense of the aims of corrective justice. Rosenfeld (1992) argues that the separability of law and politics is ultimately rendered redundant when the politics of corrective justice encounters legal corrective justice. As he expresses it, "...whereas law and politics are often close bedfellows, and whereas it may be sometimes impossible as a practical matter to disentangle one from the other, in theory law as an embodiment of corrective justice remains distinguishable from politics" (p.193). However, the connection between the political and the legal is not deniable in corrective justice (Rosenfeld, 1992, pp.193-194). The difference is in the respective functions and spheres of operation, which includes meaning and pastness.

Ultimately, for Rosenfeld, that distinction is not sustainable, and indeed, legal corrective justice, as an exercise in legal interpretation, has the potential to affect meaning by reading through and across varying texts of the past, present and future (Rosenfeld, 1992, p.193). The fundamental tool that avoids the pitfalls of the purely political is the nature of the rules and norms at play in legal spheres – universal, external, and self-referential (Rosenfeld, 1992, p. 194). It is at this point of intersection between legal corrective justice and political corrective justice that Marley's political messaging, conducted in a more radical intertextual public historicist-poeticist tradition, signals the way out via the vessel of redemption. Marley's notion of redemption is thus thoroughly fused with corrective justice. The next section takes up the methodological ground of this analysis.

Part I: Marley's Music as Texts on Justice

The argument in this chapter is premised on an examination of Bob Marley's published music produced over a 10-year period, from 1973 to 1983. This section considers Bob Marley's music in methodological terms, as text through which to interrogate the conditions imposed on justice. The lyrical content of his music is contextualised within the wider political and intellectual climate that intersected with the course of production. Put in other terms, this framework of redemptive-corrective justice is mined from the lyrical socio-political commentary that served as a strident critique of postcolonial societies. As such, it is inspired by a type of critical discourse analysis and critical theory that connect the nodes of musical texts with other textual material at specific sites of contestation.

In the case of Bob Marley's music, this methodology sits within the field that is now loosely described as Caribbean critical thought, a field that locates and localises critique and the critical dimensions of cultural texts and cultural production (Alleyne, 1994; Henry, 2000; Regis, 1988). Of course, Caribbean critical thought is much wider than this – a field that has been variously inscribed as Caribbean philosophy, set within a broader Africana philosophy, and connecting a range of disciplines that have been re-founded from Caribbean perspectives resisting imperial intellectual traditions (Bogues, 2003; Henry, 2000). While this reading of Bob Marley in terms of justice may sit within the wide outlines and methodologies of Caribbean critical thought, its aim is less ambitious and is indeed more precise. First, this repositioning of Marley is not a general account of justice. Second, this account makes specific connections with a communicative jurisprudence of harm and justice. Third, the positioning of Marley's idea of justice is as a critical lens on historical claims on human rights such as the most recent chapter in the cause for reparations for trans-Atlantic chattel slavery.

As such, redemptive-corrective justice in Bob Marley's music is constructed from his commentary on the arsenals of imperial power, systemic disempowerment, and the oppression of the peoples of African descent that urge specific claims in the name of honouring the rights of *being human*. This sets the context for a consideration of extant sets of jurisprudential frameworks that are also concerned with harm and injustice – principally (but not limited to), corrective justice in private law, and corrective constitutionalism/corrective jurisprudence. The details of such a project are wider than the scope of this chapter. Space here only allows a broad overview of the communicative technique through which this kind of critique emerges and what this says about Marley's idea of justice.

That (reggae) music is critique is also notable in Marley's work (Dawes, 2002). Music is part of the strategy for correcting injustice through raising consciousness. Marley could not be more explicit about this in "Chant Down Babylon," from the album, *Confrontation* (1983):

> A Reggae Music, mek we chant down Babylon
> With music, mek we chant down Babylon
> This music, mek we chant down Babylon
> This music, come we chant down Babylon

Chanting brings into consciousness a collective exercise in calling out oppressive regimes ("Babylon system") for their injustices. This collective activity of chanting is the vehicle through which the elements of Babylon's wrongs can be inscribed, its justifications can be challenged, and the material manifestations of oppression reversed. The weight of chanting rests on the accompanying textual content and musical aesthetics that enable affect and meditations on enduring themes and issues in the history of oppression (Hodges, 2005). This practice provides the basis for collective philosophising more generally, in the same way as other fragments of socio-political thinkers in other comparable traditions produced culturally grounded institutions and canons later marketed (if not imposed) as universal.

An important technique worth highlighting is the excavatory aspect of putting the fragments of Marley's musical texts together to construct a provisional account of his idea of justice. With the textuality of musical expression – lyrics being the most obvious, through which the practice of the written word allows for reified techniques of reading – evidence of other, otherwise hidden, currents of thought in the popular domain are significant elements of the specific textual artefacts under examination (Chevannes, 1977). In other words, to speak of fragments is not to draw attention to breakage, disconnections, loss, gaps, or unwholesomeness. Rather, to speak of fragments is to recognise the enduring cultural starting points of critical thought, of tremendous value in societies such as those forged from trans-Atlantic chattel slavery, founded on rupture, subversive coded speech acts in Glissant's (1991) sense of creole speech, and the struggles for reconstruction out of the depths of disavowal.

The tropes of imperial power, systemic disempowerment, and postcolonial state brutality are juxtaposed with prescriptions for overcoming injustice and cross-thematised in terms of redemptive-corrective justice. This conjunction of redemptive justice with corrective justice does two things. First, it teases out the density of Bob Marley's conception of justice, demonstrating the double-edged axis on which justice in postcolonial spaces is situated. Second, this conjunction disturbs the usual distinction between redemptive justice and corrective justice – the former a purely theological affair, an internal, personal path to redemption; the latter an external conception of correcting injustice that may be readily institutionalised, especially in legal mechanisms. In this sense, corrective justice would have been complicit in the kind of racial injustice that inspired Bob Marley's music, and informed the conception of justice that he sought to communicate. This conjunction between corrective justice with redemption is itself a communicative device, which is adopted in this chapter to uncover the tenets of Marley's philosophy. Corrective justice is either complicit in injustice or is too arid to be responsive to the needs of those who have been wronged, and so must itself be inoculated by another dimension of justice in order to be realigned with emancipation and reparation. To reflect the sense of pessimism in the capacity of an unjust institutional arrangement to implicate itself and do the right thing, or that the effect of injustice is entirely external to the oppressed, or that the oppressed is condemned to be always acted upon, redemptive justice is attached to corrective justice as the way out.

Music as texts of Justice

Through the communicative ethics of his music, Bob Marley transcends the geography and spaces of his immediate environs in Jamaica (Gilroy, 2005; King, 1998; King & Jensen, 1995; King et al., 2002). It is precisely with this desired effect and sense of purpose that Bob Marley positioned music as treatises of justice to move his people to a better life. The appropriate "Trench Town" on the *Confrontation* (1983) album identified this method of communication – music as a vehicle for philosophizing and raising consciousness. This disturbed the hold of mental slavery, from which he (echoing Marcus Garvey) urged his audience to liberate themselves in "Redemption Song" (Bogues, 2003). This was also a disturbance of the European enterprise of knowledge production that disavowed African capacities to reason and communicate with, and as fellow human beings. Among his messages: first, the praxis of speaking to and speaking with Africans and descendants of Africans scattered beyond the lands of Africa (the term "African" is used collectively to refer to all peoples of African origin), and second, an articulation of justice to ground and reaffirm ways out of colonisation and imperialism. It comes without surprise that Marley's body of work has been analyzed in terms of political and religious discourse (MacNeil, 2013; Toynbee, 2007), and in terms of the intellectual history of the African diaspora (Bogues, 2003). While the language, ethics, and politics of Bob Marley's music have some sources in the King James Bible (MacNeil, 2013), its radicalness is in its Afrocentric Rastafarian liberatory folk philosophy and theology (Erskine, 2005). In this, he charts the colonial and postcolonial registers of oppression and resistance, the social and political lived realities of postcolonial life in Jamaica (Edwards, 2010), national, regional and Pan-African consciousness, and the geopolitical mapping and re-mapping of Europe's enslavement, colonization, and neo-colonization of African peoples.

Marley's incantations in the song, "War," from his 1976 album, *Rastaman Vibrations*, echoing Haile Selassie's 1968 UN Speech, encapsulate the spirit of redemptive-corrective justice. Marley instantiated, through songs of this type, a body of work that grounds redemption in active agency against the forces of oppressive racial divisions. The answer to such long-standing socio-political ills captured in the song, "Babylon System," from the album, *Survival* (1979), is in unified resistance and resolve as expressed in "War" with the well-known line: "Until the philosophy that holds one race inferior than another/we say war." The consequence of doing anything less than dismantling the philosophical bases of racial injustice is war: "War in the east/war in the west/war up north/war down south." This was not reduced to the local history of racialized oppression in Jamaica or the Caribbean. This was a diagnosis of a global problem, and a call for an answer in terms of global justice – a global war against racial injustice. His music is, then, a conduit through which he sought to communicate his philosophy of justice in response to the legacy of European colonialism, imperialism, and postcolonialism, all manifesting in the contexts of Jamaica and the lands of subjected peoples throughout the African diaspora. Bob Marley sustained the connections among these themes at both the level of representation and affect. The next section explores the signification of the problem of justice through selected texts in his work.

Part II: The Signification of (In)Justice

This section explores the theme of colonial/postcolonial state excesses that blighted the lives of the peoples with whom Bob Marley sought to communicate his message of redemptive-corrective justice. It is now well-established that the colonial/postcolonial condition was (and is) a global phenomenon, with the specific context of Jamaica standing in for myriad sites. Two points are worthy of close examination through Marley's music. The first is that the postcolonial state, as a by-product of colonialism, is itself the target for claims in corrective justice. Second, for a postcolonial state to become a vehicle for emancipation, it too must ground its redemptive capacities and see to their attachment to corrective justice.

Bob Marley's first major album, *Catch a Fire* (1973), situates the founding of Caribbean societies in racialized injustice. The three leading tracks – "Concrete Jungle," "Slave Driver," and "400 years" capture life in an order that compounds a sense of hardship, destitution, and inequality. Yet this "concrete jungle," where darkness keeps the sun away, is only bearable through hope and resilience. This reliance on self-redemption carries over into the popular narrative of active slave resistance in the proceeding track, "Slave Driver." "Slave Driver" collapses the fictional break between the colonial order and its postcolonial manifestations. The oppressed in a system of trans-Atlantic chattel slavery is always capable of shaping their fate by taking steps to overturn the system. That very spirit of resistance is equally potent in an oppressive postcolonial state:

> Slave driver the table is turned
> Catch a fire so you can get burned
> Slave driver the table is turned
> Catch a fire you're gonna get burned

This inability to break the chains of 400 years of slavery, imperialism, and colonization in the postcolonial era is captured in the proceeding track, "400

Years." The consciousness of the colonial persists in the postcolonial, lost on the youth who hold the hope of freedom. Loss is part of the mentalité of the colonial/postcolonial that manifest in structures of power that see the capacity of the youth as a threat. In the youth rests the opportunity to break the chains of 400 years of slavery; a battle that is as much philosophical as it is psychosocial. The response is to shift collective consciousness by first recognising the weight of 400 years of disavowal and follow Bob Marley to liberty.

Marley communicates this redemptive level of consciousness to his audience, who share that history of oppression. To emphasize the centrality of self-reflection, Marley takes his audience through his own feeling of frustration, a recognition of the difficulties involved in shifting the hold of colonialism on the mind. So strong is this hold that Marley chants in "Stop the Train," another track on the *Catch a Fire* (1973) album:

> Stop the train I'm leaving
> It won't be too long
> Whether I am right or wrong
> Said it won't be too long
> Whether I am right or wrong
>
> All my good life I've been a lonely man
> Teaching people who don't overstan'
> And even though I have tried by bes'
> I still don't find no happiness.

The existential threat that is the predatory (post) colonial state is also poignantly expressed in "I shot the Sheriff" (not the deputy), the Sheriff who acted illegitimately. This song tells the story of extra-judicial condemnation and extra-judicial killings perpetrated against the urban poor – a marked feature and experience of life under the postcolonial state. What is prescribed in "I shot the sheriff" is resistance to this kind of injustice – a call to impose limits on the state's exercise of its monopoly on violence. Self-defence is, to Marley, a legitimate means of resistance when the state exceeds the limits of its authority and targets life without due process and the rule of law.

The propensity for the predatory postcolonial state to inflict brutality on the dispossessed is also picked up in the song, "Burnin' and Lootin,'" from the album, *Burning* (1973). Marley takes up the normalization of state excesses in which whole communities are reduced to open prisons under constant surveillance and subject to arbitrary violation of bodily integrity by agents "dressed in uniforms of brutality." Rather than submit to such daily excesses, and with avenues for redress closed, the response is to riot. "Burnin' and Lootin'" is in homage to leaders of slave revolts as significant in the tradition of resistance, and overcoming the philosophy of dehumanization: "....burnin all illusions tonight."

"No Woman, No Cry" from the album, *Natty Dread* (1974), and "Johnny Was" from the album, *Rastaman Vibration* (1976), articulate the gendered dynamics of oppression in the context of the legacy of slavery and colonization in the excess of the postcolonial state. The normalcy and systemic nature of oppression in the postcolonial scene are also captured in "Them Belly Full (But We Hungry)" from the album, *Natty Dread* (1974). This is a scene in which the disadvantaged are not passive postcolonial subjects. Rather, collective consciousness through music, and the will to strength are antidotes to the sting of oppression:

Them belly full but we hungry.
A hungry mob is a angry mob.
A rain a-fall but the dirt it tough;
A pot a-cook but the food no 'nough.
You're gonna dance to JAH music, dance.
We're gonna dance to JAH music, dance.

The postcolonial condition is diagnosed in Bob Marley's music as a political problem, and as one that demands a political solution. So acute was the level of oppression that the system could not be changed without a revolution. A radical change in the socio-political order would not be sufficient, where that means an absence of reckoning at personal and systemic human and institutional levels. In order words, as befits Marley's call to action, redemptive-corrective justice has a job to do.

Part III: The Function of Redemptive-Corrective Justice

Marley's incantations are not reducible to simple arguments about the pacification of violence or unpacked ideas about reconciliation. His is a particular notion of justice that addresses prevailing problems as lived realities; the resolution of such problems being attached to affect and historical memory. A significant refrain in his conception of justice is the call to redemption through both individual and collective action. Justice, in this sense, speaks to both the oppressor and the oppressed – the latter must simultaneously recognise what is wrong with one's condition and oneself, to reconstitute oneself and seek redress. The oppressor too is to also undertake a similar journey of self-reconstitution and, crucially, to reconcile the contradictions in the institutional mechanisms of justice (in the forms of positive law and the state), and recognise that calls and actions toward redress are inevitable and unceasing. Redemption is thus inherently relational and is the corresponding necessity of corrective action. One is entirely dependent on the Other.

In *Rastaman Vibration* (1976), Marley anchors this motif in the specific localities of slave societies and the failed emancipation project – the purported freedom to build one's own cabin and plant one's own corn against a history of enslavement is frustrated by persistent disavowal and contempt on the part of those who continue to wield the powerful tools of oppression. Yet, as injustice brought harm to the oppressed, the oppressor is also afflicted. A relational appreciation of (in)justice is the only way out.

The quality of this kind of redemption is not set apart from personal agency and collective action. Redemption is not vested out there in a savior who, being no longer with us, has already sacrificed on behalf of the oppressed, and in whom faith for justice should rest. Marley's sense of redemption grounds justice in the agency of the oppressed, first and foremost, to change their condition in the here and now. As if to signal the urgency of this imperative, Marley's iconic intervention in Jamaica's violent postcolonial history is even marked by the 1978 One Love Peace Concert. The now well-known image of Marley standing on stage holding up the hands of Jamaica's two rival postcolonial political leaders, Edward Seaga and Michael Manley, has been hailed as a significant symbol of peace and reconciliation. Placed in terms of redemptive justice, this underscored the message that redemption must come through action on both sides of injustice. Marley's "Get up, Stand Up" from the album, *Burning* (1973), is more than an affirmation of an inalienable natural right; it is more of a call to individual redemption for those who had been historically dispossessed, who must act on newly found consciousness to change their circumstances. That call to redemption is also about prevailing upon one's leaders. Furthermore, "Rasta Man Chant" from the album, *Burning* (1973), and "Exodus" from the album, *Exodus* (1977), reference the departure from Babylon (the system of oppression) to Zion (Jah's place of freedom). Crucially, this is not until after the work (on Earth) is done. Redemption is not without work; redemption is not elsewhere.

Marley's conception of justice, seen in terms of redemptive-corrective justice, was set on a different trajectory to that which has preoccupied the intellectual and political classes in postcolonial Africa and the Caribbean as well as the diasporas in major centres in the Global North (Alleyne, 1994). Indeed, the dominant theme in the justice discourse as Marley crafted his ideas was mainly in the vein of distributive justice – principally about social, economic, and political goods to be managed by the colonial-allegedly-turned-postcolonial state (Beckford, 1972; Nkrumah, 1970; Nkrumah, 2002, p. 33; Nyerere, 1969). This was the primary preoccupation of the upper, upper-middle class urban elite, focused on questions about the (re)design of the state, the (re)shaping of relations with former colonial powers, the founding of national identities, and a viable space in global affairs. This was a period (1940s – 1960s) of tremendous national and regional anxiety in the context of a post-war geopolitics that gave rise to the ideological divide of the cold war played out in former colonies, coinciding with the emergence of independent states. To those within the intellectual classes, the postcolonial condition had to be diagnosed. In the Caribbean, the impetus for redistributive justice was to be responsive to the persistence of the plantation society examined by Best (1968), Demas (1965), and Beckford (1972, 1980), and as nation-states on the global periphery - extractive economies dependent on dominant imperial states at the centre.

The implication of the diagnoses of the postcolonial condition was that the order within which forms of colonial systems existed had to be reordered by way of a more equitable variety of distributive justice. A conception of justice that would address economic and social legacies of imperialism and colonialism depended on redistributive justice. As the game of the Cold War's political and economic ideologies played out, rival conceptions of (re)distributive justice were on the offing as Nkrumah (1970) discussed.

While postcolonial states in the Caribbean and Africa experimented with these ideas, Marley had a rather different focus. For him, a first and more fundamental re-ordering is required: redemptive-corrective justice begins at the level of popular consciousness. It is first and foremost a communicative device. Effecting this consciousness through music was a more suitable democratic approach to enabling change to emerge from below – from the people who had for so long been dispossessed. Set within wider debates about justice in the postcolony, redemptive-corrective justice would give shape to the legitimacy of the design of (re)distributive justice. The musician, like the institution of the church or the revolutionary leader preparing the minds of his followers, taps into the well of texts that map the lives of the people. This was not an exercise in canonisation or textual exclusivity. Marley operated in an open field of intertextuality that drew on other (often disparate) textual fragments of the lives of the colonised: love, despair, injustice, hope, and aspiration.

Conclusion

In the current discourse on historic public wrongs, such as reparations for trans-Atlantic chattel slavery and the persistent excesses of postcolonial state institutions, Marley's idea of justice poses two crucial challenges. The first is the recognition that righting historic wrongs (corrective justice) requires a process of redemptive justice that involves self-reflection, which in turn re-orients the institutional mechanisms that have been, and remain, implicated in injustice. Redemption is anterior to corrective justice. To that end, Marley's messaging is directed at both the oppressor and the oppressed as agents of history, a history that is too often sacrificed in the name of dominant, albeit well-meaning, projects of corrective justice. Second, the relationality of justice demands an inextricable connection between redemptive justice and corrective justice. The resistance to claims for reparations for trans-Atlantic chattel slavery by former colonial powers in Europe and former colonial states such as the United States, rest on the insistence that corrective justice relies on individuality and time-barred wrongs committed in private "lawful" social and economic relations. The accountability that comes with shifting the ground for such claims to the sphere of accountability as public wrongs is too difficult a task, not least because of the weight of history. Marley's idea of redemptive-corrective justice is an invitation to begin what is, for him, a necessary journey towards justice for all concerned.

References

Alleyne, M. (1994). Positive vibration? Capitalist textual hegemony and Bob Marley. *Caribbean Studies, 27*(3/4), 224–241.

Beckford, G. L. (1972). *Persistent Poverty: Underdevelopment in Plantation Economies of the Third World.* New York: Oxford University Press.

Beckford, G. L. (1980). Socioeconomic change and political continuity in the Anglophone Caribbean. *Studies in Comparative International Development, 15*(1), 3–14.

Beever, A. (2013). *Forgotten Justice: Forms of Justice in the History of Legal and Political Theory.* Oxford University Press.

Benson, P. (1992). The basis of corrective justice and its relationship to distributive justice. *Iowa Law Review, 77,* 515–642.

Best, L. (1968). Outlines of a model of pure plantation economy. *Social and Economic Studies, 17*(3), 283–326.

Bogues, A. (2003). *Black Heretics, Black Prophets: Radical Political Intellectuals.* London and New York: Routledge.

Brickhouse, T. (2014). Aristotle on corrective justice. *Journal of Ethics,* 187–205.

Campbell, H. (1987). *Rasta and Resistance: From Marcus Garvey to Walter Rodney.* Trenton, New Jersey: Africa World Press.

Chase, A. (1986). Towards a legal theory of popular culture. *Wisconsin Law Review, 1986*(3), 527–570.

Chase, A. (1994). Historical reconstruction in popular legal and political culture. *Seton Hall Law Review, 24*(4), 1969–2029.

Chevannes, B. (1977). The Literature of Rastafari. *Social and Economic Studies, 26*(2), 239–262.

Chevannes, B. (1998). Rastafari and the exorcism of the ideology of racism and classism in Jamaica. In N. Murrell, W. Spencer, & A. Mcfarlene (Eds.), *Chanting Down Babylon* (pp. 55–71). Temple University Press.

Coleman, J. (1992). The Mixed Conception of Corrective Justice. *Iowa Law Review, 77,* 427–444.

Coleman, J. (1995). The Practice of Corrective Justice. *Arizona Law Review, 37,* 15–31.

Coombe, R. (2005). Is there a cultural studies of law? In T. Miller (Ed.), *A Companion to Cultural Studies* (pp. 36–52). Cambridge: Blackwell.

Cooper, C. (1995). *Noises in the Blood: Orality, gender, and the "vulgar" body of Jamaican popular culture*. Durham: Duke University Press.

Copp, D. (2010). Corrective justice as a duty of political community: David Lyons and the moral legitimacy of slavery and Jim Crow. *Boston University Law Review, 90*, 1731–1754.

Cover, R. M. (1983). The Supreme Court, 1982 term - forward: nomos and narrative. *Harvard Law Review, 97*(4), 4–68.

Davidson, S. (2008). Leave Babylon: The trope of Babylon in Rastafarian discourse. *Black Theology: An International Journal, 6*(1), 46–60.

Dawes, K. (2002). *Bob Marley: Lyrical Genius*. London: Sanctuary Publishing Limited.

Demas, W. (1965). *The Economics of Development in Small Countries with Special Reference to the Caribbean*. Montreal: McGill Press.

Edwards, N. (2010). Bob Marley: Two sightings and one reflection on Natty Dread. *Review: Literature and Arts of the Americas, 43*(2), 194–199.

Erskine, N. L. (2005). *From Garvey to Marley: Rastafari Theology*. Gainesville: University Press of Florida.

Gallardo, A. (2003). Get up, Stand up. *Peace Review: A Journal of Social Justice, 15*(2), 201–208.

Gardner, J. (2011). What is tort law for? Part 1: The place of corrective justice. *Law and Philosophy, 30*(1), 1–50.

Gifford, A. (2019). Key legal aspects of the claim for reparations. *Social and Economic Studies, 68*(3-4), 250-252.

Gilroy, P. (2005). Could you be loved? Bob Marley, anti-politics and universal sufferation. *Critical Quarterly, 47*(1), 226–245.

Glissant, E. (1991). *Caribbean Discourse: Selected Essays*. Charlottesville: University of Press of Virginia.

Henry, P. (2000). *Caliban's Reason: Introducing Afro-Caribbean Philosophy*. New York and London: Routledge.

Hershovitz, S. (2011). Harry Potter and the trouble with tort theory. *Stanford Law Review, 63*(1), 67–114.

Hodges, H. (2005). Walk good: West Indian oratorical traditions in Bob Marley's Uprising. *Journal of Commonwealth Literature, 40*(2), 43–64.

Kahn, P. (1999). *The Cultural Studies of Law: Reconstructing Legal Scholarship*. Chicago University Press.

King, S. (1998). International reggae, democratic socialism and the secularisation of the Rastafarian movement 1972–1980. *Popular Music and Society, 22*(3), 39–60.

King, S., Bays, B., & Foster, P. (2002). *Reggae, Rastafari, and the Rhetoric of Social Control*. Jackson: University Press of Mississippi.

King, S., & Jensen, R. (1995). Bob Marley's "Redemption Song:" The rhetoric of reggae and Rastafari. *Journal of Popular Culture, 29*(3), 17–36.

Lyons, D. (2004). Reparations and equal opportunity. *Boston College Third World Law Journal, 24*(1), 177–185.

Lyons, D. (2013). *Confronting Injustice: Moral History and Political Theory.* Oxford University Press. https://oxford.universitypressscholarship.com/view/10.1093/acprof:oso/9780199662555.001.0001/acprof-9780199662555

MacNeil, D. (2013). *The Bible and Bob Marley: Half the Story Has Never Been Told.* Eugene: Cascade Books.

MacNeil, W. P. (2007). *Lex Populi: The Jurisprudence of Popular Culture.* Palo Alto: Stanford University Press.

Marley, R.N. (1974). *Natty Dread.* New York: Island Records.

Marley, R.N (1976). *Rastaman Vibration.* New York: Island Records.

Marley, R.N. (1977). *Exodus.* New York: Island Records.

Marley, R.N. (1979). *Survival.* New York: Island Records.

Marley, R.N. (1980).*Uprising.* New York: Island Records.

Marley, R.N. (1983). *Confrontation.* New York: Island Records.

Marley, R.N & The Wailers. (1973). *Catch A Fire.* New York: Island Records.

Marley, R.N & The Wailers. (1973). *Burning.* New York: Island Records.

Nkrumah, K. (1970). *Consciencism: Philosophy and Ideology for Decolonization.* New York: Monthly Review Press.

Nkrumah, K. (2002). *Revolutionary Path.* London: Panaf Books.

Nyerere, J. (1969). Stability and change in Africa. *African Ephemera Collection.* https://collections.libraries.indiana.edu/africancollections/items/show/5798

Perry, S. (1992). The mixed conception of corrective justice. *Harvard Journal of Law and Public Policy, 15*(3), 917–938.

Podunavac, M. (2001). The future of the liberal revolution in Serbia. In I. Spasić & M. Subotić (Eds.), *Revolution and order: Serbia after October 2000* (pp. 155-166). Belgrade: Institute for Philosophy and Social Theory/ Friedrich Ebert Stiftung and Freedom House.

Pollard, V. (1980). Dread talk: the speech of Rastafarians in Jamaica. *Caribbean Quarterly, 4,* 32–41.

Posner, R. (1981). The concept of corrective justice in recent theories of tort law. *Journal of Legal Studies, 10*(1), 187–206.

Post, R. (Ed.). (1991). *Law and the Order of Culture.* Berkley: University of California Press.

Redhead, S. (1995). *Unpopular Cultures: The Birth of Law and Popular Culture.* Manchester and New York: Manchester University Press.

Regis, H. A. (1988). Calypso, reggae and cultural imperialism by exportation. *Popular Music and Society, 12*(1), 63–73.

Ripstein, A. (2006). Private order and public justice: Kant and Rawls. *Virginia Law Review, 92*(7), 1391–1438.

Ripstein, A. (2007). As if it had never happened. *William and Mary Law Review, 48*(5), 1957–1997.

Rosenfeld, M. (1992). Deconstruction and legal interpretation: Conflict, indeterminacy, and temptations of the new legal formalism. In D. Cornell, M. Rosenfeld, & D. G. Carlson (Eds.), *Deconstruction and the Possibility of Justice* (pp. 152–210). New York: Routledge.

Sarat, A. (2011). *Imagining Legality: Where Law Meets Popular Culture.* Tuscaloosa: University of Alabama Press.

Sarat, A., & Kearns, T. R. (Eds.). (1998). *Law in the Domains of Culture.* Ann Arbor: University of Michigan Press.

Sarat, A., & Simon, J. (2003). *Cultural Analysis, Cultural Studies, and the Law: Moving Beyond Legal Realism.* Durham: Duke University Press.

Savishinsky, N. J. (2014). Rastafari in the promised land: The spread of a Jamaican socioreligious movement among the youth of West Africa. *African Studies Review*, 37(3), 19-50.

Sinel, Z. (2011). Through thick and thin: The place of corrective justice in unjust enrichment. *Oxford Journal of Legal Studies*, 31(3), 551–564.

Stephens, G. (1999). *On Racial Frontiers: The New Culture of Frederick Douglass, Ralph Ellison, and Bob Marley.* New York: Cambridge University Press.

Toynbee, J. (2007). *Bob Marley: Herald of a Postcolonial World?* Cambridge and Malden: Polity Press.

Weinrib, E. (2012). *The Idea of Private Law.* Oxford University Press.

Wint, E., & Cooper, C. (Eds.). (2003). *Bob Marley: The Man and his Music.* Kingston: Arawak Publications.

Appendix: Discography

Bob Marley: Albums

Marley, R.N. & the Wailers. (1970). *Soul Rebels.* New York: Upsetter.

Marley, R.N. & the Wailers. (1971). *Soul Revolution.* New York: Upsetter.

Marley, R.N. & the Wailers. (1973). *Catch A Fire.* New York: Island Records.

Marley, R.N. & the Wailers. (1973). *Burning.* New York: Island Records.

Marley, R.N. (1974). *Natty Dread.* New York: Island Records.

Marley, R.N. (1976). *Rastaman Vibration.* New York: Island Records.

Marley, R.N. (1977). *Exodus.* New York: Island Records.

Marley, R.N. (1978). *Kaya.* New York: Island Records.

Marley, R.N. (1978). *Babylon on Bus.* New York: Island Records.

Marley, R.N. (1979). *Survival.* New York: Island Records.

Marley, R.N. (1980). *Uprising.* New York: Island Records.

Marley, R.N. (1983). *Confrontation.* New York: Island Records.

Marley, R.N. (1986). *Rebel Music.* New York: Island Records.

Marley, R.N. (1991). *Talking Blues.* New York: Island Records.

Author's Note:

A version of this chapter was presented at the Law, Religion and Human Rights conference held at the Centre for Rights and Justice at Nottingham Law School, Nottingham Trent University, England on December 16, 2019. I wish to thank the organizers for facilitating an engaging discussion, and the participants for their very helpful comments.

CHAPTER 4

Framing contesting Nationalisms, Resistance, and Triumph in Ethiopian popular music

Dagim A. Mekonnen

Vrije Universiteit Brussel, Belgium

Zenebe Beyene

University of Mississippi, USA

Abstract

Political music in Ethiopia has a long history. In an increasingly evolving socio-political environment, musicians have long used their platforms to accentuate what they perceive to be overarching issues in society. This chapter examined current political songs in the context of tectonic shifts in the Ethiopian socio-political landscape, between 2016 and 2022. Sixteen songs were purposely selected from three regional states and Addis Ababa. A qualitative textual analysis of the songs informed by framing theory indicates that most songs from regional states are deeply rooted in ethno-nationalistic themes, while those from Addis Ababa predominantly frame Ethiopian nationalism and patriotism. Other salient political themes articulated in the songs from across all study regions include resistance, speaking truth to power, poverty and maladministration, and celebration of a triumph. The study shows that the political songs reflect the ongoing political contestations between Ethiopian nationalism and ethnonationalism, as well as among different ethno-nationalist forces in the country. The exclusivity in this contestation mirrored by the political songs could further contribute to fragmentation and polarization among Ethiopians, impeding the realization of a stable polity.

Keywords: Political music, Ethiopian nationalism, ethnonationalism, Oromo nationalism, Tigrayan nationalism, Amhara nationalism, resistance

***

Introduction

Music is a powerful tool for political expression and event celebration (Munkittrick, 2010). Popular music has a strong emotional appeal and elicits instinctive responses that give musicians the ability to push for change and be "important political figures" (Perullo, 2011, p. 87). As Orgeret (2008) noted, music's political function becomes even more immense in contexts where the highly constrained traditional media fail to push for freedom of expression; thus, popular culture plays a significant role in society. From ancient times through regimes of the last century, music has always held an important place in Ethiopia (Orgeret, 2008). Music has long been integrated into social, cultural, political, and everyday life.

In Ethiopia, the EPRDF[1] enacted several draconian laws attacking free speech, democracy, and a free press (Tadeg, 2016). In addition to a handful of indomitable opposition politicians and journalists, musicians rescued the muzzled public by raising societal concerns. In a recent study of political messaging in music across the span of successive regimes in Ethiopia, Beyene (2019) pointed out that during the EPRDF era, musicians exposed corruption and poor governance and called for national unity through their art. Throughout the protests that led to Prime Minister Abiy Ahmed's election, several resistance songs supported the opposition and called for sweeping changes, leading to some musicians' arrests (Chala, 2017).

PM Abiy Ahmed was appointed to office in 2018. In the early months of his administration, his leadership enjoyed considerable recognition and praise for having made huge strides in bringing about monumental political reforms that would potentially steer the country toward democracy (Matshanda, 2020; Weber, 2018). Nevertheless, Ethiopia's socio-economic predicaments and politico-historical questions were far from resolved. Cochrane and Kefale (2018) observed the lack of an agreed-upon roadmap that clearly outlined the demands of different actors and stakeholders in the society, and how those demands would be solved, noting that the expected "political settlement" was yet to materialize (p. 4). The rampant identity-based killings, armed attacks, interethnic tensions, and the war between the Ethiopian government and the Tigray People's Liberation Front (TPLF) that broke out in November 2020, attest to the reality that a stable polity is a far cry from realization.

Despite the release of a wealth of political songs in an extremely dynamic political landscape, there is a dearth of studies that examine the interplay

---

[1] The now-defunct Ethiopian People's Revolutionary Democratic Front, a coalition of four parties representing Tigray, Amhara, Oromia, and Southern Nation, Nationalities and Peoples Region, that ruled Ethiopia from 1991 until 2019 when it was replaced by a new party called the Prosperity Party.

between popular music and politics. Several scholars (Marye, 2019; Betreyohannes, 2010) note a lack of specific studies on music vis-à-vis Ethiopia's politics, history, and society. Moreover, in a study of popular music in Addis Ababa, Marye (2019) suggested that, as the country's socio-political and economic realities were shifting, it was imperative to study popular music in different parts of the country. This research attempts to bridge these gaps.

In this chapter, the authors analyzed purposively selected popular songs and determine their overarching subtle or explicit political themes. They also examined the songs against the backdrop of the significant political developments that unfolded since the 2015 political protests in the country, PM Ahmed's ascension to power, and the subsequent political contestations faced by his regime. This study also investigated the differences and similarities between the political views expressed in the songs selected from the Oromia, Amhara, and Tigray regions, and Addis Ababa, Ethiopia's capital city. While this is not a comparative study per se, looking at the periods before and after the coming of the new administration and the different regions in which the songs were released helps to understand the variety of salient issues the musicians sought to express in their diverse communities and shifting socio-political landscapes. The study employed textual analysis informed by the framing theory and explored themes that include contestations between Ethiopian nationalism and ethno-nationalism, resistance, and patriotism.

The next section provides an overview of research on music and politics in Ethiopia and the political landscape before and after PM Abiy's political reforms that provided the context in which the songs were released.

Literature: Music, Politics, and the Political Landscape in Ethiopia

Although studies on the relationship between music and politics are generally scarce, the extant literature on the topic shows that politics and music are positively and strongly correlated. Leveraging their art and popularity, musicians "can become powerful political actors and attempt to effect outcomes through both their actions and their music" (Côté, 2011, p. 750). In a study of historical music events, *Live 8 and Live Aid*, Elavsky (2009, p. 403) asserts:

> In its transcendent power to personalize an experience, music can reconfigure one's relationship to a moment, an idea, and an outlook. In this way lies the political potential to be moved, individually or en masse, through a speaker or through the spectacle, to new modes of meaning, consciousness, and action which force us to reconsider the subject positions we occupy as well as the power we possess to reshape our world and global systems.

In general, scholarship in Ethiopian music is scant, and the interplay between music and politics in the country is one of the least researched topics. A look at the themes within this not-so-developed area of scholarship shows that the issue of Ethiopian music and musicians in the diaspora seems to have enjoyed relatively better visibility than music and politics at home (some notable examples include Alter, 2017; Djerrahian, 2018; Shelemay, 2006, 2016; Webster-Kogen, 2013, 2014). This could in part be due to the diaspora's strong presence in the Western world, where there is a well-established scholarship. In a study of the historical development of Ethiopian music scholarship, Betreyohannes (2010, p.30) observed that in general, "domination of Western scholarship in the field of Ethiopian music has continued, and is strengthened by the fact that until recently, very few Ethiopian scholars were working intensely on the subject." It is with this background that the authors of this chapter discuss four noteworthy studies that expound on (i) the role of Amharic songs in expressing people's social and political discontent between the 1950s and 1970s (Lulseged, 1994); (ii) how Ethiopian artists across generations effectively used music for political messaging when free expression was censored (Beyene, 2019); (iii) music and politics in the context of music censorship (Orgeret, 2008); and (iv) the popular music scene in Addis Ababa and its role in promoting Ethiopian identity as a rebuke to ethnonationalism (Marye, 2019).

Lulseged (1994, p. 25) notes that "the advent and development of modern music coincided with the emergence of a modern political, economic, and social order in Ethiopia" in the 1950s. Situating his study in this critical historical juncture, Lulseged (1994) analyzed Amharic songs and found that two broader themes were prevalent and raised several issues thereof: some songs addressed social and economic concerns, thereby expressing social backwardness, economic inequity and marginalization, injustices, and cultural imperialism, etc.; yet other songs voiced concerns over political developments pertinent to the 1960 coup d'état, demanded political reforms, and questioned the exclusion of the elite from critical leadership posts, etc. Similarly, songs by iconic musicians such as Tilahun Gessesse and Alemayehu Eshete exposed serious political issues, including corruption, poverty, and the quest for positive political development during Emperor Haile Selassie's reign (Beyene, 2019). Despite the practice of banning songs that expressed political messages, musicians continued to use their artistry for political purposes during the subsequent regime known as the Derg. Again, iconic musicians of the time such as Teshome Mitiku, Neway Debebe, and Tilahun Gessesse vehemently lamented regime brutality, civil war, and the ensuing famine (Beyene, 2019).

Like its predecessors, the EPRDF repressed dissent and the media, leaving no room for free expression. This heightened suppression also involved the official banning of political songs. Although there are a handful of other musicians who released political songs at the national level during this period, especially towards the departure of the regime, Teddy Afro was undisputedly a potent figure over the last two decades, an artist who spoke truth to power and preached

Ethiopian unity against an ethno-nationalist regime. Teddy Afro endured the repercussions of his impassioned songs; his music was banned on state media outlets, he was denied venues to organize concerts, and his interview with the state media was banned after its recording.

Orgeret (2008) examined music and politics in Ethiopia through the lens of Teddy Afro's political songs and their distribution and reception during the EPRDF's regime. Orgeret's (2008) note is quite revealing: a source "stated that there was a list of definite names of singers and titles of songs that should not be played; this list had been distributed to Ethiopian Radio staff members, and several of Afro's songs figured on it" (p. 234). Music censorship during the Derg regime has been noted by some studies; however, the EPRDF regime seems to have strongly perpetuated such an exercise despite fragile claims of a break from military dictatorship toward democratization. While the government exercised censorship, as evidenced in Teddy Afro's experience, the people secretly but enthusiastically listened to a diversity of (dissenting) ideas.

Censorship of political songs and expressions is not always successful in limiting their spread because there are always some outlets, such as music shops and other public spaces, that help disseminate them (Orgeret, 2008). In the face of censorship by the EPRDF, musicians covertly embedded political messages in their music (for example, using the Ethiopian Wax and Gold literary device, locally called *Qine*, a technique in which a poet uses a word having two meanings: an obvious one that the reader would discern easily and a hidden one that requires incisive attention and interpretation). The political issues they addressed included the erosion of national unity due to the ethno-federal structure that bred widespread ethnic division, censorship, bad governance, and corruption and favoritism (Beyene, 2019).

In a study of the interrelationship between popular music and Ethiopian nationalism (*Ethiopiawinet*) in Addis Ababa in 2016, when anti-government protests began across the country, Marye (2019) chronicles, "[...] though acts of resistance on the part of youth may not be clearly identifiable, popular music seems to have emerged as the most pervasive means for youth to challenge the state ideology of ethnic federalism" (pp. 97-98). Popular music in the capital is used as a platform to cultivate a sense of social responsibility informed by Ethiopianist identity (*Ethiopiwinet*) (Marye, 2019). Resistance against the EPRDF's government intensified after 2015 through youth-led protests across the country. The unrest led to the end of the three-decades-long TPLF-led rule when PM Ahmed assumed power in 2018. Throughout the protests and after the new administration was instituted, musicians supported the resistance, advocated for national unity, and voiced concerns over ongoing conflicts. It is imperative to shed some light on how these political developments came about, which informs this study as a backdrop to examine the selected political songs.

There appears to be some agreement among scholars about the political changes that occurred in the final years of the EPRDF's regime. Cochrane and Zewde (2018) characterized the changes as the result of the people's long struggle for "democracy, human rights, and human dignity" (p.3). The growing political discontent among the public due to structural and immediate causes was coupled with an internal power struggle within the TPLF-dominated ruling coalition that comprised four ethno-regional parties, namely the TPLF, Amhara National Democratic Movement (ANDM), Oromo People's Democratic Organization (OPDO), and Southern Ethiopia People's Democratic Movement (SEPDM). Zerai (2019) notes that this internal dispute stemmed from ANDM and OPDO members' change of course from previously covert displeasure over TPLF's dominance to openly challenging the status quo, while the TPLF strived to maintain dominance. The anti-government protests emerged from a stifled political space where political actors could not engage in policy deliberations, and the youth protesters filled this vacuum with the help of the diaspora and social media (Cochrane & Kefale, 2018).

Fisher and Gebrewahd (2019) opine that the 2015 and 2016 protests across Oromia and Amhara regions were about "perceived political and economic marginalization, human rights abuse by the federal military and police, federal encroachment into regional affairs and the perceived seizure of Amhara or Oromo territories by another state, or the federal government itself" (p. 200). Although there were "resentments long in the making" in the Amhara region, the arrest of Demeke Zewdu, leader of the Wolkayit Identity and Self-Determination Committee, in July 2016, prompted the Amhara protests (Tazebew, 2021). Besides, the Amhara protests were partly in solidarity with Oromo protesters (Lavers, 2018). According to Fisher and Gebrewahd (2019, p. 200), the Amhara and Oromia regions' protests were both borne out of "ethno-territorial sentiment."

The resistance continued to intensify in both regions and spread elsewhere, even after the revocation of the infamous Addis Ababa masterplan that allegedly intended to expand the city into Oromia at the expense of farmers in the surrounding areas. However, the burgeoning protests were met with a government crackdown. Hundreds were killed, thousands arrested, and free speech quelled through arbitrary detentions of opposition politicians, journalists, and activists (Amnesty International, 2017). The crackdown failed as protesters in the two regions sought to strengthen their alliance and were later joined by OPDO and ANDM cadres (Fisher & Gebrewahd, 2019). This was followed by a huge loss of public trust in the government. PM Hailemariam Desalegn resigned on February 15, 2018. In a highly anticipated Executive Committee Meeting of the ruling party, PM Abiy Ahmed was chosen as the party's leader, and assumed the premier's position in what seems to be a calculated plan by the OPDO and ANDM factions of the party.

The new PM embarked on unprecedented political liberalization, garnering widespread support across the country. The reforms included releasing political prisoners, removing the ban on political organizations that previously engaged in armed struggle (e.g., Oromo Liberation Front (OLF), Ogaden National Liberation Front (ONLF) and Ginbot 7), lifting the state of emergency decrees that were put in place at the height of the protests, and accusing some officials of having committed human rights violations (Abdi, 2019). Appointments of prominent technocratic professionals, who enjoy public confidence, to key institutions, including the Federal Supreme Court, National Electoral Board of Ethiopia, and Ethiopian Human Rights Commission, were widely commended, marking a positive step towards the institutionalization of the reform efforts. In addition, legislative reforms pertaining to the media, civil society organizations, and elections were undertaken. However, the country was still plagued by violent incidents and apparently irreconcilable contestations among nationalist forces. Yusuf (2019, p. 11) articulates it as follows:

> As the EPRDF's tight 27-year grip over the state slackened, the institutionally induced long-simmering conflicts re-surfaced, raging across the country, and with a magnitude rarely witnessed since the establishment of the Federal Democratic Republic of Ethiopia in 1995. Many of the current conflicts have either some roots in the recent past or have been largely influenced by it. Moreover, they are marked by nationalist undertones.

Similarly, Abdi (2019) saw a shift in people's consciousness about ethnic identity following the demise of the TPLF-led regime, which he characterizes as unprecedented "ultranationalism," which posed a serious threat to the PM Abiy administration's efforts to usher in stability and the rule of law. Yusuf (2019) observes highly competing nationalisms where there is contention among and within them on politico-historical questions in Ethiopia. The major nationalisms are Amhara, Oromo, and Tigrayan.

Amhara nationalism is a recent development and owes its emergence to the 2015 and 2016 youth protest movements and the creation of the National Movement of Amhara (NaMA) (Tazebew, 2021). Different Amhara-oriented organizations existed after the EPRDF's rise in the early 90s (Yusuf, 2019) that resulted in the adoption of ethnic federalism that created self-administrative (at least on paper) regions based on ethnolinguistic factors. This is also thought to have given rise to Amhara nationalism. Conversely, Oromo nationalism existed for over half a century and evolved through the Derg regime, reaching its heights during the Oromo protests beginning in 2015 (Yusuf, 2019). The third major contender is Tigrayan nationalism. It is highly influenced by the discordant relationship between the TPLF and the federal government, following certain developments in which the TPLF was relegated and publicly reprimanded. This led to the revival of ethnic nationalism among Tigrayans.

At the narrative level, there is a clash of politico-historical narratives advanced by Oromo and Amhara nationalists. "More immediate differences relate to territorial boundaries, collective rights and balance of power," according to Yusuf (2019). Furthermore, he cites the disputes over Raya and Addis Ababa, issues of Oromo ethnic minorities in the Amhara region, and rights of Amhara ethnic minorities in Oromia, as the major sites of the struggle. Similarly, Tazebew (2021) identifies inter-ethnic conflicts as one of the challenges in Amhara nationalism, where there is a clash over territories reclaimed by the Amhara conflicting with Tigrayan nationalists and the Benishangul-Gumuz region. Moreover, the conflict between Guji (Oromo) and Gedeo, between Somali and Oromo, and between Afar and Somali are all parts of the contestations that have posed an existential threat to the country. There is "considerable evidence to suggest that ethnic federalism entails conflict since it politicizes tribal identity and scholars soundly refute its applicability, especially in the Ethiopian context" (Taye, 2017). Ethiopian nationalism, on the other hand, is believed to remedy the detriments of ethnic federalism and the divisive ethno-nationalism thereof, through unity and togetherness as its hallmarks.

Theoretical Framework and Methodology

Textual analyses of political messages in music are heavily informed by framing theory, as they aim to determine how different political themes are framed in songs. Similarly, Reese (2001, p.7) notes, "Framing has been particularly useful in understanding the media's role in political life." This study builds on this tradition and employs framing as its theoretical underpinning. Entman's (1993, p. 52) definition of framing emphasizes the selection of "some aspects of a perceived reality and make them more salient in a communicating text, in such a way as to promote a particular problem definition, causal interpretation, moral evaluation, and/or treatment recommendation."

Media has long framed issues through selectivity. Musicians do so with their songs by using several techniques to underscore their core messages. Onyebadi (2018, p. 4) writes that musicians "articulate their perceptions of the existential conditions in their community or polity, highlight the importance of those issues and promote and recommend ideas and solutions to their audiences in the lyrics of their songs." Therefore, through an analysis of the selected songs, this study highlights the salient political messages Ethiopian musicians are communicating through their platform. The qualitative textual analysis method is employed to examine these political messages.

Textual analysis is used to "assess the meanings, values, and messages being sent through" texts (Smith, 2017, p. 1). These are commonly media texts in the form of writing, sound, symbols, and pictures. Textual analysis is a qualitative analysis that looks beyond the palpable media text and identifies the "ideological and cultural assumptions" that come into the texts (Fürsich, 2009, p. 240). Fürsich further explains that in addition to uncovering hidden meanings in texts, this method also gives researchers the chance to look at assumptions, implied patterns, and missing text. However, such a method is not without limitations. Smith (2017) states that textual analysis engenders multiple interpretations of a given text, making it broad and subjective. The critique also includes the fact that the researchers' bias may inadvertently seep into the analysis. As this research attempts to discern both latent and manifest political themes in the songs under study, textual analysis best fits the purpose. Aware of the limitations of the method noted here, the authors strove to be cautious in maintaining a fair representation of the meanings, thereby avoiding gross misrepresentations.

To facilitate their use of the qualitative textual analysis method, the authors constructed a set of thematic categories of political messages framed in the songs under study. Thematic analysis is defined as a method through which a data set is analyzed to identify, organize, and come up with "patterns of meaning" or themes (Braun & Clarke, 2012, p. 57). Major framing devices developed during the initial reading of the lyrics include *Amhara, Citizen, Division, Ethiopia, Ethnicity, Flag, Love, One, Oromo, Tigray, Unity, Victory*. These frames were further subdivided into categories representing major political themes that one or more frames portray. These are Ethiopian nationalism, ethno-nationalism, Ethiopian nationalism interwoven with ethnic nationalism, speaking truth to power, poverty and maladministration, resistance, and celebrating triumph. The lyrics were then analyzed and categorized based on these thematic frames. In the analysis, parts of the lyrics that signify the thematic frame under which they are classified are cited and further explained.

Sixteen songs were selected from three regions: Oromia, Amhara, Tigray, and the capital city, Addis Ababa. The rationale for selecting four songs from each region is to gain enough insight into political music and understand the diversity of issues the songs entertained. If a smaller number of songs was picked, the insights would be significantly less, and, conversely, selecting more than sixteen songs would not be feasible given the time and resource constraints for this study. The study posits that the political context in which the songs were released is essential to understanding how they frame issues that allude to what is happening in the real world. Accordingly, the authors considered two aspects of the Ethiopian political landscape in the choice of songs for analysis: time (before and after PM Abiy's political reforms) and region (different political communities and political aspirations). Thus, four songs were selected from each region, with two songs from before the 2018 political change and two songs after that date. The reason for choosing these regions is mainly due to the central role they played in the recent past and the ongoing political contests in Ethiopia.

The songs for analysis were purposively selected from each of the regions, based on three main factors: (i) the popularity of the songs in the respective regions, (ii) the political messages communicated, and (iii) the level of the artists' influence. Of the sixteen songs, four are in Afaan Oromo (from Oromia) and the other four are in Tigrigna (from Tigray). Those from Addis Ababa and Amhara are in the Amharic language. To avoid discrepancies, the Afaan Oromo and Tigrigna song lyrics were first translated into Amharic, for which the authors employed the services of two professional translators. The Amharic texts of all sixteen songs were then analyzed by the authors, both of whom are native speakers of Amharic, and also fluent in English. The songs' lyrics used to illustrate the analysis were translated into English except for Teddy Afro's song. For his songs, the authors used the English version the musician released.

Findings, Analysis and Discussion

This section presents the findings and analyzes the selected songs under the major thematic frames identified through a textual analysis of the lyrics. The seven themes are grouped into five sections. The first section – nationalism – comprises three themes: Ethiopian nationalism and patriotism (as a remedy to the ills of ethno-nationalism), ethno-nationalism (implied as an antithesis to Ethiopian nationalism), and Amhara nationalism interwoven with Ethiopian nationalism. The other themes the subsequent sections deal with include resistance, speaking truth to power, poverty and maladministration, and celebrating triumph.

Major Political Themes in the Songs

Nationalism

Widespread contentions between variations of nationalism pervade the Ethiopian political landscape. There are evident clashes and contentions among, for example, Amhara and Oromo nationalism or Tigrayan and Amhara nationalism (Yusuf, 2019). The ethnic vs. Ethiopian nationalism dichotomy only emphasizes the fact that ethno-nationalism is an antithesis to Ethiopian nationalism (Jemal, 2020), and this does not indicate the interplay within ethno-nationalist forces themselves. Furthermore, ethno-nationalism is also not always anathema to Ethiopian nationalism, as evidenced by Amhara nationalism. The burgeoning and late-coming Amhara nationalism is intensely interwoven with Ethiopian nationalism, hence, an exception to the (often discordant) relationship between Ethiopian nationalism and ethno-nationalism.

Ethiopian Nationalism and Patriotism

There are no references to Ethiopian nationalism in the songs from Oromia. Tigrigna songs, with one exception, seldom directly mention Ethiopia. In Amhara songs, as discussed below, Ethiopian nationalism is reflected as an integral element of Amhara nationalism. However, all four songs from Addis Ababa are replete with Ethiopian nationalist frames, thereby steering clear of an ethno-nationalist outlook. Ethiopian unity is depicted as a remedy to the detriments of ethnic exclusivity. In a song titled, "Tamenal" (we are sick), released a year and a half after the new administration's rise, Zeleke (2019) describes the country's continued sickness of ethnocentrism as follows:

> We're sick, we are sick, we're very sick
> Having been educated for 20 and 30 years
> How come we cannot have better ideas
> We're still tripping over the rope of ethnic lines
> Yes, we're sick, we're sick, we're very sick

Zeleke questions who will put on the people the robe of togetherness if everyone builds walls along ethnic lines. He decries the elites for failing to generate better ideas (such as unity, as could be inferred). He calls on all to distance themselves from what he termed a *disease* (the tendency to inquire about one's ethnic origin). To signify the equality of all races and ethnicities, Zeleke fiercely asks:

> Whose ethnicity is made of fire, lightning?
> Whose ethnicity is made of straw, raffia grass?
> Do not degrade one while aggrandizing the other,
> Do not worship your stomach; preach love.

The singer further interrogates ethnocentrism and the elites who advocate for it, thereby referring to a historical event that epitomizes Ethiopian unity – Adwa.

> Where were they educated?
> Those heroes of Adwa
> Where were they educated?
> Those patriots of Adwa
> Who are examples to the world
> Beyond their own
> It's because they fought for humans
> Not because they fought for ethnicity

Zeleke's (2019) depiction of Adwa as a symbol of unity transcending ethnic division matches Araya's (2005, p. 242) description that:

[...] Adwa signifies a single inescapable truth, one which the current ethnic politics tries to undermine: Ethiopia may be a mosaic of nationalities, but its people also have a collective, shared history that binds them together. Adwa represents a supra-ethnic and supraregional consciousness in search of collective freedom.

Borrowing a phrase from a British colonel, Levine (2014) once described Adwa in an online article as a "mysterious magnetism" that unites Ethiopians.

An examination of Zeleke's (2019) song highlights another important issue. By identifying the danger posed by excessive ethnic sentiment and a weak social fabric, he underscores the importance of national unity. In doing so, he appears to have echoed the principles of *Ubuntu*, a Zulu principle that encapsulates unity and togetherness, as articulated by Mamphela Ramphele. According to Ramphele (as quoted in Wernick (2021)), "The principles of Ubuntu are the original wisdom of all our common ancestors...that the only way they can not only survive, but thrive, is by working together to relate to one another in a way that says: 'I am, because you are.'" By appealing to national unity, Zeleke encourages people to embrace their commonalities as Ethiopians. This is in line with what the Ethiopianist camp advocates for in political contests – policies that could maintain unity (Yusuf, 2020).

Getish Mamo, a musician best known for his political songs, released since the protests that ended the TPLF-led administration, voiced concerns over the detriments of ethnocentrism and raised other questions. For example, Beyene (2019) analyzed one of Mamo's songs and noted that the singer referred to freedom of expression and the need to listen rather than demonize each other along ethnic, religious, and political lines. Mamo has again, in a new song titled "Zufanu New" (Minew Shewa Tube, 2020a), championed Ethiopian unity, its invincibility against all odds, and its melting pot of a wide variety of ethnic communities in contrast to ethnic purity on which ethno-nationalists base their classifications of ethnic communities.

He begins the song by reciting the infamous anthem of the Derg – "Ethiopia Tikdem," which translates to "Ethiopia First." The song alludes to Ethiopia's enemies, both internal and external, in the song's context. It foretells the country's inevitable victory that would also result in its enemies publicly conceding. Mamo does not name who the enemies are, but he insinuates that ethno-nationalist forces caused the national tragedy. The country, he noted, was plagued by ethnic-based killings, attacks by homegrown armed forces, and several conflicts. Zerai (2019, p. 8) observes that "The rule of law has been seriously tested with mob justice being carried out not infrequently, and with gun-toting vigilante groups mushrooming in various corners of the country, jeopardizing the security of citizens." However, Mamo recalls "Ethiopia's glory" and its "current greatness" to plant seeds of hope in the people that the country will be victorious. He sang:

> It was and still is great
> It is Ethiopia
> She is not new to adversity
> This will pass, don't be afraid

The musician laments that the political landscape is devoid of truth and dialogue. The song noted that the poor are bereft of any benefit, while ethnocentric elites gamble with their lives. In a passionate refutation of the ethno-nationalist theory of identity – purely an ethnicity issue – the singer describes his bloodline to justify that he is nothing but *Ethiopian*. Jemal's (2020, p. 11) observation typifies the singer's concern that "Language and 'pure blood' have increasingly become criteria for advancement rather than one's merit in most walks of life. More than ever, this is pronounced when one travels outside of the capital Addis Ababa." Mamo criticizes ethnicity by invoking his Ethiopianness and categorically says:

> My loyal grandfather, hailing from Menz
> Settled in Becho, having married an Oromo
> He had two children from the Oromo
> When the children came of age
> The woman married a Sodo Guraghe
> Married to a Tigre, the man had children too
> I am one of those children
> All say to me 'Getiye the Kin'
> You be the judge, what's my ethnicity?
> Do not ask me my ethnicity, my ethnicity is Ethiopian

One of the pressing issues in Ethiopia is the issue of the Great Ethiopian Renaissance Dam and the subsequent dispute with Egypt and Sudan. Teddy Afro released a song titled, "Demo Be Abbay" (2020), addressing this. "Abbay" is the Ethiopian name for the Blue Nile. In his song, Afro alludes to the Egyptian effort to stop Ethiopia from filling the dam through diplomacy and sometimes through threats, albeit to no avail. The singer characterizes it as a "test." In what echoes a typical Ethiopian battle song, Afro uses his lyrics to instill a sense of patriotism and push people to defend Ethiopia's national interests. He describes the current generation as children of warriors who, like their forefathers, will show no mercy as long as Ethiopian affairs are concerned. However, Afro clarifies the fact that it is not Ethiopia's choice to go to war. "I am holding back for both of our own goods," he says, but not because Ethiopia is afraid. He articulates how the Nile benefited Egypt for millennia and is now turning toward its origins. He who tries to stop it from happening by raising arms will face the consequences, the lyrics lament.

If they test us on Abbay
No relenting on Abbay
On Abbay...
No citizen will concede Abbay
[...]
Go forth, his father a warrior
Go forth, his mother a warrior
Go forth, he shows no mercy
Go forth, on affairs of country
Go forth, I own Abbay waters
Go forth, I showed graciousness
Go forth, But If Al Masr gets nauseous
Go forth, In all shamelessness
Go forth, Even love bursts into flames
Go forth, If it loses patience.
[...]
Go forth, Abbay the generous
Go forth, fertilized Egypt's banks
Go forth, but now it longs
Go forth, to see its country's shores
Go forth, If anyone aches
Go forth, over this to raise arms
Go forth, let me not be in the shoes
Go forth, of the one who dares.

As with Afro's other political songs, this one is full of Ethiopian nationalist frames. However, there is one marked difference between the song about Abbay and the other Ethiopianist songs discussed. While the other songs confront ethno-nationalism and offer Ethiopian nationalism to heal the ills of the nation, either explicitly or through allusions, "Demo Be Abbay" arouses patriotic sentiments among Ethiopians in a cautionary message to Egypt. In a study of Afro's political songs, Orgeret (2008) noted that the artist, in his two songs titled, "Yasteseryal" and "Shemindefer," challenges political authority and strives to triumph over societal divisions. In his more recent song, "Demo Be Abbay" (Teddy Afro, 2020), Afro goes beyond internal issues and engages in the transnational discourse on the Nile River. As the lyrics suggest, he not only intends to mobilize Ethiopians to defend their rights, but also directly addresses Egypt while impliedly involving Sudan. Afro himself disseminated English and Arabic translations of his lyrics, which attests to his intentions to engage in the international discourse. This finding signifies that although one sings in a local language, political music transcends borders in its quest to challenge hegemonic discourse.

Ethno-nationalism

When the Tigray region was preparing to hold its regional election in defiance of the country-wide postponement of the polls, Brhane Haile released a song titled, "Knezarbom Ena" (Semay Ent, 2020) which translates to "We will make them speak." "Them" purports to refer to Tigray's "enemies," which likely means, in the context of the defiant election, the federal government and its allies. At times, the lyrics call Tigray's enemies "chauvinists," a term that elites regularly used during EPRDF's reign, ostensibly believed to refer to the Amhara.

Beyond calling on Tigray's children to protect it and passionately aggrandizing its history, the singer expresses great certitude in Tigray's ability to shame its enemies. The song portrays Tigray not just as one among other entities in the union but as a strong independent entity. This song strongly expresses Tigrayan ethno-nationalism. Nevertheless, it also embraces Ethiopian identity by alluding to Tigray as Ethiopia's birthplace, claiming that Tigray does not deny its Ethiopianness like "them." "Them" refers to Eritrea, an ally of the federal government. The following verses exemplify the defiance, passion, and certainty that permeate the song:

> We will make them speak twice
> We will shame them
> I swear on my father's grave, we will shame them
> We will make them bite their tongue as they are accustomed to
> We will make them speak twice, as they are accustomed to
> Witness my country, chauvinists will be shamed, humiliated.
> [...]
> Those who do not bargain on our identity
> Our Salsay Woyane, Baytona Tigray
> Those in exile, but their hearts at home
> Standby for their people's redemption
> Children of the hardworking people, Tigray's protectors
> Digital Woyane, pillars of my people
> Pillars of my people
> My people's support
> Our Tigray's fortresses
> [...]
> With our TPLF
> With our Fortress of Tigray
> We will make them speak
> Yes, we will make them speak

The singer mentions most Tigrayan political parties, including the TPLF, that were set to participate in the region's election, thereby characterizing them as "those who don't bargain on our [Tigrayan] identity" and "Tigray's fortresses."

Through this, the singer accentuates the strong unity that would "undoubtedly" lead to Tigray's victory over its enemies and the shaming of the latter. This sentiment is in line with what the regional leader and chair of the TPLF said early in 2018. Fisher and Gebrewahd (2019, p. 205) noted that the "TPLF chair Debretsion Gebremichael has also come to rhetorically position the party anew as the defender of Tigrayan identity, promoting a range of slogans aimed at the federal government in July 2018 rallies included 'stop targeting Tigrayans' and 'justice for Tigrayans.'"

Even before the 2018 political changes, and notably during the protests that led to the regime's departure, another Tigrigna song by Mulugeta Kahsay hints, in the title of the song, "Yikurkoheni Allo" (Tigray Online, 2017), that "Something is making me feel uncomfortable." Considering what Gebremichael said (quoted above), and the discord between the reformist leadership and the TPLF that unfolded soon after PM Abiy's appointment, Kahsay seems to have foreseen what was at stake. He articulates Tigray's history, its ownership of Ethiopia's first civilization, and the fact that it is the birthplace of St. Yared and Zara Yakob, the Ethiopian philosopher. In a display of passionate Tigrayan nationalism, he expresses how his heart faints whenever Tigray was mentioned. Kahsay invokes Tigrayan unity and describes Tigrayans as those who do not want what is not theirs. Contrary to this, there are claims that parts of Western and Southern Tigray were annexed from the present-day Amhara region. Kahsay also expressed his concern that something is making him uncomfortable and foreshadows the coming of a difficult time for Tigray.

Another Tigrigna song by Tikue Woldu released after the 2018 political reforms titled, "Tigray Milibama" (Admas Music, 2019), meaning "Tigray's Braveheartedness," foretells the dawn of a new day for Tigray and celebrates that Tigray "survived through a lot." He portrays Tigray as having had patience despite "newcomers defaming its reputable name." The song's message parallels Brhane Haile's (Semay Ent, 2020) in that it expresses a sentiment that Tigray has been targeted, despite its historical glory, and is now on the verge of regaining its pride. Both songs emphasize a notable Tigrayan nationalist narrative. To an extent, Woldu personifies Tigray and uses the phrase "My Honey." Referring to Tigray as a 'country,' he also expresses his aspirations for Tigray's self-administration. This is consistent with the official statements Tigray has been releasing since clashing with the federal government. The next few verses further elucidate this.

> Dreaming for the country,
> Toiled in the journey
> My country put on your robe
> It is your value for all you toiled
> My country
> Precious land, after her starvation

Tigray's patience,
She does not seek more than what she deserves
Tigray's bravery
Every passerby defaming her
Tigray's patience
[...]
You traversed through all, Tigray my honey
Dawn has broken, take heart my country
You never rested from overcoming challenges
I cannot get enough of dreaming right for you

Similarly, songs by artists from Oromia passionately celebrate Oromoness (also known as Oromuma) and call on Oromos to unite and fight together and rejoice in Oromos' (political) achievements. Most of the four Afaan Oromo songs selected for the study conspicuously reflect Oromo nationalism, hence, they fall under the ethno-nationalist frame. However, two songs exemplify resistance, while the others illustrate the celebratory frame. The following verses from Caalaa Bultume's song titled, "Waggadhan Nu Ga'I" (Golden Ethio Music, 2019), illustrate how Oromo nationalism is depicted in the political landscape:

It is a mature person we have in Sheger, no one can defeat us
The place is also ours, a cruel won't hold the seat
It is a strong man we have in Sheger, no one can defeat you
A cruel won't hold the seat, not in Oromo Folles'[2] presence

By "a person in Sheger," the singer is unquestionably referring to PM Abiy Ahmed, and claims that both the PM and the place where he resides as belonging to the Oromos. One of the most heated political issues plaguing the nation's politics is the ownership of Addis Ababa. It is a point of contention between Oromo and Amhara nationalists (Yusuf, 2019). Bultume advocates for Oromia's ownership of Addis Ababa, saying: "the place is also ours." Moreover, he underscores the unity and strength of the Oromo saying, "no one can defeat us," and defiantly sings that power will not be snatched by "a cruel" as long as the *Oromo Folle* are alive. This stresses that Oromia is the "rightful owner of power" and also the country's protector, and indicates an exclusive ethno-nationalist perspective concerning national power.

Although the songs by Amhara artists, except one, depict an inextricably linked relationship between Amhara and Ethiopian nationalism, hence, fitting the third theme under nationalism discussed in the next sub-section, it is

---

[2] *Folle* is one of the age-based grades of the Oromo society according to the traditional *Gada* system and consists of young men aged between 8 and 16.

imperative to cite some examples that are similar to the previously discussed songs that display a strong sense of ethno-nationalism. Mehari Degefaw's song, "Gitem Alegn" (Heni Tube, 2019), carries a fierce sentiment of united and strong Amhara, which is similar to the Tigrayan and Oromo nationalists' depictions in the previously cited songs.

> Our word is one, more potent than iron, and no one can revoke it
> From now on, none of the coming-and-going will kill Amhara.
> [...]
> When our own are touched, when the country is undermined
> Stand up Fano,[3] the Amhara Neftenya[4]
> Destroy that narrow nationalist

As previously noted, the protests in the Amhara region in 2016 were linked with the Wolkayit issue, which purports to reclaim the Amhara identity of people in Wolkayit and demands the reinstitution of the land to the Amhara Regional State. Amhara nationalism, since then, has centered on the Wolkayit and other disputed lands in southern Tigray and the bordering Benishangul Gumuz region (for more on this issue, see Tazebew, 2021; Yusuf, 2019). One of the songs that vocally asserted this claim is by Solomon Demle titled, "Fetenegn" ("He is testing me") (Hope Music Ethiopia, 2016), which was released in August 2016, at the peak of the protests. The lyrics metaphorically allude to the Amhara's land and identity issues with Tigray and Benishangul Gumuz:

> Tell him my habit, tell him my deeds,
> I do not like it when one sees my wife and territory
> [...]
> An Evil day is better than an evil neighbor,
> It becomes less evil if you survive today.

The word "neighbor" refers to the bordering regions in territorial dispute with Amhara. They are portrayed as "evil." This illustrates the tension among ethno-nationalist forces that is on full display in the Ethiopian political landscape. By raising this issue, the song advocates for the Amhara region's territorial integrity, presenting a staunch ethno-nationalist sentiment.

---

[3] *Fano* is used to refer to the youth in Amhara region, like the *Qeeroo* in Oromia, who have participated in the protests since 2015.
[4] The word *Neftenya* literally means "Gun Carrier" and is used by some politicians to refer to the Amhara as historical enemies. In this song, the name is reappropriated and reclaimed with pride.

Amhara Nationalism Interwoven with Ethiopian Nationalism

Three of the four songs selected from the Amhara region uniformly articulate that Amhara nationalism is inextricably bound with Ethiopian nationalism. For example, Mehari Degefaw's song titled, "Gitem Alegn" (Heni Tube, 2019), raises the question of Amhara's "rightful and historical" ownership of Metekel (a place in the Benishangul Gumuz region), Wolkayit, Raya, and Tegede (districts in Tigray), which is one of the central questions concerning Amhara nationalists. Degefaw's song appears to be militant in that he expresses a desire to fight and die for this cause. According to Tazebew (2021), the beginning of the protests in Gonder in 2016 was a turning point in Amhara nationalism. It was a period when the *Wolkayit* question was gaining momentum following the arrest of the movement's leader, as noted in the literature.

Conversely, in "Gitem Alegn" (Heni Tube, 2019), Degefaw states that "everyone in my generation" has started believing in one Ethiopia as it was in the times of Emperor Menelik II. For this, he invokes the green, yellow, and red colors of the Ethiopian flag as being part of every Habesha's blood and a symbol of unity. In a display of willingness to protect his country and people, Degefaw sings, "He who touches Ethiopia, touches my eye. He who touches my people, touches my eye."

One might find this co-existence between a purely ethno-nationalist and an ardently pan-Ethiopianist expression in one song as oxymoronic. However, this is very typical of Amhara nationalism, and most songs by artists from the Amhara region reflect that. As Yusuf (2019, p. 12) notes, the Amhara's ethnic identity "was for long subsumed under the broader Ethiopian nationalism, and it was difficult to distinguish between the two." While in the contestations between nationalisms, ethno-nationalists see Ethiopian nationalism as an imposition, hence, they are diametrically opposed to it, but Amhara nationalism seems to be in a highly symbiotic relationship with Ethiopian nationalism as reflected in the songs cited here. In a verse that perfectly captures this, Degefaw vows that no one can separate his being Gondere, Amhara, and Ethiopian. This is quite vivid in his line that says: "We built it [Ethiopia] through our flesh and blood."

Similarly, Fasil Demoz, in his song titled, "Maninete" (My Identity) (Tenaadam, 2018), depicts a blended identity of being Amhara and Ethiopian. In one part of the song, he particularly appeals to the Amhara in Wollo, Gonder, Gojam, and Shoa to awaken them to fight tyranny. "Isn't what's being done [by the government] too much?" he asks and calls on the Amhara to come together. Yet, in another part of the song, he describes his Amhara and Ethiopian identities' inseparability, which is in line with Degefaw's representation of Amhara identity. The lyrics read:

My identity is Amhara
My being is Ethiopian
What is evil about choosing my country?
Amhara means to me, in the first place
He who doesn't bargain on his being Ethiopian

Like most songs that celebrate Ethiopian identity, Fasil Demoz's song articulates the flag's three colors as Ethiopia's very meaning. Demoz honors Ethiopian identity, bravery, and heroism in saving the country from the time's predicaments while he calls for divine intervention. Such a passionate love for one country is accompanied by ethno-nationalist frames that zero in on certain politico-historical questions of a specific ethnic group. Demoz also raises the same question, in line with Degefaw's advocacy for the return of what is labeled as Amhara's historical land.

A look at the third song from the same region titled, "Leblebew" by Dagne Walle (Minew Shewa Tube, 2020b), released late in 2020, reveals a similar portrayal of a healthy marriage between Ethiopian nationalism and ethno-nationalism. Although this song is best suited to explaining the theme *celebration of an enemy's defeat*, it also expresses a blend of nationalisms, and it is worth citing part of it here. It starts with describing Ethiopia as "our glory" while praising the Amhara's role in defending Ethiopia, and mentioning Amhara heroes:

If called upon in the name of the country,
War is like his wedding, the Amhara is magical
[...]
My being Ethiopian is colorful
They say it is fading, but it's now written in gold

Resistance

Some of the songs released from the Oromia region before the April 2018 political change largely invoke resistance as a major theme. These songs were said to have been instrumental in mobilizing the youth during the protests that preceded the political change. One of the songs was "Itti Muddi," by singer Tafarii (2016), which loosely translates to "Push On." The political change began in 2016 with huge protests that first started in Oromia in November 2015, and later expanded to the Amhara region in August 2016. It was reported to have claimed 500 lives, with thousands of people detained (Horne, 2016). In general, the song, "Itti Muddi," calls on the youth to intensify their struggle against the government to end its brutality and redeem the people's freedom and dignity. Tafarii appeals to, and comforts the families of the students and other protesters who were killed during the agitations, and reassures them that the rest of the youth will bring the struggle to fruition.

Why retreat having once faced the enemy?
It will reign over you more than ever.
Once you hold the tiger's tail, you do not leave it,
for if it turns, it destroys your eyes,
then there is no solution, so be strong, my kin
Speed up, push on!

...

Dear families of students, do not cry
Dear families of martyrs, do not cry
Others are in jail, others shot, and others exiled
The rest of us will retaliate
There is no doubt this year, we will hit our friends' target
Speed up, Push on!

The late Hachalu Hundessa, a young Oromo musician and the epitome of the Oromo struggle whose life was cut short by assassins in June 2020, is known for his inspiring political songs. In 2017, when the protests that swept across Oromia and Amhara regions that started in 2015 continued to flare and a state of emergency was still in effect, Hundessa appeared at a charity concert for internally displaced Oromos, organized at the Millenium Hall in Addis Ababa, Ethiopia. The event was also attended by the then government officials from the ruling coalition EPRDF. Hundessa rocked the hall with an unprecedented political song titled, "Jirtu" (Oromp3, 2017), which translates to "Are You Alive?" He passionately screamed out loud, "Are you alive? Children of Borena, Children of Wollega, Children of Arsi, Children of Tulema, Children of Mecha, are you alive? Where are you?" He posed several rhetorical questions, eliciting the youth's response in action. He asked in his lyrics, "What has Oromo done? What is Oromo expected to do?" His lyrics instill in the Oromo youth a sense of regret about the discontinuity of what Oromo forebears had accomplished. He then inflames the youth to action. The following lyrics illustrate his plea, indomitability, and rebelliousness:

When Hararghe sharpens the machete, Tulema trained the horse
When complaints were unbounded, Qeeroo decided to fight
[...]
Let alone us, they know our horses very well
In the Adwa mountains, in the Mekelle mountains
Let alone us, they know our horses very well
During the battle of Adwa, during the battle of Mekelle
[...]
Oromo, owner of Dama, Dalle, and Shanqo[5],

---

[5] These are horse names widely known among the Oromo community in Ethiopia.

Feed your horse and prepare it
Sharpen your spear, take down your shield from where it is hung
[...]
Stand up, fight with your horse, you are closer to Arat Kilo
Pick and fight with your spear, you are closer to Arat kilo
Pick and fight with your machete, you are closer to Arat Kilo

Among Tigrigna songs, Brhane Haile's (Semay Ent, 2020) contains messages of resistance. The significant differences between the aforementioned resistance songs and Haile's are whom they purport to resist and the period the songs were released. Hundessa and Tafarii's songs were released before PM Abiy's government was sworn in, and their struggle was against the TPLF-dominated ruling government. While Haile's song was released more than two years after the current PM came to power, it implicates the new administration and its allies. Furthermore, Haile's is markedly less rebellious than the two Afaan Oromo songs. For example, instead of mentioning weapons and tools of resistance such as spears, machetes, and shields referenced in Hundessa's songs or the physical fight that Taffarii summons, Haile refers to Digital Woyane, or Tigrayan nationalist cyber troops, and counts on the Tigrayan diaspora, opposing parties, and the TPLF to join the struggle. Hence, the resistance against the federal government is in terms of holding the regional election despite the HoPR's ruling that rendered it null and void.

Speaking Truth to Power

The Ethiopian government's response to the peaceful protests across the Oromia and Amhara regions in 2016 was very highhanded. Hundreds were killed and thousands detained. In a joint letter to the UN Human Rights Council, more than ten international and local civil society organizations—including Human Rights Watch, Amnesty International, Freedom House, and Reporters Without Borders—addressed the violent crackdown on peaceful protesters both in Oromia and Amhara regions, and called for independent investigations, the release of detained individuals, and maximum restraint on the use of force by government security agents (Human Rights Watch, 2016). Among the detained were journalists, human rights advocates, and opposition political figures.

In this context, Yihunie Belay, a prominent cultural singer, released a song, "Bel, Seken" (2016), with a strong political message in solidarity with the protesters. Belay begins the lyrics with an account of police brutality where peaceful and unarmed protesters who took to the streets to defend their identity were met by shooting police. As the song was released on the eve of the Ethiopian New Year in September 2016, the lyrics expressed a wish for the new year to be free of innocents' deaths, while wishing death to the killers. It then speaks directly to those in power and calls for calming down the brutality as captured in these verses:

> Listen to my people, do not shoot at them
> See my people, do not glare at them
> In the new year, new herald
> […]
> Calm
> Calm Down
> To calm down is to be polite
> To calm down is to be a hero
> The soldier, calm down
> Calm down the gun
> Do not pull the trigger
> He is shouting empty-handed
> He is your peaceful brother
> Calm down, leave my people
> Listen to his grievance
> Do not kill him
> The government should not shoot at the people

Poverty and Maladministration

"Haregu," a Tigrigna song by Solomon Yikunoamlak (Liham Melody, 2018), was released at a time when the political changes were unfolding in Ethiopia. The major political reforms in the country had yet to be implemented; hence, the song could be considered in the category of those released before the change. What is unique about Yikunoamlak's song is that it neither glorifies ethno-nationalist nor Ethiopian nationalist narratives, nor engages in a fierce confrontation with a particular political force. Instead, it discusses serious societal problems such as poverty and lack of access to water, pinpointing maladministration as the cause. The lyrics have several symbols that are open to multiple interpretations which are outside the purview of this chapter. However, symbolisms and interpretations aside, the song clearly expresses two problems in Tigray – poverty (lack of food) and acute water shortages in Mekelle, the regional capital. In the lyrics, the singer tells the story from his perspective, as someone responsible for all the problems. In doing so, he converses with his mother, who represents not just mothers, but also society:

> Mom, the believer, had faith in me
> I, your child, weak being a drunkard
> My mom, my mentor, her patience is immense
> She tells me she's eaten well while her Mesob is empty
> I fed you numbers for lunch and starved you

In the last line, he admits to starving his mother by feeding her "numbers for lunch." This is where one can infer that the singer is referring to the source of poverty or acute shortage of water. Here, "numbers" refer to government reports that are often doctored to misrepresent the reality on the ground that people are starving and dying. Furthermore, throughout the song, there is an allusion to the water facility in Mekelle. "I could forget you like Mekelle's water," he says. Again, this phrase implicates that Mekelle's water problem is forgotten, which shows that the singer believes maladministration is to blame for the cited societal problems. He used music to expose critical problems in society and bring them to public attention.

The artist played an investigative role in which he identified societal ills and exposed them. This is especially important as Ethiopia's wandering musicians/minstrels, known as *Azmari*, used to play the same roles in the country's past. They traveled extensively and talked to communities about their pain and dreams, as well as societal ills. Then they communicated those stories through their songs and shed light on people's suffering. Gebremariam (2018, p. 38) similarly observed that "Azmari music has always been a medium through which people communicate and express their discontent with political systems, economic hardship, or maladministration of any sort." What Kebede (1971) called "The artistic interaction between performers and audiences through spontaneous improvisation" helped *Azmaris* escape the censorship trap that has existed in the country for centuries. The use of "Wax and Gold" as well as the spontaneity of message crafting and storytelling in various settings contributed to *Azmari's* vital role in exposing the corruption and nepotism rampant in Ethiopia.

Celebrating Triumph

Two songs chosen for analysis in this chapter have the triumphant frame as their central theme. One of them is Caalaa Bultume's Afaan Oromo song titled, "Waggadhan Nu Ga'I" (Golden Ethio Music, 2019). It was released one and a half years after PM Abiy came to power. In the song, Bultume uses the metaphorical expression of the coming of a new season after a gloomy and turbulent winter, to illustrate the new dawn in the political landscape where "the Qeeroo protect the country" and an Oromo is in power. The "turbulent winter" refers to when the Oromo protests were at their peak and the government responded with a brutal crackdown. The lyrics recount how such a change came about and what the cost was, as follows:

> We were strewn [polarized] for long,
> Thanks to God, we came to terms now.
> We sacrificed our children, and it is the result of their blood;
> We are back to Horra Gullele.

The song mainly cites the celebration of Irrecha in Addis Ababa, following the government's decision, as tangible evidence for the triumphant success of the Oromo struggle (protests). Oromia's regional president said in a press statement that the decision to celebrate Irrecha in Addis Ababa brought an end to a 150-year period when Irrecha was not celebrated in Addis Ababa. This speech was controversial and was contested by people who said that no such celebration was banned or stopped in the period in question. Nevertheless, Bultume's take is in line with the president's when the musician sang that the "Irrecha is back to its former place."

Another song from Oromia by Jambo Jote is filled with similar celebratory frames. Entitled "Belba" (Minew Shewa Tube, 2018), the song is believed to be named after one of the five parties known as *Luba*. The current *Aba Gada* (the leader or father of *Gada*) in *Tulama Oromo* is called *Belba* and retains the name for a five-year term. Legend among the Oromo has it that Belba's era was a time of victory and change. With the choice of this word as the song's title, Jote is stressing that it was a time of victory. The song was released a few months after the 2018 political changes, and by victory, he appears to be referring to the protests and changes that led to PM Abiy's appointment. Jambo Jote further expresses this conception of victory throughout his lyrics. The character he plays in the song is depicted as having long been separated from and pitted against someone described as his lover but could also be interpreted as a metaphorical reference to the Amhara. The lyrics then describe the coming of a new day to reunite and address societal ills. The following lines capture the celebration of a new dawn, and the earnest longing to reunite:

> The star of truth is visible,
> The era of darkness has passed.
> Who is closer to me than you?
> I have seen, my true kin is you.
> Despite the long road and challenges,
> for me, nothing is better than meeting you.

Fast forward to December 2020, a song by Dagne Walle titled, "Leblebew" (Minew Shewa Tube, 2020b) celebrates the triumph of Ethiopian forces over TPLF forces in what the government calls "a law enforcement operation." The operation began on November 4, 2020, when TPLF forces attacked the northern command of the national defense. Walle describes the swift response, and the victory thereof, of the Amhara special forces who went to the rescue of the Northern Command in Western Tigray. The regional special forces were officially recognized for their role in the operation in support of the federal army. Although it is a celebration of the overall defeat of TPLF, Walle mainly tells the story from an Amhara point of view and applauds the Amhara militia and special forces. Part of the song's celebration has to do with the "return" of the reclaimed lands of Raya, Humera, Wolkayit, and Tegede. The lyrics read:

Burn him, burn him, burn him.
Block his cave, as he is doomed.
Burn him, burn him, go show him,
if he does not listen when advised and told to stop.
The militia, the special forces, Amhara's farmer,
they marched for their country along with the soldiers.

Moreover, Dagne, like many Ethiopian and Amhara nationalist musicians, invokes the three colors of the Ethiopian flag, and he poetically articulates that his blood sees nothing but these green, yellow, and red. Walle also hints that the flag is his main motivation and drive for sacrificing for the country.

The major themes that emerged from this and the resistance sub-sections appear to have some similarities with that of Rwandese singer Simon Bikindi. Like some of the singers under the two subsections, Bikindi was a famous singer who used his fame to contribute to violence, with Bikindi's effect being much more extreme (McCoy, 2009). McCoy (2009, p. 92) argues that "Though Bikindi never explicitly called for violence against Tutsi, his songs were deemed sufficiently inflammatory that on 12 July 2001, he was arrested and brought to be tried as a war criminal at the International Criminal Tribunal for Rwanda (ICTR)."

Although the songs analyzed might not have the same impact that Bikindi's had in 1994 in Rwanda, one should not overlook their potential role in inciting violence and being used as "a combat weapon"[6] in the future. In the current Ethiopian political landscape, where everything is seen through an ethnic lens, the lack of common decency could be a byproduct of excessive ethnic sentiments. In such contexts, divisive and dehumanizing rhetoric in music lyrics should not be ignored due to music's enormous power to enable artists to convey powerful messages that encourage their listeners to act, sometimes violently.

Conclusion

Against the backdrop of the Ethiopian political landscape, which (i) has significantly shifted recently and (ii) is the site of highly contesting nationalisms, this study analyzed songs selected from across three regions and a city administration and identified salient political themes in them. Nationalism, patriotism, resistance, speaking truth to power, poverty and maladministration, and celebration of triumph are the major themes identified. The findings show that music has

---

[6] The phrase was used by McCoy, 2009.

become a platform where claims and counterclaims have been made about the future of the country. Some of the songs analyzed are situated in political frames that have to do with distinct kinds of nationalisms. Songs from Oromia, Tigray, and Amhara, both from before and after the 2018 political change, strongly voiced ethno-nationalistic sentiments. They accentuated their respective ethnic communities' unity and invincibility, prided themselves in their ethnic identities, and strongly resisted real or perceived enemies that threaten their communities. They also expressed resentment, both past and present, against groups they identified as enemies to their causes. Songs by artists based in Addis Ababa and beyond an ethno-regional enclave advocated for a united Ethiopia and mostly portrayed ethnic nationalism as divisive, violent, and an existential threat to the country. They depicted Ethiopian nationalism as remedial to the dire consequences of the excessive emphasis on ethnicity that still haunts the country. Songs in this category also evoke patriotism, especially in the face of a foreign enemy.

Songs by artists from the Amhara region ardently celebrate their roots in Amhara and raise some political questions of ethnic Amhara. At the same time, they appeal to Ethiopian nationalism, in an inextricably linked manner, by proudly invoking the three colors of Ethiopia's flag as something they would sacrifice their lives for. They consider being Ethiopian an integral part of being Amhara, and celebrate both.

Before the political changes of early 2018, when protests engulfed much of Oromia and Amhara, two of the songs selected from the Oromia region strongly resisted ongoing government brutality and the singers used their music to call the youth to action. In the same period, one Tigrigna song lamented poverty and bad governance while another song from the same region expressed fear of the coming of a difficult time for the Tigrayans. In the aftermath of the political change, songs selected from Oromia and Amhara showed celebratory reactions and continued ethno-nationalist sentiment. Tigrigna songs selected from this period showed a heightened Tigrayan nationalism involving a resistance frame. The aftermath of the political change is fraught with ethnic tensions with a massive blow to cohesion among ethnic communities. Songs from Addis Ababa continued to reflect these ills and courageously advocate for national unity.

The study shows that popular political music can be a strong reflection of the political environment in which it finds itself and can be used as a powerful tool to challenge the status quo. In that sense, popular songs are fields of contestation between overarching political questions of the day. In turn, the exclusivity reflected in popular songs from certain regions could further fragment and polarize the polity, which is evident in the current Ethiopian political landscape.

References

Abdi, A. A. (2019). Ethiopia's Burgeoning Democratic Transition: New Glamour or New Statesmanship Gimmicks? *Hungarian Journal of African Studies [Afrika Tanulmányok], 13*(5), 13–31.

Admas Music. (2019, April 1). *Tikue Woldu - Tigray Milibama (Official Video) | Ethiopian Tigrigna Music* [Video]. YouTube. https://www.youtube.com/watch?v=P_j2kHBAWII

Alter, A. (2017). National Spaces and Global Imagination: 'Ethiopian Sounds' around the World and in Australia. *Musicology Australia, 39*(1), 15–28. https://doi.org/10.1080/08145857.2017.1332972

Amnesty International. (2017, February 22). *Amnesty International Report 2016/17.* https://www.refworld.org/docid/58b033ffa.html

Araya, M. (2005). Contemporary Ethiopia in the Context of the Battle of Adwa, 1896. In P. Milkias & G. Metaferia (Eds.), *The Battle of Adwa: Reflections on Ethiopia's Historic Victory Against European Colonialism* (pp. 239–252). United States: Algora Publishing.

Betreyohannes, S. (2010). Scholarship on Ethiopian Music: Past, Present and Future Prospects. *African Study Monographs, 41,* 19–34.

Beyene, Z. (2019). From an Emperor to the Derg and Beyond: Examining the Intersections of Music and Politics. In U. Onyebadi (Ed.), *Music and Messaging in the African Political Arena* (pp. 1–21). Hershey, PA: IGI Global. https://doi.org/10.4018/978-1-5225-7295-4

Braun, V., & Clarke, V. (2012). Thematic Analysis. In H. Cooper, P. M. Camic, D. L. Long, A. T. Panter, D. Rindskopf, & K. J. Sher (Eds.), *APA handbook of research methods in psychology, Vol 2: Research designs: Quantitative, qualitative, neuropsychological, and biological* (pp. 57–71). https://doi.org/10.1037/13620-004

Chala, E. (2017). *Ethiopia's Music of Resistance Stays Strong, Despite Repression.* Global Voices. https://advox.globalvoices.org/2017/07/19/ethiopias-music-of-resistance-stays-strong-despite-repression/

Cochrane, L., & Kefale, A. (2018–2019). Discussing the 2018/19 Changes in Ethiopia: Asnake Kefale. *NokokoPod, 3,* 1–16.

Cochrane, L., & Zewde, B. (2018–2019). Discussing the 2018/19 Changes in Ethiopia: Bahru Zewde. *NokokoPod, 1,* 1–16.

Côté, T. (2011). Popular Musicians and Their Songs as Threats to National Security: A World Perspective. *The Journal of Popular Culture, 44*(4), 732–754. https://doi.org/10.1111/j.1540-5931.2011.00860.x

Djerrahian, G. (2018). The 'end of diaspora' is just the beginning: Music at the crossroads of Jewish, African, and Ethiopian diasporas in Israel. *African and Black Diaspora: An International Journal, 11*(2), 161–173. https://doi.org/10.1080/17528631.2017.1394602

Elavsky, C. M. (2009). United as ONE: Live 8 and the Politics of the Global Music Media Spectacle. *Journal of Popular Music Studies, 21*(4), 384–410. https://doi.org/10.1111/j.1533-1598.2009.01209.x

Entman, R. M. (1993). Framing: Toward Clarification of a Fractured Paradigm. *Journal of Communication, 43*(4), 51–58. https://doi.org/10.1111/j.1460-2466.1993.tb01304.x

Fisher, J., & Gebrewahd, M. T. (2019). 'Game over'? Abiy Ahmed, the Tigrayan People's Liberation Front and Ethiopia's political crisis. *African Affairs, 118*(470), 194–206. https://doi.org/10.1093/afraf/ady056

Fürsich, E. (2009). In Defense of Textual Analysis: Restoring a challenged method for journalism and media studies. *Journalism Studies, 10*(2), 238–252. https://doi.org/10.1080/14616700802374050

Gebremariam, S. B. (2018). The Azmari Tradition in Addis Ababa: Change and Continuity. *Northeast African Studies, 18*(1–2), 31–57.

Golden Ethio Music. (2019, Oct 3). *Caalaa Bultume - WAGGADHAN NU GA'I - New Ethiopian Oromo Music 2019 [Official Video]* [Video]. YouTube. https://www.youtube.com/watch?v=cYtHVpHT4OU

Heni Tube. (2019, April 12). *Mehari Degefaw - Gitem Alegn | ግጠም አለኝ - New Ethiopian Music 2019 (Official Video)* [Video]. YouTube. https://www.youtube.com/watch?v=uORB6yJ-CQg

Hope Music Ethiopia. (2016, August 15). *Solomon Demle - Fetenegn (ፈተነኝ) - New Ethiopian Music 2016 (Official Video)* [Video]. https://www.youtube.com/watch?v=wUJ2KHISS4c

Horne, F. (2016, August 13). *Ethiopia Forces Kill 'Up to 100' Protesters*. Human Rights Watch. https://www.hrw.org/news/2016/08/13/ethiopian-forces-kill-100-protesters

Human Rights Watch. (2016, September 8). *Joint letter to UN Human Rights Council on Ethiopia*. https://www.hrw.org/news/2016/09/08/joint-letter-un-human-rights-council-ethiopia

Jemal, B. M. (2020). The depoliticisation of two competing nationalisms and the introduction of democratic Meritopianism as a possible way out for Ethiopia. *Journal of Contemporary African Studies, 38*(2), 205–220. https://doi.org/10.1080/02589001.2020.1774520

Kebede, A. (1971). The Music of Ethiopia: Its Development and Cultural Setting [Unpublished doctoral dissertation]. Wesleyan University, Ann Arbor, USA.

Lavers, T. (2018). Responding to land-based conflict in Ethiopia: The land rights of ethnic minorities under federalism. *African Affairs, 117*(468), 462–484. https://doi.org/10.1093/afraf/ady010

Levine, D. N. (2014). Battle of Adwa as a "Historic" Event. *Ethiopian Review*. https://www.ethiopianreview.com/index/2006

Liham Melody. (2018, April 28). *Solomon Yikunoamlak - Haregu 1 / New Ethiopian Tigrigna Music (Official Audio)* [Video]. YouTube. https://www.youtube.com/watch?v=8h0o6k-hUoY

Lulseged, E. (1994). Social, Economic and Political Discontent in Ethiopia as reflected in contemporary Amharic Songs (Mid 1950s-Mid 1970s). *Journal of Ethiopian Studies, 27*(2), 21–43.

Marye, H. S. (2019). Ityoṗyawinnät and Addis Abäba's Popular Music Scene. *Aethiopica, 96*–123. https://doi.org/10.15460/aethiopica.22.0.1048

Matshanda, N. T. (2020). Ethiopian reforms and the resolution of uncertainty in the Horn of Africa state system. *South African Journal of International Affairs, 27*(1), 25–42. https://doi.org/10.1080/10220461.2020.1736139

McCoy, J. (2009). Making Violence Ordinary: Radio, Music and the Rwandan Genocide. *African Music, 8*(3), 85–96.

Minew Shewa Tube. (2018, September 29). *Ethiopian Music: Jambo Jote (Belba) - New Ethiopian Oromo Music 2018(Official Video)* [Video]. YouTube. https://www. youtube.com/watch?v=QY5bZ9q5a3Y

Minew Shewa Tube. (2020a, October 2). *Ethiopian Music: Getish Mamo (Zufanu New)* ጌቲሽ ማሞ (ዙፋኑ ነው መሰል) - *New Ethiopian Music 2020(Official Video)* [Video]. YouTube. https://www.youtube.com/watch?v=nVZH_twyijM

Minew Shewa Tube. (2020b, December 2). *Ethiopian Music: Dagne Walle (Leblebew)* ዳኜ ዋለ (ለብለበው) - *New Ethiopian Music 2020(Official Video)* [Video]. YouTube. https://www.youtube.com/watch?v=t8t0zFgtQtM

Munkittrick, D. (2010). Music as Speech: A First Amendment Category unto Itself. *Federal Communications Law Journal, 62*(3), 665–690. https://www. repository.law.indiana.edu/fclj/vol62/iss3/6/

Onyebadi, U. (2018). Political Messages in African Music: Assessing Fela Anikulapo-Kuti, Lucky Dube and Alpha Blondy. *Humanities, 7*(4), 129. https:// doi.org/10. 3390/h7040129

Orgeret, K. S. (2008). When will the Daybreak Come? *Nordicom Review, 29*(2), 231–244. https://doi.org/10.1515/nor-2017-0188

Oromp3. (2017, December 10). *Hachalu Hundessa: Geerarsa Ajaa'ibaa! ** NEW 2017 Oromo Music* [Video]. YouTube. https://www.youtube.com/watch?v=i8 iVN8OBHSU

Perullo, A. (2011). Politics and popular song: Youth, authority, and popular music in East Africa. *African Music: Journal of the International Library of African Music, 9*(1), 87–115. https://doi.org/10.21504/amj.v9i1.1759

Reese, D. (2001). Prologue—Framing Public Life: A Bridging Model for Media Research. In Reese, S. D., Gandy, O. H., & Grant, A. E. (Eds.), *Framing Public Life: Perspectives on Media and Our Understanding of the Social World* (pp. 7–32). Mahwah, New Jersey: Lawrence Erlbaum Associates, Inc. https://doi.org/ 10.4324/9781410605689

Semay Ent. (2020, June 27). *Brhane Haile -Knezarbom ena (ብሂርሃኒ ከነዛርቦም እና), New Tigrigna music 2020 (Official Video)* [Video]. YouTube. https://www.youtube. com/watch?v=jyRmrpT-YgE

Shelemay, K. K. (2006). Ethiopian Musical Invention in Diaspora: A Tale of Three Musicians. *Diaspora: A Journal of Transnational Studies, 15*(2), 303–320. https://doi.org/10.1353/dsp.2011.0067

Shelemay, K. K. (2016). 'Traveling Music:' Mulatu Astatke and the Genesis of Ethiopian Jazz. In P. V. Bohlman & G. Plastino (Eds.), *Jazz Worlds/World Jazz* (pp. 239–257). Chicago: University of Chicago Press.

Smith, J. A. (2017). Textual analysis. In J. Matthes, C. S. Davis, & R. F. Potter (Eds.), *The International Encyclopedia of Communication Research Methods* (pp. 1-7). John Wiley & Sons, Inc. https://doi.org/10.1002/9781118901731. iecrm0248

Tadeg, M. A. (2016). Freedom of Expression and the Media Landscape in Ethiopia: Contemporary Challenges. *UB Journal of Media Law & Ethics, 5*(1/2), 69-99. https://law.ubalt.edu/academics/publications/medialaw/pdfs_ only/Vol.%205%20No.1-2%20Complete.pdf

Tafarii, I. (2016). *Itti Muddi*. Raya Studio.

Taye, B. A. (2017). Ethnic Federalism and Conflict in Ethiopia. *African Journal on Conflict Resolution, 17*(2), 41–66.

Tazebew, T. (2021). Amhara nationalism: The empire strikes back. *African Affairs, 120*(479), 297–313. https://doi.org/10.1093/afraf/adaa029

Teddy Afro. (2020, August 3). *TEDDY AFRO - DEMO BE ABAY - ይም በአባይ - [New! Official Single 2020] - With Lyrics.* YouTube. https://www.youtube.com/watch?v=btuC2IfwmfQ

Tenaadam. (2018, January 25). *Fasil Demoz - Manenete | ማንነቴ - New Ethiopian Music (Official Video)* [Video]. YouTube. https://www.youtube.com/watch?v=Riox5xJ9wc4

Tigray Online. (2017, February 2017). *New Tigringa Song 2017 by Mulugeta Kahsay Yikurkoheni Allo* [Video]. YouTube. https://www.youtube.com/watch?v=3Ou77NN04HA

Weber, A. (2018). Abiy Superstar - reformer or revolutionary? Hope for transformation in Ethiopia. (SWP Comment, 26/2018). Berlin: Stiftung Wissenschaft und Politik -SWP- Deutsches Institut für Internationale Politik und Sicherheit. https://nbn-resolving.org/urn:nbn:de:0168-ssoar-58461-1

Webster-Kogen, I. (2013). Engendering homeland: Migration, diaspora and feminism in Ethiopian music. *Journal of African Cultural Studies, 25*(2), 183–196. https://doi.org/10.1080/13696815.2013.793160

Webster-Kogen, I. (2014). Song Style as Strategy: Nationalism, Cosmopolitanism and Citizenship in The Idan Raichel Project's Ethiopian-influenced Songs. *Ethnomusicology Forum, 23*(1), 27–48. https://doi.org/10.1080/17411912.2013.879034

Wernick, A. (2021, February 8). *Joe Biden has called for unity. The African concept of Ubuntu offers a path.* The World. https://www.pri.org/stories/2021-02-08/joe-biden-has-called-unity-african-concept-ubuntu-offers-path

Yehunie Belay. (2016, September 6). *Yehunie Belay - SEKEN BEL | ሰኸን በል! NEW Music 2016.* YouTube. https://www.youtube.com/watch?v=OsGoqogXwdw

Yusuf, S. (2019, December 9). Drivers of Ethnic Conflict in Contemporary Ethiopia. *Institute for Security Studies (Monograph 202).* https://issafrica.org/research/monographs/drivers-of-ethnic-conflict-in-contemporary-ethiopia

Yusuf, S. (2020, September 21). Constitutional Design Options for Ethiopia: Managing ethnic divisions. *Institute for Security Study (Monograph 204).* https://issafrica.org/research/monographs/constitutional-design-options-for-ethiopia-managing-ethnic-divisions

Zeleke, A. (2019). Tamenal. On *Hid Zeyerat.* Abush Zeleke.

Zerai, A. (2019). Freedom of Mobility in an Ethnic-Based Federal Structure: The Ethiopian Quandary. In *Ethiopia: Social and Political Issues* (pp. 1–25). New York: Nova Science Publishers, Inc.

Appendix: List of Songs

Addis Ababa (Beyond Ethno-Regional Enclave):

1. Abush Zeleke – *Tamenal*
2. Getish Mamo - *Zufanu New*

3. Teddy Afro – *Demo Be Abbay*
4. Yehunie Belay – *Seken Bel*

Amhara:

5. Dagne Walle – *Leblebew*
6. Fasil Demoz – *Maninete*
7. Mehari Degefaw – *Gitem Alegn*
8. Solomon Demle – *Fetenegn*

Oromia:

9. Caalaa Bultume - *Waggadhan Nu Ga'I*
10. Hachalu Hundessa – *Jirtu*
11. Ittiiqaa Tafarii - *Itti Muddi*
12. Jambo Jote – *Belba*

Tigray:

13. Brhane Haile - *Knezarbom Ena*
14. Mulugeta Kahsay - *Yikurkoheni Allo*
15. Solomon Yikunoamlak – *Haregu*
16. Tikue Woldu - *Tigray Milibama*

CHAPTER 5

Interpreting Feminism through sounds of resilience in the U.S.: An analytical approach to music from the 19th to the 21st centuries

Ngozi Akinro

Texas Wesleyan University, USA

Jenny J. Dean

Texas Wesleyan University, USA

Abstract

This chapter explores sociopolitical and sociocultural messages in songs by popular female artists from the 19th through 21st century in the U.S. It adopts the identifying characteristics of the four waves of feminism and the framing theory as the backdrop for examining how the challenges faced by women have been highlighted and emphasized over time. Using qualitative textual analysis, this chapter explores the dynamics of gender, music, and messaging from the lyrics of 12 songs by 12 female artists from the United States. The chapter presents music as a platform through which the characteristics of the four waves of feminism were expressed and dominant patriarchal ideologies that mostly inhibit women are challenged. Based on the themes in the lyrics of the selected songs, this chapter suggests that although the songs across the time period convey different messages, overall they were all focused on advancing the role and place of the female gender in society. This chapter recognizes music as a tool to convey resilient messages and argues that female artists use their music as platforms for communicating messages that challenge hegemonic narratives and spread positivity about femininity.

Keywords: Feminism, framing theory, textual analysis, women's rights, music, female artists, hegemony, grounded theory

***

Introduction

Music has often played an important role toward social change and political movement in the world and specifically in the United States (U.S.), taking on an inspirational role for a group or for an individual toward social change. For instance, Eyerman (2002) refers to the American civil rights movement as the "singing movement" (p. 446), in which the song, "We shall overcome," played an important role in expressing political messages and hope. For women, music has served as a catalyst towards liberation. In her study, Arrow (2007) captured the role of the song, "I Am Woman" by Helen Reddy in the early 1970s for providing "needed clarity and inspiration" for women. One interviewee in the study mentioned that the song was "the 'lightbulb' moment, the instant a new set of possibilities—women's liberation—became visible" (p. 213). Today, this song is seen as a "feminist anthem."

Music is a powerful tool for shaping public opinion and even promoting political participation (Street et al., 2008). According to Merriam (1964), songs are critical towards leading and following political and social movements. In their study about the use of music for political participation, Akinro et al. (2019) note that music was used in "concerted attempts to persuade Nigerians through danceable songs to engage in the socio-political environment" (p. 144). Through music, artists are able to emphasize certain narratives that express social reality. Music is a key method of expression of one's identity and politics while acting as a catalyst for the exploration of the politics of identity (Hess, 2019). In fact, as it relates to women, Roberts (1994) opines that Queen Latifah's rap focuses on the importance of women and demands equal treatment of all women. Songwriters like Queen Latifah present the audience with "moments of resistance to dominant exploitative images of women" (Roberts, 1994, p. 245).

While several studies analyze music that is related to the civil rights movement (Rose, 2007) or music adopted as a feminist anthem, few of them take an in-depth approach to examining political messaging in music targeted toward women's liberation and the women's rights movement. This chapter aims to close that gap and extend the role of music targeted toward social change by gender, beyond the women's rights movement and into the society of today.

Overall, this chapter explores the dynamics of gender, music, and messaging. It focuses on providing evidence to show how music might be used to inspire social change for women, before the women's rights movement until present, redefine femininity, educate, and raise awareness about feminine social struggles (Rosenthal, 2001). Based on the various waves of feminism over the decades, this study explores changes in the focus of the music across genres.

The authors explore and comparatively analyze themes across musical genres identified by the characteristics of each wave of the feminism movement, specifically Folk, Blues, R&B, Hip-hop, and to a lesser extent, rap.

Although there is insufficient evidence that each wave of feminism explored in this chapter has a direct influence on the songs selected for this study, the chapter adopted the characteristics of the feminist movement for each period to examine the selected songs and make inferences on how they may shape perceptions and engender social change.

Framing Theory, Music and Social Movement

Framing theory is a recognized and well-used theory that is built on the concepts of emphasis and de-emphasis of elements of reality. Various scholars have explained framing theory and the concept of frames to define social issues and situations (Goffman, 1974), as well as brought attention to the influential power of frames on individual decision-making. Entman (1991, 1993), in his quantitative and qualitative works, emphasized the deliberateness in emphasizing or deemphasizing elements of reality, which can be applied to any communicative content. As Entman (1993) puts it, framing is "select[ing] some aspects of a perceived reality and mak[ing] them more salient in a communicating text, in such a way as to promote a particular problem definition, causal interpretation, moral evaluation, and/or treatment recommendation for the item described" (p. 52). The framing process involves message construction, representation, and analysis aimed at influencing the audience's behaviors (Matthes, 2012). While framing emphasizes aspects of reality, it also helps with the creation of shared meanings for a group of people. In this case, it is for women and society at large.

The framing process indicates a connection between communicators, the audience, social content, and the social context. While the audience plays roles in the framing process, it is important to note that the information begins with the content creator who actively sets the reference frames for the audience (Tuchman, 1978). Hence, this chapter focuses on the frames and messages in the songs analyzed and the ideas they convey. Music is therefore conceptualized here as communicative and persuasive texts that emphasize women's struggles, identities, and roles during the period of the release of the songs. In addition, the authors identified a variety of frames around music published in similar periods, discussing them according to their relationships to one another as far as thematic structures, messaging, adjectives, and categorizations.

Social movements are significant for social and cultural change. Eyerman and Jamison (1998) note that it is through political and cultural change that social movements take place, resulting in "traditions, music, artistic expression - to the action repertoires of political struggle" (p. 7). These movements which combine culture and politics lead to social and cultural change, acting as catalysts that may result in "...changes in values, ideas, and ways of life" (Eyerman & Jamison, 1998, p. 7). Further, Eyerman and Jamison (1998) suggest that social movements and expression is "a kind of cognitive praxis" (p. 7). They argue that their significance is more than just political, but also cultural (Darnovsky et al., 1995; Eyerman & Jamison, 1998).

Social movement frames are defining frames. Through music, artists create meaning and frame a narrative in lyrics. Their narratives revolve around how specific grievances may give meaning to a claim (Tarrow, 1994). Artists adopt frames as strategic tools to spur the audience into taking actions aimed at social change. Snow et al. (1986) refer to frames adopted by movement organizations as collective action frames. They carry potentials to motivate a group of people or community into taking suggestive action based on the selective perspectives to which they are exposed (Tarrow, 1994).

Social movement frames are informed by existing situations of injustice as well as structural inequalities. Their audience may connect to these frames through shared experiences that are simplified and problematized by movement groups in order to motivate collective actors for change.

According to Snow and Benford (1992), social movement frames are "an interpretive schemata that simplifies and condenses the situation by selectively punctuating and encoding objects, situations, events, experiences and sequences of actions within one's present or past environment" (p. 137). This indicates that through selective framing, artists may express socio-cultural and socio-political issues towards their audiences' emotions. As the audience participates in the songs, they may adopt the perspectives of the artists and share in their goals.

The singing movement for feminism began in the late 1870s and has continued through to today (Eyerman, 2002). For Eyerman (2002), music is a cultural artifact, seen and understood through collective performance that has linked the feminism movement from past, present, and into the future, as well as many other movements. This is key because even the distant observer, DuBois (2005) suggests, maintains the collective memory of songs. This indicates that the feminist movement goes hand-in-hand with songs that have kept the movement alive, and enriched the lives of women over the years.

Feminism in its entirety is built on these systems of political, social, and cultural change. Although these movements tend to be dispersed in the literature as suggested by Eyerman and Jamison (1998), this chapter attempts to bring them together.

Feminists Movements and the Waves of Feminism

The concept of feminism is built on the ideas of universalism, power, equality, and identity. This study attempts to emphasize these ideas in the waves of feminism in order to build understanding of their characteristics and adopt them in the analysis of music by female artists in the United States.

Feminism is not amenable to a specific and globally acceptable definition, as it comes in different waves through different experiences and history. Feminist issues have been passed down from generation to generation through the unfinished agendas left behind by its proponents (Hewitt, 2010). It is impossible to pinpoint the exact start of the first, second, third, or fourth waves of feminism, rather, the political, social, and cultural issues of the time experienced by women and emphasized across mainstream media have shaped what has been known as feminism waves. It is important to note that the feminist movement started much earlier than is often noted in history books (Hewitt, 2010). Each movement has been multifaceted and constitutes a campaign for women's rights in the nineteenth century through today.

Like a wave in the ocean, these different movements did not occur in isolation, but interacted with one another (Hewitt, 2010). The date most often given for the first wave of feminism is the 1840s. This coincides with the setting of the agenda for the women's rights movement which was put into motion at Seneca Falls, New York during the first women's rights convention in 1848 (Hewitt, 2010; Imbornoni, 2021). After much discussion and debate, the Declaration of Sentiments was developed, and outlined the issues that would set the agenda for the women's rights movement. This event was significant because it brought women and men together out of isolation (Hewitt, 2010). Out of this spun the first National Women's Rights Convention, held yearly until 1860 (Imbornoni, 2021). Beginning with the need for equality in opportunities and access for women, the first wave of feminism defined itself through women's suffrage. However, one of the key overview texts in this field about the women's movement that emerged during the 1800s is described as "a more multi-issued campaign for women's equality" (Hole & Levine, 1990, p. 452).

The 1800s saw social reform movements focused philosophically on individual freedom, universal education, and the "rights of man" (Hole & Levine, 1990, p. 453). The first wave of what is known as modern feminism in the U.S. was built on this emphasis. It capitalized on the abolition movement of the 1830s. The need for emancipation and freedom propelled the ideology for the first-wave suffrage; it was based on women's experiences from pursuing the abolitionist agenda. While women were actively involved in the fight to abolish slavery, research indicates that women did not receive equal respect as men (Hole & Levine, 1990). Early feminists explored concerns about the assumptions of men's natural superiority. Their work also included challenging the social institutions that predicated and promoted such assumptions, such as religious fanaticism, cultural stigmatizations, and social and legal aspects of marriage. Furthermore, their work aimed to challenge stereotypical assumptions like requirements for what is considered "proper" female behavior and attitude. They focused on equal pay for equal work. The women also enacted state legislative reforms on women's rights to properties, divorce, abortion, children guardianship, and rights within non-legislative partnerships. In addition, the activists also focused on domestic and sexual abuses by men, as a result of intoxication, hence promoting temperance. They advanced dress reform and women's suffrage (Hole & Levine, 1990; Kroløkke & Sørensen, 2006). However, after a deliberate exclusion of women from the U.S. Constitution after the Civil War and the abolition of slavery, women's quest for suffrage was strengthened (Hole & Levine, 1990). By August 26, 1920, women had gained the right to vote under the 19th Amendment to the constitution (Hewitt, 2010; Imbornoni, 2021). Despite these efforts, millions of Asian Americans, Mexican Americans, and Native Americans were denied access until the 1940s. For others, such as the African American community, most were not able to go to the polls to vote until the 1965 Voting Rights Act (Hewitt, 2010).

The 1920s to 1950s recorded a shift to Blues and Jazz music sung by African Americans, particularly women, including "Ma" Rainey, Bessie Smith, and Billie Holiday, which Davis (1998) argues has its own roots within Black Feminism. Davis (1998) writes, "what is most interesting—and provocative—about the bodies of work each of these women left behind is the ways in which hints of feminist attitudes emerge from their music through fissures of patriarchal discourses" (p. xi). It was not until the 1950s and 1960s that there was a resurgence in the women's movement. Some scholars argue that the second wave emerged from the emancipation movements in the post-war era, including the U.S. civil rights movement, the Black Power movement, student protests, anti-Vietnam war movements, lesbian and gay movements, and the Miss America Pageants protests (Gordon, 2013). Women's concerns about media coverage during these movements reenergized the women's rights movement (Kroløkke & Sørensen, 2006). The women, their goals, and actions were minimally covered and often negative, thus damaging to the cause and the women's reputations. However, the new wave of the feminist movement bordered on issues of cultural and political inequalities. Some scholars indicated that the unique and personal struggles of individual women by race, class, or age were significant drivers of this wave (Amos & Parmar, 1984). The second wave was mobilized by the 1970s and continued through the 1980s (Ferree & Hess, 1985). Between movements, social change altered women's interests. The need for diversity exposed the movement to the non-homogenized experiences of patriarchal oppression and the complex and context-bound demarcations of privilege and subjugation (King, 1988).

The third wave of feminism focused on three main paradigms— "multicultural inclusion, identity politics, intersectionality— as its dominant narrative" (Fernandes, 2010, p. 99). Fernandes (2010) notes that the third wave of feminism was much more complicated than generally appreciated. It marked the move away from second wave feminism, which was erroneously associated with only the rights of the white middle class women, to " a new phase in which feminists of color and questions of race and gender were now included" (Fernandes, 2010, p. 100).

What is referred to as the fourth and new wave of modern feminism, some scholars suggest, began in 2012. In 2013, Beyoncé declared herself a "modern-day feminist," recasting feminism in a positive light and continuing to build upon itself, a movement that had stalled since the momentum of the 1960s and 1970s (Chancer, 2019). Beyoncé's work has "helped to spread feminist ideas and destigmatize 'feminism' itself to people across races, classes, and sexualities…" (Chancer, 2019, p. 137). For example, singers like Beyoncé, Taylor Swift, and actress Jennifer Lawrence, have shown support for the f-word (Chancer, 2019; Keller & Ringrose, 2015). With focus on issues such as sexual harassment, body shaming, and rape culture, this new wave is linked to high profile incidents that gained popularity on social media platforms. This new wave is characterized by a fight for social justice, of which the "Me Too" movement, which was launched in 2006, was reportedly a part of (Britannica, 2021).

On the different waves of feminism, Fernandes (2010) writes: "Feminist thought, in retrospect, requires a conception of history that can contain both the insights of the past and the potential breakthroughs of the future within the messy, unresolved contestations of political and intellectual practice in the present" (p. 114). Within these waves, the authors of the present study argue, is how the frames of music by female artists intersect with society. This chapter suggests that through their songs, the artists attempted to redefine femininity, to educate and raise awareness about feminine social struggles (Rosenthal, 2001).

The combination of framing theory and feminist literature suggests the need for female recognition, struggles, and power control that has moved over various phases of the feminist movement, both from a political standpoint to a sociocultural perspective. From the rights to be recognized and suffrage, to that of identity, personal and contextual politics, this chapter challenges the assumption about frame staticity. There is evidence in the music produced by the singers that feminist frames are not static, but have evolved over time based on the sociopolitical and sociocultural influences of each epoch. Some of these influences that include sexual orientation, status, race, class, cultural hegemony, patriarchy and perhaps, normative assumptions, have impacted how music by feminist artists may have changed over time (Lather, 1991).

This chapter therefore combines the feminist movement and framing theory to examine how female artists used their music to represent women issues during their time of release, as well as challenge sociocultural and sociopolitical limitations to women. In addition, it assesses the themes in the music by the identified female artists from the 19th to 21st centuries and provides evidence to demonstrate how the musical focus has changed over time.

Method

This chapter adopted the textual analysis method to examine the meanings in the music by U.S. females from the 19th to 21st century. Textual analysis is a qualitative method that allows for studying, analyzing, and interpreting texts. It also allows for drawing inferences and meanings from texts such as music, films, advertisements, poetry, etc. (McKee, 2003). Fairclough (2003) suggests that textual analysis is a good instrument for studying small volumes of text. It also allows the researcher to select texts for study (Onyebadi, 2018). The use of the textual analysis instrument may suffer from a subjective interpretation by the researcher which may not align with the content creator (McKee, 2003). However, as Bogue (2007) suggests, the method is quite reliable and appropriate, especially when an in-depth and holistic approach is adopted, considering the historical period, context, and place of the text (Onyebadi & Mbunyuza-Memani, 2017).

This study used a purposive sampling method. Music selections were based on artists' fame and music popularity over time, with consideration of diversity. The music choices were determined by an Internet search by period. After searching for popular female artists and activists for each wave from the 19th to the 21st centuries, their most popular songs were selected. The researchers only selected songs that support feminism and meet the scope of this paper, though they may have been written by someone else.

The songs selected for this study were also among the first 100 titles available for each era, based on the researchers' Internet searches. The fame of these artists also indicates potential for influence in their time, meaning they stand better chances of influencing sociopolitical and sociocultural behaviors in society. The choices speak to the potential impact of the songs and the artists within the period. Between the first major wave of feminism up to the 1920s and the normative second wave period, which was thought to begin in the 1950s and 60s, there was a gap in feminist-oriented music. This was because the movement was fragmented (Hewitt, 2010).

From a total of 25 songs preselected for this study, 12 songs by 12 artists were finally analyzed. The songs and the artists include; Harriet H. Robinson- Song: "Columbia's Daughters" (1888); Marilyn Major- Song: "Ballad of a Working Mother" (1900s); Charlotte Perkins Gilman- Song: "The Women are Coming" (1913); Lesley Gore- Song: "You Don't Own Me" (1963); Aretha Franklin- Song: "Respect" (1967); Helen Reddy- Song: "I Am Woman" (1972); Queen Latifah- Song: "U.N.I.T.Y." (1993); Shania Twain- Song: "Man! I Feel Like a Woman" (1997); Alicia Keys- Song: "Superwoman" (2007); Beyoncé Featuring Chimamanda Ngozi Adichie- Song: "***Flawless" (2014); Meghan Trainor- Song: "All About That Bass" (2014); and Taylor Swift- Song: "The Man" (2019).

To examine these songs, the authors relied on the grounded theory approach (Charmaz, 2006; Glaser, 1978; Glaser & Strauss, 1967). The grounded theory "consists of systematic, yet flexible guidelines for collecting and analyzing qualitative data to construct theories 'grounded' in the data themselves" (Charmaz, 2006, p. 2). This method was used because it allows the researcher to shape and reshape their data collection, resulting in a more refined set of data collected (Charmaz, 2006; Glaser & Strauss, 1967). Like any method, this method is simply one tool for finding understanding, though it does not provide any automatic insight (Charmaz, 2006). The goal of using the grounded theory was to generate, mine, and make sense of the data (Charmaz, 2006). Significant to this approach is that preconceived ideas and theories are not forced upon the data, but emerge organically (Charmaz, 2006).

By applying the grounded theory, the authors were in a position to assess the significance of how feminism and the framing theory offer a framework from which to examine this chapter's research focus. Charmaz (2006) notes that this approach gives an interpretive perspective to understanding the past and the present, but not its exact framing (Charmaz, 1995, 2000; Guba & Lincoln, 1994). This afforded the authors an opportunity to explore individual texts, in this case the songs' lyrics. The songs selected for this study were analyzed within the framework of four waves of feminism, with emphasis on the dominant frames in the analysis as set out below.

Community and Sociopolitical Frame

This category included phrases that charged women to unite in solidarity and fight for women's rights, justice, and freedom. Examples in this category include lyrics such as "Hark the sound of myriad voices, Rising in their might!" in Harriet H. Robinson's "Columbia's Daughters" (1888). Pronouns used in such songs are often plural and sometimes third person such as "they," "their," and "them." This study considered identifiable evidence suggesting a call to action in the fight for women's rights, equality, justice, and freedom. Songs categorized here show evidence of negotiating women's visibility, will, and importance in the society. Most of the songs focused on women's rights and the suffrage movement, pay equality, justice, and freedom.

Individual and Sociocultural Frame

Songs coded into this broad theme, emphasize a belief in and love for self and self-identity. Coding for this category include texts such as in Meghan Trainor's "All About That Bass" (2014). The songs use singular pronouns such as "I" and show focus on self. Songs categorized here emphasize ideas about societal relationships and perceptions as well.

There is no claim about these categories being exhaustive. Rather, they were mostly evidenced in the songs and distinguished by the periods reviewed. The themes were used as a focal point for analysis of the song lyrics within the feminist movement and framing theory.

Analysis and Discussion

First Wave: 1800s - Early 1900s

Community and Sociopolitical Frame

Most of the songs in the period of first wave feminism and published between the mid-19th century to early 20th century emphasized a sense of community. While some of the songs functioned like anthems with a direct call to women, others emphasized other issues within the first wave of the feminist movement. Some of the songs drew attention to patriarchy as hindrance to women's progress and used pronouns such as "we" and "us" to suggest women's unity and togetherness in the struggle for women's rights. The music indicates dominant sub themes across the songs that highlight this frame.

Call to action for women's rights to vote and equality

Harriet H. Robinson's "Columbia's Daughters" (1888), published as music to *Hold The Fort*, presents women's suffrage in political terms. The suffrage song describes a multitude of women calling out for their rights. Using keywords such as freedom, liberty, great republic, and glorious nation, Robinson questions the greatness of the nation as she negotiates equality for women.

The song calls on society to listen to the sound of the women "rising in their might!" It begins with an action phrase: "Hark the sound of myriad voices," setting the stage to present women's togetherness and "rising" as a force that should be recognized. The song takes call to action a step further by calling on males to "help us." In this way, the fight is not for women alone, but a call for action across the country suggesting that everyone in the great nation of the

U.S. must be free to vote. "Columbia's Daughters" posits women's rights within constitutional perspectives, suggesting that women's rights should be a *standard*. Robinson sang:

> Raise the flag and plant the standard,
> Wave the signal still;
> Brothers, we must share your freedom,
> Help us, and we will.

For Robinson, women's freedom indicates liberty and must be seen as a fundamental human freedom and right. The song calls out the U.S. when it juxtaposes the greatness of the country and lack of freedom in the chorus, equating freedom for all as a prerequisite for a country's greatness. Without this right, the nation would fall as suggested in the lyrics below:

> O our country, glorious nation,
> Greatest of them all!
> Give unto thy daughters justice,
> Or thy pride will fall.

In "The Women are Coming" (1913), Charlotte Perkins Gilman also takes a political stance by calling out a false communal sense of care for women's participation in society. The song posits women and motherhood as positive. Taking it a notch further, the artist presents nurture as an overarching requirement for saving the world. Thus, she reclaims the power of motherhood as a redemptive frame.

Robinson and Gilman emphasize community in how their songs use plural pronouns, indicating the plight of women as a shared issue. Gilman also uses repetition to emphasize the subject. With this song, Gilman relays the power of the women's vote. To her, the women's vote is a force that must be acknowledged. She recognizes the power of women to be mothers, as well as serve the world, pushing the importance of voting forward. She repeats that:

> The women are coming to vote! to vote!
> The women are coming to vote! to vote!
> The women are coming, to set the world humming,
> The women are coming to vote! to vote!
> A million women are standing true,
> The banners of their faith unfurled;
> To show what mother power can do,
> To save the child and serve the world!

Both Robinson and Gilman emphasize strength in the united forces of women, focused on a shared goal - the women's right to vote.

Marilyn Major's "Ballad of a Working Mother" (1900s) reverses the narrative of the time by presenting women as providers. The song attacks the narrative of women as dependents and attempts to represent women's economic engagement. It captures the struggles of a working mother who must fend for her family in the absence of the father, yet must fight for a connection with her children. In this way, Major elevates the roles of women in the society beyond the domestic, and makes a case for pay equality. The song suggests that males and females experience similar struggles in the factory, yet while the female may outperform the male and receive less pay, females are told to "be happy, that my pay - it ain't too bad." The song, through the experiences of a hardworking and struggling mother, questions society as it calls for pay equality through the lyrics:

> Oh, I am a working mother,
> working hard to earn my way,
> In the fact'ry through the long dark night,
> I sleep near half the day,
> They say I should be happy,
> that my pay - it ain't too bad.
> They forget I am the only parent,
> that my kids have ever had.

Like Robinson, Major sought to share in what men already enjoyed. While Robinson asked for equality through suffrage, Major calls for workplace and pay equality.

Second Wave: 1950s - 1980s

Individual and Sociocultural Frame

The songs in this period take a personal tone and mainly challenge female disrespect. Some of the songs demand female recognition for their achievements and financial provisions. The songs use singular pronouns such as "I" to emphasize the women's personal identities and experiences.

Romance, Domestic Abuse, and Strength.

Lesley Gore's "You Don't Own Me" (1963) requests reciprocal treatment and respect from males. She emphasizes the rights to women's bodies in this song. Mostly, the song challenges the sociocultural definitions of male and female relationships and attempts to uplift the woman in a way that helps her own and appreciate her identity. She goes further to suggest that women should have independence and power in relationships as shown in the lyrics:

You don't own me
Don't try to change me in any way
You don't own me
Don't tie me down 'cause I'd never stay

Gore takes a personalized approach to emphasize women's equality. The song challenges the notion of the objectification and capitalization of women like properties. It highlights the need for equality of genders. The song requests:

And don't tell me what to do
Oh, don't tell me what to say
And please, when I go out with you
Don't put me on display

In "Respect" (1967), Aretha Franklin explores the concept of respect by gender. Franklin used a role change strategy for Otis Redding's song to suggest that women are deserving of respect. In this way, Franklin addresses a social and cultural understanding of male versus female relations and how women should be treated in relationships. Mostly, her demand for respect also draws from the economic abilities of the woman, who is a provider and the wiser, as she noted that "I'm about to give you all of my money."

Franklin pushes an individualized and personalized narrative of respect in a song that ends up as the second wave feminist anthem. She takes a song that was meant to be sung by a man and turns it into a ballad for women empowerment and to demand respect. Through changing the gender roles in this song, she challenges its original intent and the patriarchal belief about respect in the society. She sings:

All I'm askin' is for a little respect when you come home
(Just a little bit) Hey baby
(Just a little bit) when you get home
(Just a little bit) mister
(Just a little bit)

Helen Reddy's "I am Woman" (1972), which became a signature song of the women's liberation movement, presents the strength of a woman in yet a personalized form, similar to both Gore and Franklin. To Reddy, the woman should be listened to and revered. The lyrics expose the power of women through acclamation as the song negotiates identity definitions. Through this song, Reddy redefines womanhood as she artistically emphasizes the strengths of a woman. The song encourages women to appreciate their scars and pains as a definition of strength and to take pride in their abilities to go beyond to achieve their personal goals. Of course, this song stems from Reddy's progression in the music industry and the patriarchal challenges she encountered and overcame to reach the height of her career. Hence, she roars:

I am woman, hear me roar
In numbers too big to ignore
And I know too much to go back an' pretend
'cause I've heard it all before
And I've been down there on the floor
No one's ever gonna keep me down again

Reddy expresses a sense of determination and hope. As she sings from her experiences, she wears her pains with pride as a factor in how she has grown against all odds. She taps into the heroic and describes women as "invincible." This speaks to the resilience of women.

If I have to, I can do anything
I am strong (strong)
I am invincible (invincible)
I am woman

All three songs analyzed in the second wave emphasize the general theme of body ownership and explore identity politics in how they negotiate the place of the woman in relationships and the society at large. The artists explore the dynamics of power in how their songs are personalized. All three songs take a bold stance of dominance in their use of singular pronouns. Both Gore and Franklin use singular pronouns in a polite, loving, yet demanding way, while Reddy uses it in an emphatic way. The three songs represent the concept of the "personal is political," in how they portray women's personal issues of cultural and political inequalities, demanding respect in their own rights.

Third Wave: Mid-1990s to 2000s

Individual and Sociocultural Frame

Most of the songs in the third wave of feminism reinforce feminine strength and superpower. The songs combine first person pronouns such as "I" and "me" together with second person pronouns such as "you" and third person singular such as "she" when referencing the subject. The singular third person pronouns were used in such a way that the experience of an individual is generalized and projected to other women.

Strength, Self- love, and Awareness.

Queen Latifah's "U.N.I.T.Y." (1993) addresses misogyny, derogatory language, and disrespect for women. It questions the narrative that allows men to belittle women as a sign of desire and challenges domestic abuse, cat-calling, and street groping. Overall, the song challenges a sense of entitlement by the male gender, who through their actions, attempt to objectify women. Hence, Latifah reclaims the narrative and encourages women to reject sexual harassment. The song borders on cultural redefinitions and social change, referring to the African American community and the larger society. Latifah uses the song to call out questionable behaviors she had observed. She refuses derogatory words and patriarchal language among males and females and suggests it as a path to unity. Here, Latifah challenges street culture and the idea of a demur female, while presenting a black female who can care for themselves and protect themselves from sexual harassment. Latifah emphasizes the strength of women, suggesting that they should be credited more. Latifah admonishes women in her lyrics:

> U.N.I.T.Y., U.N.I.T.Y. that's a unity (You gotta let him know)
> (You go, come on, here we go)
> U.N.I.T.Y., love a black woman from (Uh, you gotta let him know)
> Infinity to infinity (You ain't a b***h or a ho, here we go)
> U.N.I.T.Y., U.N.I.T.Y. that's a unity (Uh, you gotta let him know)
> (Come on, come on, now here we go)
> U.N.I.T.Y., love a black man from (Yeah, you gotta let him know)
> Infinity to infinity (You ain't a b***h or a ho)

Continuing from the second wave, the personalized strategy in lyrics are evident in the third wave. Queen Latifah's "U.N.I.T.Y." (1993) also adopts an individual frame, which she does through a rap. This is exemplified in how she uses first person pronouns and narrates her actions after being disrespected by a man. However, the song also uses second person pronouns, in a way that addresses other women and encourages them not to settle for domestic abuse and disrespect, but instead suggests the power a woman possesses to free herself from an abusive relationship.

Shania Twain's "Man! I Feel Like a Woman" (1997) addresses sociocultural issues of patriarchy and stereotypical norms that may limit women's happiness. It encourages happiness and almost juxtaposes good time and fun with womanhood. The song emphasizes self-appreciation without political correctness. This suggests that women should not be bound by the standards society sets for them, rather, they should negotiate their own freedom on their own terms. The song breaks with the norm as Twain puts it:

> Oh-oh-oh, go totally crazy
> Forget I'm a lady
> Men's shirts, short skirts...
> Oh-oh-oh, I wanna be free

Yeah, to feel the way I feel
Man! I feel like a woman!

Twain's song deals with female empowerment from the individual perspective using female sass to convey her message. She stands up for women's rights while challenging society to step up and recognize feminine potential. For Twain, "the best thing about being a woman is the prerogative to have a little fun." Twain refutes female inhibitions in a way that transcends cultural norms when she suggests that women can wear men's shirts with short skirts, thus emphasizing free will. The song challenges patriarchy and urges social change. The lyrics encourage women to take control as it narrates below:

No inhibitions
Make no conditions
Get a little outta line
I ain't gonna act politically correct
I only wanna have a good time

In "Superwoman" (2007), Alicia Keys shines light on the strength of women. She explores the concept of resilience and the ability of women to find strength from within. She taps into the heroic as she uses the term "superwoman" to paint an imagery of a superhero, with an *S* "on my chest." Hence, she expresses that women can overcome social challenges. In this way, she reminds society to revere womanhood, while also reminding women of their power. This, therefore, expresses self-love as a dominant theme in this song:

Cause I am a Superwoman
Yes I am
Yes she is...
...I'm a Superwoman

Keys's song is also personalized and individualized. It speaks to feminine appreciation, using first person pronouns. As women sing the song, they can personalize it and have the words speak directly to them. She also uses third person singular pronouns – "yes she is" - as a way to reach all women, and also as a reaffirmation that women rise and shine irrespective of the messes they may find themselves in. This is further emphasized with the words: mother, women, and sisters. The lyrics empower the individual to maintain their identity, and also suggest a shared redemption of self-love. It creates an image that transforms pain and hurt into what is new and beautiful, leaving the brokenness behind. The song emphasizes the resilience of women, and their ability to grow stronger from their past experiences. In this way, the lyrics are hopeful, encouraging, yet reassuring of women's potential for greatness. This is Keys's call for social acceptance:

Gotta find the strength in me
Cause I am a Superwoman
Yes I am...
...Yes she is
For all the mothers fighting
For better days to come
And all my women, all my women sitting here trying
To come home before the sun
And all my sisters
Coming together
Say yes I will
Yes I can
'Cause I am a Superwoman

The three songs promote the ideas of self-awareness and empowerment. The songs define new dimensions of femininity as they break with stereotypical definitions. In this way, they promote a sense of reclaimed identity. While all three songs reinforce the image of a woman who can take care of themselves and are sufficient in their own identities, Keys continues to reimagine the woman as a beautiful and adequate emergence of all of her experiences. In Keys's sense, the woman can overcome and rise above her challenges. She represents the female body as a canvas for self-expression and a site of strength and resilience. Additionally, the songs make direct attempts at reaching other women evidenced in how they use language suggestive of women's shared experiences, hence promoting a social bond, although different from the political one in the first wave. Lastly, the songs encourage women to make their own choices about their bodies, and not be objectified, suggesting that as women's rights.

Fourth Wave: 2012 and Beyond

Individual and Sociocultural Frame

Feminine music in this period mainly revolves on reinforcing the power of femininity. The songs, built on the overarching concept of empowerment, emphasize the need to celebrate female achievements and adequacy. The ambitions of the girl child are encouraged rather than dismissed, and within those ambitions, she must learn to not be hindered by societal limitations, and must carry herself with pride. With some characteristics spilling over from the third wave, the songs of the fourth wave also combine first person pronouns such as "I" and "me" together with second person pronouns such as "you" and third person singular such as "she" when referring to women.

Self-love, Women Empowerment, and Celebration of Feminine Achievements.

Meghan Trainor's "All About That Bass" (2014) questions society's demands for perfection from women. Built on the themes of body image and self-completeness, the song emphasizes the need for self-acceptance and self-love. In a society where women are shamed for their body sizes and looks, Trainor uses her song to boost feminine confidence. In the song, she calls out fat-shaming, emphasizing that women are perfect from "the bottom to the top." According to the lyrics:

> Yeah, it's pretty clear, I ain't no size two
> But I can shake it, shake it, like I'm supposed to do
> 'Cause I got that boom boom that all the boys chase
> And all the right junk in all the right places

Trainor relies on her personal experiences to refuse body-shaming while promoting self-sufficiency and love. She attempts to empower women who face bullying because they do not conform to society's standards and definitions of beauty. The song uses first person pronouns and second person pronouns to share personal experiences and reassure other women who may be experiencing body insecurity. Trainor calls out magazines' use of technology, in this case photoshop, to create picture perfect women, emphasizing that the creations are unreal. Trainor also attacks women conformity to satisfy masculine and societal standards. She encourages women to let go of partners who would not accept them for who they are. Trainor sings:

> I see the magazine workin' that Photoshop
> We know that shit ain't real, come on now, make it stop
> If you got beauty, beauty, just raise 'em up
> 'Cause every inch of you is perfect from the bottom to the top
>
> You know I won't be no stick figure, silicone Barbie doll
> So if that's what you're into, then go 'head and move along

Beyoncé, featuring Chimamanda Ngozi Adichie, in "***Flawless" (2013), narrates about female achievements and how patriarchy and sociocultural norms and standards are often used to dampen a woman's achievement. While the song emphasizes the beauty of marriage, it also suggests that women should not be defined by marriage nor forced into marriage as though their successes depended on it. It calls out the differences in social relationships between males versus females. In this song, Beyoncé features an acclaimed and outspoken feminist who is known to question gender standards and cultural hegemony in the society. "***Flawless," which became a feminist anthem for the fourth wave feminism, centers on female empowerment. It also questions gender inequality and the differences in how boys and girls are raised. The song suggests that women can still be high achievers while being elegant.

> I took some time to live my life
> But don't think I'm just his little wife
> Don't get it twisted, get it twisted

> We teach girls to shrink themselves
> To make themselves smaller
> We say to girls
> "You can have ambition
> But not too much
> You should aim to be successful
> But not too successful
> Otherwise you will threaten the man"
> You wake up, flawless
> Post up, flawless
> Ridin' round in it, flawless

> We flawless, ladies tell 'em

Taylor Swift (2019) in "The Man" challenges sociocultural issues of patriarchy that are used to limit women. She questions and opines metaphorically that men do not go through similar challenges as women and society is structured to favor males over females. Using examples of things she would be celebrated for if she were a man, yet shamed for because of her gender, she further questions gender inequalities. Swift sings that society is structured to hinder female achievements and stardoms. As she narrates:

> I'm so sick of running as fast as I can
> Wondering if I'd get there quicker if I was a man
> And I'm so sick of them coming at me again
> 'Cause if I was a man, then I'd be the man
> I'd be the man
> I'd be the man

Narrating from a first-person perspective only, the song responds to how society might engage with her differently if she were a man. While she does not question male activities in the society, she does question why the standards are different for females. From pushing females to work harder and then questioning why they work so hard and limiting what they have achieved, to the clothes they wear, how they carry themselves, Swift suggests that women are socially and culturally hindered. She says:

They'd say I hustled, put in the work
They wouldn't shake their heads and question how much of this I deserve
What I was wearing, if I was rude
Could all be separated from my good ideas and power moves

All three songs analyzed within the fourth wave feminism emphasize the empowerment of women. They challenge the marginalization of women in society and refocus on what gender norms should be. The songs push the salience in celebrating female potentials and achievements. While Trainor and Beyoncé go from a personalized approach to making reference to other women, Taylor only used a first person approach. It is noteworthy that the personal is more dominant for both Trainor and Beyoncé. The singular third person pronouns were used in such a way that the experience of an individual is generalized to other women. The songs call for sociocultural gender equality that allows for sexual liberation and neutrality that allow women to freely partake in activities with a masculine undertone without being judged by society.

Music and preserving the Feminist Movement

The frames in the songs analyzed suggest the dynamic role of music in representing the struggles of women and thus continuing the feminist movement over time. This chapter analyzed the use of music by female artists to express the issues related to women from the 19th to the 21st century. Based on the framing theory, the chapter examined how the characteristics of the four waves of feminism are emphasized in the lyrics of selected popular music. Through framing analysis, this chapter discussed the themes emphasized in the songs in each wave of feminism. It also considered the shift in the thematic focus and meanings conveyed by the songs.

It is noteworthy that the first, second, third, and fourth waves used as a framework for this chapter, do not have clearly delineated beginning and end dates, rather, the dates were determined by the dominant characteristics of women's struggles. This indicates that the waves of feminism did not happen independently of each other, but show continual shifts and carryovers of the defining sociopolitical and sociocultural characteristics of the time. Each song tapped for this chapter moved the movement forward and sometimes embodied elements from previous time periods. This suggests that while each wave ends, women's challenges persist as new ones also emerge. Hence, the songs, even though of diverse genres, express these struggles. In addition, as the audiences engage with the music, they are reminded of the challenges and inadvertently become a part of the movement, thus supporting DuBois (2005), who alludes to the collective memory of songs. In line with Eyerman and

Jamison (1998), the social movement may lead to social and cultural change in values, systemic ideas, and overall assumptions and stereotypes that challenge women.

Songs from the first wave focused on stronger, necessary political issues of rights, freedom, equality, and encouraged community. Although Hole and Levine (1990) suggested that the first wave was about individual freedom, the music examined for this study bore communal undertones. Following the characteristics of the period, the songs called for equal rights between men and women, but this came as a call to action in the form of marching songs.

The second wave took on less political issues, focusing on equality and respect, but from their partners and in romantic relationships. As the artists began to negotiate with social and cultural stereotypes, they addressed domestic issues that were important to female well-being.

The songs analyzed in the third wave addressed challenges of "multicultural inclusion, identity politics, intersectionality" (Fernandes, 2010, p. 99). The frames with this layer were driven by addressing the issues of misogyny, derogatory language, and disrespect for women. The songs also drew attention to the strength of womanhood and the need for inclusion.

The fourth wave frame was built on the empowerment of women. It continued to challenge the marginalization of women in society and expanded on what gender norms should be. There was a call for the neutralization of gender roles, allowing men and women to share in qualities and identities. In this way, the songs suggested gender fluidity. The singers of this era framed their work around what "should" be and questioned what is. That was what Trainor did in "All About That Bass" (2014) to boost feminine confidence and what Swift did in "The Man" (2019), where she noted she would not have to struggle with hegemonic masculinity if she were a man.

Framing was an essential component as to how each wave can be seen, heard, and perceived. The way these songs are framed speaks to the active process invested into media frames to influence perceptions (Entman, 1993; Onyebadi, 2018). Going from a communal frame, in which mostly third person plural pronouns are used in response to women, to mostly the use of first-person singular pronouns, the songs admonish women to engage in personalized ways that put them in the shoes of the artists. In this way, the songs carry the potential to shape minds and mentality.

The artists' strategies in framing sociopolitical and sociocultural challenges to women show a shift over time. Beginning with a community and sociopolitical frame, the songs moved to an individual and sociocultural frame. After female music from the 19th century established the power of women suffrage as a defining political issue for all women, music from the 20th to 21st centuries tackled individual issues of identity, power, and perception.

Across all the four waves, the strength and power of women as well as gender equality are emphasized, but in different ways. As exemplified in songs of the first wave, the power of suffrage and pay equality is dominant. In the second wave, mutual respect and body ownership is reinforced. The third wave shifted to represent the strength of a woman to not only care for herself, but also as a resilient being. Although the fourth wave explores self-love and gender equality, it does not do that in regard to pay. Rather, gender equality is negotiated along the lines of the recognition of the potentials of women to work hard and sometimes outperform. The fourth wave songs, especially Swift's "The Man" (2019) and Beyoncé's "***Flawless" (2013) do not only ask to share in the rights of men like in the first wave (e.g. Robinson's *Columbia's Daughters*, 1888), but negotiates their place and identities based on their agency and achievements. Hence, after the first wave, each new wave has uniquely redefined the girl child and woman in a way that enthrones them based on their merits.

Conclusion

This chapter posits that the frames used in the music, irrespective of genre, establish the characteristics of the feminist movement, feminism wave, and period in which they were published. They actively challenge misogyny, the dominant ideology of patriarchy, and empower women at the same time in a way that redefines female roles in society. In addition, the frames across the waves of feminism are not static but have changed over time. Although showing characteristics from different waves, the frames seek to move the roles and place of women in the society even further in a way that cancels out gender limitations.

Limitations of study

This chapter is quite unique and sheds light on music by female artists within feminist framework. It considers how the music was framed to enlighten on the sociopolitical and sociocultural meanings in the songs as well as the challenges of women. However, the study heavily relied on only 12 songs. The songs analyzed in this study, though popular, are by no means the only songs that can help us explore the dynamics of music, the feminist movement, and women's struggles. Future studies must consider other artists' repertoires and perhaps expand this unique framework to explore global music and international artists. It is by doing so that we can fully understand the depth of the messages in the music of these eras.

References

Akinro, N., Nwachukwu, E., & Duru, A. (2019). Corruption sings loudest: Music, political participation, and impression management. In U. Onyebadi (Ed.), *Music and Messaging in the African Political Arena* (pp. 131-148). Hershey, PA: IGI Globals.

Amos, V., & Parmar, P. (1984). Challenging imperial feminism. *Feminist Review, 17*, 3–19.

Arrow, M. (2007). 'I am woman,' popular culture and 1970s feminism. *Australian Feminist Studies, 22*(53), 213-230.

Bogue, R. (2007). *Deleuze's Way: Essays in Transverse Ethics and Aesthetics.* Hampshire: Ashgate Publishing Ltd.

Britannica. (2021). The fourth wave of feminism. https://www.britannica.com/topic/feminism/The-fourth-wave-of-feminism

Chancer, L. S. (2019). *After the Rise and Stall of American Feminism: Taking Back a Revolution.* California: Stanford University Press.

Charmaz, K. (1995). Grounded theory. In J. A. Smith, R. Harre, & L. Van Langenhove (Eds.), *Rethinking Methods in Psychology* (pp. 27-29). London: SAGE Publications.

Charmaz, K. (2000). Constructivist and objectivist grounded theory. In N. K. Denzin & Y. Lincoln (Eds.), *Handbook of qualitative research* (2nd ed., pp. 509-535). Thousand Oaks, CA: Sage.

Charmaz, K. (2006). *Constructing Grounded Theory: A practical guide through qualitative analysis.* London: SAGE Publications.

Darnovsky, M., Epstein, B., & Flacks, R. (Eds.). (1995). *Cultural politics and social movements.* Philadelphia: Temple University Press.

Davis, A. Y. (1998). *Blues Legacies and Black feminism.* New York: Vintage Books.

Dubois, W. E. B. (2005). *The Souls of Black folk.* New York: Bantam Books.

Entman, R. M. (1991). Framing U.S. coverage of international news: Contrasts in narratives of the KAL and Iran Air incidents. *Journal of Communication, 41*(4), 6-27.

Entman, R. M. (1993). Framing: Toward clarification of a fractured paradigm. *Journal of Communication, 43*(4), 51-58.

Eyerman, R. (2002). Music in movement: Cultural politics and old and new social movements. *Qualitative Sociology, 25*(3), 443-458.

Eyerman, R., & Jamison, A. (1998). *Music and Social Movements: Mobilizing Traditions in the Twentieth Century.* Cambridge University Press.

Fairclough, N. (2003). *Analysing Discourse: Textual Analysis for Social Research.* Psychology Press.

Fernandes, L. (2010). Third wave feminism: Feminist waves, intersectionality, and identity politics in retrospect. In N. Hewitt (Ed.), *No Permanent Waves: Recasting Histories of U.S. Feminism* (pp. 98-120). New Jersey: Rutgers University Press.

Ferree, M. M. and Hess, B. B. (1985). *Controversy and Coalition: The Feminist Movement.* Boston: Twayne.

Franklin, A. (1967). Respect [Song]. On *I Never Loved a Man the Way I Love You* [Album]. Atlantic 2403.

Gilman, C. (1913). The Women are Coming [Song].

Glaser, B. G. (1978). *Theoretical Sensitivity.* Mill Valley, CA: The Sociology Press.

Glaser, B. G., & Strauss, A. L. (1967). *The Discovery of Grounded Theory.* Chicago: Aldine.

Goffman, E. (1974). *Frame Analysis: An Essay on the Organization of Experience.* Harvard University Press.

Gordon, L. (2013). Socialist Feminism: The Legacy of the "Second Wave." *New Labor Forum, 22*(3), 20-28. https://doi.org/10.1177/1095796013499736

Gore, L. (1967). You Don't Own Me [Song]. On *Lesley Gore Sings of Mixed-Up Hearts* [Album]. Mercury.

Guba, E. G., & Lincoln, Y. S. (1994). Competing paradigms in qualitative research. In N. K. Denzin, & Y. S. Lincoln (Eds.), *Handbook of Qualitative Research* (pp.105-118). Thousand Oaks, CA: SAGE Publications.

Hess, J. (2019). Singing our own song: Navigating identity politics through activism in music. *Research Studies in Music Education, 41*(1), 61-80.

Hewitt, N. (2010). From Seneca Falls to Suffrage? In N. Hewitt (Ed.), *No Permanent Waves: Recasting Histories of U.S. Feminism* (pp. 15-38). New Jersey: Rutgers University Press.

Hole, J., & Levine, E. (1990). Historical precedent: Nineteenth-century feminists. In S. Ruth (Ed.), *Issues in Feminism: An Introduction to Women's Studies.* Mountainview, CA: Mayfield Publishing.

Imbornoni, A. M. (2021, February 24). *Timeline: U.S. Women's Rights, 1848-1920.* Info Please. http://www.infoplease.com/spot/womenstimeline1.htm

Keller, J., & Ringrose, J. (2015). 'But then feminism goes out the window!': Exploring teenage girls' critical response to celebrity feminism. *Celebrity Studies, 6*(1), 132-135.

Keys, A. (2007). Superwoman [Song]. On *As I am* [Album]. J Records.

King, D. K. (1988). Multiple jeopardy, multiple consciousness: The context of a Black feminist ideology. *Signs: Journal of Women in Culture and Society, 14*(1), 42-72.

Knowles, B. (2013). ***Flawless (featuring Chimamanda Ngozi Adichie) [Song]. On *Beyoncé* [Album]. Parkwood Columbia.

Kr"kke, C., & S"rensen, A. (2006). Three waves of feminism, from suffragettes to grrls. In C. Krol"kke & A. S"rensen (Eds.), *Gender Communication Theories and Analyses: From Silence to Performance* (1st ed., pp. 1-21). Thousand Oaks, California: SAGE Publications.

Lather, P. (1991). *Getting Smart: Feminist Research and Pedagogy With/in the Postmodern.* New York: Routledge.

Latifah, Q. (1993). U.N.I.T.Y. [Song]. On *Black Reign* [Album]. Motown Records.

Major, M. (1900s). Ballad of a Working Mother [Song].

Matthes, J. (2012). Framing politics: An integrative approach. *American Behavioral Scientist, 56*(3), 247-259.

McKee, A. (2003). *Textual Analysis: A Beginner' s Guide.* SAGE Publications.

Merriam, A. P. (1964). *The Anthropology of Music.* Evanston: Northwestern Univ. Press.

Onyebadi, U. (2018). Political Messages in African Music: Assessing Fela Anikulapo-Kuti, Lucky Dube and Alpha Blondy. *Humanities, 7*(4), 129. https://doi.org/10.3390/h7040129

Onyebadi, U., & Mbunyuza-Memani, L. (2017). Women and South Africa's anti-apartheid struggle: Evaluating the political messages in the music of Miriam Makeba. In U. Onyebadi (Ed.), *Music as a Platform for Political Communication* (pp.31-51). Hershey, PA: IGI Global.

Reddy, H. (1972). I am Woman [Song]. On *I am Woman* [Album]. Capitol Records.

Roberts, R. (1994). "Ladies first:" Queen Latifah's Afrocentric feminist music video. *African American Review, 28*(2), 245-257.

Robinson, H. (1888). Columbia's Daughters [Song].

Rose, L. P. (2007). The freedom singers of the civil rights movement: Music functioning for freedom. *Update: Applications of Research in Music Education, 25*(2), 59-68.

Rosenthal, R. (2001). Serving the movement: The role(s) of music. *Popular Music & Society, 25*(3-4), 11-24.

Street, J., Hague, S., & Savigny, H. (2008). Playing to the crowd: The role of music and musicians in political participation. *The British Journal of Politics and International Relations, 10*(2), 269-285.

Snow, D.A., & Benford, R.D. (1992). Master frames and cycles of protest. In A. Morris & C. M. Mueller (Eds.). *Frontiers in Social Movement Theory* (pp. 133-135). New Haven, CT: Yale University Press.

Snow, D.A., Rochford, E.B, Jr., Worden, S.K., & Benford, R.D. (1986). Frame alignment processes, micromobilization and movement participation. *American Sociological Review, 51*, 464-481.

Swift, T. (2019). The Man [Song]. On *Lover* [Album]. Republic Records.

Tarrow, S.G. (1994). *Power in Movement.* Cambridge: Cambridge University Press.

Trainor, M. (2014). All About That Bass [Song]. Epic Records.

Tuchman, G. (1978). *Making News.* New York: Free Press.

Twain, S. (1997). Man! I Feel Like a Woman [Song]. On *Come on Over* [Album]. Mercury Nashville.

Appendix A: Songs examined in this study

Alicia K Keys – *Superwoman* (2007).
https://genius.com/Alicia-keys-superwoman-lyrics

Aretha Franklin- Song: *Respect* (1967).
https://www.azlyrics.com/lyrics/arethafranklin/respect.html

Beyoncé featuring Chimamanda Ngozi Adichie in ***Flawless* (2013).
https://g.co/kgs/iEFrp9

Charlotte Perkins Gilman- Song: *The Women are Coming* (1913).
http://www.protestsonglyrics.net/

Harriet H. Robinson- Song: *Columbia's Daughters* (1888).
http://www.protestsonglyrics.net/

Helen Reddy- Song: *I am Woman* (1972).
https://www.azlyrics.com/lyrics/helenreddy/iamwoman.html

Lesley Gore- Song: *You Don't Own Me* (1963).
  https://www.azlyrics.com/lyrics/lesleygore/youdontownme.html
Marilyn Major- Song: *Ballad of a Working Mother* (1900s).
  http://www.protestsonglyrics.net/
Meghan Trainor- Song: *All About That Bass* (2014).
  https://www.azlyrics.com/lyrics/meghantrainor/allaboutthatbass.html
Queen Latifah- Song: *U.N.I.T.Y.* (1993).
  https://genius.com/Queen-latifah-unity-lyrics
Shania Twain- Song: *Man! I Feel Like a Woman* (1997).
  https://www.azlyrics.com/lyrics/shaniatwain/manifeellikeawoman.html
Taylor Swift- Song: *The Man* (2019).
  https://genius.com/Taylor-swift-the-man-lyrics

CHAPTER 6

Broadcasting populism: An examination of Venezuelan Community TV and participatory democracy

Elena M. De Costa

Carroll University, USA

Abstract

The long-running debate over the role of the mass media appears to have reached a new level of concern in Latin America. The power, conduct, and increasingly concentrated ownership of the corporate media, the future role of public service broadcasting, the possibilities for community media, and the impact of new technology are among the key issues driving the debate. Community media is but one facet in the socialist experiment of direct democracy and worker-control that President Hugo Chávez of Venezuela promoted while in office (1999-2013). In Venezuela, a grassroots movement of community and alternative media challenged the domination of private commercial media. Part of this process was the understanding of freedom of speech as a positive and basic right of the people. In this chapter, the author examines the following: (1) the world of community television production in the era of Hugo Chávez, focusing on Catia TVe and its sociopolitical impact; (2) Venezuela's Organic Telecommunications Law (June 2000) and Articles 58 and 108 of Venezuela's Constitution; (3) participatory democracy and its promotion of and confrontation with politics and journalistic principles; (4) the role that community media play in the negotiation of local values and meanings; and (5) state-supported media's ability to criticize the state.

Keywords: Community TV, Catia TVe, The Bolivarian Revolution, Hugo Chávez, Venezuela, The New Left, Latin American TV media, Participatory Democracy

***

Introduction

I think the main intersection between art and
politics is that artists and art itself have a
huge responsibility to keep politics honest...
It comes down to freedom of speech and
keeping those in power accountable.
              —*Tracey Deer (Screening Truth to Power, p. 119)*

Participatory democracy brings community members together by using the knowledge from the community to understand problems and provide immediate benefits for planning and evaluating relevant interventions. It engages formerly excluded populations by giving them voice to express economic and social problems experienced by past exclusionary policies of marginalized groups. As a populist measure, participatory democracy appeals for mass support by championing the causes of ordinary people against powerful elites. It is designed to address the most vexing issues of underserved populations, such as poverty and unemployment, a livable wage, healthcare, education, improvement in living and working conditions, land ownership, and the promise of playing a greater political role in the direction of their country.

However, this experimental approach to democratization of Latin America's New Left[1] is not without its problems. For one, how will the greater inclusion of marginalized groups be achieved in both the short and long terms? Will the voices of the once voiceless silence the voice of the elitist class? If so, is this then an authentic form of democracy, an alternative form of democracy, or no democracy at all? In order to have a better understanding of this brand of Latin American participatory democracy, we need to turn to its iconic image in recent times, the Bolivarian Revolution of Venezuela's Hugo Chávez.[2] Social activism, popular mobilization, and advancing the interests of the urban poor

---

[1] The New Left in Latin America is a collection of political parties and grassroots social movements (indigenous movements, student movements, mobilizations of landless rural workers, Afro-descendent organizations, and feminist movements.) The term "New Left" refers to the "pink tide" of democratically elected, left-leaning governments in Central and South America, modeled on the presidency of Venezuela's Hugo Chávez. It generally advocates direct action, confrontation with state power, anti-authoritarianism, direct or participatory democracy, and/or the undermining of traditional patriarchal norms.

[2] The Bolivarian Revolution is the political process initiated by the late Venezuelan leader, President Hugo Chávez, the founder of the Fifth Republic Movement and later the United Socialist Party of Venezuela (PSUV). Its policies included nationalization, social welfare programs or "missions" seeking to reduce social disparities, and opposition to Neoliberalism. It is also referred to as *Chavismo* to reflect its identification with its founder.

were the hallmarks of this revolution. And the broadcast media gave voice to a once voiceless majority contributing to grassroots participation to promote transformative social change. Local experiential knowledge, historical memory, oral narratives, and barrio-based community media form the basis of community television production in Venezuela's most prominent community television station, Catia TVe. It was launched by activists from impoverished communities in Caracas and began transmission on March 30, 2001. Catia TVe was founded as a grassroots movement of community and alternative media to challenge the domination of private commercial media in the industry. Catia TVe is, by definition, *television from, by, and for the people.* Its original intent was one of inclusionary participation of the marginalized and self-determination. Catia TVe sought to encourage participation within organized communities by making audiovisual productions reflecting community struggles and demonstrating how to build networks within the community. Its function was clearly educational in nature in this sense.

By 2007, almost thirty community television stations and hundreds of community radio stations had begun operating across Venezuela. They identified with President Hugo Chávez's humble roots; his mestizo, black, and indigenous features; and his call for social and economic justice. The alternative media format of community television undertook sociopolitical and economic transformation as its goal. Part of this process of change was the understanding of freedom of speech as a positive and basic right of the people. This right included universal access to a meaningful space for communication in addition to freedom from censorship. Freedom of expression as a positive right, in turn, provided wide-spread access to the means of communication. Direct involvement of *el pueblo*, ordinary people, in their future, variety of formats and topics, the freedom to perform marginalized cultural expressions of music, dance, traditions, authenticity and spontaneity unrehearsed— all these characteristics were in support of Venezuela's popular Bolivarian Revolution. In realistic terms, was this political stagecraft or public television designed to educate the populace? Was Catia TVe a tool of democratic voice or a weapon of the government to undermine its opposition? Was community television an expression of democratic freedom or a means to control insurrection and gain popularity by a subversive politician and political movement? To what extent did community media and popular politics merge to solidify Venezuela's populist government? What subliminal messaging, if any, was woven into community television and communicated to the larger television audience and, if so, to what end?

The community and media movement marked an outgrowth of earlier popular ("popular" in this chapter refers to the country's poor majority) movements in the second part of the twentieth century with a surge in the Latin

American Popular Education movement, Liberation Theology[3] and a variety of liberation struggles against dictatorships in the region in the 1960s and 1970s. Latin America's popular communication programs were adapted to urban and suburban issues as well as the farming, mining, and indigenous communities across the continent.

Community media have always been identified with the struggles of marginalized groups toward the end of giving voice to the oppressed and repressed populations in whatever public means available from the simplest flyers, posters, songs, sound recordings, newsletters, popular protest gatherings in public spaces to the more complex and more widely distributed radio and television broadcasts. In Venezuela, and specifically under the leadership of Hugo Chávez in June 2000, the National Assembly passed the Organic Telecommunications Act (*Ley Orgánica de Telecomunicaciones*) and in 2002, the Free Community Radio and Television Broadcast Ruling. Both decrees were responsible for implementing two articles of constitutional reform, Articles 58 and 108 of Venezuela's Constitution. Article 58 guarantees freedom of expression as follows: "Communication is free and plural and must adhere to the obligations and responsibilities under the law. Every person has the right to objective, true and impartial information, without censorship...." Article 108 ensures that all communication media, public and private, contribute to the social development of citizens. The same articles guarantee public access to radio, television, library networks and information networks in order to permit universal access to information. Public access channels and community-based media are rights that, for the first time, were ensured under the 1999 Constitution (Venezuela. *Constitución de la República Bolivariana de Venezuela*. Caracas: Gaceta Oficial, 1999.) Consequently, these constitutional reforms gave voice to participatory government through community media for social change and through grassroots development within communities. Catia TVe was the most effective of many community initiatives in its inclusion of cultural perspectives as well as local, national, and international news programming disseminated throughout the community in live television programming. Through class alliances, Catia TVe broadcasters, who hailed from port barrios of Caracas themselves, used their cultural agency to participate in the political experiment of *bolivarianismo*, the populist brand of Hugo Chávez's socialist government, as it unfolded. It identified closely with the community video collective movement of the time. Prior to Hugo Chávez's election to the presidency in 1998, any type of community organizing process or public sharing of ideas had been discouraged by authorities.

---

[3] Liberation Theology, a movement in Christian theology, preaches that it is a Christian duty to aid the poor and oppressed through involvement in civic and political affairs. It was prevalent in Latin America in the 1970s and 1980s.

In a media context dominated by private broadcasters, several meaningful initiatives took on the public service functions neglected by both public and private broadcasters in the second half of the twentieth century under Hugo Chávez. Community media and its many initiatives flourished under the Chávez government. The reason is obvious in the context of a participatory democracy based on socialist beliefs and practices. Communities need to see themselves represented in the media in order to be validated as engaging citizens. It is the media that raised consciousness to community issues, thus empowering the community to act as protagonists in their own destiny with their achievements and conflicts aired to the larger populace.

Community media such as radio and television provide a space for local people to exercise their power. Based on this premise, a minimum of 70% of Catia TVe's programming was required to be produced from within the community. The remaining 30% of TV production came from other communities in Venezuela that shared similar programs. Most of these ancillary productions were pre-recorded in the form of full-length films, shorts or *cortometrajes*, and documentaries. All these productions engage the masses over individual interests in the true spirit of the "New Man" philosophy of socialism[4] espoused by Ernesto "Che" Guevara, first in Fidel Castro's post-revolutionary Cuba and later picked up by Hugo Chávez some 40 years later in Venezuela. While the Venezuelan radio-electric broadcast system belonged to the state, communities were encouraged to create their own TV messages without the controlling hegemonic mechanisms of the elite's interests. However, it is interesting to note that the skills workshops that were offered to community media participants served more as political and ideological meetings than media training in technology and its applications to broadcasting. This separation between the medium and the message placed political messaging in the forefront and, by default, contributed to political stagecraft or political theatre in some instances by its sheer simplicity and spontaneity of format. Overall, such media workshops were modeled on the pedagogy of Popular Education, an active learning process whose goals are to raise social awareness, stimulate critical thinking, and ultimately, lead to action for social change, reflective of the Brazilian educator Paulo Freire's pedagogy.[5]

---

[4] The New Man philosophy espoused by Ernesto "Che" Guevara in his essay "Socialism and Man in Cuba" (1965) is a utopian concept that involves the creation of a new ideal human being, who would embody a communitarian attitude of individual self-sacrifice for the good of the larger society.

[5] Paulo Freire chose the process of critical pedagogy utilizing dialogue as his pedagogical model. His approach in *The Pedagogy of the Oppressed* (1970) viewed human beings in dialogical exchanges as equals rather than the oppressive imposition of passive recipients of

Within this socialist philosophy, an individual's personal experiences were connected to larger societal problems. And, for this reason, Catia TVe broadcast numerous interviews with citizens, who aired their personal complaints and frustrations not for self-aggrandizement (although this might have been an ancillary reason), but with the goal of identifying a more widespread social ill. To this day, Catia TVe works in designated community teams called ECPAI (Independent Community Audiovisual Production Team, *Equipo Comunitario de Producción Audiovisual Independiente*), simply because its stated goal is to propitiate collective work and put it at the service of the community to fulfill its stated needs. This approach is unlike corporate media outlets that decide on what content will be aired ultimately after review. Participatory democracy in all its manifestations, from print media to audiovisual media, from declamatory speeches to mass protests, is meant to be a tool for people's mobilization. How successful it is in developing popular organizations and in supporting the struggles of the underrepresented depends on the participants, the medium of production, and the diffusion of information. In theory, community media's primary purpose is to deliver social benefits and not to operate for private commercial profit. Ideally, community media stations should be owned by and be accountable to their target community, and they should provide for participation by that community at all levels. As an independent entity, community media should be provided by and for communities in a specific geographic location or, alternatively, communities with shared interests. But this ideal scenario of independence from outside forces is not always possible due to the very nature of community media originating in communities with limited resources and little to no technical and professional knowledge.

Marshall McLuhan, the Canadian philosopher whose work is among the cornerstones of media theory, maintained that the form of a message (print, visual, musical, audiovisual, etc.) determines the way in which that message will be perceived. In 1964, he coined the iconic phrase "The medium is the message."[6] Television, unlike print or radio, requires more sensory involvement of the participant, since it is categorized as an example of "cool media" and, as

---

knowledge from hegemonic structures. To Freire, problem-posing education creates critical thinkers who challenge the power structures and patterns of inequality within the status quo. Engaged in their surroundings, they take control of their own learning, critically evaluate the opinions they have been taught, and thus partake in life-long learning.

[6] The concept that the form of a message (print, visual, musical, etc.) determines the ways in which that message will be perceived was introduced by Marshall McLuhan in his book *Understanding Media: The Extensions of Man* (1964). Due to its ability to reach large audiences and its ability to broadcast live programming, television was a powerful medium to bring Venezuela's Bolivarian Revolution to the general public. https://www.ecoi.net/en/file/local/1185288/1930_1437487822_int-ccpr-css-ven-20714-e.pdf

such, it is the world's most powerful medium of communication with the ability to educate great numbers of people around the world. The communication channel or the path through which messages are sent to their recipients needs feedback to verify that its message has been transmitted effectively by the recipient and then acted upon. Action in the form of social change is the goal of participatory democracy. The functions of the media are to inform, persuade, entertain, and transmit culture. Catia TVe defined its communicative role as placing its message of transformative socioeconomic and cultural change within the context of its poor, underserved communities or *barrios* by transmitting a shared message of upward mobility, social recognition, valuation, and equality. It advocated media production "as a process of political organizing, rather than as a means to an end." (Schiller, 2018, p. 46)

It is noteworthy that the community television station movement in Venezuela during the Chávez presidency spread throughout the country as a result of the audiovisual production workshops in Caracas where Catia TVe was based. Depending on the geographic location's demographics and local needs, topics varied —worker struggles, community struggles, the fight of rural workers, women's issues, indigenous peoples, and other exploited sectors of the populace. The television medium was perceived as an inclusive space where all the exploited sectors in Venezuela were given a venue to air their grievances and to contribute to their government's agenda. The community media sectors tended to identify strongly with the tenets of *Chavismo* and the Bolivarian Revolution by engaging in the revolution's ideal of people's power from *inside* the revolution toward building socialism with a critical, self-critical, and class-consciousness perspective. The community media messaging thus became a tool for unity that helped to strengthen and deepen Chávez's New Left revolution based on non-violence and legitimate elections—the voice of the people expressed through the establishment—the legal frameworks of constitutional law, governance, and mass communication. Articles in the Organic Telecommunications Law explicitly recognized community broadcast media in the country. Article 12 states:

> As a condition of telecommunications service, every individual has the right to exercise individually and collectively the right to free and pluralist communication through adequate conditions to create non-profit community radio and television stations dedicated to the community, in accordance with the law.

Articles in the community broadcast media law separated the media and message. Article 28 states:

> Community radio and television stations will be broadcast media with independent and community productions, from the community and

from other communities. At least 70% of a community station's daily broadcast programming must be produced within the community.

And, finally, Article 29 states:

No single producer, from the community or independent, can take up more than 20% of the daily programming broadcast at a community television or radio station. The station's paid staff may only produce a maximum of 15% of the programming with the rest to be produced by community volunteers. (*IPYS*, 2015, p. 6)

Community media thus became a defining moment in Venezuela's democratic social transformation, validated by its credentials as a community-oriented, non-profit, non-commercial citizen and volunteer enterprise not subject to censorship. When Channel Eight, the state-run television channel, was taken off the air during the coup attempt against the Chávez government in April 2002, most Venezuelans were denied accurate coverage of the events. But the coup was quickly contained with the assistance of community media stations and activists, particularly Catia TVe. They rallied their communities together to take to the streets and demand that their voices be heard. Additionally, the camera became not only a witness but a weapon to hold officials accountable for their promises.

In theory, programming should be democratic and inclusive, focusing on media participants free from government and commercial interference and free to innovate and present controversial issues. But Catia TVe made alliances with the Chávez government and the middle class against the elitist class, and this alliance of interdependency proved to be a questionable one at best in part due to the charismatic nature of Hugo Chávez in the delivery of his message and the contrasting economic resources of the middle-class station, ViVe TV. The platform of community TV broadcasting provided the Venezuelan government with a strategic amplification of its message of "twenty-first-century socialism," that is, socialism by state election instead of revolution. When Chávez's pronouncements were aired on Catia TVe, it messaged to community residents that their actions were validated from the highest echelons of society, the office of the president. And Chávez was aware of the power of words and images to shape political culture, given his populist appeal to the masses. Indeed, Hugo Chávez's consolidation of power was successful, in large measure due to media image and spectacle. Over time, a relationship of causation, not simply correlation, developed between political actions and political messaging in poor urban communities. An interdependency soon developed between the needs (both in resources and policies) of Catia TVe viewers and the outreach of its political messaging to a key component of its supporters—the urban poor, the masses. By 2007, nearly 30 community television stations and hundreds of community radio stations had begun broadcasting across the country not just in the greater Caracas area. The dissemination of the Bolivarian Revolution's political messaging was well on its way nationwide. And a significant number of poor people for whom access to the presidential palace never had been even a remote possibility, now had been given a platform in the form of media coverage of their own neighborhoods. They could air their grievances directly from their community to the ear of the country's president.

Aló Presidente (*Hello, Mr. President*), introduced in 1999, was an unscripted talk show hosted by President Hugo Chávez himself and broadcast on Venezuelan state television by Venezolana de Televisión (ViVe TV) and radio stations across the country. The program aired live every Sunday from 11:00 am with no set wrap-up time, prime time for Venezuelans. In "reality show" style, the entertaining, enigmatic, and relatable presence of Chávez not only reflected the realities of his country, but he often impacted those same realities by making policy, directing his staff to solve community problems, and critiquing his opposition both at home and abroad live on his television show. Although the show was unpredictable and tawdry, it was as fascinating and addictive as much as any soap opera or *telenovela* and attracted a vast audience of loyal viewers, particularly among the middle and lower classes.

Part variety show, part political theatre, the show brought the country's president into the homes of millions with simple-to-understand solutions to individual and community problems delivered in real time, salt and peppered with anecdotes, crooned folk songs, and digressions of all sorts. *Aló Presidente* and the many community broadcasts created a type of direct link between the leader of Venezuela's Bolivarian Revolution and the common man, thus humanizing a cult-like figure. The storytelling format of many episodes provided a very powerful way to express ideas and policies concisely and clearly to an uninformed audience. Stories are powerful because they delight, enchant, amuse, teach, inspire, motivate, and challenge. This is precisely what Hugo Chávez intended to communicate to his captivated viewers as he invited them to become *participant-observers* of an ongoing social experience and national revolutionary movement.

The show became the cornerstone of Chávez's political messaging to the nation, replacing press conferences and interviews. It included phone-in calls directly to the president with viewers sharing their ideas, emotions, and everyday life concerns. Indeed, both Catia TVe and ViVe TV as well as numerous other television broadcasts informed and defined the ideological process of the Bolivarian Revolution throughout Chávez's presidency as co-related, interdependent forces of populism. All these channels of mass media communication started as a seemingly participatory space of inclusion of formerly excluded populations of both urban and rural poor. Progressively, these broadcasts accomplished the unity of shared ideas and concerns that print media had difficulty achieving. They became a platform for mass participation and education as well as for *chavismo*. Hugo Chávez, by association, as the sole leader and authority figure of Venezuela's revolution, defined himself and his revolution through the media. Whether or not this established interdependency between host/president and audience/electorate had been carefully orchestrated from its inception is unclear. Its thirteen-year run between 1999 and 2012 coincided with and further solidified the identity of a public that shared the values and ideals of the nation's loquacious leader, a public that was in every sense of the word a *co-participant* in state formation (statecraft) with Hugo Chávez at the helm as its populist ideologue. The parallel relationship between *statecraft* and *stagecraft*, between policy formation by the state with participation of the masses and the media's role in creating a form of political theatre, is at issue here. Community television played a role in inspiring democratic inclusion in a semi-authoritarian context of cult following. But it was a gradual process that required both identification with and allegiance to the president.[7]

For all the importance of community involvement, training, and other aspects of social gain activities, it was the entertaining nature of Venezuela's community broadcasting that sustained it and attracted a wider audience. Its task was twofold. On the one hand, community broadcasting sought to be relative to the communities served and represented through the promotion of social development, cultural diversity, the strengthening of social and cultural identities, community empowerment, information dissemination, etc. On the other hand, such broadcasts also ensured that programming was as entertaining, fascinating, and useful as possible to keep its audiences switched on and tuned in. Programs such as *Aló Presidente* became *edutainment,* since varied and creative formats combined the needs of popular culture (the masses) with entertaining components.

Community television: voice for the voiceless; platform for the state

The term *community broadcasting* is applied to a wide range of noncommercial initiatives, including broadcasting that runs the gamut of rural, cooperative, participatory, free, citizens,' alternative, popular, and educational programming. Venezuela's Catia TVe represents and is directed by Caracas's urban poor neighborhoods for the most part. Its unique communication process is shaped by its communities' environment, distinct culture, history, and the reality of the

---

[7] Joseph and Nugent define statecraft as the everyday process of creating ideas and representations about what the state is and can be. It includes power-laden interactions between social actors who jointly create the state through practices that are local, regional, and global.

communities that it serves. Its humble beginnings were an outgrowth of grassroots social movements and community-based organizations seeking to highlight their own grievances. The founders of Catia TVe wanted to secure a place in Venezuela's history. They wanted calls for social and economic justice in their impoverished neighborhoods to be heard.

The creation of Catia TVe, and subsequently other community programming, provided an alternative both to public broadcasters and to private commercial media. On the surface, such programming is not under government control. But, at a deeper level, the identification of Catia TVe with socialist goals and its limited resources gradually created an interdependency between Venezuela's Bolivarian Revolution and the community television stations in service to their constituents, the communities from which they originated and vowed to serve. The political sphere made an unspoken alliance with the poor, who were seeking empowerment, a voice on the political stage. These socially and economically marginalized populations fully supported Chávez's policy of redistribution of wealth and popular power. The producers of Catia TVe viewed the Chávez state and its institutions as holding the potential to improve the lives of their impoverished communities and include their voices in the process of political participation. Hugo Chávez, on the other hand, identified with this segment of the population due to his own sociopolitical exclusion as a person of indigenous blood with mestizo and black features and humble background. The unequal relationship of interdependency between the two factions of state and community media resided not only in Chávez's powerful role as president of the Republic of Venezuela but also as a well-educated, charismatic individual with the ability to debate effectively and charm the lower classes. He displayed this charm with his folksy demeanor, often breaking out in song, reciting the poetry of the renowned Chilean poet Laureate Pablo Neruda, quoting the country's heroes, referencing folklore, engaging in humorous quips, and the like (i.e., *edutainment*).

In visual communication media, it is the *attitude* of the interlocutor based on non-verbal as well as verbal codes that conveys political messaging more than vociferous political slogans. The role of symbols in folk culture and in horizontal communication is paramount. Patterns of regional behavior are part of the communication code with base groups which politicians often seek to activate. Philosophers such as Hobbes and Kant long ago recognized the communicating function of what is called *intentional language*. Such parlance incorporates the direct vocabulary of the wants and aspirations, the thoughts and the beliefs of ordinary people with which everyday behavior is understood or explained. Since the objective is clarity and facility of communication, it would be unwise for political animators not to master the intentional language or the popular discourse of the target groups which they seek to activate. The political effects of messaging are not obtained by separating discourse from the people's concrete necessities or from their own forms and symbols of expression. Shouting slogans and hurling accusations against imperialism, for example, are ineffective among the non-politicized and disenfranchised. The desired effect of active participation in community development and social change is better obtained through a well-composed song or an inspired poem denouncing exploitation by foreign business interests. Venezuela's peasants do not identify with political terms such as "participatory democracy" and "social transformation" since they have been marginalized for so long by the political system with low levels of education. Theirs is a more direct and simple language of experiences.

CatiaTVe did play a significant role in the delivery of public service goals, not only by informing, educating, and entertaining its audiences but also by providing a platform for diverse perspectives, facilitating participation in governance, trying to hold leaders and officials accountable for their actions and policies, and contributing to equitable and participatory development. The broadcasting media gave voice to a segment of the population that would not ordinarily have been heard. And the denouncements (*denuncias*) and grievances they aired underscored the accountability to which public officials would be held by the masses. Community programming in this regard provided Catia TVe communities with benefits ranging from visibility to remedies for simple community problems. CatiaTVe gave its audiences a sense of agency and hope for advancement. Such broadcasts also provided this population with the ability to share its own culture and validate those autochthonous values that contact with other social classes had debased.

The directors of Catia TVe presented their station as a social arena in which the neighborhood *barrios* both discovered and shared their history at several levels of collective recognition: (1) the poor as visible, not marginalized; (2) the past in relation to the poor; (3) the legitimacy of the struggle to destroy the bourgeois values of corruption and exploitation; (4) the causes of injustice and marginalization, and the identification of those responsible; and (5) the people's capacity to decide, act, and transform themselves collectively.

The role of community television and the inspiring work of collective production are critical to a government that depends on grassroots support. These community stations were anchors, hubs and public spaces for the districts they represented, led and organized by people living in the community. According to the CatiaTVe Collective, "community media works to democratize communication, affecting the necessary separation of the medium and the message." (CatiaTVe Collective, 2006, para. 3). Their agenda of people's power depends heavily on socially and economically exploited grassroots groups as they articulate and systematize knowledge (both their own and that which comes from outside) in such a way that they can become protagonists or agents in the advancement of their society, and in defense of their own class and group interests. But dialectical liaisons were and are always inevitable when there is such an imbalance of power between the state and the agents for change on whom it relies. The people power agenda of the urban poor of Catia TVe and the participatory democratic Bolivarian Revolution of Hugo Chávez were aligned, so that community television served as a vehicle for the delivery of political policy. In its early years, Catia TVe and other community communication channels were careful not to form strong ties of dependence on state officials, and they worked so that their own media presence would be progressively redundant. This stance of potential redundancy —the opposite of paternalism— assures that the organized communities can both carry on alone the social changes which had been initiated and criticize the shortcomings of the revolution. This process would come to fruition without having to appeal to outside experts, intellectuals, or state agents except in special and extreme cases.

But could solidarity with and criticism of the Chávez government co-exist successfully for the long-term at Catia TVe? Could the state's vow to reject the renewal of the broadcast license of a commercial television station critical of the revolution signal censorship or, at the very least, limitations on media freedom? Could state-supported media criticize the state? Might dissident activists become government allies? In a "subliminal seduction" discrete form of coercion, Catia TVe began shaping state projects in the interest of the poor with a negotiation of meaning of community television between popular movements and state actors. In this way, Venezuela's revolution became the product of grassroots participation on full display in community television projects. *Statecraft* (the government's redistribution of wealth and its commitment to the empowerment of the poor) became political theatre, or *stagecraft*. Catia TVe and its community television affiliates were produced in the barrios with humble settings, using interviews with barrio inhabitants made for television with powerful stories. The financial struggles of community media gave way to compromise and collusion, resulting in the sway of political audience opinion and the influence of political outcomes both on and off TV. In some instances, substance was sacrificed for spectacle in the name of advancing social justice and equality for the disadvantaged in the political sphere. Patterns of dependency, authoritarianism, and paternalism inherited from the traditional exploitation systems of the past continued to flourish despite the revolution. Caracas's poor neighborhoods and their middle-class allies began engaging in what Noemi Schiller terms "mutual instrumentality" (2018, p.17) in order to achieve their mutual goals. The demarcation between community media and the state began to blur. Community media practitioners rely on state funding for their survival. State dependency, consequently, creates a problematic issue for staff and volunteers.

One major goal of the community and alternative media movement in Venezuela has been to procure institutionalized state support for a participatory media system without ceding decision-making authority to the state. The passage of the Law of Telecommunications on June 12, 2000 was an initial attempt to achieve this goal. It attempted to combine the legal recognition of the state with private sector resources. Nonetheless, reliance on state resources mitigates Catia TVe's opportunity to grow into a viable counter-hegemonic system. In his 1979 *Theory of Communicative Action*, the German philosopher and sociologist, Habermas, addresses the issue of the public sphere. Referencing "strategic action," (Habermas, 1979, p. 198), Habermas affirms that actors are not so much interested in mutual understanding as in achieving the individual goals they each bring to the situation. The "public sphere" (Habermas, 1979, p. 198) of society engages in critical public debate. In order to communicate within this public sphere, "those who enter any given arena must share a reference world for their discourse to produce awareness for shared interests and public opinions about them" (Habermas, 1979, p. 198). This world consists of common meanings and cultural norms from which interaction can take place. Habermas further considers state power as "public power" (Habermas, 1979, p. 198), but he warns that public opinion must control the state and its authority in everyday discussions. Thus, the presence of a public sphere is the basic requirement to mediate between state and society, since this public sphere permits democratic control of state activities.

In the case of Venezuela's Catia TVe, a somewhat compromising situation arose, wherein the community television staff and volunteers had a continual reliance on so-called outside experts for guidance, resources, salaries, and the like. The presence of cross-class collaboration with the working class and the intervention of official state institutions in their popular movement projects only jeopardized their autonomy. Catia TVe and other community television networks sought to democratize access to the means of media production since they viewed mass media as a vehicle of broader political and social change. Mass media was also a unique way to accelerate the process of social transformation. These efforts toward democratization aligned perfectly with Chávez's Bolivarian Revolution and its 1999 constitutional reforms toward a participatory, protagonistic democracy as opposed to a representative democracy. Centralization and constitutional reforms have been instrumental in mobilizing the once marginalized populations to defend reforms in many New Left governments throughout Latin America (Cuba, Bolivia, Ecuador, and Venezuela) for the governments' developmental plans.

Thus, the questions persist in this problematic scenario of interconnected agents: What are the boundaries between community activism and state institutions in Venezuela, particularly as they relate to community media broadcasting? How can community television maintain its autonomy and self-determination when it is perceived as "essential to the revolution" by elected officials? What tenets of press freedom and journalistic autonomy could be exercised by community media television networks if they rely on institutional support and are seen as a tool for the mobilization of their audiences to support and implement the goals of the state? And finally, how do the producers of Catia TVe and other community television networks view the state? Is the state viewed as a support mechanism of inclusion of the marginalized or a threat to their community organizations on the ground?

In 1980, UNESCO (United Nations Educational Scientific and Cultural Organization) commissioned a study known as the MacBride Report, entitled *Many Voices, One World*. The study was in keeping with the mission of the organization's initiatives to end world poverty through collaboration and exchange of scientific, cultural, and global education. The report identified unequal access to information and the commercialization of the media as significant problems in contemporary societies. It sought to remedy these problems by the democratization of communication, declaring that people have the right to bidirectional, horizontal, and participatory communication through the expansion of local and public service media without dependency on external sources. Caracas was selected by UNESCO representatives as the venue to present their findings. This proposal for a new global communications order was not taken lightly by Western superpowers. Both the United States and the United Kingdom withdrew from UNESCO on the grounds that their recommendations were a violation of freedom of the press. Nearly two decades later, the Chávez government revived the MacBride Report that had been unceremoniously rejected and left unimplemented. The Venezuelan president conceived an unprecedented cultural and media policy promoting the Venezuelan audio-visual sector in an international climate with strong emphasis on culture. In 1999, Chávez enshrined the tenets of *Many Voices, One World* in the Bolivarian Constitution as the right to "timely truthful, impartial, and uncensored information" through democratized access to the means of media production, using media as a tool for social change. In light of the vilification of the impoverished class, commercial media was deemed as dangerous, entitled, and unreasonable.

Hugo Chávez revisited a resolution of former President Caldera in 1972, which was designed to set specific norms for broadcast media to preserve Venezuela's national identity in the face of foreign media influence. Resolution #3178 affirms that "Radio and television stations should foment moral and cultural values of the nation, strengthen democratic conditions and national unity, contribute to the development and improvement of education, and affirm respect for social morality, human dignity, and family institutions" (Coronil, 1997, p. 284).

Consequently, a progressive relationship of trust, a bond of common goals, formed as Catia TVe and other community networks identified with Chávez and his Bolivarian movement. What did this identification between the state as represented by Chávez and community groups entail? The New Left promotes democratic governance based on popular participation as follows: (1) a willingness to use state power to stimulate economic growth and correct for market failures; (2) a willingness to use state power and/or social organizations to reduce social inequalities and address social deficits; and (3) a commitment to deepened democracy through various forms of popular mobilization and participation in the political process. This willingness to actively employ collective political resources to supplement or modify social outcomes is appealing to the disenfranchised because of its stance on the inclusion of lower-class constituencies against elite economic interests. There could not be any better linkage of common interests and trust between state formation personified in Hugo Chávez and popular validation of social justice demands sought after by Catia TVe and its constituents.

The left and state-civil society relations

Chávez's Venezuela presents a case of contrasts. While controlled by the state, the *círculos bolivarianos (Bolivarian Circles)* are designed to enhance the mobilization of some of the poorest and most marginalized segments of society. Created by Hugo Chávez in December 2001, these political and social organizations of workers' councils were often featured on community networks since they are a means for neighborhood groups to request assistance for community programs directly from the president's office. Such programs include issues related to health, public transportation, and urban clean-ups.

At their core, the role of these community circles is to discuss local problems and relay them to the appropriate state office to identify solutions. Their function is closely aligned with that of community television, which can provide them with a larger platform to air their views. However, membership in these neighborhood groups depends on staunch support of the ideals outlined in the Bolivarian Constitution promulgated by the state. In February 2002, a delegation from the Inter-American Press Association (IAPA) reported that there was a lack of press freedom in Venezuela. The IAPA expressed its solidarity with numerous journalists and news media executives who had been threatened, berated, and abused physically and verbally, particularly by members of the Bolivarian Circles, who echoed President Chávez's constant discrediting of the press in his public statements and radio addresses. Should civil society be autonomous from the state while echoing some of its policies and criticizing others? Should a top-down model of civic organization (as seen in the Bolivarian Circles and community broadcasting networks) be dismissed as largely authoritarian? Or might the concept of neighborhood circles and community television linked to a state entity of charismatic leadership with shared concerns be an innovative approach to organizing society? Might this arrangement harken a new order with more direct results? These questions should elicit responses that move beyond group identity and assess the effectiveness of civil society and its capacity to attain or even influence policy results in the state formation process. The actors of community groups in the case of Venezuela simply do not have the expertise to influence state policies due to their lack of understanding of government and how it works.

The unique dynamics of social mobilization, the distinct nature of linkages between social movements and the state, or the role (or lack thereof) of ethnic cleavages in shaping political outcomes cannot be captured by the designation "populism" or "people empowerment." The electoral outcomes of Venezuelan twenty-first-century socialism clearly indicate widespread popular dissatisfaction with the failure of two decades of Neo-liberal reforms to deliver broadly shared social benefits. Venezuelan socialism also demonstrates the incapacity of traditional political elites to respond to demands for greater equity, participation, and economic, political, and social inclusion. The Bolivarian Revolution owes much to the experience of the average citizen, not just the marginalized. These pre-revolutionary experiences included the persistence of poverty and inequality; the growth of the informal sector and the decline of labor unions; disenchantment with the institutions of existing democratic governance; the difficulty of establishing adequate mechanisms of participation, representation, transparency, and accountability; and dislocations related to the domestic effects and foreign policy implications of globalization. The government had operated for too long for the benefit of a powerful minority rather than for the good of the masses, "the people," according to the manifesto of Chávez's movement *by and for* the people. It was time to establish a pluralism of information and opinion and to be inclusive of *all* voices.

Tension between populism and authoritarianism

The alternative and community media movement, with considerable support from the Bolivarian government, has accrued many impactful moments of empowerment and collective knowledge production. The movement has marked decades of struggle motivated by the continued sacrifices of those working within this public sphere. There is no denying their many successes. The system of participatory media as part of a national political project in Venezuela cannot be depicted as entirely totalitarian nor naively utopian in the analysis of its actors from both sides of the divide, state and community. This would be an entirely unfair and untruthful assessment. Catia TVe and all its constituents were not just communities of place determined by the propinquity of residents within a geographic space. They were also communities of interest defined by their members' shared focus, events, ideas, and problems determined by their geographic location in the poorer sectors of society. Chávez's presidency was built on the grievances of these disenfranchised communities giving them visibility, validity, and voice.

Laudeman (2013, pp. 133-35) discusses two public spheres of influence in civil society, the *decision-making sphere* (formal organizations and government institutions) and the *meaning-making sphere* (communities of individuals linked by shared interests and decisions.) Democratic forms of government, whether participatory or representative, require interactions between both spheres of decision-making and meaning-making categories with a free flow of information between them to facilitate their dialectic interaction. Habermas refers to such a relationship as "a far-reaching publicity" (1979, p. 201). One major goal of the community and alternative media movement in Venezuela has been to procure institutionalized state support for a participatory media system without compromising its right to free speech and thus its ability to criticize the government. The Telecommunications Act of 2000 and its attendant regulations were an initial attempt to achieve this goal by combining the legal recognition of the state with private sector resources in agreement with the existing liberal model of community media. However, in December 2010, Hugo Chávez amended this law (The Organic Telecommunications Law and the Social Responsibility on Radio and Television Law) in order to limit opposition voices. The controversial change classifies the use of telecommunications networks as a "public service," of "social responsibility" among those who provide television, radio, and internet service (text, images, sound, or context sent or received in Venezuela.) As such, broadcasters and internet providers are prohibited from broadcasting anything that might be deemed to incite hate, cause "anxiety or unrest among the public order," or promote the assassination of public officials. Furthermore, the private sector's financial support for community and alternative media networks proved insufficient to bring about a determinative role in these meaning-making spheres. The wording of these media-law changes is sufficiently broad as to give the government the power to censor news content and personal communications which conflict with journalists' and the media's right to communicate freely. Yet, it might also be argued that these media-law changes align Venezuela with the media regulations of other countries in the Western world with restrictions on what language, sexual content, and violence can be broadcast at certain times. This measure might also have been a response to the 2002 coup attempt against Hugo Chávez that was broadcast on live television. And, within the context of the current restrictions and punishments of social media in the United States against those who incited violence against the Capitol lawmakers on January 6, 2021, the stance that these are protections of the many at the expense of the few is completely justifiable outside of the realm of protection of free speech argument. Freedom of speech cannot be absolute, after all, if it offends or violates the rights of the larger society.

Catia TVe and the community television movement reflect the ideals of activist-oriented components: producers, publics (audiences, communities, and collectives of people from the poor and working class), and programming, all dedicated to the effective working of political systems in their favor. As a method, participatory broadcasting of this nature provides the tools to allow practitioners to work together on pressing social issues. Structures of power should be challenged, both in the production process and in terms of who produces knowledge and how. These are laudable goals, but community broadcasting rests on fundamental political values and shared ideals which include:

> Recognizing the political nature of knowledge and its production; skepticism of positivist social science; an attempt to equalize power relations between the knower and the known; a commitment to the transformative potential of situated and subjugated knowledges; a belief in participatory democracy as the means and goal of social change; and the explicit goal of research for anti-oppressive social change. (Nygreen, K. 2009-2010, p. 14)

Yet there is an implicit naivety in Catia TVe's philosophy that simply by expressing their grievances on air, or recognizing them collectively in public spaces, marginalized communities' issues will be addressed. Surely, direct democracy is based on participation, and community television is an engaging way to activate participation. Self-recognition and empathy towards others are powerful tools in creating the groundwork for social change. Understanding that you are not alone on the issues that you experience daily can be essential to building confidence, for pursuing issues further, and building coalitions. Getting people involved in speaking and reflecting on some of the very difficult experiences in their lives is essential to participatory democracy and the outcomes of community television. Nonetheless, these community actors are working for social change. They are aware of the institutional framework that has the potential to exploit or even override the voices it was designed to uplift. Truth-speaking to power is doomed to failure under a political leader with autocratic tendencies. Catia TVe's staff did make attempts from the outset to separate community and state in well-defined arenas with broadcast requests from the community given priority over elected officials, state ministries, and other state official institutions. But the demarcation between popular movements and state institutions remained blurred.

In their attempt to build a "communal state" during a period of limited economic resources, Catia TVe encountered increasing challenges with the community-state question of autonomy. But the asymmetric relationship between these community actors and the state soon evolved into political clientelism. In this arrangement, the state provided financial support for goods, services, and salaries, and the patrons provided policy and program support. And, of course, some of those policies and programs benefited Catia TVe actors and patrons — the marginalized communities. In the twenty-first century, clientelism has come to be a social exchange, a method of mobilizing political support, a strategy to maintain power, or a method of electoral mobilization. Contemporary clientelism is anything but a social structure dictated by socio-cultural or socio-economic contexts. In other words, there were many benefits accruing from the popular media's relationship with the state that justified maintaining it, despite its drawbacks of self-censorship and subordination to the government.

The negative impact of political clientelism, such as vote-buying, patronage, and other forms of corruption are well-known. Little emphasis has been put on the more positive outcomes of clientelism. Such a practice may spur accountability if it leads to patron politicians fulfilling the identified needs of their clients. The literature of ethnographic clientelism, such as that done by Naomi Schiller in *Channeling the State*, often emphasizes the client's agency, the diverse rationales for clients to behave in the way they do. But it also shows that clientelism takes many forms and not just typical vote-buying. The trade-offs faced by the client, the political alternatives available to the client, the client's level of agency, and the trade-offs perceived by the client when making political decisions complicate the issue of political clientelism when viewed from this perspective. Catia TVe grassroots actors viewed themselves as full participants in the political process of the emerging revolutionary Bolivarian state, shaping its ideas, policies, and practices. Indeed, the physical location of the *barrio* and the command center of the station were located a short walk from the presidential palace. And it was their neighborhood of community-run media broadcasts that provided the backdrop of and validation for the revolutionary state's policies as being advanced by the people, the "authentic" popular or masses of the poor.

Consequently, it was relatively easy for Catia TVe and its allies to at long last see Chávez's revolution as *their* revolution and themselves as full participants in state formation. The homogeneity of political messaging of inclusivity (state and the popular impoverished masses) was pitted against all forces of opposition. Catia TVe identified with the idea of state as *process*—a process moving toward a just and equitable populist agenda favoring programs to advance the cause of the poor. Their imagined future of the popular state would not only serve the interests of Venezuela's poor majority but also be governed by it. That is why Catia TVe producers, staff, and volunteers have presented state and community as mutually exclusive entities advancing mutually beneficial agendas, negotiating relationships of power and empowerment. It was the *vox populi* that ultimately became the face of Venezuela's complex revolutionary process of top-down management by and for the poor, interweaving the lowly barrios and the official halls of government power.

The general concept of authentic participation as defined herein is rooted in cultural traditions of the common people and in their real history, not the elitist version. Such traditions are resplendent with feelings and attitudes of an altruistic, cooperative, communal, and democratic nature. They are core cultural values which have survived in practice despite the destructive impact of conquests and all kinds of foreign invasions. Such resilient values are based on mutual aid, the helping hand, the care of the sick, the communal use of lands, forests and waters, the extended family, kinship, and many other ancient social practices which vary from region to region, but which constitute the roots of participatory democracy. These enlightened masses, which have been given voice by community television Catia TVe, are the *real* vanguard. The *raison d'être* of these masses is to seek consensus; its members tend not to be authoritarian but act as catalysts for social transformation over time as participants in an *evolutionary* process. But these same autochthonous factors of social movements often cause communities to fall victim to the structural failures of the old order characterized by exploitation, oppression, and dependence. Under this old order, politicians simply decided what to offer to the masses according to their own superficial impressions or political platform and proceeded accordingly to dispense the crumbs of power through miscellaneous promises and some fulfilled commitments which reflect traditional subservience. It was only after Chávez came to power that dark-skinned, poor people became legitimate protagonists in Venezuelan media. Through governmental and grassroots media like the Catia TVe collective, Venezuela's most prominent (and first) community television station broadcast from Catia, a major neighborhood in the capital city of Caracas. But, whether intentionally or unintentionally, the station and its allies served as a medium for state policies, some of which benefited their communities.

In June 2015, the non-governmental organization, IPYS Venezuela (*Instituto Prensa y Sociedad de Venezuela*), published an 18-page summary report on freedom of expression in Venezuela spanning 2005 to 2014. Executive Summary point #5 states:

> From 2005 to 2014, IPYS Venezuela recorded excessive pressures that restricted the freedom of TV and radiophonic media. 52 administrative procedures, i.e., investigations on alleged technical and content-related

crimes, were applied by the entity that regulates telecommunications against the private and community-based radio-electric media, web portals and Internet and cable TV carriers. (IPYS, p. 4)

In its section on "an unbalanced media ecosystem," the organization goes on to state that "the Venezuelan government has also taken advantage of the platform of community-based and state-owned media, a large part of which are grouped under the Bolivarian System of Information and Communication...." And they conclude that, "This demonstrates the absence of plurality, freedom and autonomy in the system of state-owned, community-based and private media in Venezuela." (IPYS, p. 14)

Venezuelan community television: A retrospective and a prospective view

What kind of media policy would have best served the Bolivarian Revolution begun by Hugo Chávez to correspond with its discourse of popular power to avoid accusations of paternalism and clientelism? In order to allow popular power to be on equal footing with state power and even eclipse it, Chávez would have had to construct new media democracies in communication infrastructures that had been largely monopolized by the private sector. He would have had to prioritize an independent media over state and parastate media. Chávez would have had to eliminate controls exercised over community broadcasting stations. Media and social movements obviously fulfill different roles. The state had the potential to improve the lives of the poor and expand its access to political participation. During Chávez's presidency, community media became a vehicle for poor and elite social actors to jointly shape political policies; health and education initiatives became universal human rights for all Venezuelan citizens. State resources were invested in community media to provide the marginalized poor with a voice on a powerful media platform.

In 2003, Catia TVe community media activists and many of their allies sought to restructure their social order. Their goal was to bring sweeping societal change to their country as part of a massive movement in popular political participation. The Bolivarian Revolution was underway at the time with the same aims of establishing a new anti-capitalist cultural hegemony of socialism against the traditional power hierarchies. President Hugo Chávez led the charge, and so appealed to and inspired the poor majority by his mixed-race ancestry so that he easily engaged them in the process of state formation—the socialist ideals of his revolution. He looked like and talked like the poor, and his performative style of speaking was captivating. He empathized with the squatter town residents and created programs that gave them access to primary health care and secondary education, created social welfare institutions for them, and most importantly, gave them agency through media visibility. They told their stories, aired their grievances, and shared the uniqueness of their culture as Chávez listened and applauded them for their honesty and resilience. The poor people's movement and Chávez's twentieth-century socialist revolution shared the same commitments to progressive social change and the inclusion of once alienated populations of the urban and rural poor. But the dialectical relationship between autonomy and dependency of social actors and spheres of influence is not always clearly demarcated. So, the complexities of the community television station's relationship with the state were immense and increased over time. Collaboration with state institutions often blurred the line between the freedom to critique the government and the constraints such criticism placed upon their broadcasts whether directly or indirectly. State support of community media caused grassroots social movements to compromise their ideals in many instances. The relationship of state actors to the media and the autonomy of popular movements in Catia TVe became redefined over the years. Hugo Chávez's death in March 2013, the plunge in oil prices in an oil-dependent economy, and the rise to power of Chávez's successor, Nicolás Maduro, were pivotal factors in the temporary demise of Catia TVe in 2014. Media staff were dispersed to other media outlets or left without employment altogether as disillusionment set in. And the charismatic personality of Hugo Chávez was not replicated in the new president. The media experiment of the Bolivarian Revolution that gave voice to and valorization of popular wisdom and culture had descended to its darkest cavern in a little more than a decade.

The words of the Venezuelan singer-composer, Ali Primera, resonate here. Primera was recognized as a Venezuelan National Heritage treasure by Chávez in 2005. Like Víctor Jara and Violeta Parra in Chile, Mercedes Sosa in Argentina, and countless other singers and composers of the 'Nueva Canción' (New Song) movement, Ali Primera became a symbol of the struggle that represented the voiceless and marginalized, and thus, the Bolivarian Revolution, despite his death in 1985. Some phrases of the Singer of the People include:

> Capitalism is the root of all the problems my people are suffering.
> You can't call dead those who die fighting for life.
> Don't be fooled by those who speak of progress …you remain thin, and they gain weight.
> If the fight is scattered there will be no peoples' victory in combat.

During the social unrest of the 1990s, Ali Primera's music resurfaced in popularity. And it was that social turmoil that led to the election of Hugo Chávez. Among his most emblematic songs is 'Techos de cartón' (Cardboard Roofs), wherein he speaks about the poorest people in his country living in cardboard houses, listening to the sound of rain on cardboard roofs. Considered too radical for mass media, Primera's music was censored by the government of Rafael Caldera (President of Venezuela: 1994–1999; 1969–1974). Nonetheless, he continued to promote his own work and that of other artists with a shared commitment to his own label. His compositions made him the spokesperson for the painful realities of the neediest in Venezuela. Despite being categorized as a "protest singer," he used to say that his songs should not be considered songs of protest, but songs of necessity. Why are the lyrics of Ali Primera relevant to Venezuela's community television movement? How do they reflect the philosophy of Catia TVe and other community media?

Community media producers envision *barrio*-based television not as a mouthpiece for the government, but rather as an instrument with which to engage in statecraft, alongside with, or in radical interdependency with, state authorities. In this sense, *access* to media production may be perceived as more important to community media producers than press freedom. Historically, the masses had been marginalized communities, and so *some* voice was better than no voice. At times, Catia TVe's workers tried to erode boundaries with the state, for example, reaffirming the station's commitment to revolution through their election coverage, or supporting the government's revocation of RCTV's (a commercial channel) license. At other times, the boundaries with the state were reproduced strategically. Examples include efforts to build a collective political identity encompassing residents of poor, formerly disenfranchised communities, or considering the possibility of raising money from the local community instead of relying on an unstable and at times overshadowing state. As Schiller (2018, p. 224) asserts, Catia TVe constituted "neither watchdog nor lapdog." Community media producers were aware of the dynamics of interdependency between the organized activist poor and official state actors and institutions. They were cognizant of Ali Primera's warnings against progressives who might not deliver on their promises.

Debates about press freedom in Venezuela are highly polarized. Journalism in Venezuela can paradoxically both deepen and threaten democratic forms of expression and action. It was noted earlier in this chapter that Catia TVe, as well as other community stations, regularly aired *denuncias* or criticisms of social, political, and economic problems in the country as an exercise of press freedom and community involvement in local problem-solving. There were counterclaims and examples of censorship as well. These mass-mediated denunciations became a tool of the popular movement to make demands and suggest reforms of existing institutions. Unfortunately, the atmosphere of openness in Venezuela has deteriorated in recent years since the death of Hugo Chávez. The authoritarian governing style of Nicolás Maduro stifles criticism of his government to protect his legitimacy. Under increasing sanctions and criticism from foreign powers, Maduro, in a form of *caudillismo mediático* or media autocracy, has all but eliminated the element of popular broadcast denunciations of his government and the processes of political self-determination and accountability previously upheld. How should we evaluate notions of statecraft and the transformation of the state by participatory democracy in the context of the increased bureaucratization and suppression of popular activism in the post-Chávez administration? According to Catia TVe staff, without economic and social rights, press freedom is a luxury of the elites. And, indeed, community media producers faced enormous intransigence from their own allies in state institutions in their efforts to remake and retake media outlets in the interest of the poor.

We are living in an age of *media populism* using broadcast media, cable, satellite, and now social media to present a political agenda and to maintain a media presence to a broad audience. We need only to look at the "media presidency" of Donald Trump for the indispensable role that twenty-first-century communication has played in the consolidation of personality politics. As Hugo Chávez was forced to step down from the presidency in 2012 while undergoing cancer treatment in Havana, he too embraced Twitter as a platform to continue his populist media presidency. Chávez was a pioneer among politicians in the use of Twitter, gathering millions of followers and frequently announcing news on the platform. Maduro also uses Twitter as his main form of communication and congratulates Catia TVe staff and volunteers for their service of defending the truth of the people on their broadcasts on this medium. One of President Maduro's Twitter accounts belongs to Radio Miraflores, a station set up by Maduro himself, broadcast from the presidential palace. It appropriately includes a salsa music program that he hosts—an expression of community culture.

Celebrating almost two decades of community broadcasting, Catia TVe finds itself at a crossroads—try to defend popular democracy within the existing system and reform it despite the corruption and concentration of power, or embrace an opposition to the current power structure? Catia TVe fought long and hard to further democratize access to and socialize ownership of media resources since it was established from a simple media club. Catia TVe still maintains the hopeful perspective that the state is a process which they can shape even in the face of adversity. In the final analysis, social movements and community media, more than political movements, will redefine democracy in Venezuela.

Community media, whether broadcast or online, are crucial to ensuring media pluralism and freedom of expression, and are an indicator of a healthy democratic society. As an alternative medium to public and commercial media, as well as social media, community media are characterized by their accountability to, and participation in, the communities they serve. They have a greater focus on local issues of concern and facilitate public platforms for debate and discussion. Additionally, community media are crucial to providing an outreach mechanism for increased access to education, self-expression, and communication, particularly among underserved populations in urban poor, rural, and hard-to-reach populations.

Ideally, television stations such as Catia TVe allow communities a sense of ownership about their own development agenda, becoming self-empowered to publicly express opinion, debate issues, and promote the culture, history, and language of their community. The long-term viability of community media should be encouraged through supportive policies and strategies, including legal recognition, fair access to spectrum and licensing, sustainable sources of funding, and inclusion in consideration around digital transition. Realistically, community media independence and sustainability cannot be completely guaranteed in a country undergoing a drastic transition from Neo-liberalism to socialism with a goal of participatory democracy for all its people. Such a goal is one of inclusivity of the marginalized masses of poor and disenfranchised populations based on race, color, ethnicity, and gender. The best that can be expected under such circumstances of sociopolitical and socioeconomic instability is the creation of the necessary spaces for state criticism in order to deepen the revolutionary process according to an agenda of popular empowerment.

Should community media attempt regime change, exit its place in state alliances, or support state initiatives to respond to existing challenges in the hope of finding a stronger and freer voice? Catia TVe and its allies have chosen the latter as their course of action on their path toward participatory democracy in Venezuela despite all the challenging drawbacks that it holds. What such a decision portends for a freer, more equitable, and just Venezuelan society is for the moment a matter of conjecture. Clearly, the interlocutors in Naomi Schiller's study of Venezuela's community media fought long and hard to democratize access to and socialize ownership of media resources. Throughout Schiller's interviews with Catia TVe representatives, they argued that without economic and social rights for the marginalized, press freedom was a luxury of elites. For Catia TVe producers and their allies, Schiller asserts, "freedom meant the ability to engage in this process of statecraft, not declare autonomy from the process…" (Schiller, 2018, p. 240).

If there is a space for hope in Venezuelan community media, it can be found at the grassroots level among the media producers and journalists, the youth aboard buses ("Bus TV") using their voices and cardboard frames to bring news to the poorest neighborhoods of Caracas. To be sure, these are different visions of media and democracy. On the one hand, the fact-based reporting of professional journalists balks at political intervention and ramifications of its reporting. On the other hand, the *barrio*-based activism of Catia TVe seeks inclusion and a platform for its demands, aware of its dependence on government resources. The concluding chapter of Venezuela's community media, its successes and failures, has yet to be written.

References

CatiaTVe Collective. (2006, July 19). *Catia TVe, Television From, By and For the People.* Venezuelanalysis.com. https://venezuelanalysis.com/analysis/1843

Coronil, F. (1997). *The Magical State: Nature, Money, and Modernity in Venezuela.* The University of Chicago Press.

Habermas, J. (1979). The Public Sphere. In A. Mattelart & S. Siegelaub (Eds.), *Communication and Class Struggle: 1 - Capitalism, Imperialism* (Vol. 1, pp. 198–201). International General Publishers.

Joseph, G., & Nugent, D. (Eds.). (1994). *Everyday Forms of State Formation.* Duke University.

Instituto Prensa y Sociedad de Venezuela (IPYA Venezuela). (2015). *Freedom of Expression and the Right to Information in Venezuela.* Human Rights Committee. https://www.ecoi.net/en/file/local/1185288/1930_1437487822_int-ccpr-css-ven-20714-e.pdf

Laudeman, G. (2013). *Toward a Multilevel Theory of Learning: How Individuals, Organizations, and Regions Learn Together* [Unpublished doctoral dissertation]. University of Tennessee at Chattanooga. https://scholar.utc.edu/cgi/viewcontent.cgi?article=1458&context=theses

McLuhan, M. (1964). *Understanding Media: The Extensions of Man.* https://www.ecoi.net/en/file/local/1185288/1930_1437487822_int-ccpr-css-ven-20714-e.pdf

Nygreen, K. (2009–2010). Critical Dilemmas in PAR: Toward a New Theory of Engaged Research for Social Change. Social Justice Activist Scholarship: Possibilities of Participatory Action Research (PAR). *Social Justice/Global, 36*(4), 14–35. https://www.jstor.org/stable/29768559?seq=1

Schiller, N. (2018). *Channeling the State: Community Media and Popular Politics in Venezuela.* Duke University.

CHAPTER 7

Music and violence: The complexity and complicity of Pashto "Songs of Terror"

Muhammad Farooq

Kent State University, USA

Syed Irfan Ashraf

University of Peshawar, Pakistan

Abstract

This chapter discusses how Pashto songs eulogize and romanticize militarization, especially its twin technologies of systemic violence — Drone strikes and suicide bombing. Using Achille Mbembe's necropolitics as a theoretical lens, the authors discuss how music, politics, and destruction reinforce one another in a war zone where life is subjected to the rule of death. The authors argue that militarization in the Pashtun belt—a border region straddling Afghanistan and Pakistan and inhabited by the ethnic Pashtuns—led to the emergence of a local genre of songs, which they call "songs of terror" in this chapter. The poignant lyrics in these songs hide the power structure that imperceptibly regulates the troubled space of their cultural production. This politicization of music and musicalization of death, they argue, create a necrospace in which the cultural imagery appears in an undifferentiated role with the technologies of war. This imagery of the necrosovereigns — Drones and suicide bombing—does not only reflect the complexity of the ties between culture and politics, but also becomes complicit in reproducing and proliferating organized violence in its enunciations.

Keywords: Pashto songs, songs of terror, necrospace, necrosovereigns, drone, suicide bombing, Pak-Afghan border, terrorism

***

Introduction

The famous Pashto singer, Sitara Younis, sang: "I am an illusion, a suicide bomb" (*Khud kasha dhamaka yum, dhoka yuma, dhoka*), with the stage performance of Sonu Lal, to hundreds of Pashtuns of all ages who did not just listen to the song, but also danced to the tune and lip-sang the lyrics in unison with the singer (Zeb, 2012).

Given the popularity of this song, a couple of years later, the same singer sang another song, "My gaze is as fatal as a Drone attack" (*Za kaom pa stargu stargu drone hamla*) that also received a similar response (Zainali, 2014). This popular appearance of the imagery of suicide bombs and drone strikes, the two offshoots of the "war on terror" in contemporary Pakistan, signify the prevailing wave of militarization as a discourse in the daily life of the Pashtuns. This raises a vital question: does this form of music dilute, negotiate, and/or resist the horrible effects of the war in Pakistan? Since music is traditionally associated with resistance, therefore its celebration of militarized violence complicates its role and deserves an investigation. These responses require seeing how music, especially the lyrics, has been influenced by the persistent militarization in Pakistan. In this chapter, therefore, the authors examine a complex relationship of Pashto music with the troubled site of its emergence — the border region comprising the northwest Pakistan and southeast Afghanistan, commonly known as the Pashtun belt.

With the beginning of the "war on terror" in Pakistan's bordering tribal region in 2001, the daily lives of the local Pashtun population and their cultural space began to shrink (Ahmed, 2013). The heavy presence of Pakistan's military and the Taliban's reemergence as a political force reinforced the militarization that almost resulted in the stifling of alternative voices in the region (Siddique, 2014). In the given militarized space, the emergence of the "songs of terror" problematized the relationship between music, politics, and death. Despite the relative lull in the drone and suicide attacks in recent years, the Pak-Afghan border is still the focus of the global war and its multiple ramifications. Using Mbembe's (2003) necropolitics as a theoretical lens, this chapter focuses on the lyrics of the emergent Pashto songs to understand how music, politics, and destruction reinforce one another in a conflict zone where life is subjected to the rule of death—various sovereign powers (USA, Pakistan, and Al-Qaeda-affiliated Taliban) instrumentalizing death to control the local population. This politicization of music and musicalization of death, as argued in this chapter, create a necrospace in the Pashtun belt where the cultural imagery appears in an undifferentiated role with the necrosovereigns—drones and suicide bombers—drones representing the U.S. military sovereignty in the sky and suicide bombing ruining people's lives on the ground (Ashraf & Shamas, 2020). The textual imagery produced in such a violent troubled space not only reflects the complexity of the ties between culture and politics but also becomes complicit in reproducing systemic violence in its ramifications.

Often dismissed in Pashtun belt as too mundane[1], and thus unfit for academic inquiry, a relationship between commercial music and militarized violence (read "war on terror") is not a common theme in popular and academic discourses. This undervalued symbiotic relationship between space and violence is either generalized in the context of performing arts as the cultural voice of Pashtun nationalism (Khan & Khattak, 2014) or it is buried deep down under a militarized discourse with a focus on the legal and political dimensions of techno-savvy Drone warfare (Gusterson, 2019; Khan, 2011; Parks, 2014; Peron, 2015). A few academic inquiries have examined the violent (mis)representation of Pashtuns in a bid to dispel such myths of cultural representation (Afridi et al., 2016; Yousaf, 2019), but the approach (of such a discourse) is often apologetic in a sense that it absolves Pashtuns of colonial charges of being unruly and violent. Among the popular responses, the authors of this chapter found reports that have looked into the shrinking of space for Pashto music with focus on murders, censorships, threats, and destruction of the places of cultural production (Buneri et al., 2014).

On the whole, such cultural discourses, while attributing regional imperialist militarization to local insurgency, ignore a relationship between global power and the state's ideology in the construction of the space. It also undermines the mutation and transformation of the marginalized local cultural sphere that reveal mediation between the global forms of local violence and their attendant responses. These representations, however, do not connect the local social milieu with the systemic form of contemporary global violence in the form of "war on terror." As a result, the local agency, as well as the Pashtun belt, either submerges in a passive power of victimhood or reduces to an appendage status in cultural discourses. This dual negligence, academic inattention toward the expansive local cultural terrain in the context of the global war and generalizations around the Pashtun identity, do not only decontextualize systemic violence, but also naturalize the proliferation of the wider militarized discourse.

The main objective in this chapter, therefore, is to reveal a symbiotic relationship between imperialist violence and a local production of commercial cultural artifacts — "songs of terror." By showing how a new genre of songs has developed under the shadow of the decades-long militarization in Pakistan, the authors not only attempt to show the rising popularity of this emerging genre

---

[1] For details see *Vulgarity has destroyed Pashto music | Art & Culture | thenews.com.pk.* (n.d.). Retrieved February 21, 2021, from https://www.thenews.com.pk/tns/detail/56496 5-pashto-music; and *Violence and vulgarity: Pashto pop music reflects region's war fixation.* (2015, July 5). The Express Tribune. http://tribune.com.pk/story/915473/violence-and-vulgarity-pashto-pop-music-reflects-regions-war-fixation.

on social media but also focus on how the local cultural artifacts connect imperialist violence to everyday life in the Pashtun belt. The discussion in this chapter, however, is not limited to mere temporal conditions (trends, profit, public response) responsible for the production of the cultural artifacts; rather, it emphasizes that the emergence of this commercial text and their poignant lyrics hide the power structure that imperceptibly regulates the space of their production. This study, therefore, aims to establish that these songs do not merely depict violence at the time and place of their origin but also, through their circulation, disseminate it to the broader cultural space of the region, and consequently produce a hitherto unknown necrospace in the process.

The Pashtun Belt: A Site of Imperialist Militarization

The Pashtun Belt is a sparsely populated mountainous strip that connects Pakistan's northwestern (Khyber Pakhtunkhwa including former FATA) and southern parts (Karachi and Ten Districts of Baluchistan). It protrudes into Afghanistan's three adjacent eastern (Loy Nangarhar or Greater Nangarhar), southeastern (loya Paktia or Greater Paktia), and southern and southwestern (Loy Kandahar or Greater Kandahar) tribal regions. Divided on both sides, over 20 million ethnic Pashtuns live in Pakistan—over sixteen percent of its total 200.2 million population (*Minority Rights Group*, 2018). This belt had historically connected Central Asian states in the north with the northwestern fringes of the Indian subcontinent (present day Pakistan) via Afghanistan.

Different global powers at different ages fought for the control of this corridor for different purposes. The British regime in India, as part of its Forward Policy, initially imagined its boundary with Russia along Amu Darya (river) in Afghanistan, but their defeat in the First Anglo-Afghan war made them settle for a "closed border" policy that resulted in the Durand Line in 1893.[2] As a colonial outpost, this line separated northwestern and southwestern fringes of British India from Afghanistan, dividing Pashtun tribes, the world's largest tribal society on both sides of the Durand Line (Ahmed, 2011; Anderson, 1975; Bartlotti, 2000; Hart, 1985). In 1901, the local population along the border toward the British Indian side was further divided into North West Frontier Province (NWFP) and Federally Administered Tribal Areas (FATA). Culminating in what the British called a "threefold frontier," this division allowed the colonial administration to directly administer NWFP with Peshawar as the capital of the state and indirectly govern FATA with a separate set of laws known

---

[2] The British colonial power in India and Afghanistan fought three wars, known as Anglo-Afghan Wars or Afghan Wars (First Anglo-Afghan War 1839-42, Second Anglo-Afghan War 1878-1880, Third Anglo-Afghan War 1919).

as the Frontier Crimes Regulations (FCR). This division enabled the British colonizers to exert strategic control over Afghanistan at the extreme outer fringe of the British India (Siddique, 2014). Such layers of buffer zones facilitated the British Raj to effectively counter the growing Soviet influence in the region.

After the British withdrawal from India and the latter's partition in 1947, these administratively divided territories (NWFP and FATA) of British India fell under the control of the newly created state of Pakistan. As a result, these regions continued to be imagined as what the British called "lawless territories" (Yaghistan, subsequently *Illaqa Ghair* or the Land of the "Others"), hence the bordering tribal area was governed through FCR until 2018. Operating from this core, the colonial administration and the postcolonial Pakistani state (de)regulated life in the Pashtun belt, giving militarization a permanent form of life (Ainslee, 1977).

Using Britain's fabricated lawlessness as a framework, the Pakistani, in alliance with the U.S., appropriated the Pashtun belt for their strategic interests and legitimized their military aggression in the name of peace and stability (Ahmed, 2013; Khan, 2011; Shaw & Akhter, 2012). This imperialist alliance raised and equipped the Mujahedeen and Taliban as a proxy Islamist fighting force in the 1980s to stop the Soviet Union's intervention in Afghanistan (Crile, 2007). The current U.S-led "war on terror" is not a break from the past. Instead, this systemic violence is in line with this bordering region's almost two centuries of imperialist history. The U.S. and its allied forces (NATO-ISAF) invaded Afghanistan to eliminate the hideouts of their former Islamist proxies (Ahmed, 2013). Among others, drone strikes and suicide bombings are the most lethal technologies in this asymmetric global war (Khan, 2011; Woods, 2015). Although the "war on terror" was launched in 2001, the first drone attack was carried out in 2004 (Shaw & Akhter, 2012). Ever since, over four hundred drone attacks have targeted the Al-Qaeda-affiliated Pakistani Taliban commanders in which close to 3,700 deaths, including 245 to 303 civilians, have been reported (Bergen et al., 2021).

This war-like situation did not exist in the metropolitan areas, but in tribal regions that were considered lawless by the alliance that indiscriminately used lethal technology to prosecute their deadly war against the Mujahedeen and Taliban. The collateral consequence of the "war on terror" exposed Pashtuns living in this region to the ire of the Al-Qaeda-affiliated local Taliban groups. Unable to stop the drones, these Taliban groups settled scores with the local population by carrying out suicide attacks against soft targets such as schools, music centers, net cafes, local theaters, etc. The majority of these attacks were carried out in Peshawar, Quetta, and Kabul, as well as other major Pashtun cities, during the peak time of violence (Woods, 2015). From 2007 to 2009, for example, there was an average of two suicide-attacks each month in ex-FATA and Khyber Pakhtunkhwa (South Asia Terrorism Portal, 2018).

Due to such persistent militarization and militancy in this area, forms of cultural events were silenced, and local voices against the war and violence either emerged in the form of *Pashto tapey*, a folkloric romantic genre of Pashto literature, or found expression in commercial songs the authors call "songs of terror." Essentially, these songs highlighted drones and suicide bombings as the twin technologies of indiscriminate violence that were featured in the "war on terror." How then did this genre produce and occupy a cultural space amidst persistent imperialist militarization? This question is addressed in the sections below.

A space thriving on an economy of injury

The "songs of terror," produced in a space under the influence of high-tech warfare and its attendant responses, could best be analyzed in the light of Achille Mbembe's notion of necropolitics—a theoretical paradigm that discusses the subjugation of life to the power of death and a reconfiguration of the relation between sacrifice, terror, and resistance. Mbembe (2003) argues that Foucault's notion of biopower can no longer explain the new form of "social existence"—the creation of *"death-worlds,"* and the reduction of humans into *living dead* (p. 92). In his critical theoretical formulation, Mbembe primarily focuses on two things: the sovereign's exercise of the right to kill and the deployment of technology for maximal destruction of human life. Though these technologies are instructive here, we would like to take it further into the spatial formation that results from the incidents of destruction and their attendant responses. We argue that when an act of terrorism occurs and its spectacle subsides, a new necrospace emerges, not just in the form of deadly practices (revenge, suicide bombing, etc.), but in the speech acts (in this case the "songs of terror") that continue to proliferate and reproduce the imagery of violence and death. Thus, instead of a single event like a drone strike or suicide attack, which in itself certainly devastates human life and the conditions of their survival, the cultural proliferation and reproduction of violence in the form of these songs create an imaginary space in which death takes center stage.

Additionally, this spatial production and reproduction is useful to the necrosovereigns because it keeps the population in a state of what Jasbir Puar (2015) calls "deliberate debilitation." However, it is pertinent to mention here that debilitation is not the same as disability. Differentiating between debility and disability, Puar (2015) says that the former is a "slow wearing down of population" while the latter "hinges on a narrative of before and after for individuals who will eventually be identified as disabled" (Preface, p. xiv). Put differently, people in a state of debilitation are restricted to an open-air incarceration where all forms of life support (food, water, health, communication, and digital technology) are being constantly modulated by the technology of power. For example, Pashtuns have historically remained marginalized under both colonial (British India) and postcolonial (Pakistan, after 1947) regimes. Most wars, including those that were cultural, in both periods were fought on their soil and body (Fowler, 2007). Both regimes applied a separate set of laws on Frontier Crimes Regulation, Action in Aid of Civil Power) to maim the Pashtun body and environment in order to make available for sustaining the economy of injury.[3] Thus, debilitation is "a practice of rendering populations available for statistically likely injury" (Puar, 2015, p. xviii).

Disrupting the categories of disability, Puar (2015) uses the concept of debility to expand understanding of injury in order to encompass a wide range of people into its fold. By doing so, she also adds debility ("will not let die") as an additional component to the logic of biopolitics ("make live and let die") and necropolitics ("make die and let live"). Puar (2015) argues, "debilitation and the production of disability are in fact biopolitical ends unto themselves, with moving neither toward life nor toward death as the aim" (p. xviii). This existence between life-in-death and death-in-life is what Puar calls the sovereign's right to maim. In postcolonial Pakistan, for instance, the state machinery encourages patriarchy as a social system with focus on increased reproduction without provision of sufficient means of life support system (see Khan, 2005, 2016). In this way, a Pashtun benefits the state not only by keeping the border as an unpaid soldier (*bela tankhey mulazem*) but also the destruction of resources on their land compel them to work as laborers in the foreign countries where they earn and send back remittances to meet Pakistan's economic needs (Nichols, 2008). Thus, maiming, as Puar (2015) says, is "a source of value extraction from populations that would otherwise be disposable" (p. xviii). Produced in this debilitating space, even a text as entertaining as commercial songs could potentially be a macabre expression of this maiming. Using "drones" and "suicide bombing" as their catchwords, the emerging genre of commercial

---

[3] In 1948, for instance, the State sent a tribal militia for *jihad* in Kashmir against India and then, dispatched them against India to fight on the Lahore front in 1965. In 1979, the tribal youths were even sent to fight a US-funded *jihad* against the Soviet Union in Afghanistan. In 1998, the then military dictator Pervez Musharraf sent Pashtuns to the war against India in Kargil.

Pashto songs is one of its examples, an argument we extend below in examining the "songs of terror."

Music and Violence

As Carvalho (2013) contends, music is "born of a contract between the violence of noise and the silence of death" (p. 111). This complicated relationship between music and violence has intrigued many of its critics and researchers. McDonald (2010), for example, discusses the Palestinian wedding songs and performances (*debke, zeffa,* and *sahja*) to underscore how music assumes a political meaning in a conflict zone by forming communal connections between shared history of home and family and ideals of nation and resistance to occupation. Unlike such oft-romanticized vision of music as a voice of resistance to war and oppression, Attali (1985), by focusing on the noise and sound of music, finds music itself as an instrument of death and violence. He argues that in "its biological reality, noise is a source of pain. Beyond a certain limit, it becomes an immaterial weapon of death" (Attali 1985, p. 27). This fusion of music and violence is taken further by Daughtry (2014) in his framing of *thanatosonics,* which he says is "the acoustic instantiation of what Achille Mbembe has called 'necropolitics': 'contemporary forms of subjugation of life to the power of death'" (p.40). He argues that "the potential for violence is structurally embedded in all music...all of which have been consciously manipulated in detention centers throughout the 'war on terror'" (Daughtry, 2014, p. 42). Similarly, Cusick (2013) also highlights how "loud music" was weaponized as a technique of torture in the US-led detention centers to disorient the prisoners' subjectivity and disintegrate their psyche. Thus, music has the potential of creating solidarities among communities to form a coherent response to forces of oppression as well as the capacity of acoustic coercion and torture that play into the hands of the very forces of oppression.

However, it is beyond the purview of the present study to rehash previous research on music and violence or prove the innocence or complicity of music in itself in sustaining or resisting violence in general. We would still like to point readers to Elaine Sandoval's exhaustive review of literature on the role of music in multiple contexts including in violence and peacebuilding. Sandoval (2016) categorizes a large body of literature into "music and peace" and "music and violence" to discuss how various authors have engaged with the role of music in preventing or ending a conflict, or its traumatic and therapeutic functions in the aftermath of a conflict.

In this chapter, however, we focus on the relationship of Pashto music, especially the lyrics, with the organized global violence in the Pashtun belt to see how decades-long militarization produces a spatial mutation in local cultural artifacts. Though we partly agree with Sandoval's (2016) assertion that "understanding detailed, specific local contexts of violent conflict is crucial to thinking through music's potential role in such situations, and whether it can be one of peacebuilding or further violence" (p. 212), we would like to take it further than a mere dyadic understanding of music in terms of peace and violence. We focus on the specific context of the emergence of Pashto 'Songs of Terror' in the wake of decades-long militarization and organized global violence so as to understand how music mutates and creates a spatial contagion.

Violence and Pashto Music

This chapter was largely motivated by an article that appeared in a Pakistani English daily discussing one of these songs (Khan, 2012): "My gaze is as fatal as a Drone attack" (*Za Kaom Pa Stargo Stargo Drone Hamla*) that aroused mixed response from the song's viewers. The article claims that though "the song and video do not have anything new to offer, with an unimpressive melody and some dance moves by Dua, it seems the audience cares more about the lyrics" (Khan, 2012). According to the article, most respondents resented the trivial representation of drones and suicide attacks which they believe were otherwise meant for entertainment. Some even called for the censor board to filter out the content of these and other similar items. The article in itself generated mixed comments from its readers. One respondent, Gul, in the comment section of the article, apologetically denied the popularity of such songs. Another user, Imran Con, justified a death sentence for the musicians who sang the songs, arguing that "From what I gather, the fact they make music is enough for a death sentence from them anyways (sic)" (Khan, 2012). A couple of online users, Enlightened and Romo, however, appreciated the song and prayed for the safety of the singers.

We accessed about 20 songs in a random YouTube search that were composed in the last decade, all of which addressed the "war on terror" from different perspectives. Only five songs, however, used the metaphors of "drone strikes" and "suicide attacks." The five songs were therefore purposively selected as the data for our qualitative analysis.

Since no effective copyright regulations were in effect locally, some of the selected songs are available in different versions in Pakistan. Additionally, they are also available as playback tone in various self-promotional videos on different social media sites. Since most of these songs are recorded in small studios in the interior city areas of Peshawar and Lahore, they are also used by professional artists as background music to stage performances. This randomness makes it difficult to authenticate the original source of their creation, hence this poses a problem of proper academic citation when they are referenced. Also, it is pertinent to mention that the general fear of the necrosovereigns, owing to decades of systemic violence, conditions a forced anonymity for some musicians. For example, the Taliban destroyed many local entertainment spaces such as the commonly known "CD" shops and Internet cafes, and forced many artists either to quit the profession or seek asylum elsewhere. Authenticating the authorship of these songs, therefore, becomes muddied in the terrorized space of their production.

Some newspaper articles and reports make interesting revelations about the forced anonymity of these songs. Ali (2011), a journalist with *The Express Tribune*, a leading English Daily of Pakistan, claims that Shakir Zeb, a popular local composer, directed the song, "Khudkasha Damaka," that was written by Lyricist Rashid Johar and sung by Sitara Younis. He adds that initially Zeb refused to compose the song but "an anonymous influential figure of the Pashto film industry pressurized Zeb to work on the controversial song" (Ali, 2011). As far as these singers are concerned, they could only be guessed by their voices or appearance if available in video version. Quite often, as *YouTube* empowers people to create a channel and upload content, sometimes even without strict copyrights enforcement, the general users upload these songs to their respective channels and subsequently share them on their social media spaces in multiple forms. In this unauthorized scenario, some if not most of these songs are often duplicated, edited, and shared in such a way that it is difficult or impossible to determine their authorized and original versions. In other words, no standard repository of Pashto songs exists to authenticate the date of their composition and release.

Therefore, given the availability of these songs as multiple variants, shared on multiple platforms via multiple users, our choice was determined by the audience's maximum engagement based on the number of "views," "likes," and "comments" associated with the songs. From our investigation, we found out and determined, for example, that all the five songs discussed in this chapter had an aggregate total of 1.36 million views, with "Rolling Eyes Like a Drone" (Stargey Laka Drone Garzawey) receiving the highest tally of 773K views as of February 22, 2021. We chose and referenced the songs that were not merely depicting drones and suicide attacks—the focus of this study—but also had the most "views" and "likes" on YouTube only—a site that is popular among Internet users in Pakistan. Therefore, for more clarity, the two factors that determined the choice of songs analyzed in this chapter are: (a) songs that were about drone and suicide attacks; and (b) such songs that had the highest "views" and "likes" on YouTube.

Although it is outside the remit of the present study to dive into the parallel history of war and songs in Pakistan, nonetheless, a brief overview of the genre is instructive here so as to show how these songs have engaged with and intervened in the spatial reality of the Pashtuns. This background will be useful to the readers in understanding how these cultural artifacts adopted the imagery of drone and suicide attacks while depicting everyday Pashtun life enveloped in a state of war and terror.

"Songs of Terror:" The birth of a genre

Suffice it to say that the imagery of war and resistance in Pashto songs is as old as militarized violence in the region itself. In order to categorize these songs into their relevant time periods, therefore, we relied on the visual and textual clues of these artifacts, taking this Pashto genre as far back as the 1980s, the years in which the USSR's intervention in Afghanistan prompted the U.S.-backed Mujahedeen resistance, locally called *Jihad*. We found, for instance, one song on social media entitled, "Afghan War Song" (ABR Video, 2016), whose black and white flickering visual and textual clues could be conveniently placed into the Mujahedeen time. Sung by Afghan singers, as the edited *YouTube* video shows, the celebration of resistance in this song is supported by some blurred visuals of the armed Mujahedeen attacking the Soviets, aiming and shooting at a building where people run for their lives. These visuals also juxtapose the images of the Mujahedeen with those of Mohammad Najibullah, a pro-communist Pashtun president of Afghanistan (1987-1992), and different leaders of the Parcham faction of Soviet-backed Afghan People's Democratic Party. As no effective copyrights exist, already discussed above, almost all these songs are edited over and over to keep their appeal in contemporary "war on terror." Based on these production clues, we historicize this commercial text into their relevant time periods to trace a Pashto genre in the process of becoming.

Deriving orientation from the sacred and profane, these early Pashto songs feature the religious Islamic concept of *Jihad* as a spectacular nationalistic theme, associating it with local defiance against foreign oppression. For instance, the song, "The Brave Pashtun Freedom Fighters Resisting the Biggest Occupation of Modern History" (TheAbdaliBacha, 2011), juxtaposes the jihadist narrative with the nationalistic spirit. On the one hand the singer relies on the Islamic concept of martyrdom (sacrificing oneself in the way of God) as the lyrics glorify, "Young are martyred, orphans cry" but on the other hand, the singer claims possession of the Pashtun belt and intends to drive out all invaders (TheAbdaliBacha, 2011). The lyrics, for instance, talk about:

> Gun on my back, prayers on my lips
> I will not lay down my arms
> Until I drive enemy out of my land

(TheAbdaliBacha, 2011)

Similarly, another song titled, "Afghan War Song" (ABR Video, 2016), adopts the same approach, establishing a dichotomous relationship through lyrics such as:

Our pure land was desecrated by Khalqyan
The disheveled Russian
The disheveled Parchamian

(ABR Video, 2016)

In this song, the local jingoistic affiliations are sometimes appropriated for fomenting religious sentiments through juxtaposition of nationalistic undertones and visuals of mujahedeen era fights against the Russians. This approach of mixing the love of land (patriotism) and the imagery of jihad sometimes invokes colonial cues, a theme we found in another song entitled, "Patriotic Pashto Song/Brave Pashtunz" (Nasar, 2012). This song clearly depicts the imagery of Pashtuns as a "martial race"—a colonial objectification of the local people to use them as cannon fodder in their colonial wars. This cultural artifact invokes a nationalistic tone by emphasizing that Pashtun belong to Pakhtunkhwa and they:

Love this beloved (land)
In life or in death
This land belongs to Pashtuns

(Nasar, 2012)

By equating Pashtun identity with the space, the song makes a temporal move by claiming that their "History is a witness" to their identity as "Fearless Pashtuns," and their capacity to drive out an infidel (Russian) enemy from their land (Nasar, 2012). Despite their apparently nationalistic tone and message, these songs carry visual features that also glorify *jihad* and the Mujahedeen in the context of war. It is the juxtaposition of these four divergent elements: secular identity, ethnic identity, extremist religious ideology (*jihad*), and colonial categorization (brave and fearless race) that are mixed together to construct a *perverted* form of cultural narrative that defines Pashtuns as warriors. Ruling the Pashtun belt for many decades, this retrogressive imperialist approach is detrimental to any trace of alternative progressive worldview, yet it is also a popular myth that is reinforced in some sections of academic and popular literature as well (Fowler, 2007).

As a result of this somewhat orchestrated spatial and temporal retrogressive representation, Pashtuns' cultural identity and religious beliefs are intertwined to define their character and nature stereotypically. Most of these songs do not only serve the binary categorization of the local resistance and foreign aggression, but some of them also extend historical forms of colonial stereotyping to perpetuate contemporary war and violence in the Pashtun belt (Fowler, 2007).

Before the US-Soviet's proxy war, Pashtuns traditionally based the locus of their ethnic identity in their rich culture, commonly known as *Pashtunwali*. But the importation of *Jihad* by the Pakistan state, in conjunction with global powers (USA and their allies) into the region, instilled in Pashtuns an ethnoterritorial sensibility, and inculcated among them a sense of brotherhood across religious and national lines. Such political experiments in imperialist engineering did not only open the Pashtun belt to foreign elements (jihadists from Gulf and elsewhere)[4] but also promoted a worldview depicted in the "songs of terror."

This phenomenon was not so intensely felt during the *Jihad* years when the Pashtun belt was used for a fight between the two global powers: the U.S. and Soviets. In the Post 9/11 scenario, however, the Pashtun land and space in themselves became the means and the end of an asymmetrical war between the Mujahedeen-turned-Taliban groups and the US-led "war on terror." This contemporary imperialist violence almost permanently grounded and mutated violence into the local space, giving birth to a new category of enemy, the nonbeliever. This imperialist practice, taking up the form of local cultural narratives, reduces indigenous reality into a footnote. The spectacle of the post-9/11 Pashto songs does not just cobble Islamic *jihad* with nationalism, but also creates a spatial mutation that blurs the boundary between invasion and resistance, and the sacred and the profane. This takes a further complicated turn in the appearance of the contemporary "songs of terror," where the representation of suicide bombing and drones, the twin technologies of indiscriminate destruction, serves the same ends: systemic violence.

Post-9/11 imagery in Pashto songs[5]

In post-9/11 context, "drone" and "suicide bombing" were used for the first time as a metaphor in Pashto songs around the year 2011. Experimented in a fast musical track, "Suicide Bomb" (*khudkasha dhamaka*) (Zeb, 2012), this innovation—cooptation of the technologies of drone and suicide—brought an apparent shift in the local news and entertainment industry, inviting immediate attention of symbolic means of local representation, along with generating several responses among the viewers/readers (Ali, 2011; Khan, 2012; Shah, 2012).

---

[4] For details, watch US Secretary of State, Hilary Clinton's interview (2014, July 12). *Hillary Clinton: "we have helped to create the problem we are now fighting."* https://www.youtube.com/watch?v=AwpR6ngoSjQ

[5] This section contains close textual analysis of songs; therefore, some songs are referenced and parenthetically cited several times.

Beginning the song with the catch phrase, "Illusion, illusion," the singer adds the concept of suicide almost synonymously in the next lines, "I am an illusion/I am a suicide bomber, suicide bomber" (Zeb, 2012). This narration runs through the song as its dominant refrain. In this process, the song accommodates several aspects of a local perception of an actual suicide bomber. An actual suicide bomber, for instance, is locally taken as an uncontrollable, daringly ruthless, spontaneous, and terror-striking enemy — reducing its targets (human bodies) to indistinct smithereens. It is this perception that the song aims to capture. The essence of this local imagery is caught in the song through a series of characterizations of this phenomenon: "I do everything by force, everywhere I govern," and boasts an emotional control over people when the singer says: "Hearts I have plundered" (Zeb, 2012). As an embodiment of a suicide bomber, the female singer, therefore, assumes an absolute power over the audience/listeners.

The "suicide" song also points to the evasive, fearless and treacherous nature of the bomber, when the singer says, "None can capture me, none can scare me" (Zeb, 2012). To further reinforce her might, halfway through the song, the singer transitions from subjective empowerment to the spatial contagion in order to justify her absolute and total control over her targets. She creates a disjunction between spectacle of horror and love by saying, "Here you can merely see, here you can't love," and folds in the whole society into this collective relationship of enmity, "I am nobody's friend, I am everybody's enemy" (Zeb, 2012). The lyrics empower the singer to pinpoint the love-hate relationship between the deadly suicide bomber and the innocent masses in general when she says, "Neither can you stay away, nor get endeared," and coquettishly finishes off as a sovereign of the place and space: "I have besieged you" (Zeb, 2012). Overall, the song portrays the duplicity of the local technology of war, introducing suicide bombing as a form of lethal agency that eliminates all visible and invisible boundaries of distinction and creating a total war-like situation.

Sung by a non-Pashtun female singer, Sitara Younus, the lyrics of this fast-beat song foreground the deathly technologies of the imperialist war while signifying indiscriminate violence through a characterization of different ingredients of suicide bombing. Stylistically, this musical track also represents a war of all against all. Using the first-person pronoun "I," for example, the female singer exhibits strong agency, asserting control over the message, "I am an illusion/I am a suicide bomber." These lines, as a refrain of the song, create a powerful ambience of its own recurrent happening. The use of "suicide bomber" as an extended metaphor is also coextensive with the song's overall message and the spatial effect that it forcefully creates. This lyrical composition drags audience/listeners to clearly see the striking similarities between an actual suicide bomber and its lyrical and spatial representation. The very fact of the singer's presence on stage among a crowd of people reminds them of the devastation packaged in the lyrics.

The song also has a male chorus that compliments and enhances the singer's message by signaling the audience through an objective reference to her lethality. When the singer sings, "I am a suicide bomber," the chorus in the background repeats, "Suicide bomb! Suicide bomb!" (Zeb, 2012). The male chorus, as is typical of this literary device, both as a singer and a spectator, complements as well as enhances the enormous effect of this deathly speech act. This spectacle-spectator juxtaposition in the form of a female singer and a male chorus points to the spatial reality that thrives on a disjunction between actual experience and its remote representation. Thus, this imagery aims to represent suicide bombing as a concrete act of destruction and as a symbolic weapon of all pervasive terror. More than representing the lethality of love, the song actually seems to celebrate the loss of human relations (love) at the altar of a total war.

In another five-stanza long Pashto song, "My gaze is as fatal as a Drone attack" (*Za kawum, za kawum pa stargu stargu drone hamla*) (Zainali, 2014), also sung by a female Pashto singer, the innovative way of celebrating violence over a traditional definition of love, i.e., sacrifice, tolerance, humanity, etc., takes an unnoticeable trivial touch. Each stanza of the song picks up a different conventional metaphor of cultural aesthetics and replaces it with the imagery of a war machine in the refrain. The first stanza, for instance, while picking up the conventional association of sweetness with a beloved's lips, uses drones as a metaphor to weaponize the traditional notion of love. Similarly, the singer associates the "touch of [her] lips" and "Intoxicating wine" with the imagery of the destructive nature of drone technology: "My gaze is as fatal as a Drone attack" (Zainali, 2014). This combination of the imagery of conventional love and high-tech weapons tends to develop a new physiognomy of the "destructive" beloved that does not just skirt metaphorical death in its lethal beauty, but also emphatically enforces it by embodying the same annihilating technology.

The song continues this treatment in the second stanza as well. Picking up the beloved's traditional attributes of love, the stanza portrays a beloved's gaze and smile as "amorous pangs" that ensnare and debilitate lovers. The beloved's "coquettish stare" is presented as "a snare of beauty," and her smile as "early morning dew" (Zainali, 2014). This stanza, however, also does not leave the lover in the masochistic pain of conventional love but reminds him of the fatality of the beloved's gaze that strikingly resembles a drone strike. The third stanza moves away from suggestive language into an explicit message of torture and death as the singer says that she is "A leaping flame and a rose bud" burning a lover to death (Zainali, 2014). Such a spectacle of unforgiving death is reinforced by the imagery of drones in the refrain. The fourth stanza evokes the humming noise of drones through the clinking of the beloved's bangles that "leaves one enchanted" and "Tests lovers' courage" (Zainali, 2014). In traditional Pashto music, evoking the clinking sound of the beloved's bangles is aimed to create an evocative sensation in the onlookers or lovers, but this new mixing of the conventional metaphor of local love (clinking) and modern signs of violent global warfare (the humming of drones) could not just be dismissed as a trivial form of local representation in a state of war, but the effects of this macabre treatment go beyond the apparent. It potentially passes a chill through the spine of those affected people who actually live under the agonizing humming sound of drones, hovering 24/7 over their heads; thus, the sound of music and drone become indistinguishable from each other. Also, the next stanza rounds up the parts (lips, eyes, smile) into a whole (body and prime) that deceives and "leaves many... astray" (Zainali, 2014). This analogy between the freshness of the beloved's beauty and newness of drone technology point to the new gore and uncanny reality that apparently cannot find apt expression in the existing local cultural artifacts.

Although the song thrives on juxtapositions and subversions, this treatment rarely unearths the gruesome experience of life caught in a state of an imperialist war. The traditional imagery reflected in these songs and evoked through literary devices, such as the metaphors and similes, not only fail to grasp the essence of the gruesome local reality but also subvert the conventional notion of love by picking up metaphors of traditional aesthetics in Pashtun folklore. This treatment further romanticizes and trivializes the reality of this deathly space. By superimposing the imagery of a high-tech drone as a refrain in every stanza, the song, for instance, convolutes the experience of the deadliness of a drone as a gruesome phenomenon and mixes it up with veneration of a beloved femme fatale — a beautiful and seductive woman who charms her lover into a deathly trap. This macabre treatment, instead of representing a local, brutal reality as an experience from the perspective of local people, glamorizes drones as an unmatched weapon of total war—an innovation that helps sell these commercial cultural artifacts. As a result of such representation, two types of understanding immediately become apparent. On the one hand, the beloved's most sought-after "looks" are replaced with a "gaze" that not only changes the notion of the beloved's "looks" in itself, but also subverts the beloved's positionality from *being gazed at* into *gazing at* her lover—and that too with a formidable threat of fatality (emphasis added). On the other hand, the appropriation of drone imagery for expression of romantic love and its juxtaposition with the trite metaphors of local aesthetics normalizes the lethality of drones as the self-inflicting wounds of love.

Another song, "Never mess up with a Drone" (*Drone sara ba na cherey*) (Arts, 2020) takes this celebration and romanticization to new heights. Referring to the lethality, superiority, and invincibility of drone strikes, the song invites listeners to admit the omnipresent and godly power of this modern and destructive war technology. In the song's first stanza, perhaps for lack of a better metaphor, as is the case with the representation of this gore reality elsewhere, the lyrics compare the lethal drone with a "Thunder from the sky" (Arts, 2020). The drone and thunder have striking similarities: both strike from above, carrying out devastating effects on the ground. Yet thunder is less dangerous in the sense that it produces a harrowing and roaring spectacle attributed to nature without necessarily causing material damage to the people below, unless in exceptionally rare situations. On the other hand, the drone is a man-made indiscriminate weapon of war and destruction, known for its guided precision and creating a deliberate and targeted terrorizing effect through the subjugation of everything into its surveillance and devastation. The lyrics, referring to the drone's asymmetrical power, tout the war technology as "invincible on every front" while rhetorically inviting listeners to admit its power with the rhetoric, "Won't you admit Drone!" (Arts, 2020). A call for an all-out submission, this song represents the awesome power of drone technology commanding and dictating local life from above.

But this sovereignty in the sky is not detached from its attendant spectacle on the ground. The song's second stanza conveys this pragmatic logic. Personifying a drone as a wrestler (locally called *pahlawan*), the stanza imagines the drone's movement "with a swagger" when it "Tosses to the ground" and "Indulges in carnality" (Arts, 2020). Portraying this war technology as a master of the earth, the stanza ends this death-dance-like imagery with a different refrain: "Never mess up with a Drone" (Arts, 2020). This time, the forceful use of refrain as a literary device is an imperative that mainly attempts to secure an unquestionable acceptance for its asymmetrical power. The song's next stanza reinforces the Drone's uncritical acceptance through an in-group/out-group discourse by informing the listener that, "Everyone has recognized Drone," so as to comprehensively secure their unconditional recognition of this phenomenon. And, the stanza with the same rhetorical trope as the refrain in the first stanza, "Won't you admit Drone!" (Arts, 2020). This stanza gives permanency to the drone's on-ground rule, thus conveying that the technological might in the sky is replicated only in its act of tossing and continuity of death and destruction on the ground.

The rhetorical question, "Won't you admit Drone!" is a technique that constricts room for alternative perspectives and secures a quiet acceptance of the statement of a pliable speaker. In order to continue to establish this unquestionable superiority of this war machine, the singer projects a local understanding of power to this new phenomenon. By highlighting its uniqueness, for example, the lyrics say, "None parallels its might/ None can overpower it/ Drone is one of its kind" (Arts, 2020). The song also mentions the local people's inability to counteract this technology, saying: "None can resist it;" it is omniscient, "None can escape its gaze" and its lethality, "Drone drops atomic bombs" (Arts, 2020). Ironically, the song ends on a happy note, stating that "Drone is unparalleled, Mafroor/ Be happy forever, Mafroor" (Arts, 2020). The song's lyricist who, with an authoritative voice has robustly secured the listeners' attention and instructed them to admit the Drone's unquestionable necropower, finally partakes in its pleasure in a carnivalesque manner. The end, though it may seem baffling at first, points to an alternative reality of the use and abuse of Drones in the Pashtun belt. Some people appreciate its precision and accuracy and its capacity to kill terrorists that are hidden and harbored in their region (Khan, 2011; Shahzad, 2011; Shaw & Akhter, 2012).

A number of variations appear between this "Drone" song and the previous "Drone" and "suicide" songs. Unlike the female singer of the two previous songs who embodies the modern technologies of death and romanticizes them through her looks and gaiety, the male singer here personifies the drone and celebrates its unmatched might as a partisan spectator with a certain degree of detachment from local grievances. This gender variation also affects the style of singing. Unlike a threatening language in the first two songs, here the singer alternates between rhetoric "Won't you admit" and the imperative of "never mess up" to indulge in a dialogic way with his attentive listeners.

Like a typical drone strike, there is an impulsive and determining movement in this "song of terror." Depicted not just as a weapon of war, the lyrics portray Drone with unique predatory agency. It begins like a thunder flash in the sky, hovering up in the air with a swagger, and drops bombs indiscriminately, killing human beings on the ground below. Such a movement symbolizes the complete control of aerial and earthly local space of everyday living. No evidence of resistance seems to exist in a space where Drones are absolute necrosovereign. This celebration of the heroics of war in glorifying tones and fast beats, depicts a complete occupation of every sphere of the surrounding environment below. Like the imperceptive strike of a Drone that turns its target into ashes within a wink of an eye, the song's musicality and lyrics create a sense of total effects, filling the surrounding sphere with absoluteness, leaving no room for reflective and alternative thought.

The imagery of Drone, or the language of this macabre celebration, has so imperceptibly infiltrated into the spaces of entertainment and artistic expressions in the Pashtun belt that a new trilogy of songs on *YouTube* that appeared in July 2020 became an instant hit. Though these songs do not exactly speak to the drone technology as we found in the case of previous two songs, their mere title, "Drone Songs," and a passing mention of Drone in this series attract numerous viewers. For example, one of these songs, "Rolling Eyes Like a Drone" (*Stargey Laka Drone Garzawey*) (Khan Bangash Creation, 2020), has a single stanza about Drone in this 17-stanza long song about the clichéd expression of love and beauty. In addition to its rising viewership, this entire series is also being marketed in the name of this war machine.

The sixth stanza of this seventeen-stanza-long song, like one of the songs discussed above, focuses on the two prominent understandings of Drone: positional elevation and surveillance. The singer uses the drone analogy to discuss his beloved's bride, "Hovering in the sky" and "Rolling eyes like a Drone" (Khan Bangash Creation, 2020). The drone's appropriation of romantic appreciation of the beloved's beauty and clout, on the one hand, trivializes the lethality of this war technology, but on the other hand, romanticizes and submerges its lethality in the expression of love. As shown in the next line, "Roaming with a few scoundrels/Didn't I befriend you," the singer/lover here celebrates his friendship with a drone-like dangerous beloved, the femme fatale (Khan Bangash Creation, 2020). Interestingly, as is typical of a male singer of these songs, the singer here too, instead of embodying this war machine as female singers do, objectifies and reifies it. The lover here externalizes his emotional pain into the drone's capacity for surveillance and killing. The receding of this male subjectivity is a typical trope that emphatically recurs in much of Pashto literature in various forms, including these songs, since the onslaught of the "war on terror."

Thus, by dealing with the textual and stylistic attributes of this commercial production, we see three important threads articulated in the "songs of terror:" disarticulation of the modern technology of death, a sense of banality in responding to this gore reality, and a glimpse of receding male subjectivity—that of the traditional Pashtun patriarch. Based on these threads, we found that the immediacy and contemporaneity in the imagery of the relatively new technologies of war (drones and suicides) create a unique predicament; it seems to evade a linguistic grasp, reverses the cultural positionality of gender roles, and trivializes and romanticizes an otherwise existential threat in the commonplace language of romance and love. However, we argue that it is neither the inability of the local cultural toolkit nor a unique set of anthropological characteristics (of Pashtuns) that results in an ineffective counteractive strategy and negotiation of this deathly space. Rather, this depiction is the result of a four-decade war and the employment and deployment of absolute military means that create a spatial mutation in the Pashtun belt. Such a portrayal also completely captures the thought-making process of the subjected population and forecloses alternative possibilities of nonviolent resistance and existence. It is this spatially degenerative phenomenon that we turn to in the next analyses section, with focus on the context of the given text production.

Musicalization of death: Disarticulation, Banality, and Receding Male Subjectivity

An initial glimpse into and a peripheral understanding of the "songs of terror" may be taken as a confusing articulation of a complex phenomenon: a selective picking of the imagery of drone strikes and suicide bombers for the expression of love. Also, the relative newness of these technologies of death may mistakenly lead to the assumption that it can hardly be articulated in the available cultural discourse. A deeper look into these songs, however, reveal a temporal disconnect and a spatial collusion. In other words, Pashto songs are not a spontaneous outcome of the local cultural industry, which means that examining the given text in a temporal sense, i.e., profit-making, market trends, or mere entertainment, is a deception. Instead, we argue that meaning-making in the Pashtun belt is a contextual process that is subject to geo-strategic compulsions, a colonial legacy rooted in the history of British ideas about Pashtuns and the region itself. As a result, expression of war, such as "I am a suicide bomber" or "don't mess up with Drone," feels like either romanticizing or trivializing violence. But this self-image of the Pashtun population as a violent and belligerent people is a much talked-about colonial trope that is used by successive empires in the region to advance their hegemonic policies at the cost of the Pashtun bodies (Fowler, 2007).

This spatial realization is reinforced through the instrumental use of state apparatus in postcolonial Pakistan. In other words, history itself becomes a specter, a force to realize its existence in the structure of the state which then reduces textual production to the compulsions of a necrospace. Allowing drones in the Pashtun belt (and not outside of it) engenders not only a phenomenon of suicide bombing, but these technologies of imperialist war, while dictating everyday life, also regulate speech acts (songs in this case). This vantage point thus allows us to clearly see limitations of the local cultural industry in its continuity with its imperialist wars, a perspective to understand local violence in its colonial and postcolonial context. In other words, we maintain that the visceral realities of war and their depiction in the "songs of terror" are interconnected. Thus, the representation of the technologies of the war cannot, therefore, be taken at its face value—a rootless and temporal reality with impulsive reactions of random local singers. Moreover, the seemingly textual evasion of this organized violence should also not be taken merely as a sign of local indifference to this absolute power. Instead, these songs, associating agency with destruction and celebration of the technologies of war, need to be understood as an indication of an acute sense of spatial besiege that encloses and hinders all kinds of possibilities of a peaceful life.

That is why many songwriters engaging with this phenomenon (songs of terror) take recourse to the familiar vocabulary of the past to tease out a meaning of the profound local, lived experience in the present. However, an existing resource of symbolic expression cannot keep up with the constant spatial mutation. The decades-long total war has destroyed all possible places of local artistic negotiation, including music and entertainment avenues. A society that has lived and breathed war for years can see war as the only leading narrative and hence its tools become the elements of their communication. We call this the "musicalization of death," that is, a representation of graphic violence (or sharing its pathos) in songs that generate a musical celebration or collective nostalgia. This form of contemporary commercial music does not negotiate or resist the violent events as music traditionally does, but reproduces ennui and at times, unknowingly, glorifies the local form of the organized global violence, a phenomenon that gradually developed under spatial compulsions— that is, creating the Pashtun belt as a site and sight of militarized violence.

Interestingly, the trivialization and romanticization of violence in music and entertainment spaces is a somewhat recent phenomenon in the Pashtun belt. This has emerged in the context of "war on terror" through years of necro-linguistic engineering experiments by the Pakistani state (Khan, 2016). In this process, for instance, the local Pashtun population, among others, was force-fed with the ideology of Pakistan—erasure of local cultural differences and fostering an Islam-based religious identity—via Urdu-medium textbooks, glorification of an inorganically unified national identity through mass media, and denigration of local ethnic identities (Khan, 2016). Such experiments by the postcolonial state of Pakistan reduced Pashto, both as a language and as a mode of thinking, to a footnote. In other words, this duality—glorification of a unified and state controlled national language and denigration of the ethnic languages—on the one hand empowered the state to mediate all cultural forms of publications in Urdu language[6] and on the other hand, reduced the ethnic

---

[6] Mohammad Hanif's widely acclaimed novel, A Case of Exploding Mangoes (2008) that satirizes General Zia ul Haq, the then military dictator of Pakistan (1977-1988) remained unnoticed until its Urdu language publication that was immediately rolled back. For

languages to a mere medium of communication among the downtrodden and uneducated laypersons within their respective communities.

Consequently, music or entertainment that is being produced in these ethnic languages rarely make it to the larger society. Such a dismissive attitude about these languages creates a general indifference to their organic messages too; they are either taken as trivialization or romanticization of what seems to be a reality beyond their semantic grasp. However, as we have argued in this chapter, such an apparent disregard for ethnic and local cultural artifacts is not a sudden eruption or the inherent inability of the local languages to be effective channels of expression. This reality goes deeper into an organized political engineering by successive empires in the region and the continuity of such attitude and neglect, also by successive governments and administrations in postcolonial Pakistan.

On the issue of the context of the songs analyzed in this chapter, we note that the Pakistani state has attempted to appropriate the image of Pashtun space and body to exercise strategic control over Afghanistan. For example, their living space has been touted as the "graveyard of empires," which, in reality, has merely turned out as a graveyard of Pashtun bodies and culture. So much so that one of the primary routes, known as Khyber Pass — connecting and facilitating the business of Pashtuns on both sides of the border — has been romanticized as a passage of warriors and a gateway to the Indian subcontinent. The colonial image of the local Pashtun as a brave and ruthless imperial warrior was invoked when their body as a "mujahid" (fighter) was needed for an anti-Soviet force. When that purpose was served, their new identity as a militant facilitator and their region as the hideout of the US-Pakistan-created jihadist force were invoked as an excuse to legitimize the post-9/11 "war on terror" and its resultant mayhem.

Such successive appropriation of the local place and space has also carved out a typical image of the Pashtun male. Since the local culture is patriarchal and androcentric, therefore, underscoring or undermining its male subjectivity, either directly or in relation with women, favors the systems and structures of power at the top. Any discussion of male subjectivity in this study does not, in anyway, support or vouch for the Pashtun tribal and patriarchal culture—a great deal of which has been artificially created and officially sustained by the successive regimes of power—rather, we examine the textual representation of male

---

details see *Pakistani Author Comes Under Fire for Satirical Novel After Urdu Edition Is Published.* (n.d.). NPR.Org. Retrieved February 21, 2021, from https://www.npr.org/2020/01/10/794538415/pakistani-author-comes-under-fire-for-satirical-novel-after-urdu-edition-is-publ

subjectivity under the necrospatial condition of their existence. These "songs of terror" offer a glimpse into how the interplay between expectations and experiences operates in complex relation with factors such as gendered positionality in the officially patronized space that is thriving on local patriarchy. Whereas the pre-9/11 Pashto songs valorize male subjectivity by processing their image as the brave and fearless Pashtuns who resist the greatest occupation of the modern times, the post-9/11 contemporary "songs of terror" show a receding male subjectivity. In the post-/911 songs discussed above, we see both male and female singers. The latter assume a necroagency and take pride in their femme fatale identity in a necrospace that either shoves local men to the background or subjects them to violence, albeit in a symbolic form. The male singers/lyricists, instead of assuming agency and claiming ownership of their land and culture as was the case in the earlier songs, take recourse to a debate with their fellow men to warn and caution them about the mighty power of the foreign technology of imperialist war, a degeneration of space thriving on systemic violence and perversion of local values of resistance.

Conclusion: The Economy of Injury

Taking "drones" and "suicide bombing" as two markers of systemic violence, as we have examined in this chapter, the newly emerged genre of Pashto songs— "songs of terror"—does not only represent different stages of militarization in the Pashtun belt but it also reinforces geostrategic interests of postcolonial Pakistan. Given the subjection of local lives to the rule of the deathly technologies of "war on terror," and the resultant counter-terrorism measures, one would expect music, especially lyrical songs, to raise a voice of resistance to represent the genuine plight of the local Pashtuns. Quite the contrary, the songs under discussion valorize the imagery of imperialist violence and appropriate it for commercial purposes in the local spaces of entertainment. The singer's identification with the suicide bomber — imagery that would otherwise give shudders to listeners — is not only being welcomed as an image of a modern-day femme fatale but also internalized as a new normative standard of beauty. One may wonder whether it is the singer's physical beauty, mellifluous voice, accompaniment of music with the lyrics, the dance steps, or the crowd cheering that transforms the meaning and message of the songs altogether. But the mass media attention and the wider circulation of these cultural artifacts on social media reveal a somewhat local infatuation with their lyrics. These songs do not only empower the singer or anyone who lip-syncs them, but they also appropriate the voice of death in a troubled space that would otherwise hardly find any room in common conversation. Our emphasis on the spatial aspects of these songs was meant to connect imperialist wars with Pakistan's geostrategic compulsions in relation to regional power dynamics—to exercise strategic control over Afghanistan—continued to be imagined and shaped in line with the British colonial legacy.

The local Pashtun population, neither a counteractive force nor empowered and equipped with the latest tools of war to protect themselves, were reduced to a zombie-like existence in this foreign war on their land. Living on the cusp of Afghanistan and Pakistan, they are politically and militarily subjected to the alliance of regional and global powers. This subjugation reduces them to mere spectators to the death and destruction of their fellow Pashtuns, their land, and resources. It is this spatial contradiction that translates itself into Pashto songs and hence creates an economy of injury—that is, debilitating population and making them expendable for war economy—the representation of which reinforces and benefits the regional and global powers.

The "songs of terror," for instance, are symptoms of a contradiction between tradition and modernity that continues to converge in the Pashtun belt. In other words, the conflict in the Pashtun belt is of historical nature and needs to be understood within its own socio-cultural (ethnic and tribal complexity) and political dimensions (relationship with the postcolonial state). Exploiting this complex spatio-temporal phenomenon, the contemporary global interest in the Pashtun belt uses their geographical location and ethnic identity to the ends of free-market war economy and geo-strategic interests. Therefore, the development of the Pashtun region and understanding of their culture never capture this global imaginary. As a result, Pashtuns are either compelled to leave their space or, if they choose to stay, are treated as expendable, to be disposed of in the State's collusion with the market forces whenever needed. Drone warfare on the Pashtun land is just one example of this collusion.

In order to make sense of this complex spatial engineering, local Pashtuns take recourse to music and lyrics. This cultural engagement with the contemporary economy, as discussed above, mobilizes and appropriates the imagery of high-tech warfare, which in turn creates nercospatialization.

References

ABR Video. (2016, August 11). *Afghan war song* [Video]. YouTube. https://www.youtube.com/watch?v=MxByqa2o_J0&list=RDbqKoWIesmag&index=6

Afridi, H. S., Afridi, M. K., & Jalal, S. U. (2016). Pakhtun identity versus militancy in Khyber Pakhtunkhwa and FATA: Exploring the gap between culture of peace and militancy. *Global Regional Review, 1*(1), 1–23. https://doi.org/10.31703/grr.2016(II).01

Ahmed, A. (2011). *Millennium and charisma among Pathans: A critical essay in social anthropology.* Routledge.

Ahmed, A. (2013). *The thistle and the drone: How America's war on Terror became a global war on tribal Islam.* Brookings Institution Press.

Ainslee, E. (1977). Pakistan's imperial legacy. In A. Embree (Ed.), *Pakistan's western borderlands: The transformation of a political order* (pp. 24–41). Vikas Publishing House.

Ali, M. (2011, November 26). *Khud kasha dhamaka yama: The song's a blast.* The Express Tribune. http://tribune.com.pk/story/298042/khud-kasha-dhamaka-yama-the-songs-a-blast

Anderson, J. (1975). Tribe and community among the Ghilzai Pashtun: Preliminary notes on ethnographic distribution and variation in eastern Afghanistan. *Anthropos, 3*(4), 575–601.

Arts, G. (2020, September 18). *Drone sara ba na chere pashto song drone Garza |pashto new song 2020* [Video]. YouTube. https://www.youtube.com/watch?v=sci-Q4wkX7E

Ashraf, S. I., & Shamas, K. (2020). Necrospace, media, and remote war: Ethnographic notes from Lebanon and Pakistan, 2006–2008. In R. A. Adelman & D. Kieran (Eds.), *Remote warfare: New cultures of violence* (pp. 229–254). University of Minnesota Press. https://doi.org/10.5749/j.ctv17db42n.13

Attali, J. (1985). *Noise: The political economy of music* (B. Massumi, Trans.). University of Minnesota Press.

Bartlotti, L. N. (2000). *Negotiating Pakhto: Proverbs, Islam and the construction of identity among Pashtuns.* [Unpublished doctoral dissertation]. University of Wales.

Bergen, P., Sterman, D., & Salyk-Virk, M. (2021, June 17). *America's counterterrorism wars.* New America. http://newamerica.org/international-security/reports/americas-counterterrorism-wars/

Buneri, S., Arif, M., & Zeb, R. H. (2014). *Music and militancy in North Western Pakistan (2001–2014).* A Center for Peace and Cultural Studies.

Carvalho, J. (2013). "Strange Fruit:" Music between violence and death. *The Journal of Aesthetics and Art Criticism, 7*(1), 111–119.

Crile, G. (2007). *Charlie Wilson's war: The extraordinary story of how the wildest man in Congress and a rogue CIA agent changed the history of our times.* Grove Press.

Cusick, S. (2013). Towards an acoustemology of detention in the "global war on terror." In G. Born (Ed.), *Music, sound and space: Transformations of public and private experience* (pp. 275–291). Cambridge University Press.

Daughtry, J. M. (2014). Thanatosonics: Ontologies of acoustic violence. *Social Text, 32*(2[119]), 25–21.

Fowler, C. (2007). *Chasing tales: Travel writing, journalism and the history of British ideas about Afghanistan.* Rodopi.

Gusterson, H. (2019). Drone warfare in Waziristan and the new military humanism. *Current Anthropology, 60*(S19), 77–86. https://www.journals.uchicago.edu/doi/full/10.1086/701022

Hart, D. M. (1985). *Guardians of the Khyber Pass: The social organization and history of the Afridis of Pakistan.* Vanguard Press.

Khan, B. C. (2020, July 10). *Stargy laka drone garzawi pashto new tiktok viral song* [Video]. YouTube. https://www.youtube.com/watch?v=IrpYlfgbrhc

Khan, A. (2005). *Politics of identity: Ethnic nationalism and the state in Pakistan.* Sage Publications.

Khan, A. N. (2011). The US policy of targeted killings by drones in Pakistan. *IPRI Journal, X1*(1), 21–40.

Khan, H. (2012, September 18). *My gaze is as fatal as a drone attack.* The Express Tribune. http://tribune.com.pk/story/438610/my-gaze-is-as-fatal-as-a-drone-attack

Khan, T. S. (2016). *Pakistanizing Pashtun.* [ProQuest Publication No. 10142987] [Doctoral dissertation, American University, Washington D.C.]. ProQuest Dissertations and Theses Global. https://www.academia.edu/42225525/Pakistanizing_Pashtun

Khan, U. S., & Khattak, W. (2014). Role of Pashto theatre and other performing arts in inculcating the spirit of cultural renaissance and promoting nationalistic & ethical values among Pashtuns: An analytical overview. *Sarhad University International Journal of Basic and Applied Sciences, 2*(1), 46–57.

Mbembe, A. (2003). Necropolitics. (L. Meintjes, Trans.). *Public Culture, 15*(1), 11–40.

McDonald, D. A. (2010). Geographies of the body: Music, violence and manhood in Palestine. *Ethnomusicology Forum, 19*(2), 191–214.

Minority Rights Group. (2018). *Minority rights group international: World dictionary of minorities and indigenous people.* https://Minorityrights.Org/Minorities/Pashtuns-2/.

Nasar, S. J. (2012, July 2). *Patriotic Pashto song ~ brave PashtunZ* [Video]. YouTube. https://www.youtube.com/watch?v=KOoUQFvgIe4&list=RDbqKoWlesmag&index=2

Nichols, R. (2008). *A history of Pashtun migration, 1775–2006.* Oxford University Press.

Parks, L. (2014). Drones, infrared imagery, and body heat. *International Journal of Communication, 8*(1), 2518–2521.

Peron, A. (2015). Virtuous war and UAVs: The 'inhibition' of friction and the banalization of violence. In E. Bouet (Ed.), *The (un)certain future of empathy in posthumanism, cyberculture and science fiction* (pp. 17–28). Inter-disciplinary Press.

Puar, J. (2015). *The right to maim: Debility, capacity, disability.* Duke University Press.

Sandoval, E. (2016). Music in peacebuilding: A critical literature review. *Journal of Peace Education, 13*(3), 200–217.

Shah, S. Q. (2012, November 18). *Violence replaces romance in new Pashto songs* [Video]. Dawn. https://www.dawn.com/2012/11/18/violence-replaces-romance-in-new-pashto-songs/

Shahzad, S. S. (2011). *Inside Al-Qaeda and the Taliban: Beyond Bin Laden and 9/11.* Pluto Press.

Shaw, I. G., & Akhter, M. (2012). The unbearable humanness of drone warfare in FATA, Pakistan. *Antipode, 44*(4), 1490–1509.

Siddique, A. (2014). *The Pashtun question: The unresolved key to the future of Pakistan and Afghanistan.* Oxford University Press.

South Asian Terrorism Portal. (2018). *Suicide attacks in Khyber Pakhtunkhwa.* http://www.satp.org/satporgtp/countries/pakistan/nwfp/datasheet/suicide attack.htm

TheAbdaliBacha. (2011, April 11). The brave Pashtun-Afghan freedom fighters resisting the biggest occupation of modern history [Video]. YouTube. https://www.youtube.com/watch?v=V9VksB05VtY

Woods, C. (2015). *Sudden justice: America's secret drone wars*. Oxford University Press.

Yousaf, F. (2019). Pakistan's "tribal" Pashtuns, their "violent" representation, and the Pashtun Tahafuz Movement. *SAGE Open, 9*(1), 1–10.

Zainali. (2014, January 7). *Pa stargo stargo drone hamla Pashto new stage song* [Video]. YouTube. https://www.youtube.com/watch?v=YB8btKaMtEw

Zeb, S. (2012, February 28). *Sonu Lal—khudkasha dhamaka* [Video]. YouTube. https://www.youtube.com/watch?v=dJWvbHNH3rQ

CHAPTER 8

Political messaging in the *Anatolian-Pop*: How has this music genre transformed Turkey's socio-political landscape?

Yavuz Yildirim

Nigde Omer Halisdemir University, Turkey

Mehmet Atilla Guler

Adnan Menderes University, Turkey

Abstract

During the 1960s and 1970s, a new kind of Turkish music called, *Anatolian Pop*, created a new music genre that incorporated social and political messages. The Anatolian Pop emerged out of the political and social struggles and the need to create an independent society that was bereft of Western hegemony and capitalist contradictions. This chapter analyzed the genre to explore and understand the transformation of Turkey during the second half of the 20th century, with emphasis on examining the figures, songs, and messages contained in the lyrics. Anatolian Pop was not purely political, as it also had cultural and popular content. Using extraordinary and old-school instruments, musicians of the new genre created a new music and song atmosphere that told different stories about the daily life and history of the country.

Keywords: Turkish politics, Turkish music, protest movement, alternative music, Anatolian Pop

***

Introduction

Turkey has witnessed conflicting cultural and political traditions over the years. As a society stuck between the West and East, the Turkish people have produced some synthesis of different cultures. When the country was searching for its development patterns in the changing world order during and after the demise of the Cold War, the transformations that occurred in various areas of Turkish life were also reflected in its music. It was against this backdrop that in the 1960s and 1970s a new kind of Turkish music called the *Anatolian Pop* emerged and created a new genre that was replete with social and political messaging. This genre challenged the Western hegemony and capitalist contradictions that were creeping into and reshaping Turkey and its future.

During the 1960s, especially after 1960 when Turkey experienced its first military coup d'état and was followed by the introduction of a new constitution, the country began a new era to adapt to the changing dynamics the world. This was facilitated by the engagement with capitalism and democracy from the West. This engagement led to the transformation from the traditional agrarian economy to the capitalist economic relations with the West and changes in working conditions for blue-collar workers. It was also in this period that political parties and workers' unions also emerge, leading to ubiquitous debates on the shape and content of the economy as well as the establishment of political parties, all of which brought the societal transformation in Turkey.

The rise of the Anatolian Pop music could therefore be traced to the second half of the 20th century, and is closely related to the economic and political domestic changes in Turkey in that period as well as the in the global community. Thus, the major underlying factor that brought about the messaging in the Anatolian Pop music was about the democratic struggles within the country, especially among Turkish political groups.[1]

Several studies by musicologists such as Gedik (2018), Gedik & Ergun (2019), Baysal (2018), and also experts on cultural studies such as Yarar (2008) and Ozgur (2006), underscore the relationship between politics and music. The present study was designed to complement these prior studies from the socio-economic perspective by focusing on the fundamental messages of Turkey's Anatolian Pop music. For clarity, this study is not only about political parties in Turkey or the country's engagement with capitalism from the West but goes beyond to examine the society as a whole through the messaging embedded in and disseminated through the Anatolian Pop music that addresses salient issues in society in a nonconventional way.

This chapter employed both historical and qualitative analysis in the examination of the Anatolian Pop music in Turkey. The main argument is that when Turkey's society shifted away from the ideals of its founding era, coupled

---

[1] Anatolian Pop has been hugely influenced by national developments, similar to the folk music in the USA. But international conflicts and struggles have also been effective in its development. In this context, while examining the beginning of Anatolian Pop, the national and global environment should also be taken into consideration.

with its problematic engagement with capitalism, Anatolian Pop emerged with musical messages that addressed the concerns of the oppressed people in a nonconventional way.

Turkey: Politics and music pre-1960s

The Republic of Turkey, or the Turkish Republic as the country is also known, was established in 1923 after the collapse of the Ottoman Empire in the aftermath of World War I and under the aegis of the Treaty of Lausanne (July 24, 1923). The official proclamation of statehood and republic came on October 29, 1923, leading to the rise of Mustafa Kemal Ataturk.

Anatolia, historically known as Asia Minor, a region that shaped several civilizations and cultures over several centuries, was the main part of the homeland of the new Turkish Republic. In the multi-cultural empire of the Ottoman times, popular culture and entertainment mainly flourished in the areas dominated by minority ethnic groups. Those old songs were popularly known as *türkü*, with impacts that did not go beyond the localities where they were sung. The songs that were most popular across the empire were military or martial music and national anthems.

Among the issues that arose in the new Republic period was the reformation of the ideology of *Kemalism*. *Kemalism* somehow combined different aspects of modernization approaches and debates that traditionally existed since the Young Turk revolution of 1908 (Celik, 2000). Its main aim was to create a contemporary society based on secular values as distinct from the Ottoman heritage. This modernization process is known as the Six Arrows (meaning republicanism, statism, revolutionism, populism, nationalism, and laicism) which is also the symbol of the founding-party, *Cumhuriyet Halk Partisi* (CHP - Republican People's Party). One may argue that these principles of *Kemalism* came with state repression (Kadioglu, 1996), although the aim of his government was to modernize Turkey's economy and governance, and generally Westernize the country. Unfortunately, this quest to modernize Turkey also meant the quelling of ethnic nationalism and culture.

The new state regime's style of government and implementation of policies that sought to Westernize Turkey's culture, socio-economic, and political development also meant all sorts of state control and suppression of dissenting voices. One of the areas that suffered in this process was the abolition of Classical Turkish Music education in 1926. This was followed by banning the music on radio for a few years. On the other hand, the government supported and encouraged the establishment of conservatories and orchestras that enabled the development of Western music. Nonetheless, by 1937, a year before founding-leader Atatürk died, the restoration of suppressed aspects of Turkish culture was heightened based on the rising populism principles enunciated in the Six Arrows, leading to the Turkish Folk Music compilation being initiated by the Turkish Radio and Television Corporation (TRT) (Ozbek, 1991, pp. 140-143). These studies included a radio program called "Folk Songs with Bass-Bariton Ruhi Su" (1943). This program was an important step in the development of political music in Turkey. Ruhi Su, who performed the folk songs - using the Western technique on the official broadcaster TRT between 1943 and 1945, became the first name to influence future musicians playing Anatolian Pop in the 1960s (Canbazoglu, 2009, p. 21).

Turkey's politics after World War II were mixed, with the introduction of the capitalist form of governance and the contradictions and restrictions that came with it (Karpat, 1972; Ahmad, 1985, 1993; Zurcher, 1993; Ozbudun, 2000). In the 1950s, the shift away from the founding principles of the Democratic Party (DP) government allowed pro-US politics to affect the cultural and artistic activities in the country. Thus, the first rock orchestra was established in Turkey during this period. This orchestra was founded in 1955 by students in the country's Naval Military College. The orchestra only played English-language rock music songs, neglecting indigenous music. Nonetheless, the presence of a rock band was not welcomed by the commanders of the Naval Military College, hence the orchestra's activities were consequently prohibited on the grounds of the naval academy. As a result, some members of the orchestra members kept on staging secret concerts, while others left the academy (Erkal, 2013, p. 60; Dilmener, 2014, pp. 31-32).

In other words, rock music imported from the West had found its way into the cultural sphere of Turkey in the 1950s just as the economic and political life in the country had been impacted by Western ideology and thinking. The next decade, however, saw a resurgence of old Turkish music and culture.

The Social and Political Transformation of the 1960s

As already shown in the historical narrative above, Turkey aligned itself with the Western-style political system in the post-World War II era (Esping-Andersen, 1990; Greve, 2012; Castles et al., 2012). In order to not to encourage the reactivation of disastrous state policies like fascism, the West generally accepted and adopted liberal democracy, and some mild forms of regulatory policies and welfare-state policies. The U.S. introduced itself as the champion and defender of the free world and the capitalist form of governance. On the other hand, Russia and China took to the socialist and communist type of governments. Under the DP administration, Turkey chose to align itself with the US and Western-style liberal democracy, and also a rapid transition to capitalism. In spite of the army coup d'état against DP on May 27, 1960, the form of liberal government was enshrined in Turkey's 1961 constitution. It continued the consolidation of the country, which adopted and joined the North Atlantic Treaty Organization in 1952.

The new constitution of 1961, which was modeled after the liberal constitutions in Western democracies, unshed upon Turkey the notions and practice of expanded assertions of human and social rights. Thus, Turkey was not immune to the 1960s wave of social movements, protests, and popular demonstrations expressing and supporting human dignity at the international level (Yildirim, 2015; Pekesen, 2019). The Turkish Anatolian Pop music genre was born in this socio-political environment and can be arguably said to be the product of a series of economic, social, and political developments, all of which were framed in music and songs all over the Western world in the 1960s.

The authors of this study note that the existing pop and rock music arranged and produced by French and Italian records in Turkey had some indigenous Turkish lyrics. Other brands of music, represented by Elvis Presley (USA) and the Beatles (Britain), also made their mark in Turkey. Collectively, they were called *aranjman* songs and music in Turkish (foreign music, as replayed by locals who did not originate them). On the other hand, Anatolian Pop music represented the authentic music conceptualized, arranged, and produced in the county (Ramm, 2020, pp. 259-260). This genre is a synthesis of rock and old-style Turkish music called *türkü*. This brand of music and songs dealt with and expressed important and local issues of poverty, economic exploitation, poor conditions of working-class people, and injustice.

Birth and Development of the Anatolian Pop

The Anatolian Pop was derived from rock music. Its entry into the music scene was first made and popularized in 1969 by Taner Ongur, the bass guitarist of the band, "Mogollar." The band was founded early in 1968 by the following: Cahit Berkay (guitar), Engin Yorukoglu (drums), Murat Ses (keyboard), Aziz Azmet (vocal), and Hasan Sel (bass). Sel was later replaced by Taner Ongur.

The band's 1969 tour marked an important milestone in the history of the Anatolian Pop music. During the tour, Turkish folkloric musical instruments such as *baglama, iklig,* and *yayli tambur* were used in the new songs played by the band. Guitarist Berkay was basically responsible for the introduction and use of the instruments. For his part, bassist Ongur compiled all songs played by the band during the tour. This compilation was later titled, *Anatolian Pop,* and the name stuck as the representation of the new genre of music in Turkey. Ongur explained the essential features of Anatolian Pop as follows:

> ...what we want to prove is that our folk music has a polyphonic spirit, besides the closeness of our folklore and pop music, the unity of our backward music with our advanced technique and rich folklore.

Anatolian Pop aims to combine advanced technology with rich folkloric elements. (Meric, 2006, p. 249)

Ongur further explained that although the concept of Anatolian Pop was first used in 1969, its roots date back to the early 1960s. He drew attention to two names that were associated with the birth and development of this new music genre: Ruhi Su and Tulay German (Guler, 2018, pp. 21-22). Su had worked for the state broadcaster, TRT, in the 1940s, where he created and promoted what he called a "revolutionary music" that highlighted the life and times of the ordinary folks in the country in the lyrics and music of the songs (Su, 1985, p. 116). The content of his music so riled the authorities that they found that a reason to jail him for five years, followed by forced exile. The ostensible reason for his incarceration was that he belonged to the Turkish Communist Party.

However, Su was not deterred by his prison sentence and exile. He resuscitated his music in 1960 and later released his first record in 1962. He also established a school where he gave music lessons. One of his pupils was Tulay German. Su's teaching was focused on interpreting and universalizing Turkey's folk songs with Western techniques in a way that did not spoil or distort the essence of the indigenous songs (Canbazoglu, 2009, pp. 342-343). Ruhi Su said this about popularizing folk songs with Anatolian Pop music in the late 1960s:

The reason why folk songs are increasingly dominant in the records should be sought in the life force and life-related narration in the folk songs. The effect of culture and manners on the taste of the people living in the cities is an indisputable fact, and it is a fact that this taste has developed recently. Like all other artists, I am happy that I have contributed to the development of this applause... Everyone, from beggars and sellers on the street to symphonic music masters, benefits from folk songs within their measure...I believe that contradiction is unthinkable in a successful job done with the language of our people. (Su, 1985, pp. 98-99)

Tulay German started music by singing foreign jazz songs accompanied by a piano at famous clubs in Istanbul in the early 1960s and soon became one of the most famous singers in the city. German's musical journey changed completely after she met Erdem Buri in 1962. Buri was already a well-known name because of his jazz shows on TRT in the second half of the 1940s. After they began working together, German's music changed dramatically. Buri believed that a real artist should touch and impact people. He contended that no matter how sonorous a musician's voice was, it was not possible for someone who only sang jazz to the elite in exclusive concert halls to be a real artist. With this in mind, Buri made some suggestions to German, including singing foreign language songs with Turkish lyrics and with different arrangements in the form of *aranjman*. He also suggested arranging folk songs as polyphonic without disturbing their melodic and rhythmic structure, and their composition in Turkish. German combined Buri's suggestions with the lessons learned from Ruhi Su, and with Buri both compiled and released a repertoire of Anatolian melodies (German, 1996, p. 92). German's success with the song, "Burcak Tarlasi," in 1964 was the result of this transformation. This success, as already mentioned, was generally regarded as the first opus of Anatolian Pop music.

German's second vinyl was released in 1965 (*Yarinin Sarkisi/ Kizilciklar Oldu Mu?*). With this vinyl, the political messaging in German's music was clarified. *Yarinin Sarkisi*, whose lyrics and music belong to Buri, was used by the Turkish Workers Party in the elections held the same year. German also attended the party's concert with very powerful political figures such as Asik[2] Nesimi, Asik İhsani, and Ruhi Su (German, 1996, p. 109).

German and Buri's musical journey moved to France in 1966 because of a lawsuit. Buri had translated a work of Plekhanov's into Turkish (*Fundamental Problems of Marxism*). For this reason, Buri was sentenced to 15 years imprisonment, hence both German and Buri unwillingly settled in Paris.

One of the most important tools in the rise of Anatolian Pop was the *Altın Mikrofon* (*the Golden Microphone*) *Contests* which were organized from 1965 to 1971 by *Hurriyet*, one of the most influential newspapers in Turkey. The importance of the competition stems from its regulation, whose aim was "to give direction to Turkish music by using the rich techniques and forms of western music and playing with western musical instruments." Participants in the competitions were asked to perform two songs, one of their own and the other from traditional folk tunes (Ramm, 2020, p. 262). Although other bands won the competitions at its inception and a little thereafter, from 1967, bands or musicians who were associated with the Anatolian Pop genre won most of the competitions (Guler, 2018, p. 31-32).

In a narrow sense, the Anatolian Pop music genre can be defined as an original music movement developed in the rock genre by integrating local folkloric elements with Western instruments (Meric, 2006, p. 61). Nonetheless, and from a broader perspective, it can be argued that two factors stand out in the history of Anatolian Pop music. The first is the prominence and dominance of songs with strong political messaging which was in contrast to mainstream music in Turkey. Thus, in both content and performance, Anatolian Pop embraced the genre of *aranjman*'s that was developed by famous names such as Ilham Gencer, Fecri Ebcioglu, and Sezen Cumhur Onal (Dilmener, 2014, p.

---

[2] Asik (Aşık in Turkish, actually means "lover") is a kind of old title using for people-poet and singer who dedicated himself to music.

86). Despite pressures from well-known composers who shaped popular music of that era and also from TRT in the beginning, Anatolian Pop became popular throughout the country in a very short time, and the official state broadcaster which had initially ignored it began to air it prominently on the radio channels. The second factor which highlighted Anatolian Pop as a genre was that it fed off the socialist literature in Turkey. In this context, it was also considered the equivalent of the reality of challenging feudalism through music. The authors of the literature that got translated into music were such Turkish literary giants as Yasar Kemal, Fakir Baykurt, and Mahmut Makal in literature (Canbazoglu, 2009, p. 25).

During the 1970s and 1980s, Turkey experienced several successive political and economic crises and upheavals. The decades also witnessed the changing patterns of the Turkish economy in its transformation and engagement patterns with the West (Keyder, 1987, pp. 186-189). The oil crisis and its aftermath seriously impacted most economies in the 1970s and 1980s, and inspired similar responses practically in several parts of the world, Turkey included. Several critics in the country challenged the state government and bureaucracy for failing to regulate the market, and for abolishing social welfare policies that cushioned the sufferings of the common people (Eder, 2010). Thus, in Turkey, as in most capitalist nations, the government placed priority on market principles and determinants over ameliorating the social and economic life of the people. It was in this dire economic situation that a popular left-wing politician and young leader of the CHP, Bulent Ecevit, emerged and tapped into the music to publicize their politics. The harsh economic situation in the country, coupled with populist violence and the rise of leftish politicians and political parties with radical ideologies (Keyder, 1987, p. 209) expectedly shaped the growth of the Anatolian Pop music and the rise of other giants of this music genre.

Prominent figures in Anatolian Pop music

Anatolian Pop music in Turkey has produced a number of personalities and bands since its inception in the late 1960s. After Tulay German, Alpay is another prominent musician in the Anatolian Pop genre. Alpay's importance is related to his popularity rather than his actual works in Anatolian Pop. He was better known as the "performer of romantic songs" in and around Istanbul in the 1960s. By contrast, his song, "Fabrika Kizi" ("The Factory Girl"), released in 1967, was completely different from the previous releases. "Fabrika Kizi," whose lyrics and music belong to Bora Ayanoglu, became one of the biggest hits of the period it was published. The song was also the first work to center on Turkey's working class and its affairs. Ayanoglu describes the song as "a description of Marxism" (Dilmener, 2014, p. 157; Meric, 2006, p. 56).

Fabrika Kizi describes the Turkish working woman's experiences every day, from sunrise to sunset. According to this song, the only dream the factory girl has is to have a good marriage and income to sustain her family and daily life. However, the low income and living conditions in the country prevent this dream from becoming reality. The factory girl's destiny and experiences go through the same cycle of poverty and dashed hopes every day. Fabrika Kizi outlines this situation in the song:

> Every morning at sunrise, a girl passes by my door
> She disappears around the corner, with a head leaned forward, rather tired
> She wraps tobacco in the factory, as if it is for her own smoke
> She daydreams while wrapping, as all the people do
> She wants to own a house, and a non-drinking husband
> She gets along with whatever God gives, as long as she is happy at home…
> Every evening at dusk, a girl passes by my door
> She disappears around the corner, with a head leaned forward, rather tired.

The band, "Mogollar," published its first song in 1968. The other pieces of music released by the band between 1968 and 1974 mainly consisted of instrumental songs. The nature of instrumental songs means that there were hardly forms of vocalized political messaging in the lyrics of the songs by the band. However, members of the band appear to be the first to introduce revolutionary songs in Anatolian Pop music. Their stage performance was something that also motivated other budding musicians to take to Anatolian Pop. Even today, and in spite of the changing generations in the composition of the band, musicians still make Anatolian Pop.

Cem Karaca

Cem Karaca is undoubtedly the musician who takes the lead when it comes to the creation of works with the strongest political emphasis and messaging in Anatolian Pop's golden age with his band, the "Apaslar." Karaca and his band had come second at the *Golden Microphone Contest* held in 1967. The lyrics of the song the group played at the competition were compiled from the words of Asik Emrah, one of the greatest political figures of the 19th century Ottoman Empire. Emrah's lyrics directly focused on the contradictions embedded from the feudal order, especially the divide between the affluent members of the ruling class and the rest of the population.

In the same period, Karaca and the band produced two more hits that cannot be legitimately classified as belonging to the Anatolian Pop. They are: "Resimdeki Gozyaslari" ("Tears in Photo") and "Bu Son Olsun" ("Let This Be the End"). These two songs are arguably considered among the most important works of Turkish rock history. The band's vinyl, *Zeyno* (1969), was the closest work to

Anatolian Pop in terms of both political characteristics and musical arrangement. The inequalities of the feudal order are revealed through a love story in this song, in which farm laborer, Mehmet, and the landlord's daughter, Zeyno, are told that they could not live their lives together as husband and wife (Guler, 2018, pp. 38-39).

Baris Manco

Baris Manco started music with twist songs in 1962 and sang in English until 1966. Twist songs and music were new and quite popular at that time. Between 1968 and 1970, Manco sang Anatolian Pop songs that did not have any remarkable political underpinning. Manco's most important hit in the Anatolian Pop genre is "Daglar Daglar," published in 1970. This song is also among the biggest hits of Anatolian Pop. The term "the most famous Anatolian Pop figure who does not make political music" was used in reference to Manco primarily because of the traditional expectation that saying something political was at the core of Anatolian Pop music.

Fikret Kizilok

Fikret Kizilok is one of the most exclusive names, not only in Anatolian Pop or Turkish rock but also in country music. Kizilok had an experimental approach to music throughout his life. While Kizilok's music developed mostly under the influence of the West between 1965 and 1969, a new era began in Kizilok's music with Asik Veysel. "Uzun Ince Bir Yoldayim" ("I'm on a long and thin road"), released in 1969, is one of the first and most important works of this period. Kizilok visited Asik Veysel twice in the Sivrialan village of Sivas in the east of Turkey in 1969 and 1970. During his second visit in 1970, he had to remain in Sivas for three extra months because the road out of the city was blocked by heavy snowfall and was not motorable. Kizilok broke his *baglama* upon the death of Asik Veysel in 1973 and stopped using this instrument in his songs (Canbazoglu, 2009, pp. 118-120).

The Army Memorandum and Coup D'état

The history of the Anatolian Pop would be incomplete without reference to the unique military intervention that took place on March 12, 1971. Following the spate of right-wing and left-wing violence, insecurity, vandalism, and near total anarchy that had engulfed the country since 1968, the Turkish army chief of staff sent a memorandum to Prime Minister Suleyman Demirel, leader of the ruling center-right Justice Party government, to immediately halt the carnage in Turkey; failure to do so would oblige the the army to step in and take over power and restore order. The unambiguous order was subsequently referred to as a military "coup by memorandum" because sensing that the army was about to oust his administration, Prime Minister Demirel resigned his position after a three-hour meeting with his cabinet.

The events that followed the military "coup by memorandum" marked a turning point in the political history, character, and content of Anatolian Pop music. The new government of Prime Minister Nihat Erim of the Republican People's Party which replaced the Demirel administration, perhaps nudged by the army, quickly moved to put all leftist movements under extreme pressure. In addition to the socio-economic and political impact in the aftermath of the coup, Turkey's social and cultural life was affected, especially the Anatolian Pop musicians and other cultural organizations (Kahyaoglu, 2003, p. 86). The new names that got onto the "new" Anatolian Pop music scene included Selda Bagcan and Edip Akbayram. More importantly, however, in 1971, the leading band in this genre, "Mogollar," went to France and began producing music and holding concerts in the country. One of their famous albums, co-produced with CBS, was published in 1971 with the title, *Danses et Rythmes de la Turquie D'hier à Aujourd'hui* (Dances and rhythms of Turkey From Yesterday to Today). While in France, the band teamed up with Baris Manco, under the name Manco-Mongol, and dominated the Anatolian music scene together. But the band was to split later after a tour back home was interrupted when their minibus was burnt by arsonists. That was an unmistakable signal that the political conflict at home had spread to the Anatolian music scene. One of the great Anatolian Pop music songs the band left behind was called "Alageyik Destani" ("White Deer Saga"). It became a type of cult music for this genre.

Some memorable moments for Anatolian Pop

By the end of 1970, Cem Karaca established a new band known as "Kardaşlar" (meaning Brothers, in the old use of the word), with its most popular song being "Dadaloglu." This song was named after a bard and folk poet of the early 19th century in the southern part of Anatolia. Dadaloglu was a rebel and symbol of resistance by a nomadic tribe that fought for citizenship from the central government. "Dadaloglu" was later associated with left-wing politics and political agitation against all forms of imperialism. The popularity of "Dadaloglu" earned Cem Karaca the name, "Mr. Dadaloglu."

Early in 1971, the new band, "Kardaslar," had success with a number of recordings in Germany with Alex Viska, arguably the most famous guitarist of that period. Another important song released by the band was "Acı Doktor" ("Suffering Doctor"). It was a song about a poor peasant who was begging a doctor to take care of his sick child for free. But by 1972, however, the group disbanded, and in the same year, Karaca and "Mogollar" formed what became a famous partnership. This coincided with the period (1972-1974) when Turkey was going through various forms of political turmoil. Its best-known hit song was "Namus Belasi" ("Trouble of Honor"). The lyrics say:

My bride girl, my tall in weight, without satisfying to each other
Without opening your face with Besmele, without sitting knee to knee
They have taken you away, and hanged you in deserted
For the trouble of honor my brother, the soul that we sacrificed is ours

Several music writers and critics point out that this song really was neither about the class struggle in Turkish society nor the theme song for the country's so-called revolutionaries. In a way, the song was highly apolitical, as it was an open response to the 1971 "coup by memorandum" that ousted the elected government of Prime Minister Süleyman Demirel. The song was about the honor-murder committed by a man after the woman he loved was raped.

Incidentally, some feminist organizations in the country, against the backdrop of their opposition to the idea of honor-killing that only targeted women, were offended by the song's theme about killing women in order to maintain the masculine supremacy in the largely feudal society that presented itself to the rest of the world as democratic. Thus, the feminist organizations termed the theme of the music to be "too masculine" and produced a number of anti-honor-killing slogans. Then there was a twist with the music, as the "too masculine" slogan was appropriated by various opponents of the army's "memorandum" that resulted in the fall of Prime Minister Demirel's government and used it to campaign against the army and the coup d'état. Thus, the apolitical music became political.

Another band of note was "Kurtalan Ekspres," formed by Baris Manco in 1971, upon ending his partnership with "Mogollar" in 1971. Between 1972 and 1974, "Kurtalan Ekspres" released Anatolian Pop music that did not have political content. However, in the same period, Manco also released songs such as "Genc Osman," "Hey Koca Topcu," and "Estergon Kalesi" which are identified with Ottomanism and loved by right-wing nationalist masses (Canbazoglu, 2009, p. 42).[3]

After the 1971 Memorandum, Fikret Kızılok came to the fore with two works composed by Ahmed Arif, one of the most famous socialist poets of Turkey. Among them, "Vurulmusum" ("I Had Been Shot") was the slogan-song of the socialist youth who died at the hands of the government. Another famous song was "Anadolu'yum" ("I am Anatolia"). Both songs were published in the second

---

[3] Together with Barış Manco, Donusum was supported by the nationalist conservatives in the first half of the 1970s. Donusum defined their music as National Turkish Music and highlighted Turkish (not Anatolian) instruments such as rebap, cenk, and tar. The active period of Donusum was between 1970 and 1975.

half of 1971. Selda Bagcan is another name that became prominent with her political works in the Anatolian Pop genre in the period 1971-1974 after Cem Karaca. In her songs, she predominantly highlighted the problems of poverty and inequality in the system. Bagcan's first production in this period was about the violations of people's rights caused by the "coup by memorandum." Indeed, Bagcan drew attention to the conditions of the army's opponents imprisoned with "Mahpushanelere Gunes Dogmuyor" ("The Sun Does Not Rise to Prisons") in 1971. Another song, also published in 1971, mainly posed a question: "Adaletin Bu Mu Dunya?" ("Is This Your Justice, World?"). It was based on the problems arising from property inequality in Turkish society.

It is noteworthy that in this period of the army's memorandum, the journalists' and news organizations' integrity and loyalty were quite questionable. One of Bagcan's songs, "Yaz Gazeteci Yaz" ("Write Journalist Write"), highlights the suspicions people had about the news media and reporters regarding where their loyalties lied. In this song, she attempted to make a comparison between the deep social problems of the period and news published by the tabloid and mainstream newspapers. She sang:

> For heaven's sake, journalist, come to our village and write about our situation
> Don't write about painted fingers in the city (Write about the calloused
>   hands in our village ...
> Don't write in the suffocating language of fame
> Don't write about the roses in your garden
> Don't write about the young unjust hands of murders
> Write about those dying in the east without doctors

Edip Akbayram, who started a music career in 1970, also became famous during the Anatolian Pop period, especially with "Ince Ince Bir Kar Yagar" ("It Snows as Scattered Flurries") in 1974. The focus of this song was poverty and inequality. Akbayram was one of the most important figures of the second half of the 1970s, a period that coincided with the progressive rock era.

It is noteworthy that the rise of Anatolian Pop affected other popular singers and their music. From 1972 to 1974, many pop music singers who adopted the *aranjman style* in the past started to include folk songs and lyrics in their work. This situation caused some of the names that had already begun to push the boundaries of Anatolian Pop musically to move away from this genre and turn toward progressive rock. The transformation in the direction of progressive rock in Turkey can be seen on the political level. Politically, the second half of the 1970s was the first time when the urbanization rate exceeded fifty percent. It also meant that the process of proletarianization in Turkey was increasing, especially in metropolitan areas and cities. Thus, the proletarian problems began to replace feudalism as the theme in Anatolian Pop.

The Damping and Transformation of Anatolian Pop

Cem Karaca, Selda Bagcan, and Edip Akbayram, who were the prominent figures of Anatolian Pop, composed and released songs that can be considered political during the period that was called the "progressive rock years." During this period, Cem Karaca-Dervisan focused mainly on proletarian problems, starting with the "Tamirci Ciragi" ("Apprentice Mechanic"). "Tamirci Ciragi" is arguably a turning point in Turkey's Rock History. Its release saw the trend towards progressive rock and the emergence of proletarian problems at the forefront of society's concerns. The song is based on two themes. The first is related to the contradictions and inequalities in music production and in the country. The second is based on the contractions based on the first factor: a situation of heightened class discrepancies that made it impossible for an apprentice mechanic and a girl who came to his garage to fall in love. The lyrics of the song tell the story:

> Her car was brought into our garage yesterday for service
> I was struck as soon as I saw her and began loving
> A long skirt covering her legs, wavy hair
> The boss called out to me at a distance, 'Son, bring the tools'
> I'd read something like this in a novel
> It was an expensive book with a glossy hardcover
> Whatever or however happened, a young girl fell in love
> With an apprentice mechanic in a similar situation
> I said to the boss 'let me not wear overalls today'
> I combed my hair in my hazy mirror
> She'd come back today to take her car
> Maybe to make the dream in that novel true
> Time stopped, the earth stopped as she entered the door
> I just stood staring without taking my eyes off from her
> I opened the door of the car so that she gets on
> Her crescent eyebrows were raised and asked, 'Who's this bum?'
> She drove away with her car that was covered in her exhaust fumes
> Teardrops like buds in my eyes, I stood upright slowly
> The boss came, slapped my back, and said: 'forget the novels'
> 'You're a worker, stay as a worker,' he said, 'wear your overalls.'

Cem Karaca-Dervisan's *Yoksulluk Kader Olamaz (Poverty Can Not Be Destiny)* is also considered one of the most important political albums in Turkish rock history. Karaca-Dervisan's songs supported the socialists' position and movement in the country, and this reinforced the political polarization in Turkey. The musicians played at several events organized by trade unions and left-leaning groups. Their new songs, especially "Yuh Yuh," became some of the important political rock songs of the period. Baris Manco continued to play apolitical songs during the second half of the 1970s, just as he did in the past. In the same period, Manco-Kurtalan Ekspres released strong progressive rock songs with futuristic content such as the long plays "2023" and "Yeni Bir Gün" ("A New Day"). Although "Mogollar" released albums in France under the leadership of two founding members of the band, Cahit Berkay and Engin Yorukoglu in 1975 and 1976, this trend did not last long and the band broke up. Fikret Kizilok continued his musical searches and gradually moved away from Anatolian Pop and produced works that were pioneers of the genre to be called "new music" in the 1980s. Other popular figures of Anadolu Pop did not make any significant work during this period.

As a result of the political crisis in the country at the end of the 1970s, Turkey witnessed another coup d'état on September 12, 1980, led by Kenan Evren. As expected, the reason was to maintain national security. Nonetheless, it can be argued that this coup was aimed at suspending left-wing politics in the context of stopping the so-called communist threat in the Cold War context. Again, as expected, right-wing politicians declared their support for the military intervention. Eventually, the progressive rock years ended with the coup. Under the military-backed president, the symbolic figures of Anatolian Pop were also put on notice that the government would not tolerate them anymore. It was therefore no surprise that most of them fled into exile, Cem Karaca among them. Nothing substantial was heard about Anatolian Pop until almost a decade later.

The Anatolian Pop music genre was revived in the 1990s, but it had been transformed with another name: *Anatolian Rock*. Arguably, there are two major reasons for this revival. Firstly, Cem Karaca returned to Turkey in 1987 after a reported call and chat with Prime Minister Turgut Ozal's. Secondly, "Mogollar" was to follow in 1992.

However, the Anatolian Rock of the 1990s was remarkably different from the Anatolian Pop of the 1970s and 1980s. Without a doubt, the new names of the 1990s were not as strong as the figures of the past with regard to the political content in the music. It is true that popular figures such as Cem Karaca continued to produce songs of a political nature in the 1990s, but their impact was not comparable to what had transpired in the past. On the other hand, "Mogollar" released very strong political works, especially since 1994. They were largely about the social crises of the early 1990s, including "Issizligin Ortasinda" ("In the Middle of Nowhere") and "Bi'sey Yapmalı" ("It Must Do Something"). Baris Manco, full name, Mehmet Barış Manço, remained popular with songs that can be classified into more pop genres until his death in 1999. Selda Bagcan and Edip Akbayram spent the same period mostly interpreting folk songs in a traditional style. It can be said that the Anatolian Rock period ended with the death of Cem Karaca in 2004 if the productions of "Mogollar" were to be put aside.

Anatolian Pop became popular again in the late 2000s, this time with the works of musicians such as Gaye Su Akyol, Altın Gün, Lalalar, Hey! Douglas, Baba Zula, and Derya Yıldırım & Grup Simsek. This new era represents a period of experimental music when compared to the Anatolian Rock era of the 1990s. In searching of saying new things in a new political era, these voices symbolized the alternative way in music. Nowadays, under the conditions of globalization, the spreading of the local things around the world makes the new music valuable in terms of the market situation. In this context, the new Anatolian Pop bands turned to the local sounds to find a new commercial way forward in the music industry. In the same period, Selda Bagcan started to work with Boom Pam, returning to the past progressive approach and taking the stage at many international festivals. Bagcan gained international fame in her late age with the attention of some famous names in the movie and music industry. The latest production of Anatolian Rock was published by the old-school "Mogollar" at the end of 2020. They recorded a selection of 16 songs published between 1968 and 1996, with new arrangements in the name of *Anatolian Sun*, and continued to produce in this genre in their 52nd year.

Conclusion

Anatolian Pop is a socio-cultural, socio-economic, and political product of Turkish history. This history is traceable to the post-World War II period and the determination to create a new country in the aftermath of the turbulence created by said war. When this brand of music emerged in the late 1960s, Keynesianism and welfare-state economic policies were the dominant paradigms among the developed countries in the Western world, while import substitution was the mainstream policy in the emerging and less-developed countries such as Turkey. One can therefore make a case that Anatolian Pop was born at a time when the nation-states in the world were divided and expressed more by their economic and political systems rather than national boundaries. This made the messaging in the music very relevant and deep-rooted in the political and economic system and realities in Turkey.

As already expressed, Turkey's somewhat problematic embrace and engagement with global capitalism, a movement away from its founding principles of the DP era, partly created the environment from which Anatolian Pop emerged. The contradictions in the newly embraced capitalist philosophy necessitated the messaging in the music, as the lyrics resonated with the people at the lower end of the economic and political ladder. In the Turkish political atmosphere in which the government was under military tutelage, criticisms of *Kemalism* and its representative CHP, the election successes of the center-right, and the economic shocks brought on by the fraught transition from an agricultural to industrial society resulted in this genre of authentic music expressing new political pursuits. Different groups in Turkey, from workers in the fields and factories, activists in the streets and in political parties, as well as others who found themselves marginalized by the system, had something that expressed their sentiments and disenchantment with the system in the new music. In other words, the Anatolian Pop music genre became popular because it expressed and challenged the restrictions and deprivations of modern Turkish society.

In using the lyrics of Anatolian Pop to highlight the inequalities and deprivations in the system, the musicians in this genre found themselves in alliance with the leftists and critics of the government. Thus, the musicians were often invited to play at political rallies and other events organized by the left-leaning groups in the country. Their music also resonated with the intellectuals who were also disenchanted with how the country was governed. With the economic and political crises the country witnessed in the late 1960s and early 1970s paired with the consequent riots and mayhem that engulfed the country, the government clamped down on musicians who played Anatolian Pop, resulting in many of them fleeing into exile.

It is noteworthy that Anatolian Pop was not purely political music because it also had cultural and popular content. It was based on Turkish culture and the use of traditional instruments to play the songs. However, this apolitical origin soon gave way to the use of the music to point out the anomalies in the system, especially the burgeoning divide between the rich and the poor. To the authorities, the new music sounded as a direct challenge to their power, hence the right-wing governments attempted to do all they could to harass and imprison the musicians and restrict their songs from going on air.

Anatolian Pop was embraced by the common people because the songs told the story of their plight in Turkish society. So, from being a musical way of singing about love and entertainment, the prevailing circumstances in Turkey turned Anatolian Pop into songs that were considered to be anti-establishment. However, with the prominent musicians of this genre being forced into exile, especially after the 1971 coup d'état by memorandum, and a number of the great names dying, Anatolian Pop had to give way to the Anatolian Rock of the 1990s and beyond. Furthermore, the music was also thematically transformed by the producers' commercial interests. Thus, the music mellowed down on highlighting the distortions of the feudalism of the past and instead focused on commercialism and entertainment.

References

Ahmad, F. (1985). The transition to democracy in Turkey. *Third World Quarterly*, 2, 211–226.

Ahmad, F. (1993). *The Making of Modern Turkey.* New York: Routledge.

Akbayram, E., & Dostlar (1974). Ince Ince Bir Kar Yagar [Song]. Sayan Plak.

Alpay, N. (1967). Fabrika Kizi [Song]. Disco Plak.

Bagcan, S. (1971). Adaletin Bu Mu Dunya? [Song]. Turkuola.

Bagcan, S. (1971). Mahpushanelere Gunes Dogmuyor [Song]. Sel Plak.

Bagcan, S. (1975). Yaz Gazeteci Yaz [Song]. Turkuola.

Baysal, O. (2018). Reconsidering "Anadolu Pop." *Rock Music Studies, 5*(3), 1–15.

Canbazoglu, C. (2009). *Kentin turkusu: Anadolu Pop-Rock.* İstanbul: Pan Yayincilik.

Castles, F. G., Leibfried, S., Lewis, J., Obinger, H., & Pierson, C. (Eds.). (2012). *The Oxford Handbook of the Welfare State.* Oxford: OUP Oxford.

Celik, N. B. (2000). The Constitution and Dissolution of the Kemalist Imaginary. In D. R. Howarth, A. J. Norval, & Y. Stavrakakis (Eds.), *Discourse Theory and Political Analysis: Identities, Hegemonies, and Social Change* (pp. 193–204). Manchester: Manchester University Press.

Dilmener, N. (2014). *Bak Bir Varmis Bir Yokmus-Hafif Turk Pop Tarihi.* İstanbul: İletisim Yayinlari.

Eder, M. (2010). Retreating state? Political economy of welfare regime change in Turkey. *Middle East Law and Governance, 2*(2), 152–184.

Erkal, G. E. (2013). *Turkiye rock tarihi I - Saykodelik yillar.* İstanbul: Esen Kitap.

Esping-Andersen, G. (1990). *The Three Worlds of Welfare Capitalism.* New York: Princeton University Press.

Gedik, A. C., & Ergun, L. (2019). Looking beyond the republic of love or hate in Turkey: Studies in popular music. *IASPM Journal, 9*(2), 92–104.

Gedik, A. C. (2018). Class struggle in popular musics of Turkey: Changing sounds from the left. In A. C. Gedik. *Made in Turkey: Studies in popular music* (pp. 89–106). New York: Routledge.

German, T. (1964). Burcak Tarlasi [Song]. Ezgi Plakları.

German, T. (1965). Kizilciklar Oldu Mu? [Song]. Ezgi Plakları.

German, T. (1965). Yarinin Sarkisi [Song]. İstanbul: Ezgi Plakları.

German, T. (1996). *Erdemli yillar.* İstanbul: Bilgi Yayinevi.

Greve, B. (Ed.). (2012). *The Routledge Handbook of the Welfare State.* New York: Routledge.

Guler, M. A. (2018). *Belki gercek yapmaya - Cem Karaca'nin hayati, muzigi ve yalnizligi.* Ankara: İmge Kitabevi Yayinlari.

Kadioglu, A. (1996). The paradox of Turkish nationalism and the construction of official identity. *Middle Eastern Studies, 32*(2), 177–193.

Kahyaoglu, O. (2003). *And Dağları'ndan Anadolu'ya devrimci muzik geleneği.* İstanbul: neKitap.

Karaca, C., & Apaslar (1967). Emrah [Song]. Sayan Plak.

Karaca, C., & Apaslar (1968). Resimdeki Gozyaslari [Song]. Turkuola.

Karaca, C., & Apaslar (1969). Bu Son Olsun [Song]. Turkofon.

Karaca, C., & Apaslar (1969). Zeyno [Song]. Turkofon.

Karaca, C., & Dervisan (1975). Tamirci Ciragi [Song]. Yavuz Plak.

Karaca, C., & Dervisan (1977). Yoksulluk Kader Olamaz [Song]. Yavuz Plak.

Karaca, C., & Kardaslar (1970). Dadaloglu [Song]. Turkofon.

Karaca, C., & Kardaslar (1971). Aci Doktor [Song]. Turkofon.

Karaca, C., & Mogollar (1974). Namus Belasi [Song]. Yavuz Plak.

Karpat, K. H. (1972). Political developments in Turkey, 1950–70. *Middle Eastern Studies, 8*(3), 349–375.

Keyder, C. (1987). *State and Class in Turkey*. London: Verso.

Kizilok, F. (1969). Uzun Ince Bir Yoldayim [Song]. Sayan Plak.

Kizilok, F. (1971). Anadolu'yum [Song]. Grafson.

Kizilok, F. (1971). Vurulmusum [Song]. Grafson.

Manco, B. (1970). Daglar Daglar [Song]. Sayan Plak.

Manco, B. (1973). Genc Osman [Song]. Yavuz Plak.

Manco, B. (1973). Hey Koca Topcu [Song]. Yavuz Plak.

Manco, B. (1974). Estergon Kalesi [Song]. Yavuz Plak.

Manco, B. (1975). 2023 [Song]. Yavuz Plak.

Manco, B. (1979). Yeni Bir Gun [Song]. Yavuz Plak.

Meric, M. (2006). *Pop dedik! Turkce Sozlu Hafif Bati Muzigi*. İstanbul: İletisim Yayinlari.

Mogollar. (1972). White Deer Saga [Song]. Turkuola.

Mogollar. (1994). Bi'sey Yapmali [Song]. On *Dört Renk*. Emre Plak.

Mogollar. (1994). Issizligin Ortasinda [Song]. On *Mogollar-94*. Emre Plak.

Mogollar. (2021). Anatolian Sun [Song]. Night Dreamer & Gulbaba Records.

Ozbek, M. (1991). *Populer Kultur ve Orhan Gencebay Arabeski*. İstanbul: İletisim Yayinlari.

Ozbudun, E. (2000). *Contemporary Turkish Politics: Challenges to Democratic Consolidation*. Lynne Rienner Publishers.

Ozgur, I. (2006). Arabesk music in Turkey in the 1990s and changes in national demography, politics, and identity. *Turkish Studies, 7*(2), 175–190.

Pekesen, B. (2019). Atatürk's unfinished revolution – The Turkish student movement and left-wing Kemalism in the 1960s. In L. Berger & T. Düzyol (Eds.), *Kemalism as a Fixed Variable in the Republic of Turkey* (pp. 97–118). Berlin: Ergon.

Ramm, C. (2020). Turkey's "light" rock revolution – Anadolu pop, political music, and the Quest for the Authentic. In B. Pekesen (Ed.), *Turkey in Turmoil: Social Change and Political Radicalization During the 1960s* (pp. 256–278). Berlin: De Gruyter Oldenbourg.

Su, R. (1985). *Ezgili yurek*. İstanbul: Adam Yayinlari.

Yarar, B. (2008). Politics of/and popular music: An analysis of the history of arabesk music from the 1960s to the 1990s in Turkey. *Cultural Studies, 22*(1), 35–79.

Yildirim, Y. (2015). Social movements in Turkey: Changing dynamics since 1968. In M. B. Jogensen & O. G. Augustin (Eds.), *Politics of Dissent* (pp. 99–116). Frankfurt am Main, Germany: Peter Lang.

Zurcher, E. J. (1993). *Turkey: A Modern History*. New York: I.B. Tauris & Co.

CHAPTER 9

Praise songs amidst political chaos: Assessing the impact of "Hope Your Justice Will Arrive" on Hong Kong's 2019 Social Movement

Wendy Wing Lam Chan

The Hang Seng University of Hong Kong, China

Abstract

The World Wide Web offers innumerable avenues for audiences to listen to music on free channels. One of such channels is *YouTube*, in which one praise song became a hit among audiences during Hong Kong's 2019 social movement protests. While popular music is generally more relatable to young people, it was a surprise that a Christian praise song swayed young audiences on the Internet and resulted in instantaneous online sharing, whether or not they were part of a religious community. This research analyzed 290 comments that were left by viewers of the praise song on the *YouTube* channel to determine the levels of effects that the song had on the social movement. The data analysis revealed four important effects and outcomes: (1) arousing the public's emotion; (2) justice becoming a keyword conveying a sense of hope that a rather messy political situation will resolve itself; (3) the value of God as a sacred force that motivates the unheard and voiceless to release their emotions, and; (4) uniting the community and cultivating a collective identity. These emotions evolved from the individual level and spread to the public at large, demonstrating the intangible value of music and song alongside the sociocultural significance of God as huge factors that sustained the social unrest and political protests in Hong Kong.

Keywords: Hong Kong, online communication, political communication, praise songs, religion, sacred value, social movement, social media

***

Introduction

The social movement protests that occurred in Hong Kong in 2019 are arguably the result of many consequences of the territory's controversial extradition bill to China. Even before the government formally announced the proposal, there had already been a few rounds of street demonstrations against the idea and tensions were all the more heightened. As the legislation day drew close, more people took to the streets to voice their unsurprisingly polarizing opinions. Using second-hand or recreated lyrics and borrowed melodies, pop music filled the air as more conflicts erupted between the protesters and the police forces who were tasked with handling and containing the situation.

Amidst the various pockets of protests and scuffles with the police, what caught the attention of Christians in Hong Kong was one of their praise songs becoming a hit on *YouTube*. It was titled, "Hope Your Justice Will Arrive." Suddenly, the song hit the airwaves and recorded 766,094 views (on14th Jan. 2021) in a very short time. It was hosted on the *YouTube* channel called *Worship Nations*, owned by a musical band that composed religious songs and other related music. *Worship Nations* was established in Hong Kong in 2014 and their intention was to share and worship God through music. They always encouraged youngsters to write praise songs for their worship practice.

The song, "Hope Your Justice Will Arrive," became the first praise song to be associated with the social movement by the audiences because of its content, though no one is certain about the original intention of the team that produced this praise song. Its lyrics contain traces of Bible verses, thus making it very popular among the Christian public. It also contained some proverbial sayings that captured the imagination of the general public. Two examples will suffice: "唯願你公義 如滔滔江河" ("I truly hope that justice will flow like a river"); and "公平 如大水滾滾" ("where fairness is like the water billowing").

Prior literature account for the role of songs in social movements in many significant ways. Corte and Edwards (2008) pointed out that one of the functions of music is to recruit new youth to join, to cultivate a kind of identity, and to obtain financial resources. De Bruyn et al. (2008) also mentioned that music actually moves and synchronizes participants to a certain extent in social contexts. Eyerman (2002) and Eyerman and Jamison (1998) also shared the fact that there is a long history between social movement mobilization and music. On their part, Rosenthal and Flacks (2015) and Roy (2010) opined that music has a role to play when calling for changes in society; the genre can even be diverse too, from folk music to pop songs. What is interesting in the present study is that the praise song itself is different from other music composed specifically for the political environment. It is created only because the Christian group recognizes the oppressed group and the Bible has similar sayings about the theme of justice in times of oppression.

"Hope Your Justice Will Arrive" was specifically chosen for this study because it became a hit and the most popular praise song in the Hong Kong community in a short period of time. The praise song was written by Fong Man Chong, who was once a drug addict before becoming a Christian leader of a music band catering to the Christian community. He often incorporated Bible sayings into their praise songs. For this song, he adopted Amos 5:24, a biblical verse that reads, "But let justice run its course like water, and righteousness be like an ever-flowing river" (this English translation is from the *New Revised Standard Version*).

The praise song was written in 2017, prior to the beginning of the social movement's protests. It became a hit later in 2019 when the social movement in Hong Kong had been going on for a few months. Many *YouTube* audiences, especially among the Christian community, clicked on the song and shared it on *Facebook*, although this is not a theme song created specifically for the social movement. However, the theme of "justice" that is highlighted in the praise song appeared to have animated members of the community and the audience in general. By saying so, it gives light to the power of music as a medium of communication and how it is often regarded as a rather subtle way to transmit a message and arouse one's inner soul. It bears reiterating that while the praise song was not composed for the social movement, it still touched people's hearts because it was anchored by the concept of justice. When justice cannot be embodied in the real world, people have to rely on sacred values to release their emotions, as the political situation in Hong Kong demonstrated.

This study was conceptualized to analyze 290 plus comments on the song, "Hope Your Justice Will Arrive," left by *YouTube* listeners/watchers of the channel. The overarching aim was to determine the levels of effects the song had on the social movement. Three pertinent research questions posed in this chapter are: (1) What role did this this praise song, "Hope Your Justice Will Arrive," play in the Hong Kong community? (2) How were the effects of the song different from those of ordinary pop music and songs? (3) Was any kind of cultural identity built by listening to this praise song, especially during the time of social movement?

The content analysis method was used in assessing how listeners reacted to the song.

Literature Review

Contextualizing Music in Politics

Danaher (2010) asserted that music is a key element of social movements, pointing out that in this regard, music has four components: collective identity, emotions, free space, and social movement culture. Collective identity is fostered and nurtured via the use of music. Along the same line, Eyerman and Jamison (1995) brought up the idea about music as a culture that provides the identity of adaptation that is rather passive in the historical process, especially when we think about such questions as: what forms of social movement do cultures rearrange or redevelop, and is there such thing as cultural transformation? Their study also questioned how people transform their values and ideas, and what the social activities in the process of cultural transformation are. Therefore, when talking about the proliferation of cultural values, Roy (2010, p. 9) employed a sociological perspective concerning the spreading of ideas through music. In his study, he asserted that there are social relationships between people and their music, especially the effects music has on them. It is noteworthy that there was some form of similar spiritual support during the previous umbrella movement in Hong Kong when protesters congregated together, praying and singing hymns (Chan, 2015). Such rituals were not only found offline but also online in the social movement that started in June 2019 in Hong Kong. Christians gathered and participated in collective prayers and sang their usual praise songs.

Such gatherings and collective participation in songs and music have been identified in previous studies. The studies showed that people engaged in social movements and various types of protests often use music and songs to rally their supporters and create *esprit de corps* among themselves. For instance, Street (2003, p. 120) discussed how music has long been considered as "a site of resistance," asserting that "from the folk songs of rural England to the work songs of slaves, from anti-war protest songs to illegal raves, music has given voice to resistance and opposition." Hence, music becomes an alternative form of political participation. Taking this concept into the 2019 social movement that happened in Hong Kong, music can range from the cultural to the political, in which lyrics contain heavy elements of political phrases and intentions. However, praise songs should not be underrated as well just because they are not directly involved in politics but are "by-products" for people to soothe their emotions by composing and voicing out elements of hope, peace, and justice in the lyrics. Second, music is an instrument that stimulates and catalyzes political mobilization because it creates and sustains emotions along with providing an uplifting mood on many occasions. This is exemplified in the case of Hong Kong's social movements in 2014, when people in the areas occupied by the police and security agents sang various songs together as a way to provide support for one another and mobilize themselves for action. As for the third role of music, sound composed by human beings can convey emotions through the intentionality of the note, rhythm, and tempo—thus, offering a hint to understanding the mood of the composer. It is interesting how people interpret a song in different ways but the central theme of the song could still be traceable. It is undeniable that music is connected to politics, for it lays a strong foundation for people to share their visions and compassion about the social and political issues happening around them.

Religion, Music, and Social Movement

Back in the 1970s and the 1980s, rock music made splashes across various communities in the UK. Many fans were "die-hards" about rock music irrespective of its specific variants, such as hard rock, pop rock, or a rather gentler presentation of pop music. Rock music has played a significant role for those who are angry with society and have rage against the government, and such music has influenced a lot of audiences around the globe, especially among European countries. Lovers of this genre of music will sing ferocious songs and even put some nasty words in between to demonstrate or amplify their anger. Music is freestyle. However, people could easily be moved by the lyrics and the rhythm. Bringing such concepts into this study, music has underlying effects for every occasion and social movements are no exception. Prior studies have pointed out how music has facilitated social movements' action directly and indirectly. For instance, Turino (2008, p.1) pointed out that, "musical sounds are a powerful human resource, often at the heart of our most profound social occasions and experiences, and people in societies around the world use music to create and express their emotional inner lives." Futrell et al. (2006) shared similar thoughts - that the music scene is where songs are used as the central organizing principle and theme for a full range of social movement activities.

Such social movements could be seen as "collective enterprises to establish a new order of life." Blumer (1995) noted that the idea behind social movements could range from seeking a form of living condition or protesting a policy with a view to having it changed or moderated. According to Collins (2001), it is not new to see that there are ideologies and tactics for creating the group dynamics in social movements. These movements have created or adopted ways of making their presence and actions known, felt, and seen, especially in order to attract the attention of their target audience and especially people in powerful positions and authority. According to Collins (2001, p. 40), a social movement could adopt "its ideologies and tactics: its anti-traditionalism (for instance, Christians playing guitars in church in place of singing old hymns), its use of group dynamics and consciousness-raising techniques (touchy-feely group psychology), even its nonviolent sit-ins (in the 1980s and 1990s, used mainly by the Right to Life movement)" to achieve its objective.

With regard to the role played by music in social movements, it is noteworthy that prior studies have also specifically examined the relationship between black music and social movements, and how music is seen to be a participatory object (Redmond, 2014). Other studies that established the relationship between music and social movements include Kassam (1999), Mouw (2004), Roy (2010), Said (2012), Boots (2013), and Walters (2005).

Method

Data for this study was collected directly from comments on a *YouTube* channel in Hong Kong during the 2019 social movement protests against a law that might send people to China. According to Roulston et al. (2003), such comments are candid expressions of self or thoughts in an unfiltered manner. They represent how people truly feel, unlike interviews in which sometimes some people feel they need to express themselves in a "politically correct" way or in a way that will not offend or cause some level of discomfort to their interviewers. It also helps that such comments are often posted anonymously in the sense that the person posting it is not afraid of being identified or becoming a victim of a spiral of silence, that is, fall in line with other peoples' line of thought in a situation that requires identity disclosure.

The choice of *YouTube* as the venue for the collection of the comments used in this study was in part influenced by the fact that the channel provides a lot of video content on a variety of topics, from civic and constructive discourse to insults and uncivil communication (Spörlein & Schlueter, 2020; Uldam & Askanius, 2013). Also, in terms of social bonding and in relation to social movements at the core of this study, *YouTube* allows individual activists to communicate with the organization and to spread messages to their existing social networks (Kavada, 2012).

In all, this study relied on 290 comments posted on *YouTube*, in response to the video of the praise song, "Hope Your Justice Will Arrive," from the 9th to the 14th of January 2021. As such, purposive data was used in this research. The comments were then sorted in a descending order of the *YouTube* function that classifies entries from "top comments" to other comments that do not carry much support. In other words, a "top comment" was determined and classified as such on the basis of the number of "likes" it attracts. For clarity of analysis and ensuring a deeper understanding of the comments, the author created themes for the classification or categorization of the comments. The categories and themes are as follows:

1. Audience engagement with God. This refers to comments on the expectation that God will guide and be with the protesters.
2. Justice and praise songs. These are comments on the need for justice in society.
3. A call to action through prayer. These comments urge people to join the prayer crusade for action and divine intervention against the deteriorating conditions in Hong Kong.

4. Asking God to provide direction. Comments in this category are about reliance on God to lead the people out of their misery.

5. Songs as support therapy. These comments are about songs as therapeutic in the face of distress.

6. Skepticism about God and justice. These are comments deal with the uncertainty about God's protection and justice.

Manual coding, text categorization, and interpretations were completed by the author based on a deep understanding of the context of the social movement in Hong Kong, the author's city of residency during the social movement protests. The author also handled all translations from Chinese to English, being a native speaker of the former, with proficiency in the latter.

Findings

The comments that were downloaded from the *YouTube* channel and categorized according to the themes expressed in the method section yielded the following results. The results are presented with samples of the comments.

Audience Engagement with God

The audiences seem to hope that God could be with them. This theme constantly appeared from the pool of comments left by their authors. As "justice" is linked with God, the comments pointed out that Hong Kong people desperately needed God to be with them. Seen and likened to an idol, God could influence the audiences' buying intention, choices, and preferences. The same applies to the *YouTube* audiences; when they wish to express their emotions, they will listen to the Christian music or praise songs. Below are some of the comments that are related to this kind of emotion:

1. Hong Kong desperately needs God's help to grant us the justice. Hong Kong is not like the Hong Kong we knew before. When I watched the news, I badly want to cry. Every Hong Konger was heartbroken and I beg God to heal everyone of us.

2. I hope the justice will arrive in Hong Kong. The justice will flow like a river.

3. I am just so moved. God is not only situated at the shrine, and I hope the justice will arrive, and protect Hong Kong, Amen.

4. Hong Kong, add oil! I hope the justice will arrive.

5. God, May I know where do Hong Kong's fairness, integrity and justice go?

The comments also show that the audiences shared their concerns about Hong Kong, and that they hope to seek God's help to heal and fix the broken hearts of the people of Hong Kong:

1. God, even though the surrounding were tough, but I still wish the way we behave is within your expectation, and we could be the citizens that obliged to justice. In addition, I hope your country, your fairness, your justice will arrive. I hope your kingdom come, your will be done, on earth as it is in heaven. I hope you will bless us Hong Kong people, and help us go through the darkness, and help to fix the broken hearts of Hong Kong people and also the broken relationship, Amen!

2. Looking at the current situation of Hong Kong, we are all very heartbroken.

3. I'm confused about what God's justice is? A group of Christians exalt the name of Jesus Christ and declare that Christ leads us to war against the government?

4. So are those who support the Hong Kong police to strictly enforce the law and condemn the evil deeds of the rioters, are considered not loyal to God?

5. Why do you only see the thorns in the eyes of others without removing the beams in your own eyes?

6. What I see is that black horror is covering every place: how many students are being abused and bullied for not participating in demonstrations, how many citizens are "privileged" for expressing disagreement, and how many shopping malls are being disturbed by thugs every day. And if the police are refused to enter, how many shops may be continuously destroyed by mobs just for supporting the police's anti-riot remarks, and how many citizens dare not express their opinions publicly because of fear of being kicked out.

7. Lord, may your justice come. In the past few months, the Hong Kong police have been wronged, bullied, deprived, physically attacked, and hurt by vicious words. They just did their duty to protect the people of Hong Kong but they have to pay such a high price. May the Lord protect our policemen who uphold the law, day and night. May your righteousness be manifested on the earth, in the holy name of Jesus Christ, Amen.

Several comments under this theme ended with phrases such as "in the holy name of Jesus Christ" and "Amen" as if they were prayers to God. The prayers themselves contain very detailed descriptions of what was going on in Hong Kong. Some of the "takes" on the political issues are subtle while others are mild or even radical. Although the levels of emotion in the comments are different, the content of the prayers are more or less similar in that they all they all seek God's help.

Justice and Praise Songs

Similar to the previous theme, the comments in this category appear to be heavily focused on justice. The theme "justice is absent" is often emphasized in the comments and different forms of sayings. The murmur and complaint about the lack of justice is buried in the prayers. And the prayers are often found presented in a poetic way. Here are examples:

1. Non- stop looping of this praise song. I want to cry badly and I hope the justice will arrive in Hong Kong.

2. While I saw the news mentioning the flower arrangement sent by Taiwanese President for the bookshop, I suddenly rang the bell of this praise song, "Where the fairness, is like the big water billowing; I truly hope that the justice will flow like a river."

Some authors of the comments also asked God to help and used the term "righteously" to project similar ideas about justice. Some of the ideas are highly related to the praise song and the choice of words are similar to what the praise song uses. An example of this use of the lyrics of a hymnal is something like "please come here righteously" used in the comment below:

1. Lord
   Please come here righteously
   Please help this place in Hong Kong
   Please let the protesters have a clear heart
   See the government's conspiracy
   Don't let anger cover your eyes

2. Lord
   Please keep every protester going home safely
   The child knows that you are the god in charge of the world
   Children know you will lead us
   Only by the Lord can we overcome difficulties
   Please come righteously
   Let us have a conclusion
   Give us a real Hong Kong

3. Lord
   I hope the child's prayer can reach your ears
   I beg you to listen, help and be conservative
   Pray in the name of our Lord Jesus Christ
   Amen!

4. God is in power. The unjust government does not belong to Him. God will destroy it.

5. I hope justice can still be in Hong Kong, my Hong Kong, and the rehabilitation of the people I assist in the future.

The people who leave comments underneath the videos seem to ask for God's support and promise to return them back to a clean society and to a reliable government. This is highly related to the lyric's main theme. The theme of justice is conveyed here in a poetic way with the choice of words and the phrases. The strong use of diction such as "give us a real Hong Kong" and "Please come here righteously" have the theme of justice embedded in the prayers. With justice retuning to Hong Kong once again, the "light" and "rehabilitation" could be found eventually.

A Call to Action Through Prayer

Other than talking about the justice that is missing in Hong Kong in the days of civil strife and uncertainty, the Christian audiences as well as the rest of the populace share a number of things in common, prominent among which is about embarking on collective actions to stymie the deteriorating conditions in Hong Kong. For instance, they collectively pray for Hong Kong, hoping that Hong Kong will go back to its previous state of tranquility, peace, and progress. The call for actions expressed in the comments usually tend to be short and descriptive. Here are examples:

1. Pray for Hong Kong

2. Today when we pray, we prayed that we need to ascertain a serious way to support Hong Kong. And this praise song rang the bell, and I think this praise song is very suitable for describing the current situation of Hong Kong.

3. It has been 5 months, and I hope Hong Kong people will not give up.

4. Our beloved Father in Heaven, please save our city Hong Kong from evil. We really need you. May the glory be to You only and forever. Amen.

5. Hong Kong brothers and sisters, please keep praying until the day our JESUS returns.

The comments appear to be a call for action through prayers, where people who wrote the comments talked to God in a prayer format. In addition, the content mentioned in the prayers is about saving Hong Kong and the desperate need for God to "return" the city to its previous tranquil status, and asking for forgiveness for past sins. There are choices of diction and phrases such as "Hong Kong brothers and sisters," "Today we pray," and "pray for Hong Kong," etc. The *YouTube* platform became a forum for Christians to gather and call for action through prayers.

Asking God to Provide Direction

Some comments showed signs of hopelessness, acknowledging that God was the only solace out of the precarious situation in Hong Kong. God, seemingly, is the only one whom they can seek answers from. They asked questions to God about what they could do in such a dangerous situation in Hong Kong. Unlike the first two categories and themes, the comments in this group appear to show people who are lost and unsure what to do. The comments are also as emotionally driven as they show a people in a desperate situation:

1. After tonight, it hurts so much. What should I do, God?

2. From June till now, a lot of things (have) happened and seems it is adding up day by day.

3. The whole earth belongs to God, God will definitely work. I feel sad; God must feel more painful than me. Look up to God with faith. He knows everything.

4. Seeing the extreme power, [there is] nothing we can do. When the gun is used to fire at citizens who are holding umbrellas, tear gas can be used to attack.

These comments are more emotional. Rhetorical questions were asked. As found in the *YouTube* comments, they are asking God what they could do. These comments are often found in the middle of the social movement activities when people begin to feel the pressure, the deadlock, and the stiffness in the unstable political environment. The extent of losing hope has reached a zenith and the people seem to fall into a valley that no one could save them from, hence their supplication to God to provide the direction out of the quagmire that had engulfed the city.

Songs as Support Therapy

The YouTube comments also shed light on how the praise song has helped alleviate the pressure on the people. The praise song itself serves multiple purposes. The comments showed that by listening to the song, the people could feel some sort of alleviation from the pressure and attendant depression many of them felt. The praise song also offers a good measure of encouragement and tenderness. Some of the comments include the following:

1. When I heard about this praise song, I cried. God Bless Hong Kong.

2. This praise song has offered me a lot of encouragement and keeps enlightening my heart. Hong Kong, add oil.

3. In this age where the deer is the horse, where fewer people are bullied by more people, God, please, I hope your righteousness comes, and your children are very likely to collapse.

4. I need to listen to it once to soothe my emotion.

5. I often feel powerless and tired. Listening to this song continues to support me. I am still looking forward to the day when Your righteousness will come!

6. Put it (praise song) in Hong Kong from June to August, very meaningful!

7. I believe God will have power over Hong Kong again!

8. Willing to be a vessel of the era. May your righteousness come.

9. Add oil, the musical band of this praise song, may God bless you all.

10. Every time when I repeatedly listen to it, I have a kind of awe feeling.

By listening to this praise song, the people felt that they were being heard, and that their concerns were being shared with God. The phrases such as "soothe my emotion," "encouragement," and "keep enlightening my heart," tend to assuage their fears and offer some succor etc. The authors of the comments even offered support to the musical band that composed this praise song.

Skepticism About God and Justice

Although several voices were found underneath the praise song, with a sizeable number talking about how they trust God and believe in God to grant them justice, there were also voices that expressed some skepticism about justice and divine intervention. More specifically, some of the comments were unsure of and skeptical about whether God did listen to their concerns. Such comments had questions about whether the community of Christians was actually walking on the path that led to God. Here is a typical comment that reflects the doubts and concerns in the Christian community. Remarkably, these comments were lengthier than the ones already identified on other categories and themes:

> In the past few months, I have heard many Christians use vicious words and actions to curse dissidents. For example, those who consider themselves baptized Christians, regardless if they have talent, when they encounter demonstrators on the streets, they will be violently interrupted by the so-called Christians. In the words of the Christian person inciting violence: You will reap what you sow when you join the social movement. I never thought this threat would come from a Christian.

Some comments questioned whether they would still see justice in the near future, expressing their disappointment over some of the public actions taken by their government, and desperately looking forward to God's manifestation of justice and fairness. This skepticism was repeated a number of times in the lyrics of the praise song. Nevertheless, the belief was that listening to the praise song was a way to feel that God was with them, thus engendering some immediate calmness and soothing feeling among members of the audience. Here are examples of such comments:

1. Will justice really come?

   Looking at Hong Kong society nowadays really makes me feel desperate
   Government and police shield each other
   The government does not listen to the voices of the citizens
   The police know that they break the law, but they have no way to punish them
   If there is a God
   Can you let justice manifest?
   Can you let Hong Kong people see hope?
   I'm in such pain

2. Hong Kong is now a place where justice is very much needed. Pray for the Lord's spirit to come to this place. Sometimes why the Lord does not listen to people's prayers and does not punish sinners, why the righteous are always persecuted, the Lord has his own time to show, Hong Kong's brothers and sisters, please do not give up on God.

Such comments show a mixture of worry and hope. While some questioned when God would come to the rescue in the midst of the government's highhandedness, others appealed to endearing terms like "Hong Kong's brothers and sisters" in order to strengthen the concept of having faith in God.

Discussion

This study investigated the 2019 social movement in Hong Kong which arose in opposition to the city government's introduction of the controversial extradition bill that might send residents to mainland China. The street demonstrations that resulted were forcefully confronted by the Hong Kong police. It was in this precarious circumstance that the Christian hymn and praise song, "Hope Your Justice Will Arrive," became the most notable song and anthem for the protesters, as it hit and literally took *YouTube* by storm and went viral. This study, therefore, examined the comments left on the *YouTube* channel in response to the song by a variety of Hong Kong residents, especially people who were against the extradition law. Thus, this discussion segments the comments and contextualizes them for a better understanding of their meaning in the chaotic and often dangerous situation that occurred in Hong Kong in 2019.

Arousing and Soothing Public Emotion

Praise songs have the power to influence the public (Adey, 1986). Human responses have always been ingrained in praise songs and praise songs composed in different eras reflect the political and social conditions of those eras. In 2019, when Hong Kong residents were protesting the extradition law to mainland China, they prayed and sought God's intervention in providing an answer to their sufferings. In that circumstance, singing praise songs became a way for the public to unleash their emotions in a most difficult time.

The invocation for divine intervention was only symptomatic of the state of despair and despondency among the people. Police brutality and constant conflicts between police and demonstrators in the guise of the maintenance of law and order had reached such crescendo that it was impossible for the people to withstand the ferocity of the attacks any longer. Consequently, they turned to God in supplication. Statements such as "Hong Kong needs justice to arrive...." and "We need God to heal everyone in Hong Kong" filled the *YouTube* channel. However, other social media platforms were equally overflowing with information (and perhaps misinformation) about hatred, discontent, frustration, anger, and disappointment about what was happening to disturb the tranquil life in the city. But while the anger and disappointment raged on, some people in the city chose to listen to the praise song, "Hope Your Justice Will Arrive," to soothe and cushion their frustration. Indeed, that praise song seemed to have become one of the best ways to help people calm down their heightened emotions. Such people went on to pour out their emotions as comments on *YouTube*.

It is imperative to note the dual roles of the songs among its listeners, the protesters against the extradition law. First, the song initially turned out to be a weapon for the mass mobilization of support for the social movement protesting the city authority's new regulation. In this regard, the protesters also used the *YouTube* channel to share information amongst themselves. Second, the song turned out to be an instrument for the calming of nerves and soothing of frayed emotions. It served as a form of a lullaby that helped to alleviate the pressure experienced by those who listened to it.

Justice as Keyword/Hope in a messy political situation

For the people of Hong Kong, the song was complemented by the expectation of divine justice and the comments on *YouTube* reflected this prospect for justice. Here is what a biblical verse says about the hope for divine intervention: the book of Revelation (21:3-4) states, "And I heard a great voice out of heaven saying, Behold, the tabernacle of God is with men, and he will dwell with them, and they shall be his people, and God himself shall be with them, and be their God." Applying this to the Hong Kong situation, the comments generally indicated that in spite of their sufferings, the God of justice would eventually be their God, and rescue them from the perils they faced. In the suffocating political environment they lived, where the protesters could not do much in the face of overbearing police force, religion became a pillar of strength as people embarked on prayers, asking for God's assistance and rescue, and hoping that God will answer their fervent supplications.

Not surprisingly, the results from this study revolved a great deal on the theme of justice, which the people felt was absent in Hong Kong. One of the comments lamented that "I want to cry badly and I hope the justice will arrive in Hong Kong." Another comment enthused that, "I hope justice can still be in Hong Kong, my Hong Kong." Yet, another observed that "God is in power. The unjust government does not belong to him. God will destroy it." All these suggest that the keyword in the protests was justice. But while the protesters acknowledged that "justice is absent" in Hong Kong, the hope remained that the flame of justice would subsequently return to the city, as expressed in one of the comments that had this wish: "I truly hope that justice will flow [back] like a river to the city of Hong Kong."

Music for Communal Unity and Identity

Cultivation of identity could be a way to unite the community. In this regard, collective memory is one of the most important notions in prior studies about the relationship between social movements and music (Eyerman, 2002; Harris, 2006). While the actual grit of the social movement is what can be observed physically in the presence of a political event, music itself becomes a medium for people to express their values and those of their community.

As shown in the results, the comments written by the *YouTube* users who listened to this song showed that they shared strong feelings of sadness, disappointment, and hopelessness. At the same time, some of them still had faith and hope that peace and justice would prevail. From their comments, one can sense the dignity, pride, unity, and kinship in supporting one another as friends and colleagues do when going through some dark and harsh periods. The praise song became a source of sustaining hope, a medium to share emotions and stimulate communal support, and a call for prayer and some action against the burdens imposed by the government.

Jasper (1997) opined that the cultivation of a cultural and collective identity is mostly based on shared ideals. That was what happened in Hong Kong, as members of the Christian and non-Christian communities faced the same political turmoil, and consequently became involved in a social movement to overcome their predicament and seek God's direction and assistance in doing so. In this regard, the praise songs on *YouTube* offered a virtual space for the people to express their ideas and establish their identity as people of Hong

Kong, and more specifically, as a Christian community that pursued the ideals of peace, hope, justice, and love.

Conclusion

Evidently, the praise song, "Hope Your Justice Will Arrive," gained a lot of clicks on *YouTube* in a short period of time in Hong Kong during the 2019 protests against the extradition law to China. Traditionally, when people who belong to social movements wish to express their grievances and impact public opinion, they take to the streets in forms of demonstrations. In this study, however, some people chose to go online to listen to the praise song and leave comments right there instead of taking to the streets. These are people who felt it was best for them to leave comments on the *YouTube* channel as a form of call for action in support of the protests. To them, listening to and singing the praise song was considered the same as the ritual of physical street protests. While it is important for research to focus attention on street protests by social movements, the Hong Kong experience demonstrates that the importance of music and praise songs online should not be ignored in researching social movements and their *modus operandi*.

While the social movement in Hong Kong was most complicated and serious, the praise song actually showed a few layers of meanings and commitment throughout the span of time between June and December of 2019. The online community that listened to the praise song was far bigger than most people expected, hence the imperative to research this form of social movement. Future research can focus on the key antecedents that influenced the people to embrace the praise song and the direct relationship between listening to the praise song and the collective action that occurred in Hong Kong society of that era.

Limitations

One of the limitations in this study is the nature of data obtained and used for analysis. The data was not random, and perhaps more importantly, was limited to one platform, *YouTube*. The protesters also used other platforms to express their discontent. Again, the methodology may have impacted or affected the nature and interpretation of the findings. The use of *YouTube*, as already mentioned, and the reliance on selected comments left on the channel in response to a particular song, cannot adequately and sufficiently address what the protesters did in furtherance of their objectives. Indeed, there were other songs that gained some support in the same short period of time of the protests, but were not identified or chosen for analysis in this chapter. At best, we can assert that this study is exploratory in nature. These limitations should be addressed in subsequent studies in this genre of communication research.

References

Adey, L. (1986). *Praise Songs and the Christian Myth*. Canada: UBC Press.

Blumer, H. (1995). Social Movements. In S. M. Lyman (Ed.), *Social Movements: Critiques, Concepts, Case-Studies* (pp. 60–83). London: Palgrave Macmillan. https://doi.org/10.1007/978-1-349-23747-0_5

Boots, C. C. (2013). *Singing for Equality: Praise Songs in the American Antislavery and Indian Rights Movements*. North Carolina: McFarland.

Chan, S. H. (2015). The protestant community and the umbrella movement in Hong Kong. *Inter-Asia Cultural Studies, 16*(3), 380–395.

Collins, R. (2001). Social Movements and the Focus of Emotional Attention. In J. Goodwin, J. M. Jasper & F. Polletta (Eds.), *Passionate Politics: Emotions and Social Movements* (pp. 27- 44). Chicago and London: The University of Chicago Press.

Corte, U., & Edwards, B. (2008). White power music and the mobilization of racist social movements. *Music and Arts in Action, 1*(1), 4–20.

Danaher, W. F. (2010). Music and social movements. *Sociology Compass, 4*(9), 811–823.

de Bruyn, L., Leman, M., Moelants, D., Demey, M., & F. de Smet (2008). Measuring and quantifying the impact of social interaction on listeners' movement to music. In K. Jensen (Ed.), *Proceedings of the 2008 Computers in Music Modeling and Retrieval and Network for Cross-Disciplinary Studies of Music and Meaning Conference* (pp. 298–305). Universiteit Gent (Belgium).

Eyerman, R. (2002). Music in movement: Cultural politics and old and new social movements. *Qualitative Sociology, 25*(3), 443–458.

Eyerman, R., & Jamison, A. (1995). Social movements and cultural transformation: Popular music in the 1960s. *Media, Culture & Society, 17*(3), 449–468.

Eyerman, R., & Jamison, A. (1998). *Music and Social Movements: Mobilizing Traditions in the Twentieth Century*. Cambridge University Press.

Futrell, R., Simi, P., & Gottschalk, S. (2006). Understanding music in movements: The white power music scene. *The Sociological Quarterly, 47*(2), 275–304.

Harris, F. C. (2006). It takes a tragedy to arouse them: Collective memory and collective action during the civil rights movement. *Social Movement Studies, 5*(1), 19–43.

Jasper, J. M. (1997). *The Art of Moral Protest*. Chicago, IL: University of Chicago Press.

Kassam, T. R. (1999). Songs of Wisdom and Circles of Dance: An Anthology of Hymns by the Satpanth Ismāʿīlī Muslim Saint, Pīr Shams. *Journal of the American Oriental Society, 199*(2), 327–328.

Kavada, A. (2012). Engagement, bonding, and identity across multiple platforms: Avaaz on Facebook, YouTube, and MySpace. *MedieKultur: Journal of Media and Communication Research, 28*(52), 28–48.

Mouw, R. J. (2004). *Wonderful Words of Life: Praise Songs in American Protestant History and Theology*. Michigan: Wm. B. Eerdmans Publishing.

Redmond, S. L. (2014). *Anthem: Social movements and the Sound of Solidarity in the African Diaspora*. New York: NYU Press.

Rosenthal, R., & Flacks, R. (2015). *Playing for Change: Music and Musicians in the Service of Social Movements*. Routledge.

Roulston, K., DeMarrais, K., & Lewis, J. B. (2003). Learning to interview in the social sciences. *Qualitative Inquiry, 9*(4), 643–668.

Roy, W. G. (2010). *Reds, Whites, and Blues: Social Movements, Folk Music, and Race in the United States* (Vol. 45). New Jersey: Princeton University Press.

Said, B. (2012). Praise songs (Nasheeds): A contribution to the study of the Jihadist culture. *Studies in Conflict & Terrorism, 35*(12), 863–879.

Spörlein, C., & Schlueter, E. (2020). Ethnic Insults in YouTube Comments: Social Contagion and Selection Effects During the German "Refugee Crisis." *European Sociological Review, 37*(3), 411–428.

Street, J. (2003). 'Fight the Power': The Politics of Music and the Music of Politics. *Government and Opposition, 38*(1), 113–130.

Uldam, J., & Askanius, T. (2013). Online civic cultures? Debating climate change activism on YouTube. *International Journal of Communication, 7*(2013), 1185–1204. https://ijoc.org/index.php/ijoc/article/view/1755

Turino, T. (2008). *Music as Social Life: The Politics of Participation*. Chicago and London: The University of Chicago Press.

Walters, S. (2005). Social movements, class, and adult education. In S. B. Meriam & A. P. Grace (Eds.), *The Jossey-Bass Reader on Contemporary Issues in Adult Education* (pp. 138–148). San Francisco, CA: Jossey-Bass.

WN X 玻璃海樂團 X PHOTIC. *願你公義降臨* (Hope Your Justice Will Arrive) *(official lyric mv) // worship nations // 玻璃海樂團* [Video]. YouTube. (2017, July 31). https://www.YouTube.com/watch?v=QxDccKsJJhI

Appendix

Hope Your Justice Will Arrive (願你公義降臨)
(https://www.YouTube.com/watch?v=QxDccKsJJhI)

Music and Lyrics：Fong Man Chung

Editing: Philia Yuen
Vocal: Gabby Yeung, Yip Yan Wing

Translated by the author of this article

神求你喜悅 我們的敬拜 (I wish God will like the way we worship)

獻上誠實公義正直的心 (That we wish to devote our heart with justice and integrity)

願我們行事為人 對得起主你 (I wish the way we behave is within your expectation)

作你看為義的子民 (and we could be the citizens that obliged to justice)

唯願你公義 如滔滔江河 (I truly hope that justice will flow like a river)
   (Bible Amos, 5:24)

公平 如大水滾滾 (Where fairness is like the water billowing)

神又豈止於聖殿中 (God is not only situated at the shrine)

祂憐恤 受壓的人 (He sympathize those who are oppressed)

主帳幕在人間 (God put the tent over us)

唯願你公義 如滔滔江河 (I truly hope that justice will flow like a river)

公平 如大水滾滾 (Where fairness is like the water billowing)

神又豈止於聖殿中 (God is not only situated at the shrine)

祂憐恤 受壓的人 (He sympathize those who are oppressed)

願你公義降臨 (I hope the justice will arrive)

你的國 你的義 你公義降臨 (Your country, your fairness, your justice will arrive)

你的國 你的義 你公義降臨 (Your country, your fairness, your justice will arrive)

你的國 你的義 你公義降臨 (Your country, your fairness, your justice will arrive)

Their musical band's core values: 我們的核心價值 (Core values)

1. 召聚渴慕主的敬拜者，重建大衛倒塌的帳幕 (Gathering the worshippers who hungered for the Lord and rebuild David's fallen tent.)

2. 興起年青一代，進入主的呼召，培育他們成為神國的敬拜者 (Raising the younger generation, entering the call of the Lord, and nurturing them to become the worshipers of the kingdom of God.)

3. 成為年青敬拜者的平台，讓他們發展發揮神所賦予的恩賜 (Becoming a platform for young worshipers, allowing them to develop the gifts given by God.)

4. 擴展粵語敬拜歌的市場，推動及鼓勵創作粵語敬拜歌 (Expanding the market for Cantonese worship songs, promoting and encouraging the creation of Cantonese worship songs.)

5. 恢復及興起廣東話敬拜歌，用我們的母語帶領人與主相遇 (Resuming and raising up Cantonese worship songs, and to lead people to meet the Lord in our mother tongue.)

Acknowledgment

I would like to express my sincere gratitude to the editor of this book, Dr. Uche Onyebadi, for working with me on this chapter. My gratitude also goes to Ms. Elaine Ling for her enduring support, especially her professional advice on the perspective of religion. Also deserving of my appreciation is Mr. Kristian Jeff Cortez Agustin who assisted me with the meticulous editing of the manuscript.

CHAPTER 10

From political stump to messaging through music: A study of Madzore's political songs in Zimbabwe

Faith Bahela

National University of Science and Technology, Zimbabwe

Abstract

Popular music plays a significant role in mediating ordinary people's lives. During the liberation struggle in Zimbabwe, popular music was used to galvanize the masses for the nationalist cause. In post-independence, musicians such as Thomas Mapfumo, Leonard Zhakata, and Lovemore Majaivana emerged as subversive voices challenging the hegemony of the ruling party, Zimbabwe African National Union-Patriotic Front (ZANU-PF). Given how politics and music are intertwined in Zimbabwe, this study examines how Paul Madzore, an opposition politician in the country, uses music as a vehicle for political messaging. Drawing upon Foucault's theory of discourse and an analysis of Madzore's selected songs, this study argues that Madzore's music became a site where political identities are renegotiated and reconstructed as the opposition party is valorized whilst delegitimizing ZANU-PF.

Keywords: Madzore, ZANU-PF, political music, election, MDC, political instability

***

Introduction

This study focuses on the political discourses and identities that emerge from Paul Madzore's music post-2000. Madzore is a former Movement for Democratic Change (MDC) legislator-turned musician who has been churning out oppositional messages that reflect Zimbabwe's socio-economic and political realities. Using complex *chiShona* proverbs of his Shona cultural origin, mixed with political and religious discourses, Madzore has become the voice that articulates and reiterates the opposition party's viewpoint. Thus, he is ideologically inclined to the MDC party, as he uses his music as a mobilizing tool to garner support for the party that grew out of Zimbabwe Congress of Trade Unions (Chuma, 2005) to challenge the hegemonic status of the ZANU-PF ruling party in Zimbabwe's post-independence era. Thus, Madzore's music provides an arena to contest the ruling party's power and leadership in the country. This study therefore focuses on the politician's use of music for political messaging and analyzes the discourses and identities embedded in his songs.

Historically, music in Zimbabwe has been employed as a tool to mobilize people for the struggle for independence and speak back to the power bloc. In this regard, post-independent Zimbabwe has seen the production of music mirror the state of affairs in the country. Willems (2011, p. 147) posits that popular media such as music, videos, and comics have become an alternative arena where citizens obtain information on political issues or contest political elites' power. Thus, music has become a site where "unsayable" truths are channeled. Against the backdrop of silencing protest voices and the censorship of "protest" music in mainstream media, this study interrogates the political messages in Madzore's songs. With a view to gain political mileage for MDC, Paul Madzore employs his music to praise and give salience to the opposition party, thereby challenging reality aligned with the ruling party's discourses. Against the backdrop of socio-economic and political upheavals and heightened unrests in Zimbabwe, as well as the alleged torture and abduction of journalists and individuals deemed 'pro-opposition,' this study attempts to analyze the political messages advanced by Madzore in his music.

The ruling ZANU-PF party has used galas, jingles, music, and musicians to give salience to their political messages on nationalist discourses in the wake of growing opposition in the country. Willems (2015) argues that Jonathan Moyo, the then Minister of Information and Publicity, produced songs for the group Pax Afro with the 'Back2Black' album which promoted Pan-Africanist discourses. Willems (2015, p. 4) expounds that under the Mugabe regime, sponsored music by selected artists and politicians-turned-musicians to endorse its ideologies. These were meant to push the Pan-Africanist rhetoric to the forefront so as to counter the imperialist narrative. However, musicians such as Oliver Mtukudzi took a subtle approach (Sibanda, 2004) with political overtones whilst Thomas Mapfumo used music to challenge the power bloc. In this vein, Madzore's songs capture and expose the political landscape in Zimbabwe and are politically aligned to the MDC, challenging the grand narrative that was in support of the people in power and their surrogates.

The production of Madzore's songs was characterized by a turning point in the political landscape, which saw massive political unrest in Zimbabwe, with ZANU-PF losing massive political gains due to the formation of MDC (Mazango,

2005; Moyo, 2005). This study was conducted in this political situation and at the height of the ZANU-PF and MDC rivalry. The antagonisms between the parties grew in such intensity that the ZANU-PF operatives resorted to calling and vilifying MDC members as puppets to whites and Western nations, sellouts, and homosexuals (Meredith, 2011), and strategically constructed their (ZANU-PF) party as a revolutionary patriotic party (Chibuwe, 2017).

This intense rivalry between the two parties practically dominated the political landscape in Zimbabwe. One of the things that emerged from this situation was the notion of "inclusions and exclusions" (Ndlovu-Gatsheni, 2009), defined as "them" and "us" contestations. This division also seeped into the music industry, where musicians who identified with a certain political party produced songs that impugned on the legitimacy, leadership, integrity, and policies of the other party. In other words, the music landscape in the country, like the political terrain, also became a site for struggle to win and re-win hegemony. Given his background as an opposition legislator, Madzore obviously supported the MDC. With time, his music naturally became an alternative avenue where MDC's political messages were disseminated and reiterated, exposing and attacking the socio-economic woes that had engulfed the country.

The songs analyzed in this chapter were produced after the year 2000, a period that witnessed intensified crises and changes in political power dynamics in both the ruling party and the opposition. Thus, it is imperative to understand Madzore's framing of messages and identities in light of these shifts in power. Furthermore, this period was also marked by succession disputes and factional politics within both political parties. Ultimately, these shifting power dynamics and contestations impacted the content of the political messages in the songs. In addition, the political environment also witnessed government-controlled broadcast stations in the country downplaying songs that were deemed to be "anti-government" or avoiding them altogether. Instead, the broadcast stations only gave airtime to songs that recounted the liberation struggle, a crucial historical moment in Zimbabwe. In other words, censorship had found its way into the country, especially in state-owned and controlled broadcast media.

Simply put, the issue of censorship, the "banning" of "controversial songs" or however the action was framed by government officials, allowed those in power to determine what was "acceptable" or "unacceptable" by the government in a bid to shape messages and content broadcast on air to audiences. Through the Censorship Control and Entertainment Act (2004), government "rules in" the type of music that valorizes and praises it and "rules out" (Foucault, 1972) music that it considered anti-establishment. Media laws effectively became political assets and tools used by the ZANU-PF government to gain political mileage over its opponents.

In spite of the official censorship in the country, Madzore's songs found their way on to social media (*YouTube, WhatsApp*, etc.), where they could be accessed without much governmental interference. Thus, his music gained a huge political following, especially amongst the huge population of disgruntled Zimbabwean youths.

It is noteworthy that Madzore's songs were not the only "anti-establishment" music in the post-2000 era nor were they the only political songs released in Zimbabwe. This period also witnessed the emergence of "urban grooves," a youth-oriented music genre that also transformed the music industry in the country. The ruling party, through its Third Chimurenga ideology, also produced songs that celebrated the government's land reform program. Also, political jingles and music galas became prominent during that period as they were a strategic political advertising practice by the ruling party to market the ZANU-PF brand. Bere (2008) argues that the urban grooves genre was laced with propaganda elements, advancing the government's political messages that highlighted its anti-western rhetoric.

Popular Music as a Space for Political Communication

Swanson and Nimmo (1990, p. 9) conceptualized political communication as "strategic use of communication to influence public knowledge, beliefs, and action on political matters." In the same vein, McNair (2003, p. 4) posits that political communication is a "purposeful communication about politics." For Denton and Woodward (1998, p. 10), "the crucial factor that makes communication 'political' is not the source of the message, but its content and purpose." Thus, one notes that content and purpose of a particular message are key in political communication practices. Marongodze is of the view that "the symbiotic interrelation between politics and music reveals that music reflects politics whereas politics manipulates music" (2019, p. 62). In this regard, Madzore, an opposition politician, produces music to advance and reflect a pro-MDC political message. In an interview, Madzore claimed that "...Zimbabwe is the subject of my music because the purpose of my music is to mobilize support and votes for MDC and make sure they know the tyrannical character of the ruling party" (Marongodze, 2019, p.167). This assertion reinforces the perception that Madzore is politically inclined towards the opposition party, and through his songs he advances counter-hegemonic narratives.

Music is an integral part of political communication and acts as a space to convey messages aimed at advocating for a particular political diet. In this regard, music is a space through which political messages are asserted, with Madzore's songs challenging the negative narratives associated with the opposition party and critiquing the ruling ZANU-PF party. His music attempts to influence the political environment by communicating Zimbabwe's socio-economic and political reality from the opposition's standpoint. Thus, Madzore's songs mirror Zimbabwe's socio-economic and political woes so as to influence perceptions about people in power. Consequently, he assumes the role of the custodian of the opposition party's political conscience in addition to being its unofficial communicator and spokesperson. On the other hand, the political communication practices of musicians such as Tambaoga, Elliot Manyika, Chinx Chingaira, and Urban Grooves are intended to endorse the ruling party's nationalist's rhetoric, liberation war narratives, and the politics of land reform aimed at sustaining ZANU-PF's political power (Menon, 2008).

In Zimbabwe, music is not only for entertainment and challenging the ruling political elite, it also acts as what one of Africa's prominent writers and thinkers, wa Thiong'o, (1993) called a country's history reservoir. Applied to Zimbabwe, this means that music also serves as a vehicle for articulating the current socio-economic and political realities in the country, thereby becoming a site where contesting economic and political discourses play out. Madzore's music has come into that sphere, providing divergent views advanced by the MDC concerning Zimbabwe.

Conceptual Framework

This study was guided by the framing theory which facilitated the exploration and interrogation of Madzore's songs, unravelling the political messages and constructed identities embedded in them. The theory provided the critical lens used to unpack and interrogate how Madzore constructed identities and presented his messages about political actors in the Zimbabwean political sphere. Entman (1993) postulated that framing was a manner of categorizing aspects of reality as important. Therefore, the author of the present study assessed how Madzore gave prominence to "reality," identities and discourses through his music, by his use of language, certain socio-economic and political issues were pushed to the forefront while others were downplayed.

Also, this study is anchored upon the Foucault's theorization of discourse. Discourse is about the production of knowledge in situated historical contexts (Hall, 1997). Foucault argues that power begets counter power (1980), hence this theory is critical in interrogating Madzore's messages in the context of an environment that extols music that is pro-ruling elite. This chapter examines the knowledge that is produced and reproduced through Madzore's songs, as the politician uses songs to advance ideologies that challenge the normalised rhetoric by the powers that be, thereby fueling the assertion that power yields power. This theory is crucial in this study as it helps explore the political messages and unpack discourses that emerge in Madzore's music. This theory helps in understanding how a certain phenomenon is talked about, or in this instance, how it is sung at a particular time. For Foucault (1980), power is not monopolized, as it is everywhere and can therefore be vulnerable. This assertion fits this study's argument that Madzore's music unveils contesting truths concerning the socio-economic and political goings on in Zimbabwe by challenging the seemingly uncontestable rhetoric of the power bloc. Thus, the Foucauldian theory helps to unearth the contesting discourses in Madzore's songs and in understanding the power dynamics that emerge in the negotiation and renegotiation of the MDC identity. It is also critical in providing insights into the "truths" and "unsayable/hidden truth" in the narratives of Zimbabwean issues, from the perspective of a politician-turned-musician who is aligned to the MDC and its ideology.

Methodology

Data for this study overlaps the regimes of Zimbabwe's first president, Robert Mugabe, and his successor, Emmerson Mnangagwa. All of the songs were released after the year 2000. Over 20 songs in this period were accessed and downloaded from *YouTube* and *WhatsApp* social media platforms. Thereafter, the author purposively selected 13 songs as the samples that are relevant to the focus of the study, that is, the socio-economic and political realities in Zimbabwe. The songs are: "Saddam waenda sare Bob" ("Saddam is gone, we are left with Bob"), "Ndiyo here Zimbabwe?" ("Is this Zimbabwe?"), "Bond hatidi Musamanikidze mass" ("we do not want the bond note, do not force the masses), "Handicheuke" ("we will not turn back"), "Simuka Zimbabwe" ("Zimbabwe arise"), "Tombana" ("toddler") (2016), "G40 dedication," "Kure kure" ("very far"), "Chirangano 4" ("Agreement 4"), "Ngwena Ngainyururwe mumvura" ("remove the crocodile in the water"), "Manyararireiko Zimbabwe" ("Zimbabwe why have you remained silent"), "Niniva kure" ("Nineveh is far"), and "Mutakurei tifambe, Mutakureiwo tiyambuke" (carry him until he crosses over).

The lyrics of these songs were analyzed in relation to the socio-economic and political context in which they were produced. Corbin and Strauss (2008) argue that contextualizing text is crucial, as it attempts to insulate the distortion of meaning in texts. Thematic analysis was used to capture recurring motifs, themes, and patterns in Madzore's songs. Braun and Clarke (2006, p. 79) note that thematic analysis is a qualitative method for "identifying, analyzing and reporting themes within data." Therefore, this author used the qualitative content analysis to critically analyze Madzore's songs, with particular attention to the language used by the musician to frame his message. The intention of using the qualitative content analysis was to uncover the meaning (Corbin & Strauss, 2008) attached to Madzore's songs.

The songs were thematically categorized for analysis and discussion.

Analysis and Discussion

1st Theme: Songs on the Socio-Economic Situation Under Robert

Madzore organizes the messages in his music and songs in alignment with historical and present events. Thus, he sings from different contexts in order to expose those responsible for the calamities that have befallen Zimbabwe. In the song, "Tombana," he refers to the acts of the power elite as having fueled socio-economic and political instability in Zimbabwe:

> Takakutarisa nepa kona yeziso uchipunza dzimba dzevanhu
> Ndakati ko Bona wakabereka seiko, kuzvarira nyika muvengi

> *We watched you from an angle as you destroyed people's homes*
> *I said Bona gave birth to an enemy of the people*

He frames the late president, Mugabe, as *muvengi* (enemy) of the people due to the inhumane acts of Operation Murambatsvina (Operation Restore Order). Madzore makes a reference to the government's action to re-cast the identity of Mugabe as an enemy. During Operation Murambatsvina, the context in which the song is sung, government security agents and the police embarked on the massive demolition of structures that were deemed illegal in the urban areas, a move which scholars (Ncube & Chinouriri, 2016, p. 4) argue was the vindictive nature of ZANU-PF after losing the urbanite following an election. Madzore contends that colonial injustices have cascaded into the post-colonial era, as black-on-black oppression has become rampant. Thus, his political message uses the Murambatsvina policy and events to discredit and expose the flaws in ZANU-PF and Mugabe in order to delegitimize both ruling party and president. In this song, he continues to re-ascribe Mugabe's identity arguing that:

> Bhobho uno bhiyavha kunge pwere same same naTombana, Robert
> *Bob, you behave like an infant, Robert*

Madzore refers to Mugabe as *Tombana*, behaving like a toddler, as he chronicles instances where the late president showed little to no empathy with the plight of the masses, thus exhibiting immature traits. He characterizes Mugabe's actions and involvement in the displacement of the urbanites as childlike acts that discredit the president and showcases him as unfit and unworthy to rule. Thus, Madzore rides on that historical moment in order to criticize and tag

ZANU-PF as the engineer of instability in Zimbabwe. Madzore also uses another past event in an attempt to de-legitimize Mugabe and ZANU-PF. He sings:

> Vakangevabvuma kuuraya Morgan ukapomera treason
> Vakatotsvaga kamrungu keku Canada kainzi Ari Ben-Menashe
>
> *They agreed to kill Morgan, accused him of treason, and used the*
> *Service of a white man from Canada called Ari Ben Menashe*

His message constructs Mugabe and ZANU-PF as responsible for the death of members of the opposition and as liars for concocting a treason plot. He argues that the regime enlisted the services and testimony of a Canadian man, Ari Ben-Menashe, to eliminate its seemingly powerful opponent. Referring to the treason plot, Madzore presents Mugabe and the ruling ZANU-PF as pioneers of political instability in Zimbabwe in pursuit of eliminating its political opponent in order to create a one-party state. Foucault (1980) argues that power begets power, and in reference to this study, Madzore's songs are a point of resisting the normalised, official "truth" about MDC.

Next, the musician attempts to caricature the Mugabe-ZANU-PF brand, accusing the former president of ruining the nation and outsourcing his failures onto Morgan Tsvangirai, leader of the opposition MDC. The lyrics say:

> Takakutarisa uchiondoka nyika nhasi chashata iwe woti Morgan
> Saka unobvuma kuti ndipresident iwe unongori chitoyi
>
> *We watched as you destroyed the nation, now that things are bad*
> *You say it's Morgan*
> *So you agree he is the president and you are just a toy*

Here, Madzore also argues that Mugabe was responsible for the poorly conceptualized and implemented government policies that have subverted and dilapidated Zimbabwe. He framed Mugabe as a "toy," contrary to the "great man of golden mind" (Chibuwe, 2017, p. 176) presented in the ZANU-PF 2013 campaign manifesto. In this song, he uses the language of exclusion (Ndlovu-Gatsheni, 2009) in order to deconstruct Mugabe as unfit to rule the people. Then he called on the president to acknowledge his failures, because "now that things are bad, you say it's Morgan"

Discourses of economic ruin reverberate in the song, "Bond hatidi Musamanikidze mass" ("we do not want the bond notes, do not force the masses"). The Bond notes were introduced in 2016 to ease cash shortages, however these supplementary notes had detrimental effects on the economy with a myriad of economic challenges such as hyperinflation, heightened unemployment rate, prices of basics plummeting, and the rise of the black market. The musician framed that economic disaster this way:

Vanhu ava vanomhanikidza mass...bond hatidi
Gore riya Gono uyu akamanikidza mass gore riya
Akamanikidza povo Bearers cheque
Nhai vankomo makafira here vanhu kutambudzika
Ziyaphapha makafira here vanhu kutambudzika

These people force people, we do not want the bond
Gono once forced the mass to accept the Bearers cheque
Nkomo, did you die for the people to suffer?
Ziyaphapha, did you die for the people to suffer?

Madzore draws parallels between the economic policies of Gideon Gono (former Reserve Bank of Zimbabwe governor), Patrick Chinamasa (former Finance Minister), and John Mangundya (current Reserve Bank of Zimbabwe governor) who ushered in the Bearers' cheque and the Bond note currencies respectively without the people's consent. He depicted the government of the day as master manipulators for their selfish gains at the expense of the masses. Mangundya, Chinamasa, and Gono are presented as masters of economic manipulation due to monitory policies they implemented to benefit the elite while looting from the already poor masses. The policies that started under Mugabe have continued under Mnangagwa, hence the musician was able to draw a parallel between both governments in flawed economic ideas, and more specifically, monetary policies. He framed forcing the masses to accept whatever currency rate that was decreed by the government as a form of injustice and implied that the masses should resist it.

In the song, "Bond hatidi Musamanikidze mass," Madzore discusses state violence, arguing that the regime hides behind violence and throwing people into prisons to whip Zimbabweans in line with their policies and practices. He identifies them as *vadzwanyiriri* (oppressors) and encourages the masses to become street warriors to protest and show their discontent against state-sponsored violence. In other words, Madzore is inciting Zimbabweans to stand up against the powers that be for their economic and political emancipation.

Also, Madzore mines Zimbabwe's history for liberation struggle heroes such as Joshua Mqabuko Nkomo and Jason Ziyaphapha, posing a rhetorical question as to whether they fought for the masses to languish in poverty. He posits that the government has failed to uphold what the revolution stood for and presents members of the ruling party as having betrayed the struggle. In his songs, Madzore's recounts the history of Zimbabwe in ways that support the discourses of the opposition party, MDC, which was accused by ZANU-PF as being stooges of the West. Madzore's counterargument in his narrative is that by betraying the people, the ZANU-PF and its officials were working against the principled revolution that ushered in Zimbabwe's independence.

2nd Theme: Representation of Economic and Political Instability in the Post-Mugabe Era

Madzore's music also focuses on the social, economic, and political issues Zimbabwe continues to face after President Mugabe; his music captures both past and present topical issues that characterize Zimbabwe. Discourses of economic ruin emerge in the song "Handicheuke:"

> Handicheuke ndaramba nhamo yandakaona
> Vana veZimbabwe musacheuke Egipita musacheuke
>
> *I will not turn back to the problems I faced*
> *Zimbabwe, do not turn back to Egypt*

This song, released in the post-Mugabe era context, implores Zimbabweans not to return to Egypt (a place associated with oppression for biblical Israel). Through use of biblical frames, Madzore likens Zimbabwe to Israel, and in this instance, Egypt is characterized by socio-economic and political oppression. He appropriates religious narratives in political discourses to buttress his argument that Zimbabweans should not return to Egypt through votes, rather they should focus on changing the system altogether by voting out the ruling party. Thus, he attempts to convince the electorate to embrace change, using religious discourses to authenticate and legitimize the opposition's opinion concerning the socio-economic issues affecting Zimbabwe. In other words, he advocates that the masses should not allow Zimbabwe to return to the squalid conditions of the Mugabe era.

In another song, "Niniva Kure" ("Nineveh is very far"), Madzore continuously taps into religious frames to construct his political message, emphasizing the calamities that characterized the post-independent Zimbabwe that eventually led to its economic ruin:

> Niniva kure tinoda kuyambuka zvakaita Jonah tiyamurei Mambo
> Hutsinye hwanyanya toda kuyambuka ...
> Humbavha hwanyanya tinoda kuyambuka...
> Mhondi dzanyanya tinoda kuyambuka.
>
> *Nineveh is far, we want to cross over as did Jonah, God please help us*
> *Hatred is on the rise, we want to cross over*
> *Theft is on the rise, we want to cross over*
> *The number of murderers has increased*

Here, Madzore makes the case that the economic stagnancy and crisis in the country were the result of corrupt tendencies and practices by people in power. He bemoans the heightening malicious acts of thievery, murder, and hatred in Zimbabwe, and re-imagines a nation free of evil acts. He believes that Zimbabwe needs to cross over to better living conditions (in Nineveh), hence his plea to God to help his people in a time of need. In this connection, the singer appropriates religious imagery to express the need to cross over to better living conditions. However, underlying his political message is the need for a shift in political power to engender positive change in the country.

Discourses of political instability in Zimbabwe frequently reoccur in Madzore's music, especially discourses on political and election violence. He presents the ZANU-PF government as violent and full of inhumane attributes in its position of leadership. In the song, "Ndiyo here Zimbabwe," Madzore bemoans the fact that during elections in Zimbabwe, the armed forces and military bases were usually used by the ruling party as tools of intimidation and power retention. Thus, he sings:

> Pakuvoter munovarova muchivarovera nyaya yebato
> Ma base munowasetter muchiwa setera nyaya yebato
>
> *During elections, you beat them because of a party*
> *You create army bases because of a party*

The title poses a rhetorical question: *Ndiyo here Zimbabwe?* (Is this Zimbabwe?). The song was produced in the election context, where Madzore did some language manipulation that framed ZANU-PF as captains of violence. Human rights abuse discourse emerges in this song as noted by the creation of military torture bases in rural and urban areas for the purposes of intimidating the electorate. Furthermore, Madzore goes on to liken the killing of human beings by agents of the regime to the slaughter of animals, thereby highlighting the brutality in being killed because of one's political affiliation. The political message indicts leaders who abuse human rights and freedom of choice, particularly party affiliation, leading to political instability in Zimbabwe.

The song goes on to say:

> Mukoma wako uchamuponda uchimupondera nyaya yebato
> Dzimba dzavo makadzipisa muchipisira nyaya yebato
> Chikafu munovanyima muchivanyimira nyaya yebato
>
> Minda yavo makaitora muchiitorera nyaya yebato
> *You kill your brother because of a political party*
> *You burn their houses because of a party*
> *You deprive them of food because of a party*
> *You take their land because of a party*

In this case, Madzore identifies the calamities that befall people who are anti-establishment and argues that violence and dispossessing people are strategies the ZANU-PF employs in a bid to retain its political power. Thus, he reiterates his lamentation that black-on-black oppression and violence have remained in post-colonial Zimbabwe, especially as people are victimized for their political party affiliation. The message in this song is that the ruling regime is concerned with inflicting pain on its people in order to retain power, thus fueling socio-economic and political instability in the land rather than engaging in nation-building strategies for a better Zimbabwe.

3rd Theme: Multiple Diagnoses of the Zimbabwean Crisis

Madzore's music carries political messages that diagnose the multifaceted nature of the Zimbabwean crisis through MDC's perspective. He uses songs to bemoan the socio-economic and political crisis which Zimbabwe has plunged into, attributing it to the regime's maladministration and corrupt tendencies. In the song, "Simuka Zimbabwe" ("Zimbabwe Arise"), he makes a plea to the masses to wake up from their slumber and face the calamities that have befallen them. His message attempts to provoke and instill rebellious sentiments among the masses in the wake of instabilities in the country. He uses the term, *nhimbe*, which means collective fieldwork. Fieldwork is a way of life in rural Zimbabwe, and he uses this term as a call for help to tend the Zimbabwean fields which have been marred by socio-economic and political crises. The lyrics go on to say, *kwaya enda kure kure*, meaning, the nation has gone too far, thereby exposing the extent to which Zimbabwe has been pushed deeper into crisis. The song suggests that Zimbabwe will only be brought back when the masses are united, regardless of political affiliation:

Zimbabwe inouya takabatana
Tikasamuka tinopera muZimbabwe

Zimbabwe will come if we are united
If we do not rise, we will all perish in Zimbabwe

Madzore imagines the masses coming together to fight for Zimbabwe and gives a stern warning that if no action is taken, everyone will perish. Thus, he employs collectivization (Reisigl & Wodak, 2001) to show that it is in everyone's interest to come together and work towards rebuilding the nation. In this song, Madzore provides a constructive and transformative strategy that promotes unity towards formation of better conditions in Zimbabwe.

He sang:

Vanotibira takanyarara
Vanotirova takarara
Vanotipisira takarara
Vanotitorera takanyarara
Zimbabwe mukasamuka munopera

They steal from us while we are silent
They beat us while we sleep
They burn and torture us while we sleep
They take away our things while we are silent
Zimbabwe, if you do not take a stand, you will perish

This song uses the silence discourse to question the passive nature of Zimbabweans in the face of the myriad of injustices unleashed on them by the state. He argues that Zimbabweans have remained silent and have failed to stand up and fight for themselves in the wake of gross corruption, human rights abuses, and the looting and dispossession being inflicted on them. In this vein, Madzore employs criminalization strategies (Reisigl & Wodak, 2001) when he frames the powerful officials as thieves and looters in an attempt to challenge the state's narrative that everything was normal in the country. He warns the masses to take transformative actions against injustices perpetrated against the innocent, ordinary Zimbabweans, arguing that silence will lead to the death of many. Madzore's message urges Zimbabweans to be intolerant of politically motivated violence, presenting ZANU-PF as uncaring and only concerned with its own ends. In this song, Madzore assumes the role of a dispatcher sending the masses on a quest to bring back Zimbabwe.

The lyrics go on to say:

Vanochema varimhiri vanochema neZimbabwe, vanochema
NepaJoni, vanochema ku America vanochema Britain vanochema
KuBotswana

Those in the diaspora, i.e., South Africa, America, Britain, and
Botswana, shed tears concerning Zimbabwe

Here, Madzore depicts a collective diasporic outcry as a result of the accumulating, multifaceted crisis in Zimbabwe. In bringing in the diasporic community, Madzore shows that the crises at home negatively impact them as well, in spite of living far away from the country. He goes on remind everyone that:

Kubatana kwakanaka we, kushandira pamwe kwakanaka

Unity and working together is a good thing

"Unity" is Madzore's emphasis here, as he pleads for a joint, non-partisan action to solve Zimbabwe's crises. The musician reimagines a Zimbabwe that is united by the crisis the country faces; a country where differences are pushed aside for the greater good of the people and their nation. In a way, the singer suggests that the country's woes should be a factor to be used in promoting and harnessing national unity and rebuilding Zimbabwe. What he postulates can also be seen as a development discourse that will usher in a change that will result in a better and more attractive Zimbabwe.

In "Kure kure," released after Zimbabwe's 2018 election, Madzore deplores the persisting hardship faced by his compatriots and urges endurance and resilience as the weapons to conquer the harsh socio-economic turbulence in the country. He sings:

> Tikashinga tinoenda kure kure
> Nhamo iyi tabva nayo kure kure
>
> *If we endure, we will go a long way*
> *We've come very far with hardships*

Then he added this: *Chi government chandifungisa kure kure* (this government has pushed my thoughts far away). Quite notably, the word, *Chi*, is used to belittle and undermine the power of the government, suggesting that it was the government's ineptitude that has led to thoughts of a real change in the country.

The song, "G40 Dedication," revolves around Generation 40, a breakaway faction of ZANU-PF. Madzore reveals that factional fighting within ZANU-PF has spilled into national affairs, allegedly interfering with the nation-building process. The song gives an exposition of internal party contestations that characterize the political landscape in Zimbabwe which he argues deter development. The underlying message from this observation is that internal party squabbles destabilize a nation. He then posits that focusing on national development will help alleviate the crisis in the country rather than giving salience to struggles for power from within. He also sings, *shamwari yangu ndikuudze zvirimberi* (my friend let me tell you what awaits you ahead), in reference to what he calls an impending demise of the country, about which he claims to have alerted his G40 friends.

Madzore took issues with the government's formation of the Border Gezi army in the song, "Tombana" (2016). This army was formed under the banner of the National Youth Service (NYS) Program. The army was ostensibly set up to train youths as young as 16 years old for various skills and for leadership development. However, the government turned around to use the army to harass citizens and intimidate the opposition. In his song, Madzore lamented that "young boys are dehumanized and brainwashed to kill their parents." He then castigates the ZANU-PF for converting and investing state resources in the formation of an army that contributed little to national development while the nation was facing a deep economic crisis. Thus, he counsels the authorities to focus and invest in nation-building and rebuilding the economy rather than creating false armies to harass the opposition and stifle revolutionary sentiments among the already disgruntled masses.

The song, "Ngwena ngainyururwe mumvura," was released in the 2018 pre-election context, a period that saw changes in the ballot regarding the presidential candidates for ZANU-PF and MDC. It is important to note that Madzore uses the term, *Ngwena* (crocodile), a totem, to refer to Mnangagwa. Ordinarily, this name indicates perceived respect in the Zimbabwean context, and Mnangagwa has been known by that nickname for decades. However, it is also noteworthy that both allies and foes of Mnangagwa affectionately and mockingly refer to him as *Ngwena* (Chibuwe, 2017, p. 196). Madzore belongs to the latter group and sings:

> Ngwena iyo ngainyururwe mumvura iyo
> Ngwena iyo ngainyururwe mumvura tiyambuke
> Ngwena iyo tiyambuke naChamisa

> *Remove the crocodile in the water*
> *Remove the crocodile in the water…so that we cross over*
> *Remove the crocodile in water…so that we cross over with Chamisa*

Madzore sang about the need for the Chamisa leader and presidential candidate of the MDC to metaphorically drag, defeat, and eliminate Mnangagwa in the 2018 elections and assume power in Zimbabwe. The song argues and urges the electorate to vote out the *ngwena* (Mnangagwa) from its position of power, in order to pave way for Chamisa to lead the nation. This song frames Mnangagwa as an obstacle hindering Chamisa and the MDC from coming to power and providing solutions to Zimbabwe's crisis. In the same song, Madzore uses the MDC election tagline for 2018, *Chamisa chete chete* (only one) in his discourse to create an image and persuasive construct that there was no other candidate fit for the presidency except for Chamisa. Also, in marketing Chamisa to the electorate, Madzore embraces and endorses the MDC candidate as the legitimate successor to late Morgan Tsvangirai, former prime minister and leader of the party. Through his lyrics, Madzore thus reimagines power and authority in the hands of the MDC, specifically Chamisa, as the only means to bring meaningful change to the country. It was a political communication strategy to encourage regime change in Zimbabwe.

More importantly, Madzore identifies and mentions specific places where ZANU-PF should be voted out in the election, as he sang, *Kwa uzumba, nekwa zvimba marimbamurefu*, in Uzumba and Zvimbamurefu. These are areas that gained prominence as ZANU-PF strongholds during election time under former President Mugabe. He buttressed his argument to vote out Mnangagwa and ZANU-PF by the evidence of socio-economic and political decay in the country, saying:

Gore rino hakuna chakanaka tonosanga kumavotes
Ngwena iyo ngainyururwe mumvura iyo

This year, nothing is good, we will meet when we vote
The ngwena should be drowned in water

Thus, Zimbabweans are urged to become ballot warriors and champions of change.

In the song, "Manyararireiko Zimbabwe," released in 2020 in the context of a heightened socio-economic and political crisis, Madzore questions why Zimbabweans should remain lethargic and silent while the nation faces grave calamities. He calls on his compatriots not to be mere keyboard warriors (who just send messages online) but street warriors that foster all-around change. His message attempts to instill revolutionary sentiments among Zimbabweans to rebel against engineers of the crisis. He framed it this way:

Vechidiki manyararireiko muchirega muvengi achipinda?
Zimbabwe manyararireiko muchirega muvengi achipinda?

Youths, why have you remained silent, allowing the enemy to come in?
Zimbabwe, why are you silent, allowing the enemy to come in?

This song reiterates the collective action discourse present in the song, "Zimbabwe Arise." Madzore warns that remaining silent inadvertently fueled crisis in the country and uses the term *muvengi* (enemy) to suggest that ZANU-PF was the enemy of the people and development in Zimbabwe. The song argues for the replacement of the silence discourse with revolution discourses so as to face the "enemy" before it destroys Zimbabwe. The call, he also urged, was for all Zimbabweans to partake in the revolutionary fight against their perceived "enemy."

In a way, the musician had a major regret: He did not understand why some people could not stand up and fight the government for the mess going on in the country. He expressed his disbelief with this rhetorical question: *...iiih matongonyarara nhai?* (iiih you have remained silent?). His answer was that remaining silent in the face of hardships encountered by the people will not make those problems go away, and outlined his belief that the people had the power to overturn the situation and end the hardships if only they united and challenged the hegemonic power of the ZANU-PF government.

Overall, Madzore's music focuses on the election violence discourse to demonstrate how the ruling party had developed a culture of manipulation and election violence in order to consolidate and maintain itself in power. According to him, the only way to combat the excesses of the government was for Zimbabweans to rise and challenge their government by becoming alleviators of the crisis in the country instead of remaining docile and watching their country reduced to tatters.

4th theme: Music and Marketing the MDC, Tsvangirai, and Chamisa Brand

Madzore's political messaging in his music remarkably shared similar themes and objectives with the MDC's political manifesto. Like the MDC's platform, his songs canvassed for regime change, depicting the opposition party as the genuine merchant for positive change in Zimbabwe. In his music, he deliberately used historical symbols and recounted the liberation struggle and sacrifices made by patriotic Zimbabweans to build and market the MDC brand, thereby legitimizing the party's messages and principles. More importantly, Madzore arranged the lyrics of his songs in a way that associated them with the opposition presidential candidate, Nelson Chamisa. This was done to rally support for Chamisa during the internal MDC struggle for party leadership against trade unionist, Thokozani Khupe, in the aftermath of the death of Morgan Tsvangirai, the founder-leader of the party. For instance, in "Mutakure tifambe," Madzore sang:

> Mutakureiwo tifambe mutakureiwo tiyambuke
> Ndiyeyuwo Chamisa mutakurei tifambe
> Idziva rine ngwena nyururaiwo tifambe mambo

> *Carry him until he crosses over*
> *Here is Chamisa, carry him*
> *The water has a crocodile carry him king*

This was an outright partisan endorsement of Chamisa over Khupe, as he urged upon the Zimbabwean electorate and MDC members that Chamisa was the more suitable candidate to challenge President Mnangagwa in the 2018 election.

As alluded to earlier in the song, "Tombana," Madzore unapologetically ridicules the late President Mugabe, equating his actions to that of a toddler, and discrediting his regime in order to score points for the opposition. Through the songs, "Tombana" and "Handicheuke," Madzore assassinates the characters of ZANU-PF and Mugabe, depicting them as the pioneers and creators of the multifaceted crises in Zimbabwe. Madzore rides on this dismantling strategy to construct the MDC brand and position it as the party that was worthy of ascending to power and revitalizing Zimbabwe.

Madzore used his music and songs to renegotiate and contest the negatively framed identity ascribed to MDC by the ruling party and government. His music thus became a site for the inscription and re-inscription of political identities that serve the interest of the opposition, and he was quite successful in the manipulation of language to delegitimize ZANU-PF by constructing it as a "rotten," corrupt, and inhumane party as noted in the song, "Saddam waenda sare Bob." Also, in this regard, he presented the ZANU-PF in a very hostile language, whereas he showcased the MDC as the guardian of human rights and democracy in the country.

In the political messaging through his music, Madzore assumed the role of exposing the "hidden truths" and "reality" that are often downplayed and deliberately overlooked in state-owned media, thus framing the ZANU-PF and the regime as masters of muddying the truth to hoodwink the nation. To buttress his point, Madzore remembers certain events where the government deliberately muddled the truth, such as the charade called the treason case brought against the former MDC leader, Tsvangirai.

Unlike how he characterized the ruling ZANU-PF as the merchants of socio-economic and political discontent in Zimbabwe, Madzore packaged, branded, and presented the MDC as Zimbabwe's economic and political emancipator, and apparently the only source of economic and political freedom for Zimbabwe. He reaffirmed this branding in the song, "Tombana," where he hailed Tsvangirai as a hero, recounting the gains his administration achieved during the period of Government of National Unity (GNU) in the country.

Madzore used his music not only to characterize the ZANU-PF as made up of villains but to promote the MDC's call for regime change. This was aimed at scoring a political point for the MDC, which had suffered a great deal of historical wrongs in the hands of the ruling party since the year 2000. His reiteration of the call for regime change was also anchored on the visible failures of the ruling party to deliver on the economic promises made to the electorate. Consequently, he boldly and positively branded the MDC and its candidate in the 2018 presidential election, Chamisa, as the only solution to deliver and turn Zimbabwe into the land of milk and honey. The song, "Chamisa chete chete" ("Chamisa, the only one") was an endorsement of the candidate and the MDC, in contrast to the presentation of the ruling party's demonstrable failures to deliver on its election promises.

Madzore also strategically draws on the successes of the Tsvangirai government and brand, to align them to and market the post-Tsvangirai MDC in the election against ZANU-PF's President "Crocodile" Mnangagwa in 2018. The underlying implication was for the people to vote for regime change. In the song, "Chirangano 4" ("Agreement 4"), he quotes Tsvangirai saying: "…the change is not for Robert Mugabe, but the change is for the people of Zimbabwe…" In this song, Madzore strategically engages in the change discourse through the use of Tsvangirai's words to clarify that the change being called for by the MDC was not about the late President Mugabe, but for the people to change the system because it was just inevitable to do so. Furthermore, Madzore continues to utilize Tsvangirai's voice during rallies in order to re-build and re-shape MDC's somewhat cascading image and strengthen the party's brand.

Conclusion

This study explored Madzore's music as a form of political messaging. The message articulated in his music challenges the discourses and narratives advocated by the ruling elite in government and ZANU-PF in Zimbabwe to discredit the opposition. In this context, his songs became the ideological tool to deconstruct the negative narrative about the opposition party. In contrast, his messaging frames the ruling government as responsible for the election violence in the country and the near wholesale reversal of the revolutionary gains of independence in Zimbabwe.

Through his songs and performances, Madzore persuasively attempted to renegotiate and reconstruct the MDC's identity, presenting the party as people oriented and the drivers of positive change in Zimbabwe. His strident and strategic plans to canvass votes for the MDC during the election were aimed at ensuring that the party came to power to re-engineer the country's future. Using the change discourse, Madzore attempted to positively rebrand the MDC while presenting ZANU-PF as callous, intolerant perpetrators of violence in Zimbabwe.

There is no doubt that Madzore sings from the opposition's lens and perspectives as he tries to do multiple diagnoses of Zimbabwe's huge economic and socio-political problems and proffer solutions to them. To him, perhaps the first crucial step in getting Zimbabwe back onto its feet once again was unity and collective action for the sole purpose of dislodging the ZANU-PF government in Harare, the capital city. His songs in the pre- and post-Mugabe presidency are reflective of this same message, the ultimate goal being regime change and the condemnation of the human rights abuse, election violence, economic stagnation, and black-on-black oppression that characterized the ZANU-PF and governments of Mugabe and Mnangagwa. In place of the rickety, discredited, and glaringly unproductive policies and agendas of the ZANU-PF government, Madzore uses his songs to uplift the people and firmly put MDC's ideology and policies at the forefront of Zimbabwe's development agenda.

Overall, the political messaging in Madzore's music unambiguously places Zimbabwe's socio-economic and political discontent, violence, and other forms and symptoms of national malaise at the doorstep the ruling ZANU-PF government. According to him, the only feasible avenue to extricate Zimbabwe from the impeding decadence was a democratic regime change that will usher in a new MDC administration.

This chapter only examined Madzore's music as a representative sub-set and sample of the songs by opposition musicians in Zimbabwe. While this offers meaningful insights into the political contestation in the country on the music scene, a more comprehensive insight may lie in a study that juxtaposes pro-opposition and pro-regime songs in Zimbabwe. Doing so will further illuminate the undercurrent of power struggles in the country. Furthermore, examining the opportunities offered by digital technology for political communication in the country is another avenue through which the entire gamut of the Zimbabwean crisis can be further explored and understood.

References

Bere, W. G. (2008). Urban Grooves: The Performance of Politics in Zimbabwe's Hip Hop Music [ProQuest Publication No. 3320761] [Doctoral dissertation, New York University. New York]. ProQuest Dissertations & Theses Global. https://www.proquest.com/docview/304829992?pq-origsite=gscholar&fromopen view=true

Braun, V., & Clarke, V. (2006). Using thematic analysis in psychology. *Qualitative Research Psychology, 3*(2), 77–101. https://doi.org/10.1191/1478088706qp063oa

Chibuwe, A. (2017). The Nationalist Discourses of an African Ruling Party: An Exploration of ZANU-PF Print Media Election Advertisements for the July 2013 Elections [Unpublished doctoral dissertation]. University of Johannesburg, South Africa. https://ujcontent.uj.ac.za/vital/access/manager/Repository/uj:22950

Chuma, W. (2005). Zimbabwe: The media, market failure and political turbulence. *African Journalism Studies, 26*(1), 46–62. https://doi.org/10.1080/02560054.2005.9653318

Corbin, J., & Strauss, A. (2008). *Basics of Qualitative Research: Techniques and Procedures for Developing Grounded Theory* (3rd ed.). SAGE Publications.

Denton, R. E., Jr., & Woodward, G. C. (1998). *Political Communication in America.* Praeger Publishers Inc.

Entman, R. M. (1993). Framing: Toward clarification of a fractured paradigm. *Journal of Communication, 43*(4), 51–58. https://doi.org/10.1111/j.1460-2466.1993.tb01304.x

Foucault, M. (1972). *The Archaeology of Knowledge and the Discourse on Language.* Pantheon Books.

Foucault, M. (1980). *Power/ Knowledge: Selected Interviews and Other Writings, 1972-1977.* Harvester Press.

Hall, S. (1997). The work of representation. In S. Hall (Ed.), *Representation: Cultural Representations and Signifying Practices* (pp. 1–47). SAGE Publications.

Marongodze, R. (2019). Interface of music and politics: Versions of patriotic consciousness in Zimbabwean music, 1970-2015 [Unpublished doctoral dissertation]. University of South Africa, South Africa. http://uir.unisa.ac.za/bitstream/handle/10500/25566

Mazango, E. M. (2005). Media games and shifting of spaces for political communication in Zimbabwe. *Westminster Papers in Communication and*

Culture, Special Issue, 33–55. https://www.researchgate.net/publication/251288871

McNair, B. (2003). *An Introduction to Political Communication.* Routledge.

Menon, S. (2008). Political Marketing: A Conceptual framework. MPRA Paper. University Library of Munich, Germany. https://www.researchgate.net/publication/23779688

Meredith, M. (2011). *The Fate of Africa: A History of the Continent Since Independence.* BBS Public Affairs.

Moyo, D. (2005). The 'independent' press and the fight for democracy in Zimbabwe: A critical analysis of the banned Daily News. *Westminster Papers in Communication and Culture, 2*(0), 109–128. https://www.westminsterpapers.org/article/id/16

Ncube, G., & Chinouriri, B. (2016). Humour as support and/ or opposition: Nicknaming political personalities and movements in post-independent Zimbabwe. *IGAMA: African Journal of Onomastic, 1(1), 1–12.* https://www.researchgate.net/publication/303735838

Ndlovu-Gatsheni, S. J. (2009). Africa for Africans or Africa for "Natives" Only? "New Nationalism" and Nativism in Zimbabwe and South Africa. *Africa Spectrum, 44*(1), 61–78. https://doi.org/10.1177/000203970904400105

Reisigl, M., & Wodak, R. (2001). The Discourse-Historical Approach. In R. Wodak & M. Meyer (Eds.), *Methods of Critical Discourse Analysis* (Vol. 1, pp. 63–94). SAGE Publications.

Sibanda, S. (2004). "You Don't Get to Sing a Song When You Have Nothing to Say:" Oliver Mtukudzi's Music as a Vehicle for Socio-Political Commentary. *Social Dynamics, 30*(2), 36–63. https://doi.org/10.1080/02533950408628684

Swanson, D., & Nimmo, D. (1990). *New Directions in Political Communication: A Resource Book.* SAGE Publications.

wa Thiong'o, N. (1993). *Moving the Centre: The Struggle for Cultural Freedoms.* East African Educational Publishers Ltd.

Willems, W. (2011). Comic Strips and "the Crisis:" Postcolonial Laughter and Coping with Everyday Life in Zimbabwe. *The International Journal of Media and Culture, 9*(2), 126–145. https://doi.org/10.1080/15405702.2011.562099

Willems, W. (2015). Risky dialogues: The performative state and the nature of power in a postcolony. *Journal of African Cultural Studies, 27*(3), 1–14. https://doi.org/10.1080/13696815.2015.1026881

Appendix

Madzore, P. (2009). *Tombana*

Madzore, P. (2017) *Ninive kure*

Madzore, P. (2006) *Sadam waenda sare Bob*

Madzore, P. (2018) *Handicheuke*

Madzore, P. (2016) *Bond hatidi*

Madzore, P. (2020) *Manyararireiko*

Madzore, P. (2018) *G40 dedication*

Madzore, P. (2019) *Chirangano 4*

Madzore, P. (2018) *Ngwena Ngainyururwe mumvura*
Madzore, P. (2020) *Manyararireiko Zimbabwe*
Madzore, P. (2017) *Niniva kure*
Madzore, P. (2018) *Mutakurei tifambe, Mutakureiwo tiyambuke*
Madzore, P. (2020) *Ndiyo here Zimbabwe? (Is this Zimbabwe?*
Madzore, P. (2019) *Kure kure*

CHAPTER 11

Political songs, advertising, and development messaging: An assessment of music in promoting socio-economic growth in Tiv society (Nigeria)

Terna Paise Agba

Federal University of Kashere, Gombe, Nigeria

Abstract

Political music and songs are cursorily considered as platforms for political advertising, political entertainment, and conveying political messages, such as messages of resistance, liberation, political campaigns and mobilization, etc. However, an in-depth examination of political songs reveals that they go beyond entertainment and political messaging to embed messages that facilitate and promote human development-wellbeing. This study, therefore, explores this underexplored or often unexplored but important function of political music and songs. In this chapter, the focus is on Tiv indigenous music/songs, particularly the works of four artists of Tiv origin, namely, Tondo Kumbul, Tarker Golozo, El Stuffy, and Gabon. A purposive sample of political songs produced by these artists was chosen and textually analyzed in order to determine their relevance in facilitating human development in Tiv society. The development communication theory was used to foreground this study.

Keywords: Political music, Tiv indigenous songs, development messaging, Tondo Kumbul, Tarker Golozo, El Stuffy, Gabon, textual analysis

***

Introduction

Cultural variations and technological developments are two of the prominent factors that vitiate the conceptualization and standardization of the definition of music across the globe. Technology, for instance, influences musical instrumentations. Consequently, the instruments that may be used in producing quality music in one culture may not be adequate or even practical in doing the same in another culture. For instance, it is true that Beethoven's Gross Fuge string quartet in 1825 and Jazz in its early days in the 1900s, as well as the hard-core punk of the 1980s, were all criticized at various points in time as not being music. However, in spite of the challenge of multiple conceptualizations of music, researchers generally agree that music is an art form that is expressed through organized sound with such elements as pitch, rhythm, dynamics, and sonic qualities such as timber and texture (Epperson, 2022). It is therefore plausible to infer that music is the art of creating sounds and tones together in a concerted and orderly manner, and combining them to create organized sound that has intended meaning. Derived from the Greek word "mousike" meaning "art of the muses," music is performed with various instruments such as drums, bars, sticks, etc., and vocal techniques such as singing, clapping, and clicking of the tongue, among others. Essentially, a song is a musical composition. In its widest sense, a song entails instrumentally coordinated sounds (music). Therefore, songs and music have a coordinating, cooperative and dependent relationship.

Music and songs serve a variety of unique purposes in different communities and impact the lives of people who live in them. For instance, music permeates significant aspects of African societies, cultures, and traditions (Onyebadi, 2018). Adebayo (2017, p. 56) similarly argued that "to the African, music is not just a pastime, it is a ritual that describes the true essence and humanness in being of African origin." Music and songs are also repositories of the history of communities in Africa (Yongo and Tsenongo, 2004) and the means of passing information and oral traditions, knowledge, and wisdom from one generation to another in such communities. Above all, music and songs are vital tools for human and societal development in African and other societies.

The relevance of music and song in the development process makes them important human endeavours (Ker, 2002). On its part, development takes place in the context of politics, the latter being the art of authoritative allocation of limited resources and their judicious application within a society. This relationship between music and the various aspects of human endeavours across cultures have been underscored in various studies such as Pedelty and Keefe (2010), Bohlman (2002), Rosenthal (2001), Lynskey (2010), and Cross (2017). However, in Africa, and in spite of music's fundamental relevance to the development of her societies, not much research has been done on this subject (Onyebadi, 2018). The few existing studies on this important topic include Agovi (1989), Itiri (2015), and Onyebadi and Mbunyuza-Memani (2017). Perhaps, more worrisome in this already challenging situation is that the dearth of such research is even more noticeable in the realm of traditional African music and musical groups vis-à-vis communities' socio-political development.

This chapter was conceptualized to contribute meaningfully toward redressing this situation, by examining the political messaging in the lyrics of some selected works of Tiv indigenous music artists, Tondo Kumbul, Tarker Golozo, El Stuffy, and Gabon. All four musicians are of Tiv origin in Nigeria's middle belt region. The overarching research question is to determine how the musicians used their platforms to disseminate political messages and specifically how such messages have been relevant in stimulating the processes of human development in the musicians' society. The development communication theory was applied in this assessment.

A Discourse on Literature and Political Music in Africa

Music and songs are connected to almost all aspects of human endeavour including love, economic activities, culture, entertainment, religion, and politics. (Epperson, 2022). Owing to the universal nature of music and song, and arising from the differences in cultures, the forms of preservation, instrumentation, texture, methodologies, and their meanings, music and songs have been categorized into jazz, blues, reggae, hip-hop, folk, etc. Music or song can be labelled as political irrespective of the category or brand it belongs to, provided it carries political information and messaging. A political song is therefore any song that contains a political thread or lyrics. Examples of political songs include traditional patriotic songs, political party campaign songs, songs of labour movements, protest songs, political information/awareness songs, etc. Some societies preserve songs through writing. In others, songs are preserved and executed through oral poetry which takes the place of newspapers and other types of written documentations. "Oral poetry report and comment on current affairs, serve as medium for political pressure and propaganda, as well as reflect and mould public opinion" (Finnegan, 1972, p. 256).

One developing area in political communication inquiry is music and political messaging. This is in recognition of the fact that musicians across the globe are known to use their platforms and lyrics for political messaging (Onyebadi, 2018). For instance, King and Jensen (1995) and Zaid (2001) also made references to the late reggae icon, Bob Marley's Rastafarianism, as a force for societal change through his music. Bob Marley called attention to the squalid living conditions of people in poverty-stricken areas in Jamaica, especially in its capital city, Kingston. Another musician of international recognition is Bob Dylan, famous for his political messaging through songs. Dylan was awarded the Nobel Prize for Literature in 2016 in what the Swedish-based Nobel Prize organization described as recognition of his new poetic expressions within the great American song tradition.

African scholars have also contributed to the growing research evidence and connection between music and politics. The works of Agovi (1989), Ker (2002),

Onyebadi and Mbunyuza-Memani (2017), Amoakohene et al. (2019), and Aririguzoh (2019) who stated that "Africans are no strangers to political messaging through music" (p. 265), are just but a few testimonies in support of this contention. The link between music and politics in Africa predates the birth of modern political parties in the continent and even some African nations. Finnegan (1972) clearly stated this in his observation that "in the wider sense, it is certain that there were many political songs and poems in the past that carried unmistaken political messages" (p. 256). The author also noted that songs of insult, challenge, or satirical comment have a long history and function not only at the individual level but also as politically effective weapons in Africa. Political songs endured from one generation to another among the Griots in the West African sub-region, as were the epic narratives of political songs of praise for the legendary King Sunjata Keita who freed the Mande people from the oppressive power of King Sumanuru Kante and founded the Mali Empire around 1235 CE.

In the 1960s, Sudanese musician, Mohammed Wardi used his songs to arouse nationalistic fervor among his compatriots. Through music, he supported democracy and condemned authoritarianism and despotic leadership in Sudan (Satti, 2017). Political songs also featured in Ghana's political space as popular tunes were created and aired during the country's struggle for independence, to engender a sense of "… euphoria, confidence, and commitment to the nationalist struggle" (Agovi, 1989, p. 196). While some of the songs were new compositions or adapted from already existing euphonic tunes with new meanings, others were specifically made for the campaign of liberation from the colonial government (Agovi, 1989). Political songs were also documented in Cameroun, where some musicians sang the praise of their then president, Ahmadou Babatoura Ahidjo. Tala Andre Marie's song, "20 years of peace and progress under Ahidjo," and that of Manu Dibango, "Ahmadou Ahidjo," explicitly praised and extolled Ahidjo's leadership. Similarly, Medzo Me Nsom urged Cameroonians to vote for Ahidjo in an upcoming election to continue another term in office even though he had been the president from 1960 to 1982 (Asse, 1995, p. 126).

Similarly, in Kenya, praises of the government and its officials have been expressed in music and songs. During Kenya's independence struggle, "most Mau Mau's (freedom fighters) songs were a discourse on liberation from colonial injustices such as torture, rape, massacre, castration, forced labour, high taxation and land displacement"(Gakahu, 2017, p. 259). The Kenyan National African Union (KANU) under Kenya's first president, Jomo Kenyatta, as well as his successor, Daniel Arap Moi, was supported by musicians and singers who sang their praise and supported the status quo in Kenyan politics. In a reciprocal gesture, the government supported and materially rewarded the musicians and singers (Wekesa, 2004). At the climax of Kenya's multiparty elections in 1992, the popular musician/singer, Joseph Kamaru of the Kikuyu tribal origin, sang in all KANU rallies in the Central Province, the Kikuyu stronghold, to sell the party and its candidates. Ten years later, during the 2002 Kenyan presidential election, two hip hop musicians who went by the stage name, *GidiGidi MajiMaji*, produced and released the popular hit, "Unbwogable," which the Rainbow Coalition of opposition political parties effectively used in its campaign, and successfully defeated KANU. *Unbwogable* literally means *we cannot be silenced; we are unbeatable.*

In Zimbabwe, the link between music, song, and politics has also been articulated by Makwambeni (2017), who argued that under the late President Robert Mugabe, "Zimdance hall music emerged as an alternative public sphere separate from the state where counter-discourse was produced and consumed largely by unemployed urban youths who had been excluded from mainstream communicative spaces"(p. 246). Similarly, in South Africa, music was a powerful instrument during the liberation struggle against the White Apartheid government. South African musicians such as Miriam Makeba and Lucky Dube used their music and performances to support the anti-apartheid struggle often in spite of the personal dangers they faced from the government. Music not only aided in the struggle to dismantle the white domination in South Africa, but it also paved way for a new political order with a new constitution and Bill of Rights (Roux-Kemp, 2014). Ironically, the displaced and minority Whites in the new South Africa also used political songs to cry about what they termed as reverse social discrimination in the country under black rule. As Louw (2017) pointed out, "Twelve years after Afrikaners lost control of South Africa's political-system, music became a fulcrum for Afrikaners to begin mounting discontent about their place within the post-apartheid socioeconomic order. Their song, 'De la Rey,' which became an instant hit, broke their sullen silence, as the lyrics resonated with their alienation and frustration" (pp. 89-90).

In Nigeria, the music industry is predominantly saturated with songs of entertainment, however, songs that are aimed at educating the masses on the need for societal reforms also exist (Akinyoade, 2020). Various Nigerian musicians and singers have used their lyrics to beckon on their compatriots to react against the actions and inactions of government that are detrimental to human development. The musicians have also asked for accountability and better governance in the country. For instance, Eeddris Abdulkareem's soundtrack, "Nigeria jaga jaga," is a song that informs that the country is in disarray. It talks about corruption in Nigeria and the resultant poverty for the wider population (Akinyoade, 2020). In his other song, "Trouble dey sleep," Eeddris demands for judicious handling of public affairs in Nigeria by public office holders. He also criticized people in leadership positions for patronizing foreign establishments instead of making their local equivalent more functional and efficient (Akinyoade, 2020). Another Nigerian musician, Asa, released a song with one of the tracks, "Fire on the mountain," becoming quite popular because it clearly expressed and criticized the social, economic, and political rot in Nigeria, including the leadership which she described as mediocre. For his part, musician Daddy Showkey, whose real name is John Asiemo, in his song, "Fire Fire," also reflects on the socio-economic and political rot and the sufferings of the Nigerian masses as a result of bad leadership. He called for fire to burn all those involved in causing the poverty and underdevelopment in Nigeria. Also, Femi Kuti's musical album, *Africa for Africa*, is politically relevant as it is critical of bad governance being Africa's bane. His songs, especially "Politics Na Big Business" and "Make we remember," are reflective of bad governance all over Africa and the need for social change.

In Sierra Leone, there was an explosion of popular music by young musicians who thematically addressed some of the central retrogressive issues in the country, from rigged elections to corruption and the lack of opportunities for youth advancement (Shepler, 2010, p. 627). As noted by Christensen and Utas (2008), various Sierra Leonean musicians urged the voters not to allow corrupt politicians to rule again, the lyrics of their political songs referring to such politicians as "hypocrites," "wicked men," and "educated fools"(p.536).

Development

As a concept, *development* has multifarious meanings and interpretations (Todaro and Smith, 2011; Rodney, 1972). Generally, it evolved from the social sciences to guide new nations that won independence after the Second World War. Development is measured in a society by its individuals' ability to meet basic needs (sustenance), self–esteem (to feel like a human being), and freedom from servitude — the ability to make independent choices (Todaro and Smith, 2011, p. 21). These are termed values of development and are meant to improve human socio-economic and material well-being through increased and widened distribution of and access to basic life-sustaining goods and services, including food, shelter, health, education, and human security.

The Artists: Tondo Kumbul, Tarker Golozo, El Stuffy, and Gabon

Tondo Kumbul was a Tiv native and hailed from the Mbatierev mega clan in Gboko Local Government Area of Benue State, Nigeria. He once held the position of president of the Tiv Singers Association before his death in 1990 and was a recognized doyen in the local music industry. Yongo and Tsenongo (2004) noted that "many of his poems, especially those of the late 1960s and early 1970s, dwelt so much on the history of Nigeria" (p. 67).

Tarker Golozo, also a Tiv, hailed from the Mbatiav mega clan in Gboko Local Government Area of Benue State. According to his biography, Tarker Golozo had minimal elementary school education between 1944 and1950, a factor which only enabled him to communicate in basic English (Ker, 2002). Nonetheless, he was employed as a primary school teacher but quit after seven years on the job to become a professional singer. Golozo's songs are all rendered in Tiv language with the occasional injection of English words which, in most cases, were pronounced in an adulterated manner. To some extent, his time as a primary school teacher afforded him some exposure to national and international political and socio-economic issues which he reflected in his music. Golozo's songs are mainly about social mobilization, sensitization and awareness, and unity and economic development.

Mfater Kaha, popularly known by the stage name, El Stuffy, is another Tiv indigene from the Ipav mega clan in Gboko Local Government Area of Benue State. El Stuffy is a political science graduate of Benue State University, Makurdi, capital of his state. His education appears to have impacted his knowledge and understanding of the complex political and socioeconomic issues in his state and Nigeria. He uses his Tiv traditional music to express his thoughts. El Stuffy's messages are focused on political advertising and social mobilization.

While the stage name, Gabon, is quite popular among the Tiv people and beyond, very few of them are aware that the musician's original name is Shi-Aondo Akuhe. Gabon is a native of Naka Local Government Area of Benue State. His formal education is quite limited as he grew up assisting his parents with farm work. Later in life, he combined his passion for farming with a motorbike transportation business while at the same time being an employee of the Gwer-West Local Government Council. In spite of these engagements, Gabon found time to sing on a part-time basis with two other musicians in Gwer-West, Amo Baba and Godwin Orhena Upele (also called Mtopi). Both are said to be Gabon's mentors. The messaging in his music is about unity and cooperation as well as political advertising.

All four musicians examined in this chapter are not only of Tiv origin but also sing in the local Tiv language. Tiv is both a socio-cultural group as well as the name of the language spoken by the ethnic group. The Tiv people are predominantly found in central Nigeria and the western region of Cameroun. In Nigeria's federal structure, they are more specifically located in Benue, Nasarawa, Taraba, and Plateau States, and constitute the largest single ethnic group in the first three states.

This study is however confined to Benue state. Prior research such as Bohannan and Bohannan (1968), Makar (1994), and Agba (2010) have examined several aspects of Tiv culture, and their pre-colonial, colonial, and postcolonial history. However, research projects on Tiv songs, poetry, and oral literature are somewhat limited and include Ker (2002), Yongo and Tsenongo (2004), and Nyitse (2006). Unlike these studies, the present inquiry specifically deals with four Tiv musicians vis-à-vis the use of their music for political messaging aimed at the socio-economic and political development of their society.

Theoretical Framework

A theory is a construct that seeks to explain or predict a phenomenon. Bacharach (1989) explained a theory as "a statement of relations among concepts within a set of boundary assumptions and constraints, it is no more than a linguistics device used to organize a complex empirical word" (p. 496). Theories can be "posited as parsimonious-*sense-making* tools (they create meaning by organizing and explaining) as well as *sense-giving* tools (they communicate meaning)" (Henneberg and O'Shaughnessy, 2007, p. 6). The study of communication has thus led to the formulation of theories that are aimed at enhancing a more robust interpretation and meaning in communication and mass media discourse. Some of the theories that seek to explain studies in music include realism, anti-realism, and information, among others. Within the realist school are idealist theorists who hold that musical works are mental entities; that such works are imaginary objects and experiences. Such conception of music, however, has been challenged over time, based on the prepositions that it fails to make works intersubjective and renders the medium through which the work is expressed irrelevant toward understanding it. This is so in that one may be having the same imaginative experiences in response to both a live performance and recorded music, yet the question regarding whether the two media platforms are aesthetically equivalent may seemingly hold (Kania, 2015).

There is also the development communication theory that is also known as development support communication. Development communication theory is linked to the development information theory which originated in the early 1920s by scholars who include Harry Nyquists, Raph Halp Harlday, and Alan Turning. The primary thesis behind this theory is that communication is the only source of promoting development; without communication, development can be scuttled. Communication is therefore a societal and an individual need that that can be equated with the hunger for food and drink, perhaps even more so. Development communication theory argues that the media should undertake the role of promoting and evaluating developmental programs for society (Blumber, 2015).

Human beings are at the center of development in every society. They form the linear chain that comprises development planners, executors, and beneficiaries.

Consequently, there is the need for continuous information flow along the chain in a back-and-forth manner to cause a top-bottom and bottom-top approach in the development process. Such an approach allows for feedback along the chain, hence facilitating desired outcomes of the development objective(s). It is only through this process that development administrators can identify areas of need and attend to them. Also, the process allows for the beneficiaries of development to inform and educate the planners/executors on the challenges that impinge on the sustainability of any development priority. Applying this idea to the focus of this chapter, we note that musicians use their songs to pass messages relevant to their specific social, economic, political, cultural, and technological milieu in order to educate, inform, and create awareness of development issues and facilitate their actualization. In this regard, Ker (2002) opines that artists also contribute to the general development of society by mobilizing their audience for societal change, especially by exposing the ills of society through their songs. The artists examined in this study - Kumbul, Golozo, Stuffy, and Gabon - have produced songs that align with the development communication theory, as their political music is replete with messages that touch on the issues that affect or facilitate development in Tiv land.

Method

This study adopted the qualitative textual analysis method of inquiry, which in general terms involves examining, interpreting, and making inferential meaning to texts including films, music lyrics, advertisements, and graffiti (McKee, 2003); it is reliable and appropriate for research, especially if the user pays attention to the texts and the nuances that underlie them (Bogue, 2007). In order to further strengthen this method, Onyebadi and Mbunyuza-Memani (2017) argued for the need to understand the texts in the context of the time and environment in which they were composed and published, as well as their targeted audiences. Nonetheless, the major weakness in the use of this method is that the user is susceptible to misinterpreting the original intentions of the message composer, especially when it comes to cross-cultural studies (McKee, 2003).

Tiv indigenous music and songs have been in existence for centuries. For this study, the authors used a purposive sample of Tiv songs by prominent Tiv musicians who primarily sing in the local Tiv language. Thus, fifteen songs that underscore development and political messaging by Kumbul, Golozo, Stuffy, and Gabon, were chosen for analysis. The songs were selected owing to the fact that they convey relevant themes that fit into the scope of this book and address issues of development in Tiv society. The author, a seasoned researcher, is a Tiv indigene with sufficient proficiency and knowledge of Tiv language both in written and spoken forms. He therefore attentively listened to the songs, meticulously read their transcriptions and translations from other sources, and conducted his own translations into English language for comparison and use in this chapter. Thereafter, the author created and coded for the political nature and development nexus in the songs under various themes as follows:

a) **Power, Corruption, Political Advertising, Political Mobilization, and Development.** These are songs that essentially admonish political leaders over mismanagement, corruption, and abuse of power while urging the people to challenge such malfeasance by their leaders.

b) **Unity/Co-operation and Development.** Songs under this theme call on the people to unite and work for the economic uplift of their society.

c) **Conflict, Peace, and Development.** Songs addressed in this theme show the debilitating effect of conflict in Tiv society and extol the need for peace for the development of Tiv land.

d) **Sensitization, Mobilization, and Development.** Here, the songs explore the salient issues gripping society and attempt to mobilize the people for positive developments.

e) **Political Participation/Civic Duty and Development.** These are songs that urge the people to become politically engaged and not sit on the sidelines of the movement to revitalize society.

Analysis and Discussion

This study is about the underexplored but important function of the use of political music and songs by prominent Tiv musicians in criticizing and publicizing the wrongs in their society and calling on the people to unite, challenge their leadership, and embark on projects that will lead to economic development in the Tiv region of Nigeria. This section of the chapter collectively examines the works of the four musicians of Tiv origin (Tondo Kumbul, Tarker Golozo, El Stuffy, and Gabon), assessing their contributions to their society on the themes identified below.

Power, Corruption, Political Advertising, Mobilization, and Development

Across Africa and Nigeria in particular, musicians have been obsessed with fighting corruption and abuse of power by singing about it and its inherent implications on human development (Akinyoade, 2020). In Tiv society, Tondo Kumbul is famous for passing messages on corruption and abuse of office by people who wielded political power, especially between the late 1960s and early 1970s (Yongo and Tsenongo, 2004). The intent was to inform his audience and listeners about the negative actions and activities by government officials and perhaps spur action by the governed toward holding those in power accountable for their nefarious actions. The manifestation of the implications of corruption on human development includes various forms of poverty. This was clearly understood by Kumbul's 1977 song entitled, "Janala Yakubu Gawan," which indicated his belief that it is only when the society does not tolerate corruption that life will be better for the citizens. "Janala Yakubu Gawan," addressed this as follows:

WonYamakaa	*In law Yamakaa*
Kaana u hen wee	*Who do you think is it*
Naan vihi Nigeria?	*That has damaged Nigeria?*
I kôr Yakubu Gawan	*Yakubu Gowon should be arrested*
...man Dinmka	*...And Dimka*
Ato a faa mimi	*Ears would discern the truth*
Akosu Geeci	*Akosu Geeci*
Ken 1960 yange Nigeria ve dzua	*It was in 1960 Nigerians came together*
Ve ngohol independence	*They got independence*
Shie u Genela Yakubu Gawan	*When General Yakubu Gowon*
Hingir head of State	*Became head of State*
A kula mbaiv ke gomonti na;	*He packed thieves in his government*
Mba Ukpabi Asikas' man	*The likes of Asika and*
Abba Kyaris' man Musa Usman's	*Abba Kyari's and Musa Usman*
Man Ugbemudia gbaa inn	*And Ugbemudia were stealing*
Nyaregh ki gomoneti.	*Government's money*
Aper Aku wazwa shamin	*Aper Aku complained*
[Kpa] Gawan yôô ier i kôr i wuhe	*But Gowon announced that he should locked*
Ke '75, Muhamadu Mutala	*In '75, Muhammed Murtala*
Kaa tile sôôr tar chukuu	*Came in and improved the country a bit*
... i kôr Gawan...	*[He] Gowon should be arrested*

The relevance of the lyrics to development is apparent. Corruption erodes the strength of a society's institutions and therefore weakens their efficacies in initiating and executing profitable human development policies, programs, and projects. It impinges on quality services and infrastructural provisions such as education, health, roads, employment, economic opportunities, etc. Tondo presented Gowon's regime as one that did not experience much growth due to corruption by government officials, hence the need to arrest them and institute punitive measures to forestall future occurrences. However, as Yongo and Tsenongo (2004) suggest, "some people might disagree with Tondo's interpretation of Gowon's regime concerning corruption ... it should be remembered that the artist's submissions represent analytical approaches contemporary to the event described" (p.67).

In another song named, "Dzasha Jos, Hide Ke Benue," of the same album, Kumbul (1977) described corruption and human retrogression, where he decried the corrupt activities such as embezzlement and enrichment, impunity, marginalization, exclusion, power drunkenness, and unfairness by Joseph Gomwalk, military governor of what used to be Benue-Plateau state. He sang thus:

Dzasha Jos tsa u nenge	*Go to Jos and you will see*
Hide ke Benue tsa shi u nenge	*Come back to Benue and you will see*
Kwagh u Gomwalk aeren a vese	*What Gomwalk has been doing to us*
A kula nyaregh ki Benue	*He diverted Benue's money*
Man de wa usugh sha Jos man Pankshin	*And electrified Jos and Pankshin*
Or Tiv ka nan wa dzwa shamin	*When a Tiv man would complain*
...I gbidye i wuhe	*...He is beaten and imprisoned*

A bit of history needs to be put in perspective here in order to fully comprehend the above lyrics. Joseph Gomwalk, a non-Tiv man but an indigene of Benue-Plateau state, was appointed the military governor of the state by the then head of state, General Yakubu Gowon. Gomwalk was accused of corruption, embezzlement of state funds, nepotism, ethnic chauvinism, and favoritism in the course of discharging his duties as the then Governor of the state. Aper Apollos Aku, a Tiv native, petitioned Gomwalk over these allegations. Instead of responding to the petition, Aku was arrested and jailed for daring to challenge the military governor. The relevance of this political song in development engineering lies in the fact that it stressed the implications of denial and deprivation of facilities and services for human wellbeing, as also expressed in his earlier song on the negative implications of corruption on development. The denial of electricity, safe water, education, and the embezzlement of public resources for selfish aims against the common good deprived the citizens of Benue-Plateau state, particularly those in the Benue region from accessing the required conditions that would enhance their capacity for community development and save them from poverty.

El Stuffy's music similarly fits in this theme and also extends to political sensitization and advertising. Stuffy (2011) is infuriated by the errant and malevolent behavior of people in power, particularly in Benue state, and was critical of the then commissioner of lands from 2011 to 2015, whom he tagged in the song, "Kômishiona u teen inya"— "Commissioner that sells land." The commissioner, through government fiat, embarked upon fraudulent land grabs from communities by way of creating new settlement layouts particularly in Makurdi, the Benue state capital and its environs, without any form of compensation to those whose lands were grabbed for the purpose of urban expansion. This led to the displacement of several people. In his popular, hit 2015 song, "Kômishiona u teen inya," he voiced his anger:

Idyu ka inya i teen ga	*Parliament is not selling of land*
Iharev mba vaan inya ve ooo	*Iharev are crying of their land ooo*
Idyu ka inya i teen ga	*Parliament is not selling of land*
Masev mba vaan i nya ve ooo	*Masev are crying of their land ooo*
Idyu ka i nya i teen ga	*Parliament is not selling of land*
I tyô ipusu mba ke kungur ooo	*Ipuusu people are displaced ooo*
Komishiona u teen inya	*Commissioner that sells land*
Shangen ka inya iteen ga ooo	*Representation is not selling of land*
Hide se a inya yese ooo	*Return our lands ooo*
Ungu or u dedoo ga	*You are not a good person*
Votu wase ka u Tarkighir	*Our vote is for*
Dickson a ooo	*Dickson ooo*
Ityô you soo u	*Your people like you*
Or a soo bikon	*Somebody that love going about*
Izenden manden	*Mounting beacons*
Yô nan a lu her aa amande	*Should remain with beacons*

The message in this song tells of the importance of land in the socio-economic development of people and the implications of its dispossession, which include several forms of poverty (Agba, 2020). El Stuffy demands that the government should reverse this arbitrary action of land-grabbing without measures to mitigate the challenges faced by the displaced persons. Again, the song relays political advertisement and message of mobilization toward effecting socio-political change.

El Stuffy reminds his audience about the unethical and corrupt land-grabbing behaviour of the Commissioner for Lands, *Kômishona u teen inya*, who was aspiring for the Guma-Makurdi federal constituency seat in Nigeria's House of Representatives, under the People's Democratic Party (PDP), in the 2015 federal elections against Dickson Tarkighir of the opposition, All Progressive Congress (APC). The musician reminded everyone about the untold sufferings of those whose lands were forcibly taken away from them by the commissioner for lands, and vehemently demanded that the seized lands be returned to their original and rightful owners. He also mocked the former commissioner by reminding him and the audience that parliament was not a home for people who forcibly and illegally sell others' lands. He pointedly told that Mr. *Kômishona u teen inya* was not a good person and should not be voted into office. He advised voters to instead vote for the commissioner's opponent, Dickson Tarkighir, who according to him was more responsible. Clearly the song is a piece of political advertisement for the APC and its candidate and a forceful message of sensitization against bad governance, mobilizing the people not to embrace bad and corrupt leadership. Tarkighir eventually won the seat.

In the next song, "Or igyoo," El Stuffy (2015) is equally vehement about the corruption of a former Benue state governor whom he referred to as Or *igyoo* (Man of pigs), and his drive at imposing a candidate that would succeed him, as he sang thus:

U tôô se nyaregh u da yam igyo a min	*You took our money, you, and bought pigs*
Uvihi ki gen sha kwagh u pepa la	*You expended another on the paper issue*
Higen yô we saa Tiv a vine a lu azonto	*You are now insisting that Tiv should dance azonto*
Ortom yange se ishor i baja la	*Ortom prevents us from that baja dance*
Benue a va lu kwagh u kunya	*Benue will become ridiculed*
Gomna se venda or u pamen ityough	*Governor we reject the man that perms head*

The idea of *man of pigs* originates from the story about the governor's alleged money laundering activities abroad. The Nigerian anti-graft body, the Economic and Financial Crimes Commission (EFCC), was said to have learnt about the money laundering allegation and was about to investigate the matter, but the governor was one step ahead of the body and hurriedly used the funds to purchase pigs from Brazil under the guise that his government was promoting pig farming in Benue state. The mention of "expended another on the paper issue" in the song is also a reference to another shady issue associated with the same governor. After his re-election victory in 2011 under the Peoples' Democratic Party (PDP) platform, the governor was sued for alleged presentation of a fake high school certificate to the Independent National Electoral Commission (INEC) in order to meet the requirement for contesting the election. It was also alleged that as governor, he used state funds to buy justice in the litigation process. It is the certificate that was referred to as the "paper issue." Accordingly, El Stuffy's message informs about the governor's misappropriation of state funds to "buy" pigs and defend himself against the certificate saga, thus criminalizing him.

Also in the song, El Stuffy used the governor's alleged financial impropriety to challenge his attempt to impose his "anointed" successor on the state at the end of his tenure in 2015, saying in the lyrics that "now you are insisting that the Tiv should dance *azonto*." The metaphorical implication is that the governor was not satisfied with embezzling state funds and wanted to extend his brand of corruption and mismanagement by insisting that the Tiv accept the candidate of his choice as the next governor of Benue state. Stuffy's message rejects this attempt to impose the "man who perms his hair" on the people, a reference to the candidate's artificial curly hairstyle. In the song, the musician says, "Ortom prevent us from *baja* dance" because by having the "man who perms his hair" as the new governor, a show of irresponsibility and immaturity, "Benue will become ridiculed" in the eyes of the world. El Stuffy ended on a caustic note, saying: "...Governor we reject the man that perms head." The song became a campaign jingle for political advertising by all opponents of the governor's candidate. In the end, "the man who perms hair" lost the election.

In another of his songs, "Inima," released in 2011 during the general elections in Nigeria, El Stuffy articulated how the ruling Peoples' Democratic Party's (PDP) retrogressive governance had caused underdevelopment in Benue State and called on the people to vote for the opposition, All Progressive Party (APC). He sang:

...inima lu tan ityô yam shaluwa	...*umbrella was ridiculing/mocking/suffered my people*
Zum la se tôô ichan	*We were grasped with poverty that time*
Se gba lun ken toho er akange tso	*We remained in the bush like guinea fowls*
Lun er ka Dajo gayô	*If not for Dajo*
Or igyoo lu timin se	*The pigs' man was annihilating us*
Kera gba u se yer a yer	*We are to no longer hide*
Iember ne ga	*This joy*
...Angbianev ve mough cica	*...Brothers/Sisters should all stand*
Seneto u ngutor	*Senator you are king*
Or u doon ooo	*Good man ooo*
Hiee or la gba ishor	*Hiee(mockery) that man has lost the election*
Or igioo se venda	*We reject the pigs' man*
Ishor ka i Ugba	*Our candidate is Ugba*
Or la ngu u zendan wen	*That man out to be sent away*

The lyrics showcase the PDP, referring to it as umbrella (*inima*), the PDP's logo, as having thrown Benue people into poverty through bad governance. The singer contended that "We were grasped with poverty that time we remained in the bush like guinea fowls." He then sang in praise of the opposition's (All

Progressives Congress, APC) candidate as a good man with unblemished credentials, unlike the "pig man" — the governor. This song was meant to spur people to aspire to have good leadership that would be pro-development in terms of providing social, economic and political infrastructure capable of uplifting the living standards of the masses.

Unity/Co-operation and Development

Unity/co-operation and development was addressed by Gabon's 2015 song, "Awashima U Minda," in the following lyrics:

Tyô- Minda	*My people of Minda*
Aondo na ian nyian	*God has given me the chance today*
Me ôô kwagh alum	*I will say what*
Ke shima aven	*Is in mind with you people*
Ganden Cletus Tyokyaa a!	*Elder Cletus Tyokyaa a!*
Tyokyaa ka we	*Tyokaa when you*
Kegh toho	*Lay in hunt for game*
A or nan alu a hough baa	*With a tuberculosis infected person*
Ufa mtile wough a nan	*You distance yourself from him*
Ganden Domimic Ajom an oo!	*Elder Dominic Ajom an oo!*
M kaa me tyô yam minda kegh	*I say my people of minda lay*
Toho daban daban	*In hunt for game unorganized*
Ka sha fa tilen	*It is how well we organize*
Wese se wua sôsu ye (x2)	*That we'll be able to kill an animal*

This song was released against the backdrop of the expectation that all the other four mega clans-Kwande, Jechira, Jemgbagh and Sankera, in Tiv land, except Minda, have won the governorship seat of Benue state over the years. There, during the 2015 election, the Minda mega clan fielded various candidates for the governorship slot in different parties. There appeared to be bickering and acrimonies among the candidates and their supporters along party lines. Meanwhile, even the other mega clans that had earlier enjoyed the governorship position also featured candidates in various parties. Gabon sensing the danger of what disunity would cause the Minda mega clan in the election, used this song to mobilize her members to unite in order to emerge victorious at the polls. When he sang, "I say my people of Minda have laid in hunt for game *daban daban* (unorganized). It is how well we organize ourselves that we'll be able to kill an animal." Gabon urged the Minda people to unite and support one contestant instead of splitting their votes among several candidates and lose the election. The song is also interpreted as Gabon's counselling to the illustrious sons of the axis not to fight each other but imbibe unity and remain focused. Arguably, unity is a strong tool for promoting development in society;

it is also the hallmark of socio-economic, political, and cultural wellbeing of human societies.

In the next song, "Ka a kperan ikpa i ande," released in 2015, Gabon outlines his message for mobilization and unity. He sang:

Or ganden wam dokoto Nyitse	*My elder Dr. Nyitse*
Dokoto Nyitse mfe wam yô	*My understanding is that*
Man se lu imo mom	*We should be one voice*
Or puun or ivaan i urugh ga	*No one undermines another's pull of an arrow*
Onerabul John Tondo Agbum	*Honorable John Tondo Agbum*
Onerabul Alex Adum se lu zwa mom	*Honorable Alex Adum, let's be one voice*
Se urugh nyam inyor timbe	*We'll pull the animal to our house*
Samuel Ortom onorabul minista	*Samuel Ortom, honorable minister*
Shie la se kase timbe	*Then we'll create a trap house*
Nyam a nyôr	*The animal will be trapped*
Or Tiv kaa ye	*Tiv say an adage that*
Ka a kperan ikpa i ande	*A contested bag gets torn in the process*
Se kperan ikpa ga	*Let's not contest for a bag*
Ikpa ande senenge	*And we'll see if it will be torn*
Ipka i a ande shaapera ga…*	*…The bag won't tear by force*

In this song, Gabon reiterates the importance of unity as he calls on prominent Minda sons and daughters to be united for the political and overall development of their clan, emphasizing that in unity lies enormous strength. His statement that "no one undermines another's pull of an arrow" is a local metaphor that although the impact of an arrow pulled by an individual can be enormous, the pull that is executed by two or more persons would have an even greater impact. And in singing and urging people to "let us be united to pull the animal into our house," he was sending a message to the Minda people to unite and win (pull in) the governorship seat into their house (clan). Gabon used the hunting metaphor to reiterate his point, saying, "That time, we will surround the house and the animal will be brought in." This means that when the Minda people are purposefully united, one of them will win the governorship seat. He also framed and illustrated the message with a Tiv adage that says, "When a bag is dragged in contestation, it tears," that is, if the Minda people bicker and fight among themselves over the governorship seat, they will lose it to their rivals. At the end of the campaign, a son of Minda, Dr. Samuel Ortom, won the election.

Conflict, Peace, and Development

Conflict largely becomes inevitable when human interests are divergent. In this study, the notions of conflict and peace are relevant in that while conflicts impinge development, peace promotes it. Tiv artists, including Tarker Golozo, are not unaware of the intrinsic value of peace in the development of their community, and have made tremendous contributions to the issues of peace and conflict prevention through their music. At the end of the political violence in Tiv land between 1960 and 1964 (Abeghe, 2005; Anifowose,1982), which resulted in large scale destruction of lives and property, Golozo in his 1980 song, "Tyo-or Amasetimin Bai," sang against future violence thus:

Tor Bai pati yô bee	*Chief Bai party politics is over*
Mase shin atsaase	*Only the chaff is left*
Or dan ker waningbian ihom gaa	*Let nobody consider a brother as an enemy*

It is clear that this message is about peace against violence.

In the same title, the recurring violent conflicts among individuals, families, religious groups, clans etc., across Nigeria, especially in Tiv land, prompted Golozo to counsel the public about the implications of violence on human development in the following song:

Ne zua mzough ne doo	*Your gathering at this meeting is good*
U nengen sha ashe yô doo	*It is good by the eyes seeing this*
Man asema ga zuan ga	*But your hearts are not agreeing*
Or ngu a kengee sha or u nan	*Another person will look his kinsmen in the*
I lu angbian un nan je kpa	*Even when it is his own brother*
Nan cia tan ivaan ga	*He shoots an arrow without fear*
Nan cia hônon gbuuka sha nan ga	*He is never afraid to point a gun at him*
Nan cia gberen ishom ga	*He is never afraid to machete*
Nan cia nanden ga	*He burns without fear*
Ijen kporom nyôr ken tar Tiv…	*Hunger has now grasped Tiv land…*

The song explicitly outlines the dire consequences of violence in Tiv land and beyond. While human capital is critical in the development process, its destruction forestalls the execution of projects, programs and policies that could bring progressive change. In the last stanza of the song, Golozo laments that "hunger has now grasped Tiv land…" and attempts to create awareness that only peaceful and harmonious coexistence can help encourage and sustain development among his people.

Sensitization, Mobilization, and Development

Sensitization and mobilization are crucial in facilitating development. While mobilization inspires and spurs the society to take actions on issues of societal change, sensitization informs and educates society, and thus molds opinion. All of these are therefore ingredients in promoting development. As Naylor (2016) contends, food security is an important factor in development. Therefore, in his role of promoting food security in Tiv society and Nigeria at large, Golozo sensitized the need for the society to engage in agricultural production, in his 1980 song, "*Aglogoco*" ("Agriculture"):

M ngu gberen imo	*I sing*
Kpa m ngu kahan sule	*But I also farm*
Yan m yam agugu ngula	*I bought that motorcycle*
Mn na wanigban	*I gave my brother*
Kpa lu he sule ne	*But it was from my farming*
M yam ungun m lu hendan ne kpa	*I bought the one I am riding now also*
M za tee suanbin	*Upon selling soybeans*
Kua an bali	*And small rice*
M lu hendan ye	*That's why I am riding (the motorcycle)*

In this song, Golozo simply explains the socio-economic benefits of agricultural production to humanity using his personal story. He says that proceeds from his farm facilitated his purchase of motorcycles to ease his transportation problems. In line with the importance of transport infrastructure to human development as argued by Gannon et al. (2002, pp. 323-269), Golozo informed that his motor bike eased his movement and made it easy to sell his farm produce. On the whole, the message tells much about the important relationship of agricultural and food production with other aspects of economy and how such aspects enhance the socio-economic wellbeing of man.

In another song, "Gogolo," Golozo (1978) warns against habits that are inimical to agricultural production and invariably promote poverty. He is particular about the excessive and pervasive alcohol consumption problem in Tiv land and in Nigerian society as a whole, with its attendant negative impact on the people's ability to pursue positive developmental activities, similar to the effects of the Chinese opium crisis of the late 1830s (Hall & Kirk, 2005, pp. 545-548). The consumption of *gogolo*, a highly concentrated alcohol and intoxicating local brew distilled from palm trees, became so destructive of human capacity and capability in Tiv society to the point that the paramount (traditional) ruler of the Tiv people, the Tor Tiv, His Royal Highness Dr. James Akperan Orshi, outlawed its consumption in Tiv kingdom. Golozo therefore lent his voice in re-echoing this warning as he sang:

Tor Tiv Akperan Orshi	*His Highness Akperan Orshi*
Ngu yôôn er	*Is announcing that*
I de man gogolo	*They should stop consuming gogolo*
I kaha a kaha kwagh	*But rather farm*
Gogolo doo ga	*Gogolo is not good*
Gogolo vihin or aa or u nan	*Gogolo spoils relationships between people*
Shi gogolo panden tahav	*Andgogolo reduces strength*
Or gogolo yan tsa hen amo	*Anogogolo man once spent the night in my house*
Kper nan mgba yaren shin tiev	*The next day I was going to the farm*
Mkaa me a mough sha se yar	*I asked him to accompany me*
Venda kpa m sendegh yo gba yaren	*He refused but on my insistence*
Sha lan shima tsô	*Reluctantly followed me*
Za ngurum u kahan yo	*As he bent to turn the soil*
Sen tume zwa inya oo	*Fell hitting his mouth to the ground*

This song gives a succinct description of the impact of the *gogolo* drink on the physical wellbeing of its consumers, especially people who do so excessively. Such consumption patterns erode physical strength, weaken and leave the consumer powerless and senseless, and at times lead to several health issues that leave the victim incapable of productive activity, including and especially agricultural production. The obvious outcome is a huge shortfall in agricultural production and food shortage in Tiv land. Golozo highlighted these adverse consequences of *gogolo* consumption in his song.

Still on the issue of food security, Golozo (1979) also highlighted the importance of applying organic fertilizer in crop farming and encouraged farmers to use it in the following song titled, "Fetalaiza:"

Fetalaiza u a lu er ka baa dam ne kpa	*Fertilizer that looks like udam salt*
Yange la yô or u tesen se lu ga kpa	*Previously, we had no one to teach us but*
Kwa ne yô m tagher a Aor Mningem	*Now I have met Aor Mningem*
Or u ke Mbaya	*A man from Mbaya*
Pasem vievie bee	*Explained to me in detail*

M wa yô mnenge doo:	*I applied and it is fantastic:*
Mba mondo kaka nan kpa wa kongôr	*Even common cocoyam yields smooth*
Shi m hile m yam ki	*I again bought it*
Mza wa suanbin	*I applied to soybean*
M er m bee ga kpa	*I did not finish but*
M zuaa ubufu ikyundu-gber	*I got thirty bags (the soybean yielded much)*
U a hile akor la mde	*The one that yielded again, I left it*
Ngu la saa ashe	*That one wasted*
Mza yam icii	*I went and bought fertilizer*
Er me za naha naha	*As if I was going to prepare porridge*
Tso myila Awuhe Pever…	*Then I called Awuhe Pever*
Tesem er me wa ve	*To teach me*
Me kera wua sha ibumega yô.	*How to apply correctly*
M wa chi yô m ndugh doya	*I applied fertilizer and harvested yam*
Kwagh hingir kongloo	*The thing yielded well*
Agbo ngu kongoloo	*Water yam is smooth*
Logo wam kpa kongoloo	*My cassavas too, smooth*
Kua di mondo kaka kpa	*Even common coco-yam*
Mondo ngu alu kôngolôô	*Coco-yam is smooth*

The strength of this song lies mainly in the fact that Golozo provided his personal example of applying fertilizer to the crops he planted in his farm. Doing so, he had a bumper harvest of crops such as cocoyam, soybean, yam (*doya*), and noted that such high yields had never been recorded in years prior to his use of fertilizer. More importantly, he sold some of the yields and used the money to take care of other aspects of his life.

Political participation, Civic duty, and Development

Essentially, political participation entails involvement in political processes such as contesting elective positions, voting and voter registration, and carrying out other civic duties. Golozo links these forms of political participation to development because by engaging in them, people will elect people who will work toward society's development. During the 1979 military transition to democracy in Nigeria, Golozo (1978) encouraged the Tiv and all Nigerians to actively participate in the voters' registration exercise. In his 1978 song, "Asembeli," he sang as follows:

Aboki wou a tile asembeli gay ô,	*If your candidate is not vying for state assembly*
Alu shin i yough i reperezentativ laa	*It may be house of representatives*
Ulu a kaadi ga u votu aboki wou zee	*Without the card you cannot vote for your candidate*
A lu wea votu shagba or	*Even if you don't vote the person*
Unan tile President u Nigeria ga kpaa	*That is contesting for the presidency of Nigeria*
Nongu u votu or u steeti ne oo	*Try and vote the person for state assembly oo*
Nyamkume Amenge oo	*Nyamkume Amenge oo*
Icia I ka or ta ere:	*The reason a person gives that*
Me kera votu or mee	*I won't again vote in someone*
Nan a yam mato nan haam ihundu ga	*To buy car and throw dust at me*
Icia la ka igban tar	*That reason is against development*
Nongo u na iti yough	*Try and give your name (register)*
Hegen ka shie u zuan a iyenge	*Now is the time to get the number (registration)*
Pati ngu ke hemen oo	*Voting is ahead oo*

Golozo's message makes the case that one of the surest ways to qualify to vote is the possession of the voter's card; the only way to possess the card is to register and obtain it. The song also carries a subtle criticism of elected officials who subsequently neglect their constituencies and warns voters about such politicians, stating that "I won't vote someone again to buy a car and throw dust at me." In this regard, Ker (2002) noted that voter apathy is directly linked to voters' experience that once politicians assume power, they become selfish and neglect the people who helped them gain political power. Nonetheless, Golozo urges people to vote because it is only by voting for the right candidates that development will be achieved and that the standard of living given a boost. It is this idea of electing credible candidates into leadership positions and ensuring good governance that Golozo in 1978 sang the song, "Ishangen ngi van," thus:

Tyo yam ishangen ngi van	*My people, election is approaching*
Yo de veren kwagh u nyar ken hemen	*Don't let money influence your choice*
I sangen ior mba ve lu a inja yo	*Elect people of good behavior*
Or a lu a naira kpa	*If a candidate is rich but*
Nana doo yum yô	*Is of good behavior*
Tyo yam ne sange nan	*My people, elect such person*

In this song, Golozo also talks about money-bag politicians (as they are locally known), and warned the electorate not to be deceived or accept money from selfish politicians who want to buy their votes. Rather, he counselled that voters should only consider electing people of proven integrity, whether they are poor or rich. He notes that poor contestants should be given a chance if they show some integrity and credibility. During the 1979 transition to democratic rule in Nigeria, Golozo was conscious of the need for good governance towards facilitating development. He was equally aware of past failures by Nigerian politicians in promoting development and warned of their deceitfulness when canvassing for votes. This is how he put it in his 1978 song, "Mba tsughun ior" ("deceitful politicians"):

Ne mba tsughun ior	*You deceitful people (politicians)*
Yange yen shi due ve	*The time has come again for you*
U tsughun an gbianev u kimbir ôron ere	*To keep deceiving your brothers/sisters that*
A lu ne nam yô	*If you vote me in*
Me er sha shima i ityô yam I soo yô	*I will be accountable to you*
Man a sangen nan yô	*But when voted in*
Nan yem a gba sôron ice i ter u nan	*He/She abandons the people for private gains*

Conclusion

This study explored political music in Tiv society where traditional musicians and singers have used their platform to disseminate messages on multiple issues related to socio-economic development. It highlighted the works of four popular Tiv musicians, Tondo Kumbul, Tarker Golozo, El Stuffy, and Gabon by categorizing and textually analyzing their music under the following themes: abuse of power, corruption, peace and conflict, unity, sensitization and mobilization, and good/poor governance. The themes were examined in relation to socio-economic development.

Whereas Tondo Kumbul and El Stuff's songs dwelt on power, corruption, political advertising, political mobilization, and development, Gabon's dealt with the importance and relevance of unity in the development process. Golozo's music highlighted the linkages between conflict and peace, political participation/civic duty, and economic development. Whichever angle each of the musicians chose to make his point, the overall thrust in their works aimed at the Tiv society, and what can be extrapolated to the rest of Nigeria is that music can be an effective platform to reach audiences with political messaging for both human, infrastructural, and society's economic development.

What is perhaps quite noticeable and salient is that all four musicians deliberately and wisely sang in the local Tiv language, which is well-understood by the audiences they were addressing. This crucial factor largely eliminated the need for translations and foreclosed the misunderstanding of the nuances expressed in the music and songs. The musicians addressed a particular audience and sang in the best and most intelligible way possible for them to comprehend and appreciate the meaning they tried to convey on the issue of Tiv society's development. In other words, all four musicians understood that communication is best approached when there is shared meaning between the encoders and decoders of messages, thus largely eliminating the distortions in the information being passed along.

While this study attempted to showcase the relationship between political music and development in society, its focus on only four Tiv musicians and a selection of their music as a purposive sample for analysis limit the generalizability of its findings, even among the Tiv people. The chapter has not and cannot exhaustively discuss all the music of Tiv traditional songs, even of those artists that have being discussed in the present limited space. For instance, anyone who reads Ker (2002) will agree that only a little of Tarker Golozo's music has been touched in this chapter. Numerous other Tiv traditional musicians, for example Iyough Ute, Atayo Koko, Kwaghbo Gari, Obadiah, Agugu Igbakumbul, Anche, and a host of others also exist. Future studies in this genre, therefore, should expand the number of musicians as well as the songs used for analysis for more robust findings and conclusions.

References

Abeghe, T. (2005). *Tiv Riots and the Aftermaths*. Makurdi: Oracle business limited.

Adebayo, J. O. (2017). 'Vote not fight:' Examining music's role in fostering nonviolent elections in Nigeria. *African Journal of Conflict Resolution, 17*, 55–77.

Agba, T. P. (2010). *A History of Poverty Reduction Strategies in Tivland, 1986-2010*. [Unpublished Master's Thesis]. Benue State University, Makurdi, Nigeria.

Agba, T. P. (2020). Displacement and confinement: Voices from Abagana and Daudu IDPs camps. In A. Philip, N. Attah, & A. Otoabasi (Eds.), *Fortress of Tents: Dynamics of Population Displacement in Nigeria* (pp. 417–443). Abuja, Nigeria: Brandmore Communication.

Agovi, K. E. (1989). The political relevance of Ghanaian high life songs since 1957. *Research in African Literature, 20*(2), 194–201.

Akinyoade, A. (2020, September 30). *7 Nigerian singers advocating for sociopolitical change through music*. The Guardian (Nigeria). https://guardian.ng/life/5-nigerian-singers-advocating-for-socio-political-change-through-their-music/?fbclid=IwAR3t5kXTbt8AnUAJU-RFhEyt66HpjPUfRoz—DLwQgmUgb-nPvO5z6piqGo

Amoakohene, M. I., Tietaah, G. K. M., Normeshie, F. E., & F. Y. Sesenu. (2019). Campaign songs and Political Advertising in Ghana: Analyzing the Use of Biblical Imagery, Testimonials, and Repetitions. In U. Onyebadi (Ed.), *Music and Messaging in the African Political Arena* (pp. 108–130). Hershey-PA, USA: IGI Global.

Anifowose, R. (1982). *Violence and Politics in Nigeria: The Tiv and Yoruba Experience*. Lagos: Nok publishers.

Aririguzoh, S. A. (2019). Music, Political Messaging and Nigeria's 2015 Elections. In U. Onyebadi (Ed.), *Music and Messaging in the African Political Arena* (pp. 261–282). Hershey-PA, USA: IGI Global.

Asse, M. (1995). La chanson dans la communication politique au Cameroun. (The song in political communication in Cameroon). *Friquence Sud, 13*, 121–131.

Bacharach, S. B. (1989). Organizational theories: Some criteria for evaluation. *Academy of Management Review, 14*, 496–515.

Blumber, J. G. (2015). Core theories of political communication: Foundational and freshly minted. *Communication Theory, 25*(4), 426–438. https://doi.org/10.1111/comt.12077

Bogue, R. (2007). *Deleuze's Way: Essays in Transverse Ethics and Aesthetics*. Hampshire: Oxford University Press.

Bohannan, L., & Bohannan, P. (1968). *Tiv Economy*. Evanston: Northwest University Press.

Bohlman, P. (2002). *World Music: A Very Short Introduction*. Oxford: Oxford University Press.

Christensen, M. M., & Utas, M. (2008). Mercenaries of democracy: The 'politricks' of remobilized combatants in the 2007 general elections, Sierra Leone. *African Affairs*, 515–539.

Cross, S. (2017). The enduring culture and limits of political song. *Cogent Arts & Humanities., 4*(1). https://doi.org/10.1080/23311983.2017.1371102

Epperson, G. (2022, March 21). *Music*. Encyclopaedia Britannica. Retrieved May 9, 2022, from https://www.britannica.com/art/music

Finnegan, F. (1972). *Oral Literature in Africa*. London: Oxford University Press.

Gabon. (2015). Awashima U Minda [Song]. On *Awashima u Minda* [CD]. Terry Music.

Gabon. (2015). Ka a kperan ikpa i ande [Song]. On *Awashima u Minda* [CD]. Terry Music.

Gakahu, N. (2017). Lyrics of Protest: Music and Political Communication in Kenya. In U. Onyebadi (Ed.), *Music as a platform for political communication* (pp. 257–273). Hershey-PA, USA: IGI Global.

Gannon, C., Gwilliam, K., Liu, Z., & C. Malnberg-Carlo. (2002). Transport. In J. Klugman (Ed.), *A Sourcebook for Poverty Reduction Strategies: Macroeconomics and Sectoral Approaches*. (Vol. 2, pp. 323–620). Washington DC: The World Bank.

Golozo, T. (1980). Tyo-or Amasetimin Bai [Song]. On *Tyo-or Amasetimin Bai* [CD]. Gbahakon Ikyaabo.

Golozo, T. (1980). Aglogoco [Song]. On *Aglogoco show* [CD]. Terry Music.

Golozo, T. (1978). Gogolo [Song]. On *Gogolo* [CD]. Gbahakon Ikyaabo.

Golozo, T. (1978). Asembeli [Song]. On *Ishangen ngi van* [CD]. Gbahakon Ikyaabo.

Golozo, T. (1978). Ishangen ngi van [Song]. On *Ishangen ngi van* [CD]. Gbahakon Ikyaabo.

Golozo, T. (1978). Mbastughun ior [Song]. On *Mbastughun ior* [CD]. Gbahakon Ikyaabo.

Golozo, T. (1979). Fetalaiza [Song]. On *Imburvungu ka cigh* [CD]. Gbahakon Ikyaabo.

Hall, J. W., & Kirk, J. G. (Eds.). (2005). *History of the World: Earliest Times to the Present Day*. North Dighton: Oxford University Press.

Henneberg, S. C., & O'Shaughnessy, N. J. (2007). Theory and concept of development in political marketing. *Journal of Political Marketing, 6*(2), 5–31.

Itiri, U. N. (2015). From entertainment to politics: Nigeria celebrities and the 2015 general elections. *VUNA Journal of History and International Studies 2*(2), 249-257.

Kania, A. (2015). An imaginative theory of musical space and movement. *British Journal of Aesthetics, 55*(2), 157–172.

Ker, A. (2002). *Tiv Poetry and Politics: A Study of Tarker Golozo*. Abuja: Akia Books.

King, S., & Jensen, R. J. (1995). Bob Marley's "Redemption Song:" The Rhetoric of Reggae and Rastafari. *The Journal of Popular Culture, 39*, 17–36.

Kumbul, T. (1977). Dzasha Jos, hide ke Benue [Song]. On *Gomwak* [CD]. Terry Music.

Kumbul, T. (1977). Janela Yakubu Gawan [Song]. On *Janela Yakubu Gawan* [CD]. Gbahakon Ikyaabo.

Louw, P. E. (2017). Afrikaner music and identity politics in post-Apartheid South Africa: Bok van Blerk and De la Rey phenomenon. In U. Onyebadi (Ed.), *Music as a Platform for Political Communication* (pp. 89–108). Hershey-PA, USA: IGI Global.

Lynskey, D. (2010). *33 Revolutions per Minute: A History of Protest Songs, from Billie Holiday to Green Day*. London: Oxford University Press.

Makar, T. A. (1994). *A History of Political Change Among the Tiv in the 19th and 20th centuries*. Enugu: Fourth Dimension Publishing Company.

Makwambeni, B. (2017). Zimbabwe dancehall music as a site of resistance. In U. Onyebadi (Ed.), *Music as a Platform for Political Communication* (pp. 238–256). Hershey-PA, USA: IGI Global.

McKee, A. (2003). *Textual Analysis: A Beginner's Guide*. London: SAGE Publications.

Naylor, R. L. (2016). The many faces of food security. In R. L. Naylor (Ed.), *The Evolving Sphere of Food Security* (pp. 3–30). New York: Oxford University Press.

Nyitse, M. L. (2006). *Form and Content of Tiv songs*. Makurdi, Nigeria: Aboki Publishers.

Onyebadi, U., & Mbunyuza-Memani, L. (2017). Women and South Africa's anti-Apartheid struggle: Evaluating the political messages in the music of Miriam Makeba. In U. Oneybadi (Ed.), *Music as a Platform for Political Communication* (pp. 31–51). Hershey-PA, USA: IGI Global.

Onyebadi, U. (2018). Bob Marley: Communicating Africa's political liberation and unity through reggae music. *International Communication Research Journal, 52*(1), 56–78.

Pedelty, M. & Keefe, L. (2010). Political Pop, Political Fans? A Content Analysis of Music Fan Blogs. *Music & Politics*, *4*(1). https://doi.org/10.3998/mp.9460447.0004.103

Rodney, W. (1972). *How Europe Underdeveloped Africa* (2009 Ed.). Abuja, Nigeria: Penaf Publishing.

Rosenthal, R. (2001). Serving the movement: The role(s) of music. *Popular Music and Society*, *25*, 11–21.

Roux-Kemp, A. (2014). Struggle music: South African politics in song. *Law and Humanities*, *8*(2), 247–268. https://doi.org/10.5235/17521483.8.2.247

Satti, M. A. (2017). Musical messages: Framing political content in Sudanese popular songs. In U. Onyebadi (Ed.), *Music as a Platform for Political Communication* (pp. 187–203). Hershey-PA, USA: IGI Global.

Shepler, S. (2010). Youth music and politics in post-war Sierra Leone. *The Journal of Modern African Studies*, *48*(4), 627–642.

Stuffy, E. (2011). Inima [Song]. On *Inima* [CD]. Terry music.

Stuffy, E. (2015). Kômishiona u teen inya [Song]. On *Kômishiona u teen inya* [CD]. Terry music.

Stuffy, E. (2015). Or gyoo [Song]. On *Or gyoo* [CD]. Terry music.

Todaro, P. M., & Smith, C. S. (2011). *Economic Development* (9th ed.). England: Pearson.

Wekesa, P. W. (2004). The politics of marginal forms: Popular music, cultural identity and political opposition in Kenya. *Africa Development / Afrique et Développement*, *29*(4), 92–112. http://www.jstor.org/stable/24484553

Yongo, I., & Tsenongo, M. T. (2004). Oral artist as historian: Examples from the Tiv. *Journal of Historical Society of Nigeria*, *1*(1), 65–74.

Zaid, B. (2001). Bakhtin's dialogic model and Popular Music: Bob Marley and the Wailers as a case study. In A. R. Humphrey (Ed.), *Culture and Mass Communication in the Caribbean: Domination, Dialogue, Dispersion* (pp. 139–148). Gainesville: University Press of Florida.

CONTRIBUTORS

Terna Paise Agba (Ph.D.) is an Associate Professor in the Department of History and Diplomatic Studies, Federal University of Kashere, Gombe State, Nigeria, where he has been teaching history and related courses since 2015. Between 2009 and 2014, Dr. Agba lectured at his alma mater, Benue State University as well as at Alex Ekwueme Federal University, both in Nigeria. His research focus is on interdisciplinary themes that are connected to poverty and human development, particularly environment, food and human security, urbanization, and governance/policy studies. Dr. Agba has published in both local and international journals, including *Bingham Journal of Economics and Allied Studies*, *ANSU Journal of Arts and Social Sciences*, and the *Journal of Intra-African Studies*.

Syed Irfan Ashraf (Ph.D.) is a graduate of Southern Illinois University, Carbondale, USA. He is an Assistant Professor in the Department of Journalism and Mass Communication, University of Peshawar, Pakistan. Dr. Ashraf is the author of *The Dark Side of News Fixing: The Culture and Political Economy of Global Media in Pakistan and Afghanistan*. His work has also appeared in numerous national and international journals and edited collections. Before immersing himself in the academic work, Dr. Ashraf worked as a professional journalist with numerous national and international print and electronic media organizations, including co-producing *Class Dismissed: In Swat Valley*, an award-winning *New York Times* documentary featuring Malala Yousufzai, the Nobel Peace Prize winner in 2014.

Faith Bahela holds an M.Sc. Degree in Journalism and Media Studies from the National University of Science and Technology, Zimbabwe. Her research interests include popular music and political communication.

Kevin Barker (Ph.D.) is a legal scholar and criminologist. He is currently a senior lecturer in the School of Law, Social and Behavioral Sciences at Kingston University (UK) and former founding director and senior lecturer in law and criminology at the University of Suffolk (UK). He is a graduate of UWI, London (Birkbeck and King's), and Cambridge.

Zenebe Beyene (Ph.D., University of Nebraska, 2012) specializes in media in conflict and post-conflict societies. He has taught, researched, and provided training in Ethiopia, Kenya, Rwanda, Uganda, and the United States. Dr. Beyene has published or co-published work about building peace through listening, the role of the Ethiopian diaspora in political affairs of the homeland, tolerance and online debates in Ethiopia, the role of TeleCourt in changing conceptions of justice and authority, the role of ICT in peacebuilding in Africa, media use and abuse, *From an Emperor to the Derg and Beyond: Examining the Intersection of Music and Politics in Ethiopia*. He was also one of the four panelists at the 2019 Nobel Peace Prize Ceremony in Oslo, Norway. The event was organized by PRIO.

Dorothy M. Bland (Ph.D.) is a Journalism Professor at the University of North Texas' Frank W. and Sue Mayborn School of Journalism, and a former Dean of the same school. She has more than a decade of experience in higher education and more than 25 years as an award-winning journalist and media executive. In 2019, she was honored as one of the top 35 women in higher education by *Diverse Issues in Higher Education* magazine. Under her leadership, the Mayborn School of Journalism launched its 100% online master's degree in digital communication analytics and earned the Association for Education in Journalism and Mass Communication's Equity and Diversity Award. Her research interests include diversity in media, digital/social media, and management/leadership.

Wendy Chan (Ph.D.) is an Assistant Professor in the School of Communication, The Hang Seng University of Hong Kong. Prior to joining the academia, she worked in various news organizations, including Radio Television Hong Kong, Travel QnA, and Island East Markets, where she gained practical media experience. Dr. Chan completed her Ph.D. in Communications at Hong Kong Baptist University in 2017. In addition to teaching in Mainland China and Hong Kong, she taught and carried out research in London as a visiting researcher at the University College London (2016). Dr. Chan's research interests are on media writing, journalistic presentations, and consumer behavior. Her peer-reviewed publications can be found in SSCI and AHCI journals, such as *Journalism Practice*, *Visual Studies*, and the *International Communication Research Journal*.

Jenny J. Dean is an Assistant Professor of Mass Communication at Texas Wesleyan University (USA). She received her Ph.D. in 2016 from the School of Journalism and Communication at the University of Oregon. Dr. Dean has a Master's degree in journalism from the University of Colorado—Boulder (2011) and a Master's degree in photography from Syracuse University (2004). Her undergraduate degree is from Luther College (2002). Her research interests include newsroom routines and culture, digital media, credibility of information, the audience, and visual communication.

Elena De Costa (Ph.D.) is an Associate Professor of Spanish at Carroll University. She holds a, Ph.D. in Spanish/Comparative Literature from the University of Wisconsin-Madison. She teaches language, literature, history, and politics; edits the student magazine *El Coloso*; and directs the annual bilingual theatre production. She is the author of a book on contemporary Latin American theatre (*Collaborative Latin American Popular Theatre)* and numerous articles in scholarly journals and book chapters on the literature and politics of Latin America. Her areas of research interest include Contemporary Literature and Politics of Spain, Latin America & the Caribbean; Latin American Popular Theatre for Social Change; Human Rights and Civic Engagement; and Foreign Language Pedagogy. She was the recipient of Wisconsin's Civic Engagement Practitioners Award and Carroll University's Exemplary Contributions in Service Faculty Award.

Muhammad Farooq is a Ph.D. candidate and Teaching Fellow in the Department of English at Kent State University, Ohio, USA. Mr. Farooq is currently on study leave from the University of Peshawar, Pakistan, where he taught various courses of English literature for 8 years. His research interests include Postcolonial Theory, South Asian Literature, and Necropolitics.

Mehmet Atilla Guler (Ph.D.) is an assistant professor in the Department of Labor Economics and Industrial Relations at Aydin Adnan Menderes University, Turkey. Dr. Guler obtained his master's and doctoral degrees from Gazi University, Ankara, Turkey. His dissertation was on the transformation of the social state in the axis accumulation and regulation. Dr. Guler's research interests are on the welfare state, social democracy, and Turkish politics. His publications include comparative social policy, welfare regimes, social exclusion, and critical labor market studies.

Dagim Afework Mekonnen earned his BA and MA degrees in Journalism and Communication from Addis Ababa University, Ethiopia, in 2010 and 2013, respectively. He worked at Addis Ababa University for about a decade where he taught, researched, and consulted on areas of media, journalism, and communication. At the time of writing, he was pursuing an Erasmus Mundus Joint Master Degree in Digital Communication Leadership offered by Universität Salzburg and Vrije Universiteit Brussel (VUB) and graduated in 2021. His research interests include media and democracy, computational propaganda, hate speech, digital equality, and media literacy.

Marquita Smith (Ed.D.) is Assistant Dean for graduate programs and an associate professor at the University of Mississippi. She is a former Fulbright Scholar who has lived and worked in Ghana and Liberia. As a Knight International Journalism Fellow, Smith created a judicial and justice reporting network in Liberia which continues to operate at the university. She previously served as Division Chair for Communication and Fine Arts at John Brown University, USA. She has more than a decade of experience in higher education and more than 15 years as an award-winning journalist. As a former Chair of the Association for Education in Journalism and Mass Communication's Commission on the Status of Minorities, Smith's research often centers on diversity and media.

Ann White-Taylor (Ph.D.) is an Associate Professor and Interim Chair of the Department of Multimedia Communication at the University of Arkansas at Pine Bluff. A graduate of the University of Arkansas at Little Rock, she earned a master's degree in journalism at Arkansas State University and a Ph.D. in journalism at the University of Iowa. Before joining the faculty at the University of Arkansas at Pine Bluff, she taught journalism at Alcorn State University and Southeast Missouri State University. Her research interests include representation of African American women in popular culture and is currently working on a book about images of women in African American historical romance novels. A former journalist, she has worked as a news reporter for the *Arkansas Gazette* in Little Rock and the *Savannah Morning New and Evening Press.*

Yavuz Yildirim (Ph.D.) is an Associate Professor in the Department of Political Science and International Relations at Nigde Omer Halisdemir University, Turkey. He obtained his doctoral degree in political science from Ankara University (Turkey) with his dissertation on the anti-globalization movement. Dr. Yildirim is interested in researching issues on social movements, populism and urban politics.

INDEX

R

Ramotswe, Precious, 30, 31, 33, 36, 47
rap, 119
Rapsody, 11
Recording Academy, 2
Red Ink, 48
Reddy, Helen, 106
redefine femininity, 106
redemption of self-love, 120
redemptive constitutionalism, 58
redemptive justice, 54, 56
redemptive-corrective justice, 57, 61
reggae, 11
reparations, 57
Reserve Bank of Zimbabwe, 235
resilience, 120
Resistance, 92–94
respect by gender, 117
respectable, 31, 32, 33, 38, 41, 46, 50
Ricch, Roddy, 14, 17
Rice, Tamir, 2
Robinson, Harriet H., 113

S

Saddam, 232, 244
Samanga, 48, 50
Sapphire, 40
Scholarship in Ethiopian Music, 75–77
Scott-Herron,Gil, 6
second wave, 110
self-awareness, 121
self-completeness, 122
self-love, 120
Sensitization, 258, 267
SEPDM, 78
Sephodi, Malebo, 48

sexual harassment, 119
Sheard, Kierra, 14
shebeen queens, 31
Shohat, 39, 50
Simms, 41, 50
Simone, Nina, 6
Sirius XM, 2
Sisters of the Screen, 47
Snead, 41, 51
Snow and Benford, 108
social and cultural change, 107
social change, 106
Social movement frames, 108
Social movements, 107
Sociocultural Frame, 114
Sociopolitical, 113
songs of terror, x, 159, 160, 161, 164, 166, 167, 169, 171, 177, 178, 179, 181, 182
Songz, Trey, 8
Sony Music, 2
Southern Rhodesia, 31, 35
Speaking truth to power, 94–95
Spotify, 2
Stam and Spence, 38
Stellar Awards, 1, 3, 14, 20, 21
stereotypes, 29, 30, 37, 39, 40, 41, 43, 47, 48, 50
Stewart, Jon, xiv
Street, J., xxiii
Su, Ruhi, 190, 192, 193
subaltern, 29, 34, 36, 50
subjectivity, 166, 177, 180
Subjectivity, 178
suffrage, 111
suicide, 159, 160, 163, 164, 165, 167, 168, 169, 171, 172, 173, 176, 178, 181
superpower, 118
Support Therapy, 217
Swift, Taylor, 113

Printed in the USA
CPSIA information can be obtained
at www.ICGtesting.com
LVHW011736140724
785479LV00010B/38/J